LOCATING THE TRANSATLANTIC IN TWENTIETH-CENTURY POLITICS, DIPLOMACY AND CULTURE

LOCATING THE TRANSATLANTIC IN TWENTIETH-CENTURY POLITICS, DIPLOMACY AND CULTURE

Edited by Gaynor Johnson

BLOOMSBURY ACADEMIC
LONDON • NEW YORK • OXFORD • NEW DELHI • SYDNEY

BLOOMSBURY ACADEMIC
Bloomsbury Publishing Plc, 50 Bedford Square, London, WC1B 3DP, UK
Bloomsbury Publishing Inc, 1385 Broadway, New York, NY 10018, USA
Bloomsbury Publishing Ireland, 29 Earlsfort Terrace, Dublin 2, D02 AY28, Ireland

BLOOMSBURY, BLOOMSBURY ACADEMIC and the Diana logo
are trademarks of Bloomsbury Publishing Plc

First published in Great Britain 2024
Paperback published in year 2025

Copyright © Gaynor Johnson, 2024

Gaynor Johnson has asserted her right under the Copyright,
Designs and Patents Act, 1988, to be identified as Editor of this work.

For legal purposes the Acknowledgements on p. xii constitute
an extension of this copyright page.

Cover image © Tetra Images/Getty

All rights reserved. No part of this publication may be: i) reproduced or transmitted in any form, electronic or mechanical, including photocopying, recording or by means of any information storage or retrieval system without prior permission in writing from the publishers; or ii) used or reproduced in any way for the training, development or operation of artificial intelligence (AI) technologies, including generative AI technologies. The rights holders expressly reserve this publication from the text and data mining exception as per Article 4(3) of the Digital Single Market Directive (EU) 2019/790.

Bloomsbury Publishing Plc does not have any control over, or responsibility for, any third-party websites referred to or in this book. All internet addresses given in this book were correct at the time of going to press. The author and publisher regret any inconvenience caused if addresses have changed or sites have ceased to exist, but can accept no responsibility for any such changes.

A catalogue record for this book is available from the British Library.

A catalog record for this book is available from the Library of Congress.

ISBN: HB: 978-1-3502-2782-8
PB: 978-1-3502-2785-9
ePDF: 978-1-3502-2783-5
eBook: 978-1-3502-2784-2

Typeset by Integra Software Services Pvt. Ltd.

For product safety related questions contact productsafety@bloomsbury.com.

To find out more about our authors and books visit www.bloomsbury.com
and sign up for our newsletters.

Essays in Honour of Professor Alan Dobson

CONTENTS

List of Figures	ix
Preface	x
Acknowledgements	xii

INTRODUCTION   1
    Gaynor Johnson

Chapter 1
THE POLITICAL SCIENTIST AS HISTORIAN: REFLECTIONS ON THE
LINK BETWEEN CULTURE, 'STATUS ANXIETY' AND THE AMERICAN
DECISION FOR WAR, APRIL 1917   15
    David G. Haglund

Chapter 2
SIR RONALD LINDSAY, THE UNITED STATES AND THE OUTBREAK OF
THE SECOND WORLD WAR   31
    Gaynor Johnson

Chapter 3
QUIXOTIC CALLING: ROBERT AND MARION MERRIMAN IN THE
SPANISH CIVIL WAR   49
    David Mayers

Chapter 4
JOHN BASSETT MOORE AND THE MODEST VIRTUES OF
INTERNATIONAL LAW   67
    David Clinton

Chapter 5
ROCA-RUNCIMAN REVISITED: ANGLO-AMERICAN RELATIONS AND
ARGENTINA DURING THE 'INFAMOUS DECADE', 1933–43   83
    Tony McCulloch

Chapter 6
THE OTHER ROYAL DIMENSION TO THE TRANSATLANTIC
RELATIONSHIP: FDR AND THE DUTCH AND NORWEGIAN ROYAL
FAMILIES DURING THE SECOND WORLD WAR   101
    David B. Woolner

Chapter 7
RE-ESTABLISHING THE HONOUR OF FRANCE IN THE AIR: FRANCOPHONE AVIATOR LITERARY FIGURES DURING THE SECOND WORLD WAR 117
    Andrew Williams

Chapter 8
THE BRITISH ROYAL AIR FORCE: OPERATIONS OVER LAOS AGAINST THE HO CHI MINH TRAIL, 1962 135
    Priscilla Roberts

Chapter 9
BRITAIN, THE US BICENTENNIAL AND THE STATE VISIT OF QUEEN ELIZABETH II TO THE UNITED STATES, 1976 153
    Jonathan Colman

Chapter 10
REAGAN'S INCOHERENCE: NICARAGUA IN THE REAGAN DOCTRINE AND THE END OF THE COLD WAR 169
    David Ryan

Chapter 11
NORTH GEORGIA, THE AMERICAN SOUTH, AND TRANSATLANTIC CULTURE AND HISTORY 187
    T. Christopher Jespersen

Chapter 12
PERSONALITIES AND POWER WITHIN THE SPECIAL RELATIONSHIP AT THE COLD WAR'S END 197
    Jeffrey A. Engel

Chapter 13
THE ANGLO-AMERICAN SPECIAL RELATIONSHIP: PAST, PRESENT, FUTURE 211
    Steve Marsh

Chapter 14
UK–US RELATIONS: CAN SUBNATIONAL DIPLOMACY SAVE THE 'SPECIAL RELATIONSHIP'? 229
    Alison R. Holmes

Index 243

FIGURES

0.1	Professor Alan Dobson	2
3.1	Robert Merriman, Marion Merriman and Dave Doran in Spain, 1937. Abraham Lincoln Brigade Archives, New York University	61
5.1	The signing of the Roca-Runciman agreement, 1 May 1933	85
11.1a and 11.1b	The Beatles in Atlanta, 1965. 18 August 1965; Atlanta, GA, USA; Beatles' only Georgia show took place half a century ago in Atlanta. © Augusta Chronicle – USA TODAY NETWORK	193

Preface

Alan Dobson's life was too short. But as was clear to all who knew him, it was a life lived with purpose, curiosity and joy. This volume serves as a tribute to that life. With fourteen chapters exploring topics ranging from royal diplomacy to the culture of the American South, it reflects the breadth and depth of Alan's scholarly legacy. The chapters are bound together by common themes of the modern Anglo-American 'special relationship', diplomatic and cultural exchanges between the United States and Europe, as well as a nod to Alan's passion for the history of aviation. As such, the book speaks to the central preoccupations of Alan's academic career.

At first glance, Alan could appear a rather conventional figure. With his leather briefcase, neatly trimmed moustache and softly spoken manner, Alan did not immediately strike those he met as a rebel. These characteristics were of course a facet of many of his most virtuous traits – a straightforward honesty, integrity and dignity that defined his personal and professional relationships. But just as Alan revealed a more mischievous and playful side as one got to know him (particularly if conversation was lubricated by a glass of something), at the heart of Alan's scholarly interests was a fundamentally radical approach. As Gaynor Johnson correctly makes clear in her introduction to this volume, the central focus of Alan Dobson's work – the modern transatlantic world – challenged conventional approaches of History and International Relations by studying a transnational region that was remarkably diverse, but simultaneously bound together by strategic interests, diplomacy, culture and history. The extent to which Alan was able to advance our understanding of the modern transatlantic world, particularly through the realms of diplomacy concerning economics and civil aviation, is remarkable.

As Gaynor Johnson also makes clear, Alan's legacy goes well beyond his published work. In establishing the *Journal of Transatlantic Studies*, and serving as editor until his death, Alan created an enduring outlet for the publication of leading research in this area. In the Transatlantic Studies Association (TSA), Alan created an interdisciplinary academic society of global reach that not only has provided the platform for thousands of academic papers, roundtable discussions and keynote lectures, but has acted as a forum to initiate and develop countless academic projects. Always so much more than a professional association, the TSA has served as an academic family for scholars from all over the world, with Alan at its helm for the first decade of its existence.

The strength of admiration and affection for Alan was evident at the special roundtable session on his life and work held at the TSA's annual meeting in Canterbury in July 2022. When I learnt of Alan's death a few months prior to this meeting, I knew that the news would elicit such warm sentiments from those who knew him. I was, however, overwhelmed by the sheer volume of scholars from all over the world who expressed such strong feelings of respect and fondness for Alan. Notable among the tributes paid to Alan on his death was the large number of academics who remarked on how instrumental Alan had been in supporting them in establishing their own careers, whether in writing supportive references, meticulously reading draft manuscripts, or simply lending a sympathetic ear and words of wise counsel. As one of those individuals who was able to benefit from Alan's generosity of spirit as I tried to establish a career in a sometimes-unforgiving profession, I am acutely aware of his legacy. In serving as the current Chair of the TSA, I feel enormously privileged to be able to benefit from, and hopefully perpetuate, the academic community that Alan established.

In featuring contributions from many others who I know benefitted from Alan's legacy and feel the same sense of loss but enduring affection for Alan that I do, this book is a fitting tribute to our departed friend.

Thomas Mills, Lancaster, April 2023
Chair, Transatlantic Studies Association.

ACKNOWLEDGEMENTS

In many respects, of course, the principal debt of honour that I must make in the production of this book is the person for whom it is dedicated, Professor Alan Dobson. Without him, quite simply, this book would not exist. Without his support, friendship and inspiration, the lives and work of a great many of us would have been very much the poorer, and that, I know, is a view that is shared by many people well beyond the pages of this book. I am especially indebted to Alan's wife, Beverly, for her help in gathering the biographical information about Alan together and for her warm encouragement of the project from start to finish. And for keeping the initial secret of the book so well until we were all overtaken by events. I know too that this book means a great deal to Alan and Beverly's daughters, Rebecca, Jessica and Naomi, who I had the pleasure of meeting last year, albeit in circumstances that none of us would have wished for. I hope that they think that we have done their dad justice.

This book is also testament to the robustness of Alan's legacy through the Transatlantic Studies Association, and I wish to thank Professor Christopher Jespersen and Dr Thomas Mills for their kindness to me when putting this book together during their respective periods as former and current presidents of that organization. We are an association of friends as well as colleagues, which only serves to enrich who we are as well as what we write.

Lastly, I am extremely grateful to the publishers, Bloomsbury Press. In particular, I would like to thank Abigail Lane, Maddie Holder and Megan Harris for their extraordinary patience and good humour in what has been quite a long haul. And, also, from a personal perspective, I wish to express my gratitude to my friends and family who for some reason continue to put up with me and my foibles. I am immensely fortunate.

Gaynor Johnson
February 2023.

INTRODUCTION

Gaynor Johnson

The circumstances surrounding the production of this book have changed dramatically since the project's inception in 2020. But the purpose of it has always been the same: to pay tribute to the work of Professor Alan Dobson, an internationally known scholar of Anglo-American relations in the Cold War era and the history of aviation. He was also known to many as the founding president of the Transatlantic Studies Association (TSA). As the TSA approached is twentieth birthday in 2022, I thought that it appropriate to mark the occasion by putting together a festschrift by those closest to him academically and those with the deepest connection with the association. However, in the spring of 2021, Alan was diagnosed with a rare form of lung cancer. In a nutshell, it was unlikely that he would live to see the publication of the book, although for many of the months that followed, he seemed to beat the odds and, more importantly, appeared to be beating the cancer. As an insurance though, I decided to tell him about the book; the most important thing being in my mind that he knew the high regard in which he was held. I am glad that I did because, on 7 April 2022, after a short spell in hospital, he died suddenly at home in his sleep. Consequently, this book, which began life as a tribute to Alan, has become part of a memorial to his work.

Alan Dobson was Honorary Professor of History, Swansea University, a post that he had held since 2014, a year after his retirement as Professor of Politics at Dundee University. He read Law and Politics at Durham University, graduating in 1972, where he returned a year later to begin his doctoral work, completing a thesis entitled *The Politics of Anglo-American International Economic Relations 1941–45* in 1978. Thus began the interest in all aspects of Britain's relations with the United States in the twentieth century that was to so influence the remainder of his career and his life. Alan soon secured his first academic post, as Lecturer in the Department of Political Theory and Government at what was then University College Swansea, and rose through the professional ranks, leaving there as Reader in 1999 for a chair in politics at Dundee University. He remained at Dundee until his retirement in 2011, after which he relocated his family to the place where he had always been most happy, the Welsh city of Swansea.

Figure 0.1 Professor Alan Dobson (1951–2022).

Alan was a prolific scholar. He was also committed to bringing his scholarship to as wide an audience as possible, writing as enthusiastically for undergraduates as for professional scholars. He was the author and co-author of some ten books. Alan is most widely known as an expert on Anglo-American relations in the era after the Second World War, especially in the area of commercial and economic policy. Both *The Politics of the Anglo-American Economic Special Relationship 1940–84* (Brighton: Wheatsheaf, 1988) and *Anglo-American Relations in the Twentieth Century: Of Friendship, Conflict, and the Rise and Decline of Superpowers* (London: Routledge, 1995) helped to define their field, especially for British scholars. However, what fewer people realized was that Alan was also an expert on the history of aviation. Indeed, he wrote more on these topics than on anything else. One thinks especially of his *Globalisation and Regional Integration: The Origins, Development and Impact of the Single European Aviation Market* (London: Routledge, 2007); *Franklin D. Roosevelt and Civil Aviation 1933–1945: Flying High, Flying Free* (Basingstoke: Palgrave, 2011) and *A history of International Civil Aviation: From Its Origins through Transformative Evolution* (London: Routledge, 2017). He published widely in all of the major international history and international politics journals, and his expertise was recognized through the award of a number of scholarships and fellowships, including a Fulbright Teaching and Research Scholarship which he held at Baylor University in 2012. He was the winner of the Virginia Military Institute Adam's Centre Annual Cold War History

Essay Prize in 2014 and was a member of the organizing committee for a NATO-sponsored project on Political and Social Impact of Military Bases, in 2007.

The legacy of most scholars is in their published work; they hope that future generations will have some interest in what they had to say. Alan's contribution to his discipline was and remains so much more than that. In the TSA, he founded an organization in 2002 whose principal purpose is to celebrate the transnational and the international in the people who study such things as well as in what they study. It was due to Alan's example that the TSA has become a community of friends as well as a community of scholars, and one which embraces new members with the same friendly enthusiasm as it does the more senior and well established. His leadership of the TSA consistently provided a reminder of what scholarship is really for. That its value is intrinsic; that it creates its own purpose. His academic vision was of the entire Atlantic world, not just the popular, well-trodden area of Anglo-American relations, but the history and culture of Latin and South America and of Africa. He also had the breadth of intellectual ambition and insight to understand that the transatlantic world is about more than history, diplomacy and commerce; it is a vast, complex web of formal and informal networks and disciplinary and interdisciplinary perspectives. Cultural historians informed the dialogue of political and military historians, and vice versa; all rightly treated as being of the same importance. A further reason for this success was that Alan treated those he knew both in and outside the academic world with good manners, good grace, good humour, tolerance and respect. He was immensely loyal, but stubborn and tenacious when it mattered. He was also fair minded, kind and possessed a great generosity of spirit. He was an astute reader of people. As such, Alan was a man with many long-lasting friendships, and a great many of those friends have kindly contributed to this book.

****

Notions of the transatlantic have long been present in modern history, especially during the twentieth century. They are similar to other broad-brush approaches to writing history; the global, the continental and intercontinental as well as the regional have formed an important part of the discourse in political, social, diplomatic and strategic history. And these debates reflected the reality on the ground, as nations grappled with the tensions between national self-interest and international responsibility and co-operation that were thrown up by responses to the two world wars and the Cold War, as well as the numerous political and ideological conflicts that beset the world. They recast and were extensions of the much older dilemma for the Great Powers in the eighteenth and nineteenth centuries of the balance between nation and empire, and the nature of those two constructs. In the minds of many, the word 'transatlantic' is a synonym for the Anglo-American relationship, especially in the second half of the twentieth century. It is as if the relationship between Britain and the United States is so important that it has its own adjective to describe it. The word often appears in association with other vocabulary that seems to have a similar rationale, such as 'special relationship'. It implies closeness; as one of my students put it to me recently, the phrase 'UK-US' as shorthand for the Anglo-American relationship contains abbreviations that are so similar as be only one letter different from one another.

But while we focus on the definition of some of the key terminology used in this book, it is as well to remember that the prefix 'trans' means to cross. If 'studies' is placed after the word transatlantic, then we have the term used to describe a relatively new interdisciplinary and cross-disciplinary area of academic investigation that examines the social, political and cultural interactions of the nations that border the Atlantic Ocean. Geographically, it is not merely about the relationship between Europe and North America, but also embraces African and Latin American dimensions. Transatlantic studies embraces regionalism but is not exclusively regionalist. The Atlantic world is viewed as outward facing; its importance being reinforced by its location in most map projections at the centre of the world, and from which so many global influences have stemmed. It is also a region of extraordinary diversity in terms of social and economic opportunity, embracing the world from the poles to the Equator. But the transatlantic world is also united by a number of important factors: in the twentieth century, most countries along the seaboards of the Atlantic were or tried to be primarily Christian and democratic in culture. Social scientists, of whom Alan was one by training, tend to be better than historians at seeing and embracing cross-disciplinary themes in their work. Introducing historians, especially those of Anglo-American relations, to these and their intellectual possibilities through the TSA, is one of Alan's most important intellectual legacies.

The chapters within this volume broadly fall within two categories: those that deal with the nature and development of the Special Relationship and those which do not. Or, perhaps expressed differently, they all deal with notions of exceptionalism and specialness in the Anglo-American relationship in the twentieth and early twenty-first centuries, but some authors write about a period before that apparent transatlantic rapport had been given a name. And much like that other label that lingers on in British foreign policy, the so-called *entente* with France, questions can be asked about whether that concept only existed in the minds of those who wished it to do so, and whether it reflected reality. Does something that could be defined as a special relationship with the United States continue to exist in the second decade of the twenty-first century, or should it be called something else? Did it disintegrate some time ago, and if so when? Does the phrase's continued currency stem from a form of political and diplomatic embarrassment where it is used because neither country has the courage to abandon it? The answers to these questions, which many of the chapters take on directly and indirectly, point to an Anglo-American relationship that is constantly reinventing itself, like a chameleon, changing colour constantly to blend in with its surroundings. Its strength is partly found in its fluidity but that, crucially, neither Britain nor the United States is totally defined by the relationship.

In the 1980s and 1990s, Alan was one of the first to define these fields of Anglo-American diplomatic and commercial relations, especially in the period after the

Second World War from the European side of the Atlantic. In so doing, he was not afraid to swim against the historiographical current.[1] In an academic culture where books that cover the broad sweep of history are often viewed pejoratively, Alan reminded us that without defining the shape and makeup of the forest, the significance of the individual trees within it is much more difficult to ascertain. And for him, Anglo-American relations were made up of a lot of trees, indeed a more-or-less infinite number.[2] In the 1990s and in the first decade of the twenty-first century, when most historians focused on the high politics, diplomacy and strategic dimensions of the relationship, Alan encouraged the incorporation of cultural and inter-disciplinary synergies into the field and did so, crucially, without denigrating the importance of the more well-established approaches. The cultural turn in international history was not shrouded in controversy nor a phenomenon that should be seen as a sudden, jarring innovation, but was a natural part of how a historian should approach the study of any topic; that is, from as many perspectives as possible. This multi-layered and multi-perspective approach underpinned an essentially positive view of Britain's relations with the United States.[3] That the culture and diplomatic priorities of the two countries did more to unite them than to divide them. Their mutual belief in capitalism and in the promotion of democracy as bulwarks against the different forms of ideological tyranny that emerged in the twentieth century provided the basis for a solid rapprochement that culminated in the 1980s in the famous Thatcher-Reagan special relationship. While some questioned the existence of any kind of special relationship between Britain and the United States, then and have done so since, Alan's account is one of organic evolution.[4]

Steve Marsh's chapter continues this broad-brush approach to evaluating the Special Relationship. To him, the Anglo-American relationship in the twentieth century was not only multidimensional but one that was constantly evolving. The diplomatic relationship between Britain and the United States today, in the twenty-first century, would, he argues, be unrecognizable to the world inhabited by that great champion of closer ties between the two countries, Winston Churchill eighty years ago. For Churchill, the Anglo-American partnership was just that, a partnership, based on equality of status. Since then, Marsh states that the relationship has become asymmetrical, with no political leader, either in the White House or in Downing Street holding sway in shaping it or conspicuously benefitting from it. That said, there is little chance that the occupant of either of those locations would abandon the use of the phrase 'Special Relationship' altogether because it has become too culturally embedded in explaining and defining the connection between Britain and the United States. Any obvious unwillingness to move away from the use of the phrase could also be detrimental to, for example, the stability of NATO and undermine a common approach to dealing with Islamic terrorism.

But for Alan, the Anglo-American relationship is not cosy and free from tension. Importantly, his work on economic diplomacy makes it clear that that closeness was quite remarkable, unexpected, even counter intuitive.[5] That while Britain and the United States were united by more than divided them, those divisions where they existed were profound, even seismic. Alan's numerous articles emphasize how enormous the transformation of the relative fortunes of Britain and the United States was, especially in the first half of the twentieth century. Few scholars realize just how rapid and extensive the decline of British commercial power was during that period, and that it was largely at the expense of the massive expansion of the economy of the United States. This is a particularly important point because Britain's commercial prowess was central to her identity as an imperial power and as a European Great Power; indeed, there was no other country for which the stakes in these respects were higher.

Another dimension that Alan's work brings into the spotlight is the tensions caused, ironically, by both countries being victorious allies in the First and Second World Wars. The same tensions also existed with Britain's relations with France and for similar reasons. In practical terms, the two world wars did little to give the promotion of democracy in the post-war eras a particular Anglo-American identity, even though it had been central to the war aims of both countries. The relationship was also resistant to the prevailing culture of internationalism, especially before 1945; another irony, given that the League of Nations, the organization created to promote this, was an Anglo-American construct.[6] Both Britain and the United States were realist states who believed that national self-interest trumped any other kind of responsibility. So what, according to Alan, was the glue that held the Anglo-American relationship together? His answer returns us to the study of culture. It was the many small, soft diplomatic dimensions; the common language, the shared experience of being dominant world powers; the common history of the two countries before the American Revolution; the British and Irish ancestral roots of many American citizens by the start of the twentieth century. T. Christopher Jespersen's chapter on the long history of literary ties between Britain and the American South provides excellent illustration of this point. His contribution to the book also makes it clear that those roots were long and deep and survived the vagaries of the changes in the diplomatic relationship between Britain and what became the United States over two centuries. This emphasis on the human dimensions of the relationship was also underpinned as the century progressed by a mutual advocacy of liberalism and human rights; the emergence of a common ethical framework to their military and strategic activities, for example, through NATO and the United Nations and also as individual state actors.[7]

David Clinton's chapter reminds us of the dimensions that that Anglo-American ethical commitment to 'police' international relations took in the twentieth century. Notions of international law and its enforcement existed before then, of course, but it was the impact of the First World War in particular that led to its development as part of as well as processes that existed alongside formal diplomatic relations between states. Clinton's chapter is concerned with the contribution made to the study of American foreign policy in the twentieth century by the jurist and academic, John Bassett Moore. The interface between the United States' emerging role in global affairs and the growing field of international law is one not often discussed by scholars. Moore believed that international law would supersede diplomacy, making the latter redundant, ironically, by making use of diplomatic processes concerning, for example, the use of mediation and arbitration. He also anticipated that the international community would accept principles about which there was a universal consensus, such as the principle of 'right'. Moore was an advocate of diplomatic neutrality, arguing that the adoption of any other approach made war more rather than less likely. Clinton's chapter, casting new light on Moore's thinking, places particular emphasis on the way in which his views were interpreted by his contemporaries, notably, the distinguished historian and former American diplomat, George Kennan.

The chapters by Clinton and others demonstrate therefore that foreign policy cannot be understood entirely outside its domestic context. Although Alan was not given to writing at length about the internal politics of the countries central to his work, he did pass comment on the way that the different political cultures within Britain and the United States had a bearing on their relationship. Both had a bicameral system, with an upper and lower house.[8] However, it was the federal nature of American political organization that interested Alan the most. The advantages and disadvantages of this system to the United States offered important lessons to Britain on matters of sovereignty and national identity in the decades after the Second World War as the British government grappled with membership of the European Economic Community, the forerunner of the European Union.[9] Alison Holmes' chapter develops these themes as she debates the extent to which the Anglo-American relationship has become almost a redundant turn of phrase and an historical anachronism as the devolved states within Great Britain, especially Scotland and Wales, seek their own relationships with the United States. It is a little over twenty years, that is since 1999, that Wales, for example, has had its own *Senedd*, or National Assembly. But as Holmes points out, Alan had been discussing the implications of a 'devolved' relationship with the United States for more than thirty years. It is not the role of an historian to predict the future, but, as her chapter demonstrates, scholars can often anticipate the direction in which diplomacy and politics will take based on their knowledge of the patterns that emerge from the study of the past. Like Alan, Holmes sees what for convenience's sake we will continue to refer to as the Anglo-American relationship as a complex portfolio of inter-related issues, and one that continues to expand in remit to include such pressing matters for twenty-first century politicians as international human rights abuse and climate change.

Culturally and politically, the version of the Anglo-American relationship, and especially of the United States' role as a bastion of liberal, democratic values that David Ryan and Jeffrey A. Engel present in their chapters is a world away from that which became evident during the Trump era forty years later. Born in what proved to be the final decade of the Cold War, the Reagan Doctrine was the antithesis of the Trumpist 'America First' mantra. As Ryan shows, there was a nobility to Reagan's desire to assist those countries that wished to shake off the communist yoke while, at the same time, using President Gorbachev's rise to power in the Kremlin to build diplomatic bridges with the Soviet Union. Although Ryan wishes us to think again about whether it was the aim of the Reagan administration to bring about the end of the Cold War, that is, to go that far, his vision of the

United States as a global actor, the last remaining superpower, is one that is similar to that of a pre-First World War Great Power. With power came responsibility; especially the scale of influence the United States exercised in the world in the last two decades of the twentieth century. And to the United States in the 1980s that power and influence was welcome and essential to keeping the communist threat at bay. Engel's chapter extends the analysis to include a discussion of one of the most celebrated dimensions to Ronald Reagan's period as American president; his close rapport with the British prime minister, Margaret Thatcher. It was their personal chemistry combined with commonality of purpose that helped to define the term 'special relationship'. But, as Engel demonstrates, these synergies are often transient and brief. When George H. W. Bush replaced Reagan as American president in 1989, the dynamics of the Anglo-American relationship changed considerably, and not for the better, being only re-stabilised when John Major succeeded Margaret Thatcher as prime minister the following year.

Central to Engel's chapter is a discussion of the role played by the vagaries of individual relationships, good and bad, on the course of international affairs. Despite the breadth of our vision as scholars, it is impossible to escape the frailties of human nature. Yet, as human beings ourselves, it is with this basic unit of society, the human being, that we can most relate. While Alan's work tended to focus on the broad sweep of Anglo-American relations, he had a deep appreciation of the significance of this point. He also understood that the study of the past, necessarily, contains the unique perspective of the person writing it. That may be self-evidently important, but Alan was interested in the different ways in which Americans viewed their own history in all its dimensions as well as that of other countries; he also issued the same challenge to British and other non-American scholars. To Alan, Trump was as historically interesting as any of his predecessors in the White House for these reasons.

Alan's personal engagement with the community of scholars in the field through the TSA and as founding-editor of the organization's academic journal led him to have a deep affection for and appreciation of the contribution of individuals to history and to its scholarship. A number of the chapters are on what could be termed ambassadors of the transatlantic relationship; people who, often in different, sometimes eccentric ways, promoted liberal values and democracy on the international stage. And the notion of an ambassador can take many forms. My chapter discusses Sir Ronald Lindsay's stint as British ambassador to Washington during the 1930s. Among its themes, it highlights the inter-personal dynamics of his dealings with the American president for much of this period, Franklin Delano Roosevelt, as they grappled with the increasingly grave diplomatic situation in Europe. Their formal dealings were underpinned, as is always the case in modern diplomacy, with many subtle forms of soft diplomacy.

And those areas of diplomatic interaction also spilled over, and were often motivated by international trade, as Tony McCulloch's chapter on the Roca-Runciman trade agreement of May 1933 demonstrates. The Anglo-American relationship in the twentieth century was driven by many issues on which it was often possible to reach a harmonious consensus, such as peace making and the promotion of democracy and capitalism. However, a much more bitter pill for Britain was the emergence of the United States as the dominant power in world trade after the First World War. And as McCulloch suggests, that domination was truly global in extent, and included South America, a region, especially Argentina, that had long been a source of lucrative commercial opportunities for British companies. His re-examination of the negotiation of the Roca-Runciman agreement and its context also shows what happens when confronting such seismic issues is played out through the interaction of two men; the enormity of the political and commercial stakes boiled down to the effectiveness or otherwise of inter-personal dynamics. These areas of human interaction make the case more strongly than any other dimension for adopting a multifaceted approach to the study of international history; a point which, as has already been indicated, Alan not only appreciated but was an active advocate.

The book contains two chapters that deal with that other most personal example of Anglo-American diplomacy: official or state visits by European royalty to the United States. As David Woolner argues, the most well-known example was the state visit to Washington by the British head of state and his wife, King George VI and Queen Elizabeth, in June 1939.[10] The occasion when, famously, the king and queen ate hot dogs as the guests of Franklin and Eleanor Roosevelt on the lawn of their Hyde Park home.[11] While this event, just months before the outbreak of the Second World War, has been viewed as an important step towards creating the 'Special Relationship' that emerged during that conflict, Woolner shows that it was not the only important piece of royal diplomacy of Roosevelt's presidency. In the spring of 1939, the Roosevelts hosted visitors from three continental European houses: Crown Prince Olav and Crown Princess Martha of Norway, Crown Prince Frederick and Crown Princess Ingrid of Denmark, and Queen Wilhelmina of the Netherlands. Like the British royals, part of the attraction in visiting the United States at this time was the World's Fair, held in New York that year. Woolner argues that Roosevelt was keen to use the presence of the royal visitors in the United States for his own purpose; to show the human face of requests by the countries they represented for American assistance as Europe prepared for war.

The symbolic face of national identity is also at the heart of Jonathan Colman's account of the state visit to Washington of Her Late Majesty, Queen Elizabeth II, in 1976, to mark the American Bicentennial, provides another example of how the operation of the Anglo-American relationship should be seen through the lens of both hard and soft power. His work also taps into the growing literature on the importance of state visits to the study of twentieth-century international history.[12] It also contributes to the under-sung field of royal diplomacy; the notion of the British Head of State 'embodying' Britain, Britishness and British values, whether it be through a speech, smoothing the path to a trade agreement or through the brand of clothing worn on the visit. There was and still is much more to visits by the British royal family than photo opportunities, the presentation of bunches of flowers, unveiling of plaques and shaking of hands.

While members of the British Diplomatic Service and the royal family have long understood the importance of soft power, they nevertheless represent a rather formal, official and often closely choreographed version of both of those dimensions; their worlds being closely regulated by protocol and tradition. A significant number of the chapters in the book broaden that view to include much less well known and more informal contributors to our understanding of the transatlantic world. Each one of them also speaks either to Alan's own work or on topics on which he was interested. The Anglo-American relationship is often associated with a form of liberal idealism for which, as Clinton's chapter reminds us, it is often criticized, especially the contribution of American citizens to that image. The stereotypical of the export of the American dream abroad: morality, ethics, Christianity, democracy, capitalism. Values deemed to be universal, self-evidently the sign of a modern civilized society, as obvious in their virtue as motherhood and apple pie. David A. Mayers' chapter is about Robert and Marion Merriman, two Americans who were prepared to go to Spain during the Civil War in that country and to die, if necessary, in the defence of democracy as part of the famous International Brigades. The Merrimans were the embodiment of this spirit and ethical point of view. Mayers' chapter also taps into the important narrative in the international history of the interwar period and that is about the respective merits of diplomacy and war as means of providing lasting solutions to tensions between states. One thinks of Richard Overy's wonderful book, *The Morbid Age* on this subject; the social and moral impact of the long shadow cast by the carnage and destruction caused by the First World War and its psychological impact of those remaining and on subsequent generations.[13]

Ethical questions have long been asked about the conduct of modern warfare. The study and deployment of airpower in the twentieth century has been of particular interest to scholars. Priscilla Roberts' chapter argues that the role played by the British Royal Air Force (RAF) in conjunction with its American counterpart during the early decades of the Cold War has not been well studied. She demonstrates that the RAF did much to assist United States forces during the Vietnam War by attacking the supply lines of Ho Chi Minh; indeed that that role was crucially important to forging a closer relationship between the British and American military that had wider implications for the strength of NATO and for the wider waging of the Cold War. Her work also reminds us that one of the most unique characteristics of the Anglo-American relationship after the Second World War was that robustness of that relationship had global implications; if it was stable and worked well, then the non-Communist world benefitted politically and commercially. If the opposite was true, then the prognosis especially for Europe, the main nexus of the Cold War, was equally bleak.

Roberts' chapter, of course, deals with Cold War diplomacy, but the role played by aviation in international relations during the earlier part of the twentieth century is mapped by Andrew Williams' chapter. His lens is broader than that used by many students of Anglo-American relationship as it also includes the French perspective. His work provides an important reminder that we study the interactions between Britain and the United States in isolation at our peril. Churchill may have thought such an approach legitimate, even desirable, but this fails to appreciate the real dynamics of the international system after the First

World War. Williams' chapter about international aviation and the role played by several notable French aviators also depicts them through literary as well an historical perspective what Alan would have seen as one of the prime purposes of transatlantic studies. Students of Anglo-French relations in the twentieth century would also learn much from the content and the approach taken by this chapter.

While one of Alan's primary focuses as a scholar was on the history of civilian aviation, he was more than aware of the importance of studying the military deployment of airpower. And it was one famous air raid, the Japanese attack on Pearl Harbor, in December 1941, that brought the United States into the Second World War. The British and French governments had been lobbying for much of the decade before to secure assurances of American support should another global conflict break out, but with limited success.[14] This is part of a larger diplomatic problem that predated the First World War and had its roots in the American policy of isolationism and in a reluctance to abandon neutrality. Whether this pattern strengthened or undermined the Allied cause during the two world wars and in the interwar period is not something that Alan concerned himself with directly. However, as David G. Haglund's chapter argues, Alan also applied his training as a political scientist to his reading of history. Haglund builds on recent literature on the relationship between 'emotion' and foreign policy decision-making and explores the concept of 'status anxiety' in Anglo-American relations, in his example, during the debate surrounding the decision of the United States government to go to war in April 1917. Emotions broadly defined are, by their very nature, subjective phenomena. They are associated with human responses to the world. By attributing such characteristics to states in explaining how they act on the international stage, a partial process of anthropomorphism is taking place. But there is a logic to it; state actions are determined by people and people are subject to emotions and other forms of fallibility. Haglund argues that there were two principal factors that contributed to United States 'social anxiety' about entering the First World War. The first concerns the global balance of power. American commercial power and political influence were such that any action taken by the United States would have significant long-term as well as short-term consequences to the international order. This proved to be a legitimate concern if it is accepted that the twentieth century proved to be the 'American century', whether for good or ill. This then leads to Haglund's second factor. If the scenario outlined in the first point came to pass, what were the implications for the Anglo-American relationship? One of the central themes of Alan's writing, as has been argued elsewhere in this introduction, was the evolution of the notion of a Special Relationship between Britain and the United States. Did the massive expansion of American influence in global affairs during the twentieth century help or hinder its evolution? Haglund also makes a compelling case for encouraging historians and political scientists to talk to each other about such issues.

While the primary purpose of this book was an appreciation of the contribution to the study of the transatlantic world that Alan made and encouraged others to make, it also serves as a useful overview of the diversity and health of the field. He would have liked nothing more than for the chapters to stimulate further debate, still more, to inspire others to become scholars of transatlantic studies themselves, especially in a multi-disciplinary or interdisciplinary way. Festschrifts are always about debts of honour and legacy, and when the recipient of it dies during its production, it gives that aim and that perspective particular poignancy. In my obituary for the British International History Group, I wrote that Alan was in the enviable position of having secured his legacy firmly and securely before the end of his life.[15] Consequently, this book is also a tribute to the TSA on its twentieth birthday and to its current and future membership.

Gaynor Johnson
Bolton, January 2023.

Notes

1. A useful overview of Dobson's views on the developments and trends within the Anglo-American relationship can be found in the journal of the Transatlantic Studies Association, an organization he founded in 2002. 'The Evolving Study of Anglo-American Relations: The Last 50 Years', *Journal of Transatlantic Studies* 18, no. iv (2020): 415–34.
2. A.P. Dobson, 'The Years of Transition: Anglo-American Relations 1961–67', *Review of International Studies* 16 (1990): 239–58.
3. A.P. Dobson, *The Politics of the Anglo-American Economic Special Relationship 1940–84* (Brighton: Wheatsheaf, 1988); Anglo-American relations in the twentieth century. Of friendship, conflict and the rise of the superpowers (London: Routledge, 1995).
4. A.P. Dobson, 'The Reagan Administration, Economic Warfare and the Closing Down of the Cold War', *Diplomatic History* 29, no. iii (2005): 531–56.
5. For example, A.P. Dobson, 'Economic Diplomacy at the Atlantic Conference 1941', *Review of International Studies* 10 (1985): 143–63.
6. Dobson, *The Politics of the Anglo-American Economic Special Relationship 1940–84* and *Anglo-American Relations in the Twentieth Century*, op.cit.
7. A.P. Dobson, 'When Strategic Foreign Policy Considerations Did Not Trump Economics: British Cold War Policies on East-West Trade', in *The Foreign Office, Commerce and British Foreign Policy in the Twentieth Century*, ed. J. Fisher et al. (London: Palgrave, 2016), 361–81.
8. A.P. Dobson, 'Labour or Conservative: Does It Matter in Anglo-American Relations?', *Journal of Contemporary History* 25 (1990): 387–407.
9. A.P. Dobson, 'The Special Relationship and European Integration', *Diplomacy and Statecraft* 2 (1991): 79–102.
10. P. Bell, 'The Foreign Office and the 1939 Royal Visit to America: Courting the USA in an Era of Isolationism', *Journal of Contemporary History* 37, no. 4 (October 2002): 610–12; G. Johnson, 'Royal Diplomacy: British Preparations for the State Visit of King George VI and Queen Elizabeth to the United States, June 1939', *Diplomacy and Statecraft* 32, no. 2 (2021): 330–50.
11. P. Conradi, *Hot Dogs and Cocktails. When FDR Met King George VI at Hyde Park on Hudson* (London: Alma Books, 2013).

12 For example, E. Goldstein, 'The Politics of the State Visit', *The Hague Journal of Diplomacy* 3 (2008): 153–78.
13 R. Overy, *The Morbid Age: Britain and the Crisis of Civilisation, 1919–1939* (London: Penguin, 2010).
14 There is a very large literature on this, but see, *inter alia*, D. Reynolds, *The Creation of the Anglo-American Alliance, 1937–1941: A Study in Competitive Co-operation* (Chapel Hill: University of North Carolina Press, 1981).
15 Professor Alan Dobson (1951–2022) – British International History | BISA.

Chapter 1

THE POLITICAL SCIENTIST AS HISTORIAN: REFLECTIONS ON THE LINK BETWEEN CULTURE, 'STATUS ANXIETY' AND THE AMERICAN DECISION FOR WAR, APRIL 1917

David G. Haglund

Introduction

Recent years have witnessed a resurgence in scholarly inquiries into the relationship between the cultural construct of 'emotion' and foreign policy decision-making, with much of this attention being accorded to choices of states to go to war. One emotion in particular is often said to occupy pride of analytical place: 'status anxiety'. This chapter draws upon recent scholarly research into the postulated connection between emotion and war, in a bid to assess whether the American decision to enter the First World War might be said, at least in part, to have been contingent upon status considerations, and if so, how.

This particular case is chosen for three reasons. First is the April 1917 decision's obvious importance to the global balance of power, as this latter would be made manifest throughout the ensuing century, down to the present time. Second, and related to this, is the impact that America's entry into the war would come to have upon the eventual establishment of the geostrategic institution that became the 'Anglo-American special relationship', one of the core intellectual foci of Alan Dobson's scholarly corpus. Third, discussions of status, while they may not compel a reliance upon 'history', certainly are bolstered by such a reliance, and this too reflects Dobson's epistemological approach to his own discipline of international relations (IR), one in which diplomatic history is given prominence, in keeping with broader trends in the field.[1]

America's decision to enter the war that had begun nearly three years earlier constituted a jettisoning of its long-standing and revered grand strategy of aloofness from the European balance of power, otherwise known as isolationism.[2] Although the decision has been studied and debated from a variety of perspectives, not much attention has been allocated to the impact of status anxiety upon the choice for intervention. Usually, when status anxiety is under examination by IR scholars, the focus is squarely on the level of analysis that Kenneth Waltz so famously labelled the 'third image'. This chapter will be no exception to the tendency to situate status anxiety within the third image.

Waltz introduced this and two other analytical images in his first and in some ways most influential book of the late 1950s, *Man, the State, and War*, which had been based upon his Columbia University doctoral dissertation from earlier in the decade.[3] His objective was to contribute to the systematic study of the causes of war, by disaggregating the numerous explanations of war's origins into 'three levels of analysis', which he called the first, second and third images. Respectively, those images anchored the main cause(s) of war in the quality of individual leaders, attributes of domestic state and society, and systemic arrangements and processes. Waltz clearly, even in those early years, preferred to lodge his understanding of causality mostly at the systemic level – that is, the third image – in which the ultimate source(s) of international conflict would be traceable to the international distribution of relative capability, or 'power', within an international system characterized by anarchy and energized by the principle of self-help on the part of states questing after security. In a later, and more famous – or at least, more controversial – work he would express so robustly this preference for third-image explanations of international phenomena that henceforth his brand of IR theory would become known, properly, as 'structural realism', and less properly as 'neorealism'.[4]

Thinking about status and political action is nothing new among the IR professoriate, for whom it has regularly popped into and out of fashion. But, as noted above, over the past couple of decades, it has come roaring back, in keeping with a more general scholarly interest in the role that 'emotion' might be said to have in state decision-making.[5] The particular emotional trait known as status anxiety has garnered a heightened amount of attention, and not just on the part of scholars who concentrate upon relations between the great powers. Indeed, it might even be remarked that status anxiety, like SARS-CoV-2, is ubiquitous in the international system. Unlike the novel coronavirus, however, most of the time status anxiety is fairly inconsequential. Things are otherwise, however, when status anxiety can become linked to certain foreign policy aims of great powers.

Take just the contemporary discussion swirling around the prospects of a future war between the United States and China, in no small measure for reasons derivative of the logic of 'power transition theory'. One claim made by theorists of power transition is that 'rising' powers almost always prove troublesome for international peace and security, as they pursue policies fuelled by 'hubris', which is a short-hand way for expressing the thought that they are recklessly anxious to enhance their status in the eyes of the peer competition. The implication is that their anxiety grows in proportion to the growth of their power, with war in the offing unless some means of 'accommodating' or otherwise assuaging their status anxieties can be arranged.[6]

But one need not conjure up hypothetical future wars, or even be a power-transition theorist, to connect status anxiety with state decisions to go to war. There have been many occasions on which it could be and has been said that states were 'fighting for status'.[7] None of those occasions have come remotely close to matching, in magnitude and consequence, the First World War, this chapter's focus

I pursue my inquiry in two subsequent sections, each staying within the confines of the third image. One examines an aspect of the debate over intervention that leaves little if any room for the insertion of status anxiety into the analysis; it is the contention that the 1917 decision represented the first instance in which America chose to act as an 'offshore balancer'. The other continues the third-image focus, only this time what is being demonstrated is just the opposite of what the offshore-balancing perspective maintains; in that section, it will be shown how status anxiety can be argued to have had a 'causal' significance in the war decision, even if it so rarely portrayed in this light.

But before getting to those two third-image discussions, it is necessary to address the explanatory (and even normative) context for assessing the American intervention by introducing other hypotheses, drawn from other levels of analysis.

The debate over American intervention in 1917

Although more than a century has passed since President Woodrow Wilson made his historic decision to ask congress for a declaration of war upon Imperial Germany in early April 1917, questions continue to be raised as to why he did this. Among the questioners are those whose interest lies in trying to demonstrate the unwisdom of the decision. They are more interested in the normative than in the explanatory side of the debate, and to a large extent they are carrying on an earlier normative tradition prompted by anti-war sensibilities at the time the decision was made. Illustrative of this more normatively charged discussion was an opinion piece published by the *New York Times* in April 2017, on the hundredth anniversary, to the day, of the declaration of war. In it, Michael Kazin made some important, even if counterfactual, points that are worth quoting here:

> [M]ost Americans know little about why the United States fought in World War I, or why it mattered. The "Great War" that tore apart Europe and the Middle East and took the lives of over 17 million people worldwide lacks the high drama and moral gravity of the Civil War and World War II, in which the very survival of the nation seemed at stake .... But attention should be paid. *America's decision to join the Allies was a turning point in world history.* It altered the fortunes of the war and the course of the 20th century – and not necessarily for the better. Its entry most likely foreclosed the possibility of a negotiated peace among belligerent powers that were exhausted from years mired in trench warfare .... How would the war have ended if America had not intervened? The carnage might have continued for another year or two until citizens in the warring nations, who were already protesting the endless sacrifices required, forced their leaders to reach a settlement. If the Allies, led by France and Britain, had not won a total victory, there would have been no punitive peace treaty like that completed at Versailles, no stab-in-the-back allegations by resentful Germans, and thus no rise, much less triumph, of Hitler and the Nazis. The next world war, with its 50 million deaths, would probably not have occurred.[8]

To say the least, Kazin's is a powerful normative indictment of Wilson's decision to take his country into the war, and it is surely possible that in the absence of that decision, European and global security affairs would indeed have progressed on a far more happy and irenic course during the remaining decades of the twentieth century. But maybe they would not have, because resorting to counterfactuals necessarily opens the door to other, competing, counterfactuals. For when we start to experiment with one version of the past that we never did have, we need always to realize that other plausible paths can also be injected into the argument. For instance, if one were to substitute a different counterfactual antecedent for Kazin's preferred antecedent (i.e., of no intervention in April 1917), it would still be possible to arrive at the same counterfactual consequent: no German revanchism, no rise of Hitler, no Second World War, no Holocaust, no 50 million dead overall. This alternative counterfactual antecedent (no armistice in November 1918) would have featured the continual counter-offensive that military officials such as General John J. Pershing, who commanded the American Expeditionary Force, had been promoting following the failure of the Germans' final offensive in July 1918.

This counterfactual antecedent would assume the war's prolongation for at least a year, with the launching in 1919 of a great offensive into the very heart of Germany itself, propelled by an American military force that by then would have swollen to four million soldiers. In this alternative counterfactual antecedent, Germans would have come to understand in the clearest manner possible that they had been thoroughly beaten, rather than 'stabbed in the back' by dastardly socialists and Jews, as the revanchist legend of the interwar years insisted. That knowledge of utter defeat would, presumably, have had the same impact in the counterfactual past that the knowledge of utter defeat of *Stunde Null* (May 1945) had upon German thinking in the real post-1945 past.[9] It would have led sentient German policymakers, and masses alike, to develop a radically different understanding of the role of military force in their country's grand strategy. Thus one reading of the no-armistice counterfactual is that it would have eliminated the problem of German militarism, and would have led to the socialization of Germany into the Western political order a generation earlier, without all the horrors of the 1930s and 1940s.

Of course, we understand only too well what the 'real' past implied for subsequent generations in Europe and elsewhere. Equally, there can be no dissenting from Kazin's claims about the real-world significance of the American entry into the war. It truly did represent a 'turning point in world history'. But as important as is the normative debate, no less important is the *explanatory* debate, upon which the following two sections focus. Why did America go to war? Over the years since the decision was made, there have been countless attempts to answer this question. At the risk overgeneralizing, we can say that these attempts fall into four major clusters of explanation, located within all three Waltzian images.

Only one of these clusters puts security considerations front and centre in the president's decision-making. The other three concentrate on other 'causal' considerations. Much scholarly ink has been spilled trying to demonstrate the impact of economic forces upon the choice for intervention.[10] The same can be said for the claim that Americans were simply hoodwinked by clever allied propagandists, who made them believe that the war was nothing short of a crusade for morality and civilization.[11] And then there are the explanations that trace the war decision to flaws in Woodrow Wilson's psyche.[12] It would require a long book rather than a short chapter to begin to do justice to these three clusters. Accordingly, my approach in these pages is a much-restricted one, in which I only examine a competing pair of third-image arguments. Each of these links security rationales to the intervention decision, but only one of them leaves room for incorporating status anxiety into the explanation. These competing arguments will be outlined in the following two sections.

The intervention decision as offshore balancing?

In the scholarly writing on US foreign policy, systemic variables have figured regularly in the assessments of many realist analysts, especially as they might be pigeonholed as 'structural' realists. And among this latter group, no political scientist has attained greater prominence, some say notoriety, than John Mearsheimer. In his view, the understanding of America's (or any country's) foreign policy starts with the recognition that the overarching objective of decision-makers is survival. For a great power such as the United States became by the early twentieth century, this goal has entailed the prevention of any rival great power's gaining regional 'hegemony' over its own neighbours, which if obtained would render it, inevitably, a worrisome problem in locales closer to the American homeland. Thus the objective has been to keep the danger as far away as possible. Doing this obliged America to act as an 'offshore balancer'.

In Mearsheimer's own words,

> Every great power would like to dominate the world, but none has ever had or is likely to have the military capability to become a global hegemon. Thus, the ultimate goal of great powers is to achieve regional hegemony and block the rise of peer competitors in distant areas of the globe. In essence, states that gain regional hegemony act as offshore balancers in other regions.[13]

And this logic is what drove the United States, the world's only 'regional hegemon' according to Mearsheimer, into the First World War, just as it impelled it once again to play the part of offshore balancer a generation later, during the Second World War. He may well be correct insofar as concerns the latter war, but it is highly doubtful that offshore-balancing precepts prompted the intervention decision in 1917.

There is nothing new about the argument that the April 1917 decision had to have had security concerns – meaning, physical security concerns – as its motivating condition. Even during the neutrality months between August 1914 and April 1917, there had been numerous enthusiasts insistent upon augmenting

America's 'preparedness' in the likely event of a conflict with a country few of them needed to bother identifying by its name, Germany.[14] Some of these enthusiasts' successors a generation later, as the world once more descended into a war in which Germany featured centrally, contemplated retrospectively the April 1917 decision, and with their minds concentrated upon the predicament facing America in the early 1940s, concluded that the earlier decision simply *must* have been taken for reasons of national security.

Whether they dressed up their case in the conceptual garb of offshore balancing or not, it only made sense to these later policy analysts and advocates that intervention in the First World War at Britain's side had been the sole course of action imaginable if the nation's vital interests were to be protected. Walter Lippmann, writing during the midst of that second global upheaval, was certain that, just as during the current crisis, so too in 1917 did an American president understand the necessity for entry into the European balance of power, because in 1917 America's physical security depended upon the Royal Navy every bit as much as it came to do in 1941. Take the Royal Navy out of the equation, and water would turn out to have no stopping power, at all.[15]

But if a certain structural logic seems to be on the side of the Mearsheimer thesis regarding the April 1917 decision, the same cannot be said of the evidence. Here is the problem: there simply exists no solid evidentiary basis, archival or otherwise, to substantiate the argument that policymakers in Washington *perceived* a threat to American security in 1917 so grave as to have compelled the United States to play the role of offshore balancer. It is not as if, over the years, no one had ever tried to find such evidence. Foremost in this regard has been Daniel Malloy Smith, who, in an important review article published at the time of the Vietnam War, drew readers' attention to some accounts of Wilson's decision-making that had appeared 'recently' in print, meaning since the 1950s. Smith's search for a clear security rationale had been motivated, in part, by a desire to debunk claims about Wilson's having been a clueless idealist, oblivious to the realities of power politics in April 1917, a criticism not infrequently made of the twenty-eighth president, both during his lifetime and after his death.[16] Notwithstanding his intuitive sympathy for the security explanation, Smith still drew back from fully endorsing the claims by scholars who thought they had found, in threat perception, the answer to the question of why America intervened in April 1917. Instead, he concluded that the 'hypothesis that the United States went to war in 1917 to protect its security against an immediate German threat lacks persuasiveness'.[17]

In this conclusion, Smith was seconding results that a fellow diplomatic historian, Richard Leopold, had published a decade and a half earlier, in the pages of the IR journal, *World Politics*. Although he could hardly employ our contemporary term of art, offshore balancing, to account for decision-making in Washington, Leopold was dismissive of the notion that preventing the rise of a European regional hegemon setting out to challenge the United States was what determined the issue. For while deductive logic seemed to be on the side of this security paradigm, where was the evidence supporting it? Leopold found none, and did not expect much ever to turn up. His pessimism was reflected in a comment made in one of his article's footnotes, to the effect that 'a member of my graduate seminar at Harvard in 1947, Robert E. Osgood, was unable to discover in a semester's search any substantial amount of contemporary evidence to support the Lippmann thesis'.[18]

Much more recently, another scholar has cast a critical glance at the notion that Woodrow Wilson asked for intervention because he worried that Germany would attain regional hegemony in Europe. That scholar is the political scientist Galen Jackson, who, like fellow political scientist Alan Dobson, actually has spent a great deal of time doing archival research. What Jackson's study of the documents of the period showed him – or more accurately, *failed* to show him – is troubling for the Mearsheimer/Lippmann theses. For those theses to be sustainable empirically, there would have to be a documentary trail of presidential thinking revealing that by April 1917 Woodrow Wilson regarded the situation of the British and French as being particularly parlous; that he believed Russia's revolution of the previous month would detract from the Allied war effort rather than support it; that he was convinced that the situation in Germany and Austria-Hungary was especially favourable to the strategic interests of both those powers; and that he believed only a massive American injection of force on the side of the Allies could save the day.

Jackson found evidence for *none* of these suppositions in the documents he examined, leading him to conclude:

> Regardless of what the true balance of power in Europe was in early 1917, from Washington's perspective there did not appear to be any reason to think Germany was on the verge of achieving a position of regional hegemony on the continent. To put it in somewhat different terms, there was a world of difference between Woodrow Wilson and Franklin Roosevelt – 1917 was not 1941.[19]

The offshore-balancer argument does not have a monopoly on third-image accounts that invoke security as a motivation. Other security-related arguments have also been made, and as we are about to find out, one of these can be made to fit comfortably with arguments about the causal prowess of status anxiety. Let's see what this entails, by adverting to a scholarly dispute over Wilson's leadership that erupted in the decade following the Second World War's ending.

Security, status anxiety, and April 1917

If this scholarly dispute of the 1950s drew obvious attention to the president's post-1918 vision (as it had to have done), it was no less concerned with the question of why Wilson took his country into war in the first place. It was a controversy unleashed by analysts associated with an innovative IR paradigm imported from Europe, one that came to be called realism, albeit shorn of such more current modifiers as 'structural' or 'neo'. This earlier variant of the paradigm is usually termed 'classical' (sometimes 'liberal') realism. Prominent among this realist cohort was Robert Endicott Osgood, the very same Harvard graduate student whom Richard Leopold recalled as having spent an entire semester looking in vain for evidence that security rationales had prompted Wilson's decision for war. After receiving his doctorate from Harvard, Osgood took up a teaching position in the Department of Political Science at the University of Chicago, whose press brought out his first book, based on the Harvard dissertation. That book, focused as it was upon a keen debate in IR theory circles during the 1950s about the ethical basis of American foreign policy – should it be predicated upon the country's ideals, or upon its interests? – set the standard for much of the early Cold War discussion of Wilson's intervention decision.

Wilson's policymaking was faulted because it betrayed far too much idealism and hardly enough self-interest for it to have served as an adequate safeguard for America in the international anarchy at a particularly momentous time. 'Wilson's conception of foreign relations', wrote Osgood, 'was remarkable not so much for its neglect of the problems of power as for its conscious subordination of national expediency to ideal goals.' Wilson was too much of a dreamer and do-gooder to ensure that America's legitimate physical security interests could be protected. Worst of all, Wilson 'coveted for America the distinction of a nation transcending its own selfish interests and dedicated in altruistic service to humanity'.[20]

For Osgood and other classical realists, the Wilson who emerges from their research is unrecognizable to latter-day cousins such as Mearsheimer. Far from seeking to balance power from 'offshore', the classical realists' Wilson wanted to abolish the balance of power completely, replacing it with a novel arrangement known as collective security.[21] It is for this reason that so many of them consider Wilson to have been such a disaster for American foreign policy. They think that had he been more attentive to global power realities during the war itself, he would have intervened sooner than he did, and for the right reasons instead of intervening later, and for the wrong reasons. Even more, had he been attentive to global power realities of the early post-war period, he would have realized that at the Paris peace conference in early 1919 he should have been prioritizing the promotion of a healthier European balance by committing America to an ongoing alliance with Britain (and France), rather than propagating the misguided idea that stable peace required replacing that balance with collective security.[22] He gambled on the will-o'-the-wisp of collective security, they say, and in the bargain ended up losing American 'internationalism' for another generation. He was, therefore, a victim of his own preening ambition for an impossible world order, a tragic figure in a Shakespearian sense, of having been responsible for his own undoing.[23]

The charge that Wilson ignored security interests in favour of altruism is understandable, even if it is not completely fair. For if it is true that Wilson's war decision was not intended to assure America's security through its action as an offshore balancer, it does not follow that security interests did not figure in the president's decision-making. Importantly, they did so, and in a way that, ironically, testified to more than a little status anxiety in Washington. The latter is revealed in respect of two other claims about why Wilson took the decision to intervene in the fighting. Neither of these other two claims is new. One is that Wilson had to ask for a declaration of war upon Germany in April 1917 (he would not make a similar request in respect of the Austro-Hungarian Empire until the end of the same year) because Germany's resumption of unrestricted submarine warfare shortly before had forced his hand, leaving him no option but war. The other argument is that he took his country to war because he wanted it to be the key actor in the post-war peace negotiations. Each can be said to have security implications, even if not those contained in the offshore-balancing contention. Both can also be connected with status anxiety, the second one much more than the first. Let us take the two claims, in turn.

The first claim is that the president felt himself to be honour-bound to declare war on Germany once Berlin resumed unrestricted undersea warfare on 1 February 1917. Even if this did not directly endanger America's own physical security, it assuredly could and did pose mortal peril to individual Americans, and therefore constituted an affront to the country's sense of honour. No president, in this view, could turn a blind eye to such an affront, not even one so dedicated to pacifism as Wilson was often considered to be. Those scholars (and they are many) who have Wilson being, ultimately, forced by events to take the United States into war, rely on one of the oldest and most widely accepted causal arguments about April 1917, namely that the U-boat brought America into the fight.

This explanation for the war decision would have needed no amplification for Americans in April 1917, but during the revisionist onslaught launched in the early interwar period what has become known as the 'submarine school' appeared to have sunk without a trace from popular discourse. Of course, the submarines never did slip entirely beneath that era's explanatory waves among specialists in diplomatic history; they remained important staples of analysis for some professional historians and political scientists largely owing to a study published in 1934 by one of the twentieth century's leading scholarly authorities on Wilsonian diplomacy, Charles Seymour.[24] This work may not have swayed the public debate at a juncture when isolationist sentiment was at fever pitch, but it certainly did make a lasting mark among diplomatic historians, many of whom heralded it as the most definitive study of American entry published up until then.

By and large, the submarine school, which stresses the importance of Wilson's determination to protect America's 'neutral rights'[25] (not the same thing as protecting its physical security by balancing anyone's power), continues to hold pride of place among interpretations of American involvement in the war. In the words of Robert W. Tucker:

> [The] oldest explanation of America's entrance into World War I remains the most satisfactory. It was the challenge of the submarine to America's right as a neutral that left no alternative save war. In the absence of that challenge, the country would in all likelihood have remained a nonparticipant ... despite the prospect of being excluded from the peace settlement and despite the prospect of Allied defeat.[26]

The other credible security-related argument concerns Wilson's determination to preserve (or re-establish) America's credibility as the last best hope for peace. According to this argument, Wilson understood that only America could make possible the transformation of world politics from a zone of war to one of peace, but – tragic as it was ironic – for this to happen, the United States must first enter the war. Wilson, it has been said, realized America's credibility needed to be preserved, not just in a military sense, but perhaps even more importantly in a moral one, if the country was to be able successfully to leverage its consummate ethical capital at the post-war peace table. But to be at that table, the United States, in this view, had to have some skin in the game, and that implied intervention in a winning cause.[27]

Of this pair of security-related contentions, it is the second that can be most closely associated with status anxiety. Of course, it might be claimed that if the submarine thesis is the most compelling explanation, and if honour is simply one aspect of status anxiety, then the case should be an open-and-shut matter: this emotion drew the United States into the war. Alas, things are a bit more complicated, for if status anxiety is clearly an 'emotion', not all emotions take the form of status anxiety. Honour and status anxiety might be similar, but they are hardly identical constructs. The latter is a *positional* attribute before it is anything else. This means that to assert, as I do in this section, that Wilson's decision-making was shaped in no small way by status anxiety, it is really to the salience of the post-war peace that our attention should be drawn, rather than to the wartime combat on the high seas.

Woodrow Wilson had his own clear sense of America's 'rightful' place in the construction of a new and better international security system. His challenge was to convince leaders of the other great powers to envision America's status in the international hierarchy the same lofty way that he did. In brief, as Wilson was wrestling, at the beginning of April, with the intervention question, he knew one thing: should the United States continue to absent itself from the fighting, it would inevitably suffer a status diminution in the sight of its great-power associates – and this diminished ranking would doom the president's noble dream of a reconstructed world, from which war itself would be expunged. Thus, persuasive as the submarine thesis of American intervention might otherwise be, it is incomplete.

The competing account of April 1917 introduced in the above two paragraphs speaks more directly to the impact of status anxiety upon Wilsonian diplomacy. This account also presupposes that the president sensed America occupied – or at least deserved to occupy – an exalted place in the international pecking order, as nothing other than *primus inter pares*. However, in order for there to be a reconciliation between what America deserved to be able to do and what it actually might be able to do, as the president imagined things, it had to enter the war. For without being involved in the war-making, America would have little chance of dominating the peace-making. And on the issue of peace-making, Wilson, no one would deny, had some very lofty goals in sight.

In this version, Germany did not so much take the war decision out of Wilson's hands as it provided the rationale he needed for realizing his newly emergent, inspirational goals. What were these? Nothing other than to enshrine a 'new diplomacy',[28] from which would be banished the timeworn and, to the president's thinking, highly dangerous mechanisms of power balancing and alliances, to be replaced with a startlingly new vision for lasting peace. Now, all realists, no matter how they might otherwise choose to interpret, qualify, or even 'redact' their favoured paradigmatic catechism, would agree that power balancing remains the fundamental tenet of the faith, the mechanism that enables the continued functioning of the international anarchic system.

This is why the periodic debates over the meaning of Wilsonianism for America's foreign policy have routinely pitted, in one corner, realists against, in another corner of the ring, liberals and much more lately, constructivists. Wilson's image has risen and fallen on at least three separate occasions since April 1917, each time triggering debates over whether he was a great, or a disastrous, president.[29] He has not lacked for defenders, among whom Arthur Link has been the most prepared to fire back against the realists that it was they, not the twenty-eighth president, who suffered from delusionary, hence un-realistic, visions. In this retort, Wilson was presented as someone with preternatural insight into the 'true' structural preconditions for peace. Seeing him in this manner, Wilson's defenders argue he was actually quite a realist in his own right, and not at all the 'utopian' of caricature. Admittedly, Wilson's represented a 'higher' realism,[30] which has even been likened by one scholar to a kind of Waltzian structural realism *avant la lettre*, save that unlike Kenneth Waltz, who saw in the bipolar balance of power a structural remedy for the dangerous defects of multipolarity, Woodrow Wilson would go the whole hog and solve the world's structural dilemma by replacing the balance of power altogether with the apparatus of collective security.[31]

Conclusion

Status anxiety, as argued above, has frequently been associated with two things. The first of these is rising powers. And the second is motivation for mounting a military intervention. Because the United States has for so long (close to eighty years) been so evidently the strongest power in the international system, it has been easy for scholars to overlook the pull exerted by status anxiety upon its foreign policy decision-making. But as this chapter has argued, the decision to cast aside a venerated tradition of eschewing involvement in the European balance of power, while it can be traced to numerous factors, certainly deserves to be examined from an emotional perspective. Specifically, that emotion was status anxiety, highlighting the objective of enhancing America's status so that following the war, the world could be made 'right'. That Woodrow Wilson failed so spectacularly in this undertaking is not a reason to overlook the importance of his vision, or the contribution of status anxiety to his intervention decision. In this case, the United States truly was, to use Renshon's words, fighting for status.[32]

Notes

1. See Dennis Kavanagh, 'Why Political Science Needs History', *Political Studies* 39 (September 1991): 479–95; and Colin Elman and Miriam Fendius Elman, eds., *Bridges and Boundaries: Historians, Political Scientists, and the Study of International Relations* (Cambridge: MIT Press, 2001).
2. See Manfred Jonas, *Isolationism in America, 1935–1941* (Ithaca: Cornell University Press, 1966); and Charles A. Kupchan, *Isolationism: A History of America's Efforts to Shield Itself from the World* (New York: Oxford University Press, 2020).
3. Kenneth N. Waltz, *Man, the State, and War: A Theoretical Analysis* (New York: Columbia University Press, 1959). Also see J. David Singer, 'The Level-of-Analysis Problem in International Relations', *World Politics* 14, no. 1 (October 1961): 77–92.
4. Kenneth N. Waltz, *Theory of International Politics* (Reading, MA: Addison-Wesley, 1979). 'Less properly', because neorealism is a marvellous example, in IR, of the application of what economists call Gresham's Law, save that in the case of the political scientists it is a good word rather than good money that ends up being driven out by the bad. That original good word, neorealism, has become debased to such an extent that it now ends up standing for the virtual opposite of what it had originally been intended to represent, which was the disaggregation rather than the aggregation of 'capability'. That this debasing was in some large measure the doing of Robert Keohane, one of the pioneers of 'complex interdependence' theory, only adds to the curiosity. For early applications of neorealism as a means of assessing the relative merits of a variety of 'power assets' (including 'soft power' ones) in an era in which *aggregate* capability was said to have lost relevance, see Robert Lieber, *No Common Power* (Glenview, IL: Scott Foresman, 1988); Richard Feinberg, *The Intemperate Zone: The Third World Challenge to US Foreign Policy* (New York: W. W. Norton, 1983); and David B. Dewitt and John J. Kirton, *Canada as a Principal Power* (Toronto: John Wiley and Sons, 1983). The work most often associated with the distortion of the concept was Robert Keohane, ed., *Neorealism and Its Critics* (New York: Columbia University Press, 1986).
5. For instance, Neta C. Crawford, 'The Passion of World Politics: Propositions on Emotion and Emotional Relationships', *International Security* 24 (Spring 2000): 116–56; Roland Bleiker and Emma Hutchison, 'Fear No More: Emotions and World Politics', *Review of International Studies* 34 (January 2008): 115–35; and, especially, Todd H. Hall, *Emotional Diplomacy: Official Emotion on the International Stage* (Ithaca: Cornell University Press, 2016).
6. See Graham Allison, *Destined for War: Can America and China Escape Thucydides's Trap?* (Boston: Houghton Mifflin Harcourt, 2017).
7. See, especially, Jonathan Renshon, *Fighting for Status: Hierarchy and Conflict in World Politics* (Princeton: Princeton University Press, 2017). Also see Michelle K. Murray, *The Struggle for Recognition in International Relations: Status, Revisionism, and Rising Powers* (New York: Oxford University Press, 2019); and Tudor A. Onea, 'Between Dominance and Decline: Status Anxiety and Great Power Rivalry', *Review of International Studies* 40 (January 2014): 125–52.
8. Michael Kazin, 'The Great Mistake in the Great War', *New York Times*, 6 April 2017, A28 (emphasis added).
9. For the impact of *Stunde Null* on subsequent German attitudes towards the use of force, see Thomas F. Banchoff, *The German Problem Transformed: Institutions, Politics, and Foreign Policy* (Ann Arbor: University of Michigan Press, 1999).

10 See Benjamin O. Fordham, 'Revisionism Reconsidered: Exports and American Intervention in World War I', *International Organization* 61 (April 2007): 277–310. Earlier instances of the economic explanation include John Kenneth Turner, *Shall It Be Again?* (New York: B. W. Huebsch, 1922); Edwin Borchard and William Potter Lage, *Neutrality for the United States* (New Haven: Yale University Press, 1937); and Alice Morrissey, *The American Defense of Neutral Rights, 1914–1917* (Cambridge: Harvard University Press, 1939). For a contemporary critique of this hypothesis, see Denna Frank Fleming, 'Our Entry into the World War in 1917: The Revised Version', *Journal of Politics* 2 (February 1940): 75–86.

11 See Harold D. Lasswell, *Propaganda Technique in the World War* (London: Kegan Paul, Trench, Trubner, 1938; orig. pub. 1927); Horace C. Peterson, *Propaganda for War: The Campaign against American Neutrality, 1914–1917* (Norman: University of Oklahoma Press, 1939); Charles Callan Tansill, *America Goes to War* (Gloucester, MA: P. Smith, 1963; orig. pub. 1938); James M. Read, *Atrocity Propaganda, 1914–1917* (New Haven: Yale University Press, 1941); and Stewart Halsey Ross, *Propaganda for War: How the United States Was Conditioned to Fight the Great War of 1914–1918* (London: McFarland & Company, 1996).

12 Examples include Sigmund Freud and William C. Bullitt, *Thomas Woodrow Wilson, Twenty-Eighth President of the United States: A Psychological Study* (Boston: Houghton Mifflin, 1967); and Alexander L. George and Juliette L. George, *Woodrow Wilson and Colonel House: A Personality Study* (New York: John Day, 1956). For a hearty endorsement of the latters' findings, see Bernard Brodie, 'A Psychoanalytic Interpretation of Woodrow Wilson', *World Politics* 9 (April 1957): 413–22. Much less exuberant is Robert C. Tucker, 'The Georges' Wilson Re-examined: An Essay on Psychobiography', *American Political Science Review* 71 (June 1977): 606–18. A judicious summary is Dorothy Ross, 'Woodrow Wilson and the Case for Psychohistory', *Journal of American History* 69 (December 1982): 65–8.

13 John J. Mearsheimer, *The Tragedy of Great Power Politics* (New York: W. W. Norton, 2001), 236–7. For a recent combined restatement of the assumed strategic merits of offshore balancing, see Mearsheimer and Stephen M. Walt, 'The Case for Offshore Balancing: A Superior U.S. Grand Strategy', *Foreign Affairs* 95 (July/August 2016): 70–83. Individually, the two structural realists have championed this grand strategy in Walt, *The Hell of Good Intentions: America's Foreign Policy Elite and the Decline of U.S. Primacy* (New York: Farrar, Straus and Giroux, 2018); and Mearsheimer, *The Great Delusion: Liberal Dreams and International Realities* (New Haven: Yale University Press, 2018).

14 On those campaigns of the neutrality years, see John Patrick Finnegan, *Against the Specter of a Dragon: The Campaign for American Military Preparedness, 1914–1917* (Westport, CT: Greenwood, 1974); George C. Herring, Jr., 'James Hay and the Preparedness Controversy, 1915–1916', *Journal of Southern History* 30 (November 1964): 383–404; and Michael Pearlman, *To Make Democracy Safe for America: Patricians and Preparedness in the Progressive Era* (Urbana: University of Illinois Press, 1984). On the singling out of Germany as the foe against whom one needed to be prepared, see Alfred Vagts, 'Hopes and Fears of an American-German War, 1870–1915: I', *Political Science Quarterly* 54 (December 1939): 514–35; and more generally, Clara Eve Schieber, *The Transformation of American Sentiment Toward Germany, 1870–1914* (New York: Russell and Russell, 1923). German activities in the United States, including espionage, propaganda and sabotage initiatives, did little to win a place of affection for the country in the hearts of preparedness advocates,

always more than 'prepared' to put those initiatives in the most sinister possible light, as not just annoying (which they were), but also endangering. For a critical assessment of German attempts to influence developments in the United States, see Reinhard R. Doerries, 'Imperial Berlin and Washington: New Light on Germany's Foreign Policy and America's Entry into World War I', *Central European History* 11 (March 1978): 23–49; and Idem, *Imperial Challenge: Ambassador Count Bernstorff and German-American Relations, 1908–1917* (Chapel Hill: University of North Carolina Press, 1989).

15 Walter Lippmann, *U.S. Foreign Policy: Shield of the Republic* (Boston: Little, Brown, 1943). Also see Forrest Davis, *The Atlantic System: The Story of Anglo-American Control of the Seas* (New York: Reynal and Hitchcock, 1941).

16 See John Milton Cooper, Jr., *The Warrior and the Priest: Woodrow Wilson and Theodore Roosevelt* (Cambridge, MA: Belknap Press, 1983).

17 Daniel Malloy Smith, 'National Interest and American Intervention, 1917: An Historiographical Appraisal', *Journal of American History* 52 (June 1965): 5–24, quote at pp. 23–4. Also see Idem, *The Great Departure: The United States and World War I, 1914–1920* (New York: John Wiley and Sons, 1965).

18 Richard W. Leopold, 'The Problem of American Intervention, 1917: An Historical Retrospect', *World Politics* 2 (April 1950): 405–25, quote at p. 423, n52.

19 Galen Jackson, 'The Offshore Balancing Thesis Reconsidered: Realism, the Balance of Power in Europe, and America's Decision for War in 1917', *Security Studies* 21 (July 2012): 455–89, quoting from pp. 488–9.

20 Robert Endicott Osgood, *Ideals and Self-Interest in America's Foreign Relations: The Great Transformation of the Twentieth Century* (Chicago: University of Chicago Press, 1953), 175.

21 Collective security is often, sloppily, used as a synonym for a different, and competing, sort of security dispensation, collective defence. The biggest difference between the two security arrangements concerns the place of alliances, forbidden in the former, essential in the latter. A good analysis of the concept remains Inis L Claude, Jr., 'Collective Security as an Approach to Peace', in Claude, *From Swords into Plowshares: The Problems and Progress of International Organization*, 4th edn. (New York: McGraw-Hill, 1964), 353–64. Also see Roland N. Stromberg, 'The Idea of Collective Security', *Journal of the History of Ideas* 17 (April 1956): 250–63.

22 Lloyd E. Ambrosius, 'Wilson, the Republicans, and French Security after World War I', *Journal of American History* 59 (September 1972): 341–52. Wilson agreed, reluctantly, that the tripartite alliance so desired by France should be incorporated into the Versailles treaty, but when the US senate failed to ratify the latter, the former also became a dead letter. See Louis A. R. Yates, *The United States and French Security, 1917–1921: A Study in American Diplomatic History* (New York: Twayne, 1957); and Walter A. McDougall, *France's Rhineland Diplomacy, 1914–1924: The Last Bid for a Balance of Power in Europe* (Princeton: Princeton University Press, 1978).

23 Thomas A. Bailey, *Woodrow Wilson and the Great Betrayal* (Chicago: Quadrangle, 1963).

24 Charles Seymour, *American Diplomacy during the World War* (Baltimore: Johns Hopkins Press, 1934). A generation later, at a time when criticism was again mounting against Wilson's legacy as a diplomatist, this same historian would continue to fight the good fight on behalf of Wilson's strategic acumen. On the occasion of the centenary of the president's birth, he published an account praiseful of Wilsonian diplomacy, writing that '[e]ven those who today believe that only a compromise

peace would have provided the base for a permanent settlement admit that Wilson's hand was forced and that the Germans left him no alternative but to enter the war'. Seymour, 'Woodrow Wilson in Perspective', *Foreign Affairs* 34 (January 1956): 175–86, quote at p. 179.

25 See John W. Coogan, *The End of Neutrality: The United States, Britain, and Maritime Rights, 1899-1915* (Ithaca: Cornell University Press, 1981).

26 Robert W. Tucker, *Woodrow Wilson and the Great War: Reconsidering America's Neutrality, 1914-1917* (Charlottesville: University of Virginia Press, 2007), 204. Also see Justus Drew Doenecke, *Nothing Less Than War: A New History of American Entry into World War I* (Lexington: University Press of Kentucky, 2011), 249: 'Germany's public announcement of unrestricted submarine warfare marked the beginning of the end of peace with the United States'; and Gideon Rose, 'The Fourth Founding: The United States and the Liberal Order', *Foreign Affairs* 98 (January/February 2019): 10–21, where it is asserted that '[u]nrestricted submarine warfare was designed to squeeze the Allies into submission. Instead, it pulled the United States into the war, and the world, for good' (p. 12).

27 Arguing that Wilsonian decision-making was motivated by idealism born of moral certainty rather than any power-based calculations is Robert H. Ferrell, 'Woodrow Wilson: Man and Statesman', *Review of Politics* 18 (April 1956): 131–45. 'The immediate occasion for American entrance into the war was the German declaration of unrestricted submarine warfare, which to Wilson's way of thinking was a criminal act. He seems to have gone into the war under the feeling that the balance of justice in the world was being sacrificed to the unjust Central Powers. There is no proof as yet that Wilson led the country into war with a clear determination to preserve the balance of power in Europe .... The "new diplomacy" – a weighing of good against evil, rather than power against power – dictated his decision for war in 1917' (quote at pp. 143–4).

28 Robert W. Tucker, 'Woodrow Wilson's "New Diplomacy"', *World Policy Journal* 21 (Summer 2004): 92–107.

29 On this cyclical pattern, see Lloyd E. Ambrosius, 'Woodrow Wilson, Alliances, and the League of Nations', *Journal of the Gilded Age and Progressive Era* 5 (April 2006): 139–65. The three cycles of rise and decline in his image were: (1) from the earliest days of the post-First World War period to the onset of interwar revisionism; (2) from America's entry into the Second World War to the commencement of the Cold War; and (3) from the ending of the Cold War to the current angst regarding the shaky future of the 'liberal international order' (or LIO). Recent survey data indicates that Wilson is today recognized by scholars as neither great nor disastrous, but simply fair-to-middling, a president ranking alongside William McKinley and John Adams as second-tier leaders, good but not great; see 'C-Span Presidential Historians Survey 2021', available at https://www.c-span.org/presidentssurvey2021.

30 Arthur S. Link, *The Higher Realism of Woodrow Wilson* (Nashville: Vanderbilt University Press, 1971). Also see William G. Carleton, 'A New Look at Woodrow Wilson', *Virginia Quarterly Review* 38 (Fall 1962): 545–66.

31 For this intriguing claim, see Ross A. Kennedy, 'Woodrow Wilson, World War I, and an American Conception of National Security', *Diplomatic History* 25 (Winter 2001): 1–31. Also see Idem, *The Will to Believe: Woodrow Wilson, World War I, and America's Strategy for Peace and Security* (Kent, OH: Kent State University Press, 2009).

32 Renshon, *Fighting for Status*.

Chapter 2

SIR RONALD LINDSAY, THE UNITED STATES AND THE OUTBREAK OF THE SECOND WORLD WAR

Gaynor Johnson

The diplomatic relationship between Britain and the United States during the twentieth century is often described as being one of great closeness and intimate friendship; as though their national outlooks and cultural similarities were so closely aligned as to be almost synonymous with one another. Britain has even been referred to as the fifty-first state. So much so that when students first come to study Anglo-American political and diplomatic relations in that period, it often comes as a shock to discover that the so-called special relationship that defined the Thatcher-Reagan era in the 1980s was the exception rather than the rule.[1] Indeed, there is now so much academic comment about why the relationship between Britain and the United States was not actually that 'special' for much of the twentieth century that one wonders why the point is still debated. The phrase was first coined in 1946 by Britain's famous wartime prime minister, Winston Churchill, and for him it had both personal and professional resonance.[2] As Alan Dobson and Steve Marsh have written, to Churchill, it was the common commitment to the promotion of democracy in the world, and with that, resistance to all forms of political repression that defined the essential tenets of the Anglo-American relationship.[3] His personal rapport with the American president, Franklin Delano Roosevelt, was another important part of the description, and few scholars have doubted that the similarities between their world views contributed significantly to the Allied victory in 1945. This closeness was at its most intense during the first eighteen months of American involvement in the war, from the bombing of Pearl Harbor in December 1941 until the summer of 1943. And yet, if one turns back the clock further a similar length of time, to the spring of 1938 until the outbreak of war in Europe in September 1939, the tone and emphasis of the Anglo-American relationship was very different. Then, only the most optimistic would have described it as close or harmonious. Furthermore, during the 1930s, it became increasingly clear that the response of the European democratic powers to the rise of fascism in Italy and Germany would have to be very different to that of the United States. While the American government grappled with possible neutrality in the likely forthcoming conflict, Britain and France hoped to achieve peace through appeasement while simultaneously preparing for war.

Although written more than thirty years ago now, David Reynolds' analysis of the Anglo-American relationship during the decade preceding the American entry into the Second World War remains the standard work.[4] He described the 1930s in Anglo-American relations as a prelude to the wartime Grand Alliance; a time for setting the groundwork, of testing the nature and strength of the bond between the two nations. That said, Reynolds' focus is primarily on the view from London rather than from Washington. The view from the White House and Capitol Hill has been well documented by the extensive scholarship on Roosevelt, especially those seeking to understand his thinking as a wartime president.[5] But they lack the equivalent of Reynolds' detailed insight into the key personalities as well as the policies; his understanding of the statecraft of foreign policy. Indeed, most of the analyses to date have been made through the prism of the words and actions of British and American politicians. With the exception of David A. Mayers' wonderful book on American diplomats during the Roosevelt era, we know little of that important perspective.[6] Diplomats possess an intimate knowledge of the countries they serve as well as those to which they are posted. They are also foreigners abroad, ideally neutral players in international diplomacy, never in reality being entirely of their own country or belonging to the other. Within the historiography on British foreign policy, there is an even greater yawning gap on the activities of Britain's diplomatic representatives in the United States, in Washington and beyond. With the exception of Brian McKercher's biography of Esme Howard, most of the holders of the post of British ambassador to Washington have had little more written about them than an entry in the *New Oxford Dictionary of National Biography*.[7]

It is a rather grand ambition for a book chapter to try and correct this skewing of the historical picture. Nevertheless, it does seek to show some of the important insights into the Anglo-American relationship that are revealed when the influence of British ambassadors to Washington is factored into the analysis. Space prohibits a comprehensive overview of every dimension; indeed space only permits examination of the smallest tip of the iceberg. Having spent most of my career as a scholar examining the impact of individual personalities on the international history of the twentieth century, there seemed a natural logic to writing about Sir Ronald Lindsay (1878–1945), who was British ambassador to Washington in 1930–9. Not only was his stint in Washington the longest in the twentieth century, it covered a period of immense change in the international diplomatic landscape as well as in Anglo-American relations. Surprisingly, nothing to date has been written on this, although there are studies of other periods of his career. Nevertheless, there are several reasons for studying Lindsay's Washington embassy. He had already enjoyed a distinguished career that had included a period as ambassador to Berlin and as Permanent Undersecretary in the Foreign Office. The Washington embassy was seen as the plumb posting in the British Diplomatic Service, and in his case was a fitting culmination to his career. Indeed, it became his swan song, as he retired upon his return to London in 1939. Lindsay's career and actions also provide a case study in the culture and values of the British Diplomatic Service. Like many of his contemporaries, he was from an aristocratic background; he was part of the old Etonian milieu that dominated the Foreign Office at the time. He was also a career diplomat, and did not share the background in commerce and international law that was such a feature of the formative training of younger members of the Diplomatic Service. That said, he was a man of few pretensions, who took a phlegmatic, practical view of his work and who had little time for the socializing, although he was a close confidant of King George VI. He seldom formed close relationship with foreign dignitaries, although, as this chapter will illustrate, he enjoyed a cordial relationship with Franklin D. Roosevelt.[8]

When Lindsay arrived in Washington in 1930, he had accrued more than thirty years' experience as a diplomat. His appointment not only marked the pinnacle of his career – the Washington embassy was widely viewed, along with Paris – as the most prestigious diplomatic post in the pantheon of British diplomatic appointments. His arrival as the first occupant of the new embassy building, designed by Sir Edwin Lutyens, was also seen as the start of a new era of British diplomatic representation in Washington.[9] Born in 1877, the fifth son of the 26th Earl of Crawford, Lindsay was the classic younger son of an aristocrat who was unlikely to inherit the family title and wealth but who felt compelled to earn his living through a career in public life. Lindsay was educated at Winchester, part of the British public school system that educated a great many of his peers within the Diplomatic Service. That said, and while his career path suggested a fairly seamless rise to the top of his profession, temperamentally Lindsay did not conform to what one might think of that of a natural diplomat. Often gruff and complaining, his correspondence with his brother reveals a man who disliked the constant upheaval and travel that his work involved, who possessed a general suspicion of foreigners and who did not suffer fools gladly. Yet he appears to have been universally liked and respected. Some of the most important reasons for this are discussed elsewhere in the chapter, but also include a shrewd intelligence that showed a solid, balanced judgement of issues and people. Lindsay seems to have been a man with few friends and confidants; unlike many of his generation, he was not a great social letter writer. The correspondence that has survived is overwhelmingly concerned with his professional life. He married twice, both his wives were American: firstly Martha Cameron, the daughter of Senator James Donald Cameron of Pennsylvania, whom Lindsay had married in 1909; she died nine years later. His second wife, Elizabeth Sherman Hoyte (1885–1954), was a celebrated landscape gardener and close friend of the First Lady, Eleanor Roosevelt, and had been an executive of the American Red Cross during the First World War. Lindsay had a brief stint in Washington in 1919–20, which afforded him an insight into American attitudes towards the First World War and the role the United States intended to play in the reconstruction of the international order in its wake. The remainder of his career involved posting to most of the major capital cities of the Great Powers, for example, a period as ambassador to Berlin in 1926–8, preceded by a brief period as ambassador to Constantinople.[10] His solid relationship with the Foreign Office in London was built on a period as Assistant Undersecretary for three years from 1921 and his two years as Permanent Undersecretary prior to his appointment as ambassador to Washington.

In his assessment of others, Lindsay usually acknowledged personal and political strengths and weaknesses, successes and failures, in equal measure. His dislike of hyperbole and effusiveness can be seen throughout his career; for example, he very consciously adopted a more phlegmatic and practical style in his interactions with the German government during his brief stint as ambassador to Berlin in the late 1920s, than his predecessor, Lord D'Abernon.[11] He also disliked fuss and pomposity; valuing instead directness, intelligence and personal integrity. He thought it important that an ambassador should be on cordial terms to the government to which he was accredited, but criticized those, such as his Italian counterpart, Nobile Giacomo de Martino, for wanting to be regarded as a '"regular guy"', that is, someone who practised excessive personal informality in his interactions with the American government. Their colleague, the German ambassador, the aristocratic Friedrich Wilhelm von Prittwitz und Gaffron, was also guilty of this faux pas in Lindsay's eyes, commenting 'he allows rather too many people to call him "Freddy"'.[12] Both the German ambassador and his successor, Dr Hans Luther, were in Lindsay's assessment, deluded in thinking that they were viewed with favour by the American government.[13] Many of Lindsay's evaluations of the political and diplomatic milieu in Washington contain descriptions of the mismatch between actual and perceived levels of influence. As will be seen, he believed that Roosevelt was as guilty of making that mistake on occasions as anyone else. However, the ambassador believed that this kind of error of judgement would define the historical reputation of Roosevelt's predecessor, Herbert Hoover.[14] With characteristic bluntness, in 1934, Lindsay told the Foreign Office that Hoover was now a spent force; that he 'is generally held to have no skills in "politics"'.[15] When it came to assessing his own level of influence both in London and in Washington, Lindsay is very difficult to read. He was not given to statements of self-promotion or to bragging. To the Foreign Office, he was viewed favourably throughout his embassy. Indeed, it could be argued that a reason for the length of his embassy was because the Foreign Office and its political chiefs trusted Lindsay's judgement so much that they did not wish to replace him. This was a cause of frustration to Lindsay himself, who, by 1938, was plotting his departure from Washington and planning his retirement, but still no word about the name and date of arrival of his successor was forthcoming. In London, Lindsay was also seen as a 'Foreign Office man'; he was one of the few diplomats of the period who had also served as Permanent Undersecretary.[16] This was not a position that Lindsay coveted but his practical, no-nonsense approach to the role won him the respect and confidence of his subordinates. And, almost uniquely, Lindsay's influence extended beyond Whitehall, into royal circles, indeed, it was not since the days of Sir Charles Hardinge's stewardship of the Foreign Office before the First World War that a diplomat with such senior, diverse and important connections had been in post.[17] Hardinge had famously been known for his personal sense of entitlement and vanity.[18] Lindsay was the antithesis of this. The importance of his connections was what other people made of them, rather than what he bragged about himself.

Life for Lindsay in Washington appears to have been convivial. Often the epitome of the dour Scot in his written communications, Lindsay nonetheless admitted that he and his colleagues in the international diplomatic corps enjoyed a harmonious relationship with the State Department. In fact, he went as far as to say that they enjoyed 'all the courtesy and consideration which we could possibly expect at any other post in the world'.[19] That happy state of affairs also existed beyond the confines of Washington, where he had found himself 'very cordially welcomed as valuable adjuncts to any public ceremony which may be forward'.[20] Within the portals of the State Department itself, Lindsay developed a close and profitable relationship with both the secretaries of state that were in post during his embassy: Henry L. Stimson and Cordell Hull.[21] Of the two men, Lindsay rated the former as more effective than the latter. Stimson, he wrote, was 'quiet, frank and friendly in manner, and inspires confidence by his equanimity and all absence of fuss and by his evident simplicity and straightforwardness'.[22] Hull, on the other hand, while being 'amiable and courteous' was 'not a man of action'. He was 'diffident and timid and … hardly dares to come to the point … '.[23] Crucially, Lindsay thought Hull was too dependent on the patronage of Roosevelt to be an effective independent mouthpiece on American foreign relations. In 1936, Lindsay wrote: 'Mr Hull is a man of the utmost integrity, dignity and charm. He behaves with great courtesy to heads of missions, and replies at great length to any question they may put to him, but when they return to their houses, they usually have difficulty in remembering anything he has said that deserves to be reported.'[24] A more serious problem in Lindsay's view, however, was that Hull's anti-isolationist views were too out of kilter with that of the American government for him to make him an effective force in Washington. The growing international crisis of the 1930s tended to highlight these points with increasing frequency.

Lindsay's relations with the American press were much more complex, as indeed was the experience of the majority of the international diplomatic corps in Washington. During the early years of his embassy, Lindsay exuded the aura of a celebrity. He appeared to the gentlemen of the press 'as a thing out of a fairy story, or as something halfway between a film star and an animal in a Zoo; [he was] treated with a strange mixture of awe and impertinence'.[25] Three factors combined to change that situation in the years that followed. The first was the belief among leading American journalists, many of whom were Jewish, that the British government and those who represented it were covertly antisemitic. There is little evidence to suggest that this was true of Lindsay. He used racial labels in his descriptions and analyses which to today's sensibilities tend to jar and appear inappropriate, but which were crucially completely commonplace and acceptable during the 1930s. For example, he wrote of his Belgian opposite number, Paul May: 'he is Jewish by race and by religion, but being affable and agreeable has been well received by Washington'.[26] The second factor was the negative American public response to the abdication crisis in 1936, especially British establishment hostility towards Wallace Simpson and the snobbery that surrounded her being both an American and a divorcee.[27] This matter came to a head in the spring of 1939 during the plans for the state visit of King George VI and Queen Elizabeth to Washington.[28] Wallace Simpson, now the Duchess of Windsor, was seen as a much more glamorous alternative to her sister-in-law, and memories remained strong of the hugely successful visit her husband made to the United States when he was Prince of Wales, in 1924.[29] Lindsay was faced with an American press corps who viewed the British monarchy as arcane, dull and out of touch with the real world. His response was to give a number of press conferences prior to the visit in which he explained the constitutional importance of the monarch as head of state and the importance Britain placed on maintaining a good relationship with the United States. As it was, the state visit was a resounding success, largely because of the personal chemistry between the King and Queen and the Roosevelts.[30] But it did little to improve relations between the embassy and the American press. This was because there was a third factor influencing the relationship, and this by far the most significant. It concerned the decision by the British and French governments to adopt a policy of appeasement in their dealings with the European fascist dictators.[31] To many American sensibilities, any policy that appeared to offer concessions to aggressor powers was wrong and spineless. American press responses tended to support the isolationist view favoured by Roosevelt. That a war in Europe was inevitable but that Britain and France were not deserving of American support and assistance because their methods of trying to maintain peace were so wrongheaded.

Lindsay assessed Roosevelt as a person and as president for the Foreign Office in his annual 'Personalities' report, a set of opinions that he never felt compelled to revise or to supplement for the remainder of his embassy.[32] He saw Roosevelt as, essentially, a series of 'baffling' contradictions. Although he had been made frail by polio, the president was also 'as strong as an ox'. He courted public opinion and knew how to manipulate the press to his advantage but was also sensitive to press criticism. His role as president showcased his 'sanguine, optimistic and adventurous' personality; characteristics substantially enhanced by his 'irresistible' personal charm.[33] This ability to win over critics enabled Roosevelt to keep a tight grip on what Lindsay termed his 'official family', that is, members of his government. Tactics that also worked well in the wider Washington political milieu, for example, in the president's dealings with Congress, which Lindsay described as 'masterly'. Roosevelt was better informed about the internal dynamics of politics and commerce in the United States than any of his predecessors and had 'shown a power of leadership and of inspiring confidence and devotion to a degree which is almost miraculous'.[34]

However, Lindsay believed that there were other, less palatable reasons for Roosevelt's political success and popularity. The first was his propensity to surround himself with advisers of 'second-rate ability' in order to enhance his own status, to hide his own 'moderate' intellect and to deflect attention from his merely 'superficial' knowledge of key policy areas, especially relating to finance and economics.[35] Roosevelt's dislike of political discord made him prefer the company of what today would be termed 'yes men'. The reason why these issues never reached the public domain was because of his 'amazing political acumen' and by a 'complete absence of personal vanity'.[36] Lindsay tended to view Roosevelt as being somewhat in his predecessor's shadow, possessing 'all of the qualities which Mr Hoover lacked, but deficient in some of the finer qualities of his predecessor'.

Roosevelt's unwillingness to commit the United States to involvement in the event of the outbreak of another global war also meant that he remained 'untested' as a statesman. Furthermore, the passage of time did not fundamentally alter Lindsay's view of Roosevelt the man and the politician as a cocktail of extraordinary brilliance and bruising, fundamental flaws. In briefing notes to the Foreign Office prior to the royal state visit to Washington in June 1939, Lindsay wrote:

> After his re-election in 1936 Mr Roosevelt would have been wise to devote his attention to the consolidation of the gains achieved. But with all his gifts he is not an administrator. He does not choose good advisers, he is unmethodical in his work and mercurial in his temperament. He seems to do too much himself and grasps at tasks and at decisions which he would do better to leave to administrators. I think he likes to show off before his subordinates. The result is that all his laws are in a mess and all would have been indefinitely better if the four years of his second administration had been devoted to putting them in order.[37]

A pivotal event in the evolution of the Anglo-American relationship in the late 1930s was the approaches that each country took to the policy of appeasement. This difference culminated in a serious diplomatic rift that followed the Anglo-French decision to allow the cessation of the Sudetenland to Germany at the Munich conference in 1938.[38] Conventionally, this has been seen as a difference about whether it was appropriate to make diplomatic concessions to an aggressor nation. In Washington, the position taken by the British prime minister, Neville Chamberlain, and his French counterpart, Édouard Daladier, was viewed as weak, spineless even. Suggesting that the likely Anglo-French response to any subsequent acts of aggression by the Third Reich and its allies would also lack robustness thus increasing the probability that the United States would have to intervene to shore up the most important democratic relationship in Europe in its hour of need.[39] However, analysis of the British papers relating to Lindsay's Washington embassy suggests that the differences between Britain and the United States had a deeper, more intractable origin. In summary, it revealed a difference in the understanding of the purpose of foreign policy. Furthermore, that there had been a complete reversal in the approach taken by each country to European diplomacy since the peace-making process at the end of the First World War. In 1919, American foreign policy had been imbued with the idealism Woodrow Wilson's new liberal world order that would banish war and allow democracy to flourish. Almost twenty years later, Chamberlain was much too much of a pragmatist to be seen as another Wilson, but he did share the same spirit of optimism that, ultimately, rationality would prevail in international diplomacy, and that, in the final analysis, no power would be foolish enough to ignite another large-scale European war. In Paris in 1919, it had been the British who had done most to turn Wilson's intellectualist diplomacy into real, workable plans of action; in 1938, that task was performed by the Roosevelt administration. Lindsay's analysis suggests that he was fully aware of this. He refused to be drawn on his views on morality of appeasement when in February 1939, the Foreign Office notified him that his opposite number in London, Joseph Kennedy, was openly in favour of the policy.[40] Kennedy's apparent willingness to go native led to his recall in disgrace and to the end of his career in public life. Lindsay steered a more careful course. He reported with approval but without endorsement Senator Key Pittman's comment that the policy of appeasement 'encouraged the ambitions of the dictator states'.[41] He focussed instead on reporting signs of a closer rapprochement between Washington, Paris and London where he saw them.[42] By emphasizing the desirability of closer Anglo-American relations at a time when it was not clear in what circumstances that would come about gave Lindsay something constructive, even optimistic, to report to the Foreign Office, rather than the opposite.

That said, Lindsay's optimism was not boundless. When in March 1939, the former first lord of the Admiralty, Duff Cooper, suggested to the British foreign secretary, Lord Halifax, that 'the moment has come for a resolute attempt to break the axis', and that the British government should do all that it could to persuade Italy to remain neutral in such a conflict, Lindsay invoked the opinion of the influential American journalist, Walter Lippman. He had warned that a second Munich-style agreement with the fascist dictators would probably permanently destroy any hope of American support for Britain and France in the event of another war.[43] Lindsay was keen to underline the word 'permanent' in that advice; he believed that in such an eventuality, the United States would become irreversibly isolationist and even hostile to Britain.[44] Foreign Office reactions to Lindsay's observations and to the contents of the Lippman article revealed the full range of opinion to the policy of appeasement and demonstrated how deep the divisions were on that subject. Unsurprisingly, within the Foreign Office, it was Robert Vansittart, the former foreign office permanent undersecretary, and an arch anti-appeaser, who was most responsive to Lindsay's thinking. He minuted: 'I think they will not only talk but do a great deal, and do it quickly, if we have no more Munichs. We nearly lost the USA over that: but if we now make it clear that henceforth we really are going to stand up, we can have much confidence in the attitude of the USA. Anyhow it is our only chance.'[45] The remainder of Vansittart's colleagues, however, viewed Lindsay's thinking very differently. Alexander Cadogan, Vansittart's successor as permanent undersecretary, saw the American government's criticism of the Munich crisis as a temporary blip in a relationship with Britain and France that appeared to becoming closer rather than the opposite. He particularly believed that the Americans would be swayed by the moral issues surrounding the policy of appeasement and the prevention of war. He wrote: 'I am sure the Americans are frightfully keen that we should "fight for the right" and I know it is unfair – and useless – to ask them what they are going to do. But with much more talk about "moral issues" it will begin to be a fair question.'[46] However, some, such as the more junior Gorell Barnes, were openly critical of the American response to the outcome of the Munich conference. To him, the 'cardinal point' was that the inhabitants of the Sudetenland were ethnically German. Consequently, restoring them to the German Fatherland was natural self-determination, not as the 'myth of Munich' would have it, an act of betrayal.[47] He concluded waspishly, 'If we seem to them sometimes to falter in our championship of these ideas, it is not that we are abandoning our passionate love of liberty in its various desirable forms, but that, so far as Europe is concerned, we, unlike the Americans, have to face the practical means of giving effect to and maintaining our ideals.'[48] In other words, Britain was prepared to be a proactive defender of peace, freedom and democracy, the United States was not.

Of course, part of Gorell Barnes' thinking stemmed from the British and French decision to guarantee Polish sovereignty in March 1939 in the wake of the German invasion of the remainder of Czechoslovakia.[49] Lindsay was keen to capitalize on this development as evidence of the robustness of Britain's commitment to the 'traditional policy of preventing any one single Power from dominating the Continent'. It also, he argued, that it provided proof that the British government had abandoned the policy of appeasement.[50] Initially, the American response had been lukewarm; further evidence was needed to demonstrate that Britain and France really were prepared to go to war with Germany should Polish sovereignty be breached. However, Lindsay reported that many of those doubts had been dispelled by Neville Chamberlain's speech on 3 April. Indeed, greater concern had been expressed in Washington about Polish diplomatic thinking; it was unclear how far the Poles regarded Britain and France as natural allies and thus guarantors of their independence; that the Poles were more likely to look to Moscow than to London or Paris for assistance in the event of a German invasion. But he was keen to emphasize to Halifax that 'the air has been cleared and the fact made plain to Herr Hitler that he will not be allowed to pursue his aggressive career unchecked'.[51] The pre-Munich equanimity of Anglo-American relations had, he believed, been restored. And this was a point of view that the Foreign Office understandably willingly embraced. Acting on the information provided by Lindsay, on 6 April 1939, Scott of the Foreign Office produced a minute outlining the importance of maintaining the current and apparently newly improved relationship with the United States.[52] Eight days later, his colleague, John Balfour, produced another draft policy document that argued that particular attention should be paid to American public opinion as a barometer of the likely attitude of the US government towards making any further concessions to the fascist dictators.[53] Scott suggested that Lindsay and his staff travel round the United States as much as possible to gauge the attitude of ordinary American citizens to the growing crisis in Europe, and that this should be done at regular intervals to ensure that their findings were up to date.[54]

Rather than take on this work himself, Lindsay marshalled the network of British consuls and consul-generals serving across the United States. The results did not always yield what the Foreign Office was hoping to hear. For example, on 28 April 1939, Lindsay communicated a memorandum by the consul-general in Chicago, detailing American public responses to Roosevelt's most recent statement on foreign affairs. It indicated, *inter alia*, that German Americans, not surprisingly, viewed the policy of appeasement favourably and continued to advocate a policy of American isolationism.[55] However, in general, the intelligence that the Foreign Office received as a result of Scott and Balfour's initiatives was of the kind that at least offered hope for the future. Less than a week after he had submitted this report, Lindsay communicated an article with the title 'What We, the People, Think about Europe' that had been published in the *New York Times* on 30 April 1939 by Dr Gallup, the director of the American Institute of Public Opinion, that stated that the American government should give as much assistance to Britain and France in the event of a war in Europe; assistance, that is, that fell 'short of actual participation'.[56] The article was a long way from offering the British government the assistance and alliance that so many in Whitehall wished. It was also similar to many other statements in the American press in the previous half dozen years. Nevertheless, Lindsay believed that because the policy of appeasement appeared to have been abandoned the most recent statements of the American government position and public opinion was now more representative of American actual views.[57]

As April gave way to May 1939, Lindsay continued to offer a steer to the Foreign Office on how best to deal with the Roosevelt administration in the event of the outbreak of war. To ensure the support of the American government, it was essential to win over American public opinion. He recommended that, on the declaration of any hostilities, a statement should be made in the House of Commons outlining Britain's war aims specifically in a way that would appeal to and be understood by ordinary American citizens.[58] It should explain not only why the war was being fought, but give an indication of the shape of the 'new world' that would emerge from the 'ruins' of the old.[59] In what proved to be a particular prescient insight, Lindsay argued that the democratic powers should undertake not to construct a network of peace settlements similar to those concluded at the end of the First World War because American public opinion viewed the Treaty of Versailles in particular as '100% failure'.[60] Instead, and again Lindsay's thinking was to prove to be insightful here, the statement should emphasize the importance of the United States in the economic reconstruction of the world after the war. Creating some form of post-war commercial hegemony for the United States was vital, indeed inevitable, if the democratic order was to prevail during the war and after it.[61] Lindsay's recommendations resonated well with the Foreign Office; with a general consensus among officials on both the American and Central European desks that he should closely advise on the text of the Commons statement if not be asked to write it himself.[62]

Lindsay's despatches and telegrams during the last year of peace on Europe can therefore be seen as offering a cautiously optimistic view of the likely course of Anglo-American relations in the near future at least. One expects to see nuance and deftness of argument in such communications, and, as has already been indicated, this approach resonated naturally with the man himself. However, if one examines the Annual Reports from the Washington embassy in this period, the tone is far more bullish. It is notable how few scholars make use of such documents because all British embassies and legations produced them, certainly during the interwar period, and they offer a very useful overview of the mission's assessment of the issues that were of concern in Britain's relations with that country as well as including valuable comment on the domestic history of that country. The reports also cross-reference other key documents produced either by the embassy staff or by the Foreign Office, creating a useful intellectual map of the thinking of both. The document reviewing the events of 1938, written in January 1939, claimed that the American 'public conscience' had moved away significantly from support for a policy of isolationism. Although it was conceded that it was as yet too early to predict when proof of this shift would be seen, it was clear, in the assessment of the Washington embassy staff, that Roosevelt had already come round to the idea: 'It has long been the President's firm conviction that a time will come when deeds rather than words will be required to halt the flouting of international engagements and prove to the Dictator Powers that democracy is capable of a strong policy.'[63] A 'speeding up' of Anglo-American relations was advocated, especially the development of commercial relations between the two countries and the creation of other, soft power, connections that would further bind Britain and the United States together. Appeals to the American political elite about potential or actual breaches of international law by the fascist dictators were likely to have particular resonance because most of them were lawyers by training. When asked whether the United States should stay out of a war in Europe, this same elite would answer in the affirmative but, would concede, when asked whether the United States could remain on the sidelines, the answer was a hesitant but clear, no. Jewish Americans, many of whom had fled Germany to escape persecution, were particularly vocal in lobbying for US support for a British and French stand against the Nazis. They were also able to give direct voice to their views as many American newspapers had Jewish owners. Within their pages, Halifax's predecessor as foreign secretary, Anthony Eden, had become something of a hero, especially in his opposition to the policy of appeasement.[64] His decision to resign about this issue, the report argued, marked a low point in Anglo-American relations, although the absolute nadir came because of the British and French decision to concede the Sudetenland to Hitler at the Munich conference. This assessment is not inconsistent with other assessments of the dynamics of American politics and diplomacy from the pens of Lindsay and his colleagues. But it does suggest that Roosevelt was more favourably disposed towards the British and French stand against fascism than Lindsay's later despatches tended to indicate.

Another important dimension to Lindsay's work in the spring of 1939 was preparations for the state visit of King George VI and Queen Elizabeth to Washington in June. The present author has written elsewhere about the preparations for the visit from the British perspective.[65] The visit itself has somewhat passed into historical folklore with many generations of American children having been raised on the story of how President Roosevelt served root beer and hotdogs to his British guests on the lawn of the White House.[66] At the time, however, the principal debate was about the purpose of the visit. The initial invitation to the royal couple had been made by the president at the time of their coronation in 1937.[67] It was practical logistically because a trip to Washington could easily be slotted in alongside the visit to Canada planned as part of a tour of the dominions. However, for a variety of reasons, both the tour of the dominions and consequently the visit to the American capital were put back to the summer of

1939. By then, the international diplomatic climate had deteriorated dramatically. Furthermore, the state visit coincided with the most recent efforts by Lindsay to secure American support for Britain and France in the event of a war. Those scholars who have mentioned the state visit in their analysis of this period have argued that its purpose was to add royal weight to attempts to secure American support.[68] That Lindsay was a personal friend of the king also enhances the significance of his already important role at this time, and it was he who liaised directly between Buckingham Palace and the White House regarding the plans. David Reynolds has argued that if the purpose of the state visit was indeed to apply further pressure on the Roosevelt administration, it failed to work.[69] While this is true, Lindsay's perspective was different. With an eye on his by then long overdue retirement, he saw the state visit more as a goodwill gesture, which had been its original intention, rather than as a lever to exercise political pressure.[70] He recognized that what could be termed the Munich episode had caused a serious rift between Britain and the United States; a state visit from the king and queen could potentially do much to repair any residual diplomatic damage. The royal couple had embarked on a hugely successful state visit to Paris the previous year that had done much to help shore up the battered Anglo-French entente; there was every reason to believe, in Lindsay's view, that something similar could be accomplished in Washington.[71]

The state visit of King George VI and Queen Elizabeth coincided with Lindsay's retirement. He had long requested to be allowed to resign, indeed, his intention was to retire completely; he was sixty-one in 1939 and complained of physical and intellectual exhaustion. For as long as a year before, Philip Kerr, now Lord Lothian, the former confident of the British prime minister, David Lloyd George, had been mooted as Lindsay's replacement. Lothian had more liberal political inclinations than Lindsay, but it is clear that the time of the arrival of the former and the departure of the latter in Washington, they both viewed the Anglo-American relationship in broadly similar terms.[72] This was strategically vital, of course, but it is striking how alike their thinking was. In July 1939, with his personal possessions already on their way back to London, Lindsay reported with pride that it was clear that Lothian agreed with him about the contents of the statement to be made in the House of Commons for the benefit of American public opinion in the event of the outbreak of war.[73] That they were in agreement that there was 'undoubted underlying unity' between Britain and the United States.[74]

Underlying unity was one thing; for the US government, offering direct assistance to Britain and France in the outbreak of a war in Europe was not simply about recognizing the legitimacy of their cause and acting accordingly. As Lindsay's Annual Report for 1938 had indicated, most of the American political elite realized that, like it or not, if a war was to break out, it would be difficult if not impossible for the United States not to become involved at some point. It was also unclear how that assistance could be offered without there also being an American declaration of war on Germany and her allies. Between 1935 and 1940, several attempts were made to amend the American Constitution to ensure that a national referendum took place before the US government issued a declaration of war.[75]

The Ludlow Amendment, put forward by Representative Louis Ludlow of Indiana, also contained the important caveat that this condition would not apply should the United States be the victim of an act of aggression.[76] This highly democratic approach to the decision to go to war had a longer history and had first been mooted in 1914, prior to the First World War.[77] But it gained particular traction among those who favoured American isolationism in the face of the growing tensions in Europe during the 1930s. In 1935, a Gallup poll suggested that as many as three-quarters of Americans were in favour of the Ludlow Amendment, although by September 1939, at the time of the German invasion of Poland, that figure had dropped to only half. Important opponents included the influential journalist, Walter Lippmann, whose assessment of the American political landscape Lindsay held in high regard. Lippmann believed that, if passed, the Amendment would discourage the United States from preparing for war, a situation that would leave the country at the maximum disadvantage should she indeed be the victim of an act of aggression. Lindsay was keen to downplay the significance of the Amendment in his despatches to London; and as early as January 1938, he reported that it had 'lost traction' with the American people and was unlikely to be represented to Congress again in the near future.[78] Foreign Office opinion thought the reasoning behind the Amendment noble but impractical, leading one official to comment that it represented the kind of democracy that 'passed away with the Greeks'.[79] As it was, the Amendment was never passed, although the debate about it does provide an interesting additional dimension to the analysis of American attitudes towards the growing crisis in Europe. Lindsay's assessment of it largely chimed with that of the Foreign Office.[80] With the growing threat to peace posed by the fascist regimes in Germany and Italy, 'there is no doubt whatever that the country's sympathies are engaged on the side of the democracies'.[81] Lindsay believed that Roosevelt had with 'well judged frequency … warned the American public of the Nazi peril' and had 'urged the importance of military preparedness'.[82]

Alan Dobson's work on Anglo-American political and diplomatic relationship tended to have a focus on the macro rather than on the micro; the broad sweep of the dynamics that shaped it during the twentieth century.[83] Given the importance of that shared bond during that period, as it rebuilt and shaped the international order after the two world wars and the Cold War, such an approach is often essential. This chapter, along with a number of others in this volume, has taken a very different view, and examined the role played by an individual in shaping the mood music and the direction of the Anglo-American relationship. But when one does so, nothing of the significance of the bigger picture is lost. Those commitments to liberal ideals of democracy and the prevention of war as well as a desire to maintain the post-First World War international order are just as present and as a visible on the micro level. Lindsay's embassy illustrates that there were important differences of perspectives on how the Anglo-American relationship should work, but that none was so divergent as to undermine it. There is also a calmness to Lindsay's reports from Washington during the period discussed in this chapter; that is, at a time when a second larger war in Europe was looming, and both the British and French governments were keen to obtain American assurances of assistance in such an eventuality. This can be explained partly by Lindsay's temperament and because he was on the point of retirement; the long term would be someone else's problem to deal with. But it is unlikely that a diplomat of Lindsay's skill and experience would be quite so cynical. He was also not given to complacency. Nevertheless, at heart, he realized that the Anglo-American relationship had firm foundations; that it was a solid friendship. That any disagreements, and many of them were quite profound, for example, that over the advisability of the policy of appeasement, would be set aside if the post-war international order did actually collapse. In this he proved to be right. Lindsay's embassy also demonstrates that the Anglo-American relationship was based on an honest assessment and awareness of the strengths and weaknesses of both powers. Neither was obsequious to the other; this was a relationship of equals. But it is doubtful whether he would have described it as special, important yes, but no more important than, for example, the *entente* with France. However, Lindsay's reports from Washington, especially his assessments of key 'personalities' and his Annual Reports show that he took a holistic view of the study of diplomacy. An understanding of American culture was as desirable as an understanding of American politics and foreign policy priorities. Lindsay and Alan Dobson had much in common.

Notes

1   D. Reynolds, 'The "Special Relationship"? America, Britain and the International Order since the Second World War', *International Affairs* 62, no. 1 (1985): 1–20; J. Cooper, *Margaret Thatcher and Ronald Reagan: A Very Political Special Relationship* (London: Palgrave, 2012).
2   A. Marchi, S. Marsh, 'Churchill, Fulton and the Anglo-American Special Relationship: Setting the Agenda?' *Journal of Transatlantic Studies* 14, no. 2 (2016): 265–82.
3   A.P. Dobson and S. Marsh, eds., *Churchill and the Anglo-American Relationship* (London: Routledge, 2017).
4   D. Reynolds, *The Creation of the Anglo-American Alliance, 1937–1941: A Study in Competitive Co-operation* (Chapel Hill: University of North Carolina Press, 1981).
5   Especially, R. Dallek, *Franklin D. Roosevelt and American Foreign Policy, 1932–1945* (Oxford: Oxford University Press, 1979).
6   D.A. Mayers, *FDR's Ambassadors and the Diplomacy and Crisis: From the Rise of Hitler to the End of World War II* (New York: Cambridge University Press, 2013).
7   B.J.C. McKercher, *Esme Howard: A Diplomatic Biography* (Cambridge: Cambridge University Press, 2006). See, for example, McKercher's entries on Howard and Lindsay in the *ODNB*. These can be accessed online by payment of a subscription through the *ODNB* portal: https://www-oxforddnb-com/.
8   Of the extensive literature on Roosevelt the man, see especially, A.M. Schlesinger, *The Age of Franklin D Roosevelt*, 3 vols. (New York: Houghton Mufflin, 1957–60); R. Dallek, *Franklin D Roosevelt: A Political Life* (London: Penguin, 2018).
9   E. Wilhide, *Sir Edwin Lutyens. Designing in the English Tradition* (London: Abrams, 2000), 9, 53, 183; C.M. Highsmith and T. Landphair, *Embassies of Washington* (Washington: National Trust for Historic Preservation, 1992), 99–102; A. Seldon and

D. Collings, *The Architecture of Diplomacy. The British Ambassador's Residence in Washington* (London: Flammarion, 2014).
10   G. Johnson, 'Sir Ronald Lindsay and Britain's Relations with Germany, 1926–1928', *Diplomacy and Statecraft* 25, no. 1 (2014): 77–93.
11   G. Johnson, *The Berlin Embassy of Lord D'Abernon, 1920–1926* (London: Palgrave, 2002).
12   Report on the heads of missions at Washington for the Year 1930, enclosed on Lindsay to Henderson, 23 January 1931, TNA/FO371/15133/A795/795/45.
13   Report on the heads of missions at Washington for the Year 1934, enclosed in Lindsay to Simon, 1 January 1935, TNA/FO371/18761/A634/634/45.
14   D. Burner, *Herbert Hoover: The Public Life* (New York: Eastern Press, 1979).
15   List of leading personalities in the United States, undated, TNA/FO371/15136/A1592/1592/45.
16   T.G. Otte and K. Neilson, *The Permanent Under Secretary for Foreign Affairs, 1854–1946* (London: Routledge, 2008).
17   Lord Hardinge of Penshurst, *Old Diplomacy* (London: John Murray, 1947).
18   B.C. Busch, *Hardinge of Penshurst: A Study of the Old Diplomacy* (London: Archon, 1980).
19   Lindsay to Simon, 5 January 1933, TNA/FO371/16613/A588/588/45.
20   Ibid.
21   D.F. Schmitz, *Henry L Stimson: The First Wise Man* (London: Rowman and Littlefield, 2000); J.W. Pratt, *Cordell Hull, 1933–44*, 2 vols. (New York: Cooper Square, 1964).
22   List of leading personalities in the United States, undated, TNA/FO371/15136/A1592/1592/45.
23   Ibid.
24   US personalities report, 1 January 1936, TNA/FO371/19832/A308/308/45.
25   Lindsay to Simon, 5 January 1933, TNA/FO3716613/A588/588/45.
26   Reports on the heads of foreign missions at Washington for the Year 1932, enclosed in Lindsay to Simon, 5 January 1933, TNA/FO3716613/A588/588/45.
27   M. Bloch, *The Duchess of Windsor* (London: Weidenfeld and Nicolson, 1996); S. Williams, *The People's King: The True Story of the Abdication* (New York: Palgrave, 2004).
28   S. Bradford, *George VI* (London: Weidenfeld and Nicolson, 1989).
29   Josef Israels II, 'Selling George VI to the US', *Scribner's Magazine*, February 1939, in Lindsay to Halifax, 23 May 1939, TNA/FO371/22800/A3879/27/45.
30   Eleanor Roosevelt, *This I Remember* (New York: Greenwood Press, 1949), 183–4; John W. Wheeler-Bennett, *King George VI. His Life and Reign* (London: Macmillan, 1958), 382.
31   Within the now-vast literature on appeasement, see especially, D.C. Watt, *How War Came: Immediate Origins of the Second World War, 1938–39* (London: Heinemann, 1990); R.A.C. Parker, *Chamberlain and Appeasement: British Policy and the Coming of the Second World War* (London: Macmillan, 1993); D. Faber, *Munich, 1938: Appeasement and World War II* (London: Simon and Schuster, 2009).
32   Personalities in the United States, 1 January 1934, TNA/FO371/17588/A420/420/45.
33   Ibid.
34   Ibid.
35   Ibid.
36   Ibid.
37   Lindsay to the Foreign Office, 23 May 1939, TNA/FO371/22800/A3879/27/45.

38 The best multinational assessment of this pivotal event in the history of appeasement and the origins of the Second World War remains E. Goldstein and I. Lukes, eds., *The Munich Crisis: Prelude to War* (London: Taylor and Francis, 1998).
39 On Chamberlain's evolving historical reputation on this issue see D. Dutton, *Neville Chamberlain* (London: Edward Arnold, 2008).
40 Halifax to Lindsay, 20 February 1939, TNA/FO371/22829/A1385/1292/45.
41 Lindsay to Halifax, 24 February 1939, TNA/FO371/22829/A1692/1292/45.
42 Ibid.
43 Duff Cooper to Halifax, 22 March 1939, TNA/FO371/22829/A2914/1292/45.
44 Lindsay to Halifax, 23 March 1939, TNA/FO371/22829/A2439/1292/45.
45 Minute by Vansittart, 9 April 1939 on Lindsay to Halifax, 23 March 1939, TNA/FO371/22829/A2439/1292/45.
46 Minute by Cadogan, 7 April 1939 on Lindsay to Halifax, 23 March 1939, TNA/FO371/22829/A2439/1292/45.
47 Minute by Gorrell Barnes, 25 March 1939 on Lindsay to Halifax, 6 April 1939, TNA/FO371/22829/A2584/1292/45.
48 Ibid.
49 S. Grant Duff, *Europe and the Czechs* (London: Penguin, 1938).
50 Lindsay to Halifax, 4 April 1939, enclosed in Minute by Mr Scott, 6 April 1939, TNA/FO371/22829/A2693/1292/45.
51 Ibid.
52 Minute by Mr Scott, 6 April 1939, TNA/FO371/22829/A2693/1292/45.
53 Minute by Mr Balfour, 14 April 1939, TNA/FO371/22829/A2856/1292/45.
54 Minute by Scott, 11 May 1939, on minute by Bruce Lockhart, 15 April 1939, TNA/FO371/22829/A3017/1292/45.
55 Lindsay to Halifax, 28 April 1939, TNA/FO371/22830/A3596/1292/45.
56 Lindsay to Halifax, 4 May 1939, TNA/FO371/22830/A3486/1292/45.
57 Ibid.
58 Lindsay to Halifax, 8 May 1939, TNA/FO371/22830/A3314/1292/45.
59 Ibid.
60 Lindsay to Halifax, 8 May 1939, TNA/FO371/22830/A3314/1292/45.
61 Ibid.
62 Minute by Perowne, 11 May 1939, on Lindsay to Halifax, 8 May 1939, TNA/FO371/22830/A3314/1292/45.
63 Annual Report on the United States for 1938, TNA/FO371/22832/A1882/1882/45.
64 Ibid.
65 G. Johnson, 'Royal Diplomacy: British Preparations for the State Visit of King George VI and Queen Elizabeth to the United States, June 1939', *Diplomacy and Statecraft* 32, no. 2 (2021): 330–50. See also P. Bell, 'The Foreign Office and the 1939 Royal Visit to America: Courting the USA in an Era of Isolationism', *Journal of Contemporary History* 37, no. 4 (October 2002), 610–12.
66 P. Conradi, *Hot Dogs and Cocktails. When FDR Met King George VI at Hyde Park on Hudson* (London: Alma Books, 2013).
67 Roosevelt to King George VI, 17 September 1938, TNA/FO371/21548/A7769/7643/45.
68 See, Bell.
69 D. Reynolds, *The Creation of the Anglo-American Alliance, 1937–1941* (Chapel Hill: University of North Carolina Press, 1988); 'FDR's Foreign Policy and the British Royal Visit to the USA, 1939', *The Historian* 45, no. 4 (1983), 461–672.

70 Lindsay to Balfour, 11 January 1939, TNA/FO371/22799/A316/27/45.
71 J. Herman, *The Paris Embassy of Sir Eric Phipps, 1937–1939* (Brighton: University of Sussex Press, 1998); G. Johnson, 'Sir Eric Phipps and the Appeasement of Germany, 1933–1937', *Diplomacy and Statecraft* 16 (2005), 4, 651–69.
72 D. Reynolds, 'Lord Lothian and Anglo-American Relations, 1939–1940', *Transactions of the American Philosophical Society* 73, no. 2 (1983), 1–65.
73 British Library of Information, New York, to Leeper, 14 July 1939, TNA/FO371/22830/A5068/1292/45.
74 Ibid.
75 Ronald E Powaski. *Toward an Entangling Alliance: American Isolationism, Internationalism and Europe, 1901–1950* (New York: Greenwood, 1991) p. 4.
76 A. Scherr, 'Presidential Power, the *Panay* Incident and the Defeat of the Ludlow Amendment', *International History Review* 32, no. 3 (2010), 455–500.
77 Benjamin D. Rhodes. *United States Foreign Policy in the Interwar Period, 1918–1941: The Golden Age of American Diplomatic and Military Complacency* (The Hague: Praeger, 2001), p. 151.
78 Lindsay to Halifax, 11 January 1938, TNA/FO371/21525/A196/64/45. O. R Holsti, *Public Opinion and American Foreign Policy* (Chicago: University of Michigan, 2004).
79 Minute by Beith, 24 January 1938 on Lindsay to Halifax, 11 January 1938, TNA/FO371/21525/A476/64/45.
80 Bell, p. 601.
81 Ibid.
82 Ibid.
83 For example, A.P. Dobson, *The Politics of the Anglo-American Economic Special Relationship 1940–84* (Brighton: Wheatsheaf/St. Martin's, 1988).

Chapter 3

QUIXOTIC CALLING: ROBERT AND MARION
MERRIMAN IN THE SPANISH CIVIL WAR

David Mayers

The violence that swept Spain in 1936–9 reconfirmed the essence of every civil war: a sum of all political calamities, fratricide compounding the shock and destruction normally associated with interstate violence. The senior military officers who spearheaded the *pronunciamiento* neither anticipated nor desired a protracted nor internationalized civil war. Generals Emilio Mola (plot director), José Sanjurjo, Francisco Franco (proclaimed *Caudillo* in 1939) and their confederates expected to wage a quick coup d'état. Consequently, they reckoned, the country – numbering 24 million souls – would be spared further indignities perpetrated by reckless parliamentarians and heedless left-wing governments. To stanch anti-clerical outrages, church burnings, political killings and confiscations of private property, all of which had had rocked the Second Republic since its 1931 inception, the nation's uninformed protectors would establish safety and restore decorum.[1] The February 1936 election, in which Popular Front parties (liberal, socialist, communist, anarchist) headed by Manuel Azaña won a thumping victory, caused the conspirators to implement the earlier-concocted plans. Contrary to calculations, alas, stubborn Republican resistance stymied the plot. Instead of promptly returning Spain to stability, the insurgent generals precipitated warfare that lasted for the better part of three years.

The precise number of casualties remains uncertain; controversy among scholars and vying partisans continues to this day. A common estimate is that half a million deaths resulted from the fighting. Among the first fatalities were José Antonio Primo de Rivera, founder of the Falange (fascist) party and the poet/playwright Federico García Lorca. Of the roughly 200,000 Spanish combatants who died, 110,000 fought on behalf of the Republic and 90,000 against. The civil war left countless other people maimed, homeless, displaced and orphaned. A minimum of 300,000 Republicans took refuge abroad following the cessation of hostilities.[2]

The main European powers – France, Germany, Italy, USSR and United Kingdom – adopted in August 1936 a non-intervention policy, eventually endorsed by twenty-seven governments. The United States aligned itself with this programme, premised on prudence and the idea that Spaniards alone should determine their national fate, and enacted an arms embargo in January 1937.

Famously, the German and Italian administrations broke faith with non-interventionism. They lavished men, war machines and moneys on the insurgency as it dethroned Spain's democratically elected regime. Stalin's Soviet Union meanwhile provided varieties of aid to the Republic, although not of abundance or calibre comparable to that shipped to the Nationalists. In contrast with the three meddling powers, and despite periodic hesitation, the governments in Paris, London and Washington remained in compliance with the non-interventionist protocol. Yet their citizens volunteered – as did people of forty-five additional nations – to trek to Spain to bolster the Republic. Of the nearly 40,000 men and women who went, 2,800 came from the United States. They travelled by ships and trains and over steep Pyrenees footpaths patrolled by French border guards. The first American contingents arrived in Spain in January 1937 (a few persons having previously come in late 1936). These people were soon caught in a mesh of competing ideas, unforgiving politics and bewildering history irreconcilable with glossy fables about crusaders on errand to save democracy.

A third of the Americans died in combat or from related causes. Most survivors suffered wounds or other disability and received scant courtesy or sympathetic reception upon US repatriation. Moreover, their practical military contribution was negligible, although their presence helped boost Loyalist morale. Still, few volunteers doubted the rightness of the Republican cause or regretted placing what strength they possessed at its disposal. Donnish Robert Merriman, lost in the Spanish maelstrom, allowed that 'I am willing to die for my ideas'.[3]

Volunteers

The civil war struck most Americans who thought about it as not only tragic but also baffling. First Lady Eleanor Roosevelt in June 1938 expressed this dismay: 'Why everybody should want to kill everybody else is just beyond my comprehension.'[4] The broader public concentrated on dramas closer to home: FDR's Supreme Court packing manoeuvre, New Deal improvisations and the president's effort to rid the Democratic party of recalcitrant conservatives. Opinion polls indicated that the majority of Americans approved of neutrality in the matter of Spain hardly cared that nearby Mexico provided the Republic with 20,000 rifles and ignored Texaco's granting of generous credits to Franco's armed forces to purchase crucial oil (which ultimately involved transactions totalling 3.5 million tonnes).[5]

To the degree that Americans registered a preference for one or another Spanish side, they tended towards the Loyalists.[6] This partiality, though lukewarm, did support the White House outlook, forbearing of persons such as Ambassador Claude Bowers who lobbied on behalf of funnelling aid to the Republic. Not wholly averse to circumventing the embargo, FDR investigated modes by which US materiel might be surreptitiously transferred to Spain, which resulted in modest supplies of transportation equipment and wheat getting through via third countries.⁷ But FDR proceeded with circumspection. He did not want to act, nor be so perceived, in ways offensive to American Catholics, many alarmed by the atheists and anti-clerics who populated Republican ranks. Figures such as Father Charles Coughlin naturally numbered here. So did the handful of Americans who enlisted on the Nationalist side, such as the pilot Vincent Patriarca, or those filtered through Ireland's Eoin O'Duffy and his band of 700 Catholic men of Eire who appeared (ineffectually) on Franco's behalf in 1937 combat.⁸

More worrisome to FDR than such outliers was the potential mutiny of New Deal stalwarts who, like Joseph Kennedy, were incensed by Republican curtailment of the Church and furious over cases of violence against nuns, priests and laity. Very likely FDR exaggerated the hazard posed by Kennedy and others to the New Deal coalition. Opinion polls indicated that American Catholics were hardly monolithic in their attitude towards the civil war. True, 39 per cent sympathized with Franco. Thirty-one per cent were neutral, however. And 30 per cent identified with the Loyalists, among whom Dorothy Day of the Catholic Worker Movement.⁹ In any event, hoped Roosevelt, matters in Spain would somehow come out right for humanity, an unwarranted attitude that he belatedly amended but too late. In March 1939, he admitted to Bowers that adherence to neutrality and the restrictive embargo had been in error.¹⁰

By the time FDR confessed regret to Bowers, the surviving American volunteers were homeward bound from Spain or had already been repatriated. The same applied to thousands of people from other countries that had served the Republic – larger congregations being French (10,000), German-Austrian (5,000), Polish (5,000), Italian (3,400), British (2,000), Canadian (1,200).¹¹

The international volunteers who fought for the Republic did so under Comintern authority and sponsorship. These auspices did not mean that all who went were communists or beholden to the Soviet Union. Some became disillusioned. These included such estimable writers as France's André Malraux, who organized a small volunteer air force (Escuadrilla España), and Germany's Gustav Regler, who served as a political commissar in one of the Comintern's brigades. Of Americans who enlisted for Spain, a fourth were not communist party members. Only a minority fair to say, whether committed Marxist or other, fully grasped Stalin's mixed Spanish motives or, for that matter, appreciated the links between Soviet-orchestrated terror in Catalonia and the concurrent Moscow purge trials.

Americans in Spain became known collectively as the Abraham Lincoln Brigade, a slightly fanciful appellation. It entered into parlance to enhance the impression of élan and formidableness. No such combat unit ever existed, in fact. The Americans served in numerous formations but never assembled into an identifiably national brigade. Like other foreign volunteers in Spain, most Americans received assignments according to language. Thus, German speakers were concentrated in battalions constitutive of the 11th Brigade. The 12th Brigade drew from battalions of mainly Italian speakers. Battalions made up of Polish speakers (and Balkan tongues) formed the 13th Brigade. French-language battalions composed the 14th Brigade. Applied to Americans, this language principle placed them in the predominantly English-speaking 15th Brigade, other members drawn primarily from Canada and the British Isles.

Commanded until mid-1938 by incompetent Lieutenant Colonel Vladimir Ćopić, a Yugoslav communist, the 15th Brigade stabilized with these battalions: the Abraham Lincoln (American), the George Washington (American), the Mackenzie-Papineau (American/Canadian), British (United Kingdom/Ireland) and Spanish (Cuban, Mexican, South American). With allowance for fluctuation among casualties, replacements and rotations each battalion numbered 700 officers and men, supplemented by support personnel. Other Americans staffed the John Brown Artillery Battery and the First Transport Regiment; 150 US doctors and nurses invigorated the medical corps of the international brigades. After incurring appalling casualties, around 50 per cent in July 1937 in the Brunete offensive, the Lincoln and Washington remnants merged into a new designation, the Lincoln-Washington Battalion.[12]

By autumn 1938, the Lincoln-Washington and Mackenzie-Papineau outfits could not rely upon intakes of fresh US recruits to replenish the ranks. Consequently, Spanish conscripts, typically adolescent peasants without English-language proficiency (and condescendingly viewed by the wearied Americans), filled the rising vacancies.[13] This process resulted in the assimilation of nominally American units into the Republican army. Before which time, they had participated in several engagements: Jarama, Brunete, Aragon, Teruel, the Ebro. Even when successful, the Americans, like the rest of the internationalist and Loyalist units, could not sustain a strategic initiative. They were outdone by the Nationalists' material advantages, outclassed by Franco's professional armies and routed by German-Italian enormity.

A diversity of American histories and mix of motives formed the volunteers. Substantial numbers came from the white labouring class (factory workers, farm/ranch hands, miners, mechanics, seamen, longshoremen) and immigrant families recently arrived in America. The Great Depression took a toll on these people with high rates of divorce, children fostered to institutions and law breaking. To these people, Spain was an extension of US social struggles centred on labour organizing, picket line violence and unemployed councils.

White-collar occupations were represented by schoolteachers, office clerks, journalists and college instructors. A few volunteers traced their lineage to the Colonial era and sprang from the privileged or professional classes, sporting Ivy League pedigrees and fancy club memberships. Although all regions of the United States contributed, north-eastern urban areas pulled heavily, with New York City accounting for 18 per cent of the inductees.

About ninety Black Americans volunteered in Spain. To them, the Spanish fight constituted another front in the war for civil rights and stood as a proxy for Italian-captive Ethiopia. In the words of one Black soldier in Spain, 'I wanted to go to Ethiopia and fight Mussolini … This ain't Ethiopia, but it'll do.'[14]

A third of the American volunteers in Spain were Jewish, an arresting statistic given that Jews accounted for less than 3.5 per cent of the total US population (128 million in 1936).[15] Political preferences played a role, shading from liberal to militant left. So did the desire to land a blow for antisemitism, this when anti-Jewish feeling was rife in the United States, to say nothing of the virulent strain coursing through Franco's German ally where prohibitions on Jewish participation in social-political-economic life multiplied yearly. As African American views of Spain intertwined with Jim Crow conditions and Ethiopia, disgust with the Nazis shaped Jewish sympathy for the Republic.

As for commonalities among the volunteers, these stood out: The Americans were relatively young (median birth year being 1910), albeit no longer definable as unwary youth. They had little or no prior military experience. Just a small fraction was married or affianced.[16]

From Nevada to Spain – Robert and Marion Merriman

Committed to the scholarly vocation, Robert Merriman additionally possessed a penchant for strenuous action with requisite stamina. This combination of qualities impressed people he encountered, including Ernest Hemingway. His protagonist in *For Whom the Bell Tolls*, Robert Jordan, sufficiently resembled Merriman to suggest to aficionados that Jordan was a fictionalized Merriman.[17] Both were fledgling academicians endowed with egalitarian principle. Both reflexively sided with the weak against the overbearing. In the circumstances of combat, each struggled to retain moral footing yet could not help slipping, evidenced in the shooting of unarmed prisoners – more proof to Hemingway, were it needed, that war is a 'lousy enterprise'.[18]

Among Americans in Republican Spain, Merriman occupied loftier status than most. At the time of his death (likely early April 1938), he held the rank of major and responsibility as chief of staff for the 15th Brigade. Just twenty-seven when the Spanish Army rebelled, Merriman and his wife, Marion, were living in Moscow. A PhD student in Economics at the University of California-Berkeley, on foreign travel fellowship, he had devoted himself to studying Soviet agricultural policies, specifically the collective farms. To make ends meet, he also tutored Russian pupils in English and worked for the Soviet Ministry of Information as it constructed a telephone system between Moscow and New York.[19] Marion for her part took assorted office jobs, most importantly with the *Moscow Daily News*, a Kremlin-subsidized publication to interpret Soviet realities to English-language readers residing in the USSR.

Without subvention but at personal expense, and after overriding Marion's objections, Robert travelled alone to Barcelona, arriving in early January 1937. Comintern operatives then involved him in their organizing of the International Brigades. In mid-February, he assumed command with rank of captain of the hastily formed Abraham Lincoln Battalion.

Nothing in Merriman's background signalled that he would qualify for service in an army beholden to powers beyond the United States. He was born in the rugged California coastal town of Eureka but reared in San Jose and on a marginal Mojave desert homestead. He came of age in scenic but patchy Santa Cruz, where he graduated from the local high school at sixteen. His father worked as a lumberjack and at sundry trades plus farming. Merriman's mother wrote Sunday school primers and anodyne romances for public libraries. Money and other family resources were chronically scarce. After Santa Cruz graduation, Merriman clerked in a grocery store, 'lumberjacked', and did heavy lifting at a paper mill, all of which delayed his college matriculation. Eventually, the University of Nevada-Reno (UNR) recruited him to play football, the coaches evidently approving his tall and muscular frame, more hulking than agile. A gridiron injury ended his athletic career. He subsequently earned wages at a mortuary and a J.C. Penny's store, dug ditches, and did well at craps in Reno's gambling saloons. He also enrolled in the university's Army R.O.T.C. programme that carried a stipend, $7.50 per month. He meanwhile raced about Reno in a Dodge roadster, joined a fraternity and participated in thespian productions. Popular, handsome, a "straight arrow" man, he seemed destined to fit into the comfortable middle class that had eluded his parents, assuming of course that the Great Depression proved a temporary condition. He kept this counsel: 'Sit tight and wait for the breaks.'[20]

Imperceptibly at first, but obvious by his senior year, Merriman deepened. Progressivist solutions to the nation's political-economic agony caught his attention. He left the fraternity scene, dismissing it as unwholesome and elitist.[21] He applied his intellectual energy to academic studies, the payoff being admission to Berkeley's creditable Economics department. On UNR commencement day in 1932, he received his BA and commission as a second lieutenant in the Army Reserve. The same day he wedded Marion Stone in an Episcopal rite arranged by her employers. Like her groom, she had of necessity worked varied jobs – domestic and secretarial – to pay student fees and otherwise depended on university financial aid. Not all, though, was dully earnest or stuck on penny-pinching frugality. There was joy of life: a self-described 'playgirl', she had joined a sorority. Dances and parties were her milieu. She reigned as Queen at UNR's 1932 R.O.T.C. Military Ball. She also acquitted herself well in the study of English and Spanish. Having thrived on the staff of UNR's undergraduate newspaper, she entertained hopes of becoming a writer.[22]

At Berkeley, the Merrimans rented a poky one-room apartment. It housed them, Marion's two younger sisters, and an impecunious Economics graduate student who had nowhere else to turn. Financial constraints and lack of privacy aside, Robert luxuriated in his courses and assumed responsible teaching assistantships. Another Economics graduate student, John Kenneth Galbraith, fated for fame, testified that Robert was the most respected person in the department's PhD programme.[23]

Temperamentally unsuited for a purely ivory-tower existence, Merriman engaged political-labour questions that percolated near Berkeley. He helped organize assembly-line workers at a car manufacturing plant in Richmond, where incidentally he also laboured for low hourly pay in unsafe conditions.[24] When in summer 1934, stevedore actions in San Francisco led to a general strike of 130,000 workers in the Bay Area, with concomitant violence between National Guard troops and unionists, he lent his talents to the latter's publicity drives.[25]

Fed up with bromides about US resilience and Washington's assurances that prosperity would soon return, Merriman wondered whether America had become a spent force. Millions of unemployed people, destitute families, shantytowns, soup lines, idle factories, failed banks, farm foreclosures and crackdowns on organized labour comprised bleakness evidently impervious to repair by the old ways. As perceived by Merriman in Berkeley, the USSR was mercifully free of such miseries. State planning had dislodged the vagaries of unpredictable markets, dispensed with reckless stock buying and eliminated greedy finance. Industrial production climbed ever upward. Agricultural quotas were exceeded. Surplus foods were exported. The yawning gap closed between the rural poor and urban dwellers. The Soviet system of scientific management had things to teach, he therefore reasoned, and worth incorporating to salvage the United States. Hence the Merrimans, having never wandered east of Nevada, journeyed in January 1935 to the USSR.[26]

Conveniently perched at the Moscow Institute of Economics, Merriman conducted research into the theory and practice of Soviet collective farming, subject of his prospective PhD dissertation. This study also entailed excursions to the Ukrainian and Russian countryside, which displayed its cornucopia.[27] After one such visit, he exclaimed:

> The peasants ... showed me food stores that were greater than their needs required. In some cases they half-apologized for having so much ... They insisted on feeding me so often that even I, with my famous appetite, couldn't keep up. Milk, eggs, butter, cream, potatoes, chicken, pork, fish, all kind of cookies, puddings, blini with sour cream, preserved fruits, tomatoes, salads, wines, it was all there.[28]

Merriman had not noticed, or perhaps did not care to comment upon, the lingering effects of Stalin's war on the kulaks and the man-made famine occasioned by terror-enforced collectivization. In the early 1930s, this caused five to six million people to die by violence and starvation.[29] No doubt Merriman's Intourist minders explained away anything untoward that by chance he encountered. And like most people most of the time, this Moscow newcomer believed what he wanted and screened out the rest. Reports on Ukrainian famine retailed by the Hearst newspaper syndicate were a deliberate fabrication, he charged.[30] Respected members of the Anglo-US community in Moscow with whom the Merrimans mixed – the *New York Times's* reporter Walter Duranty, the indomitable Anna Louise Strong who supervised Marion at the *Moscow Daily News* – abetted this obliviousness. Duranty and Strong praised the Soviet Union's transformative agricultural achievements and scotched doubts.[31]

The wonders of Soviet life never ceased to impress the Merrimans. Robert sent 'bulletins' to readers of the *Pacific Weekly* (left-wing California publication) on the construction of the Moscow subway, Soviet building boom, cultural and recreational packages for workers, public health programmes and Red Army élan.[32] In one dispatch he confessed that he and Marion toyed with the idea of remaining in Moscow, a temptation overcome only by the felt need to return home to further justice's cause:

> Like everyone else who has ever lived here we are inclined at times to consider staying here definitely, since life is so much easier than it is in America. Not only is it easier to make a living but it is easier to do what you want. And everyone is optimistic because the growth of the country is so rapid and evident, month by month. We [discard] such an idea [however] since we realize the tense situation in America and the need for working and fighting.[33]

Anxieties about freedom of expression in the USSR and the legal system did gradually seep into the Merrimans' awareness. But these were allayed in 1936 by promulgation of the impeccably democratic Soviet constitution; it delivered humanity to 'a new stage' of 'historic importance' (Strong's words) and dignity.[34] As to the sensational purge trials of 1936 – centred on Lev Kamenev, Grigory Zinoviev and company – they also ruffled the Merrimans' serenity, but the couple's confidence in the proletariat's promised land did not wane. No less a personage than Ambassador Joseph Davies, appointed by FDR in 1936 to Embassy Moscow, publicly championed the scrupulousness of the Soviet assizes.[35]

Going to Iberia and immersion in war distracted Merriman from any misgivings. Whatever appeared slightly out of joint in the USSR, presumably correctable in the fullness of communist time to come, was trivial compared to the imperative of checking Franco and Nazi/Italian aggression. In the meantime, Merriman reflected, the USSR alone of all the main powers, to its infinite credit, fought to preserve Spain. On the eve of his first battle, Jarama (more below), he exclaimed in his diary: 'Long live the Soviet Union! Men may die but let them die in a working-class cause.'[36]

Merriman's certainty about his Spanish calling did not differ from that of other American volunteers. But unlike the majority, he also possessed a smattering of military proficiency. Admittedly, this was inferior to that of many Europeans in the International Brigades. Yet his Reserve commission and R.O.T.C. credentials elevated him among his compatriots, additionally respectful of his Moscow sojourn that implied a Soviet imprimatur. Conscientiousness and regard for the well-being of his men also commended him to his brother officers. They frequently remarked upon his clarity of mind – evident in his instructions to subordinates and reports to superiors – and his professorial tone, enhanced by thick-framed glasses and occasional preoccupation.

Colonel Stephen Fuqua, military attaché of Embassy Madrid, thought Merriman exceptional among the Americans, whom he judged generally hearty but also slovenly. Fuqua penned the following assessment after meeting Merriman:

> [He] is the backbone and moving spirit of the XV Brigade; he is addressed as *Camarada* by all except those near to him and to these he is known as 'Bob.' He is a fine manly type, over six feet in height, physically sound with the endurance of an ox, pleasing personality, filled with initiative, overflowing with energy, he

moves about everywhere in the command honored and respected by all, he is unquestionably the dominant figure of the brigade, and the 'Star' American in the 'Volunteer' group.[37]

So taken was Fuqua by Merriman, a man more than three decades his junior, that he gave Merriman a leather jacket that he had worn in France during the Great War. To Merriman's staff, Fuqua also remaindered a pair of pistols and US Army manuals, a token of favour that transgressed strictures on neutrality, which controlled in the case of all US Embassy personnel, military attachés included.[38]

Normally too self-absorbed to notice anyone outside his entourage, Hemingway encountered Merriman after he led (September 1937) a breathless house-to-house grenade attack in Nationalist-occupied Belchite. Splinters had struck Merriman half a dozen times in the face and hands; he had not stopped for dressing until after the town's cathedral, bristling with rebel machine guns, had been captured. Even as corpses strewn the streets, Merriman the Berkeley pedagogue elucidated for Hemingway the plan of attack and its progress. His meticulousness and his courage, corroborated by other Belchite participants, moved Hemingway.[39] In one of his dispatches, he wrote of Merriman and his men, whose acquaintance he had earlier made:

> Since I saw them last spring, they have become soldiers. The romantics have pulled out, the cowards have gone home, along with the badly wounded. The dead, of course, were not there. Those that were left were tough, with blackened matter-of-fact faces, and after seven months they knew their trade.[40]

This 'trade' had been earned at steep cost. Seven months prior, the 15th Brigade's American units had been thrown into the front line to defend Madrid and its communication/transportation link to the Republican leadership huddled in Valencia: the Jarama campaign. Concentrated in the Abraham Lincoln Battalion (consisting at the time of two infantry companies, one machine-gun company), the volunteers had only weeks before, in some cases just days, arrived in Spain. They had received little training in equipment, tactics and standard drill, or even the proper wearing of uniforms. Ammunition and weaponry were scant, strictly rationed among the men. Firing-range practice in this circumstance constituted an uncommon frill. The battalion was also poorly officered until Merriman, at the critical hour, relieved the Lincolns' manifestly unfit commander, frazzled Captain James Harris. On the road to Jarama, Merriman paused the battalion and allowed the soldiers to discharge their weapons, a measly five rounds each.[41] Until then, most of the Lincolns had never fired shots, felt the recoil, or sniffed the acridity, let alone heard live volleys or machine-gun staccato.

Immediately after reaching the Jarama line, the Lincolns were ordered forward, despite the protests of Merriam to Brigade headquarters. Such an advance was premature and contrary to the original plan, he argued: formations on the Lincolns' flanks had stalled; aerial and artillery support went absent. Only when threatened with court martial by Ćopić did Merriman lead his men headlong into a storm of shell burst and bullet spray. Of the 450 men, two-thirds were killed or wounded. Merriman was hit instantly, his left shoulder smashed. Ćopić later endeared himself to Merriman by calling the Americans 'cry babies'. Merriman grew to loathe the man as a bully and bungler.[42] Ćopić's just reward came in mid-1938 when called to the USSR, into which miasma he forever disappeared.

Shortly after his wounding, Marion Merriman got permission to leave Moscow and join her husband, his arm set in heavy plaster during convalescence. He thereupon assumed duties in the training depot for incoming volunteers at Tarazona. In this task, he proved adept while also liaising between battlefield commanders and Brigade seniors. Marion in the meantime assumed miscellaneous jobs in nearby Albacete: nurse's aide, office factotum, then escort to war tourists, among whom Sherwood Anderson, Dorothy Parker and Anna Louise Strong.[43] Despite grumbling by soldiers prohibited from bringing wives or sweethearts to Spain, Marion eventually enlisted (rank of corporal) in the Lincoln Battalion, the only American woman so allowed. She learned to handle a pistol. On official business, she ran urgent errands, organized personnel files (pertaining to casualties, replacements, assignments) and performed varieties of confidential work. These demands and mounting privations, primarily lack of adequate nutrition, came at cost. She developed a case of hepatitis that almost killed her. Life under bombardment and the death or suffering of friends rattled her. With her husband in Madrid in late April 1937, when he joined Hemingway to broadcast a radio appeal to the States, she experienced raw fear. Shells from a Nationalist artillery barrage collapsed nearby buildings and people's lives: 'I was terrified.'[44]

While assigned in late May to investigate rumours of demoralization and subversion at a hospital in Murcia, and in company with two male comrades (identified only as 'Slav' officers), Marion endured another trauma. Late in the evening, one of the men raped her. Furious, frightened and weeping, she scrubbed into the long night. The assailant's nonchalance next morning astonished her, but too unnerved she did not confront him. She then lived for weeks in trepidation that she had contacted venereal disease or been impregnated. In the event, she had not. Nor did she tell Robert of the violation. 'I must not hurt Bob with this,' she reasoned. 'If I tell him … Bob might kill the man. Or one of the other Americans would, for sure. There would be great trouble. No, this must be my secret burden. I cannot tell anyone – ever. What has been done cannot be undone.' She concluded in self-abnegation: 'The war filled Bob's mind. I could not trouble him further, and I did not.'[45]

Despite promotion to chief of staff of the 15th Brigade, Robert Merriman remained attached to the enlisted soldiers. He frequently dined among them rather than in the officers' mess. He discouraged them from calling him 'sir'.[46] As the Belchite action demonstrated, he did not hold back from the riskiest combat from which rank and commensurate duties could have excused him. Still, he did not invite intimacy nor the kind of fraternization between officers and men that numerous volunteers expected in a people's army assembled to defeat privilege and despotism.

In tandem with battlefield reverses, increased desertions, disobedience to orders and declining recruitment, Merriman's 'can do' optimism wilted. Nor could he relax but became more insistent on the imperatives of 'rigid control' and 'intense political work'.[47] Lapses in his usual composure occurred. He became markedly sterner. He decreed that men who lost their rifles or failed to march against the enemy should not await court martial but be shot on the spot.[48] Despite residual qualms, he countenanced the mistreatment of enemy POWs; he did not interfere with – at times authorized – their execution. The nickname conferred on Merriman by some bitter survivors of the Jarama fiasco echoed in 1938: 'Murderman'.[49]

Scrappy Dave Doran, an Albany communist (Jewish with family origins in Russia), served as commissar for the 15th Brigade. He came out of what can be called the backbone of the American brigades: committed white working-class communists without college or professional training. Alas, he was also a pre-emptory man who inspired resentment; he worked closely with Merriman, whom incidentally he outranked. Doran apparently pushed Merriman hard in dictatorial directions against the grain of his essential self.[50] Records reveal that Doran never questioned the techniques associated with André Marty, the mentally unmoored senior commissar/chief organizer of the International Brigades, who boasted of personally shooting suspected deserters, Trotskyites and other miscreants.[51] To Comintern directors in Moscow, Marty meanwhile insinuated that Merriman was unreliable, prone to 'deviationism'; he certainly warranted scrutiny, given that he held a commission in the army of the world's foremost capitalist power and accepted favours from the dubious Colonel Fuqua. For good measure, Marty had termed Merriman's Americans as spoiled brats.[52]

During the Republican retreat of March–April 1938 from Gandesa, Doran and Merriman and the foraging party they led got disoriented in night-time fighting. They inadvertently separated from the 15th Brigade's main body. The exact circumstances and timing of their fate remain a mystery. Perhaps Doran and Merriman were killed amidst this confused action. Perhaps they surrendered only to be instantly shot by their Nationalist captors, a sentence routinely meted out by the rebels to international volunteers. Perhaps Doran and Merriman were detained for an indeterminate time in a Nationalist camp, and then executed, again as normally done to foreign POWs.

Berkeley academics, US diplomats and news services mounted repeated inquiries but in vain. The corpses of Merriman and Doran were not recovered but deposited somewhere in unmarked graves.[53] Rumours and alleged sightings abounded for decades. Even Marion saw her phantom husband: 'I knew, very soon, that he was dead. And yet, in the middle of the night, I could hear his voice. For many years, in San Francisco, I would catch a glimpse of him and would run to catch up with him. But he always disappeared in the crowd.'[54]

Coda

Marion Merriman had left Spain a few months before disaster overcame her husband. In December 1937, she disembarked from the SS *Manhattan* in New York City and mustered out of the 15th Brigade (but on account of being a married woman was denied the $25 given to men upon severance).[55] When in April news arrived of Robert's battlefield disappearance, she was already resident in a low-rent San Francisco apartment. During the intervening time, she undertook a speaking tour – orchestrated by the CPUSA – to expound the Republic's cause, counter Francoist propagandists and raise funds to aid the international volunteers. Her engagements entailed stops in north-eastern cities, then in the Midwest, finally to the Pacific coast. In Hollywood, Dorothy Parker sponsored an elegant entertainment with 150 guests that featured such celebrities as Edna Ferber, Dashiell Hammett, Lillian Hellman and Ira Gershwin. Merriman spoke with zeal and the authority of a tested participant. Her southern California audience, as ones elsewhere, responded with gratifying support, moral and material: 'Checks were written for several thousands of dollars.'[56] Thereafter, once settled in San Francisco, she and a handful of comrades endeavoured to help the brigaders readjust to civilian life, find jobs, and remedy physical and psychological injuries.[57] Her organization also provided occasions and places for the returnees to gather, otherwise isolated by their incommunicable experiences from a society that was anyway indifferent. She eventually became commander of the San Francisco Bay Area Post of the Veterans of the Abraham Lincoln Brigade. 'We're not simply survivors,' she told the membership in 1985, dwindling from age and illness. 'We are and *always will be* part of the future that will be better thanks to our efforts.'[58]

Until her death (1991), Merriman remained in the San Francisco region, employed as an administrative assistant by Stanford University and arranged aid for the veterans. She also fostered public awareness of their legacy via writings and lectures, a task made timely when President Ronald Reagan pronounced that those who had gone to Spain were guilty of 'fighting on the wrong side'.[59]

As needed, Marion deflected FBI sleuths interested in the doings of survivors, which point leads to a speculative matter. Had Robert survived Spanish combat and completed his Berkeley dissertation, what kind of academic life might he have enjoyed? In this connection, it is useful to recall that faculty members of his University of California were required in 1949 to take a loyalty oath that turned on whether they were communists. Thirty Berkeley professors who refused to take the oath were fired, others penalized in lesser but humiliating ways.[60] In the middle of Spanish dangers, Hemingway's Robert Jordan halted long enough to wonder about his future Stateside life: 'I don't know whether I'll be able to be a professor when I get back. They will probably run me out as a Red.'[61] Surely, Robert Merriman's career would have been further hobbled had he, as planned, also studied with the socialist Professor Harold Laski of the London School of Economics, whose lecturing/appearance at UCLA needed in 1949 to be cancelled lest he corrupted California youth.

On the sound assumption that Robert had died, Marion remarried. She and her lawyer-businessman husband, Emil Wachtel, had three sons and lived comfortably in Palo Alto. Of her Spanish time, she considered it the high point of her life: it contained excitement, nobility and a broadening. This last obliged her to interact with compatriots of whom she lacked prior acquaintance, namely Blacks and Jews. Into old age, she reminisced fondly about Jewish repartee and humour and the singing of spirituals by African American soldiers, notably Sergeant Joseph Taylor (a Lincoln-Washington scout).[62]

The rector of the University of Salamanca, Miguel de Unamuno, delivered a brave speech in October 1936. In the presence of General José Millán Astray, a Francoist adviser and founder of the Spanish Legion, Unamuno, predicted: 'You will win, because you possess more than enough brute force. But you will not convince. For to convince, you need to persuade. And in order to persuade you would need what you lack: reason and right in the struggle.'[63] That reason and right would triumph the American volunteers believed, even in 1939 as Franco declared victory. The years involved in the waiting would, though, have stunned the volunteers had they known in advance that more than three decades would elapse before the Francoist regime ended and the octogenarian Caudillo passed to what he anticipated: encounter with his Maker and divine judgement, but escape from human tribunals. Franco's mortal remains were interred in 1975 in the stygian Santa Cruz Basilica located in the Valle de los the Caídos, earlier built by Republican prisoners and authorized by Franco to memorialize the civil war dead. (Not until October 2019 did Spain's socialist government effect the Generalissimo's exhumation and reburial in the Franco family vault in Madrid's Mingorrubio cemetery.) The basilica also housed, and still to this writing, the body of the Falange's José Antonio Primo de Rivera.

Figure 3.1 From right to left: Robert Merriman, Marion Merriman and Dave Doran in Spain, 1937. Abraham Lincoln Brigade Archives, New York University.

In 1996, amidst remembrances of the sixtieth anniversary of the civil war, Madrid offered rights of Spanish citizenship to those surviving internationals who had defended the Republic. This constituted fitting if belated tribute to aged people, who, when young, had soldiered with an enthusiasm that typically outstretched their military expertise, as the Americans at Jarama. Of the slain in that and other battles, appropriate utterances were made during the 1996 commemorative exercises. But the most fitting words for those entombed in Spain, some like Robert Merriman in sites unknown, were actually composed back in 1939 by Hemingway. His lines, their epitaph:

> The first American dead have been a part of the earth of Spain for a long time now ... and the earth of Spain can never die ... The dead do not need to rise. They are a part of the earth now and the earth can never be conquered. For the earth endureth forever. It will outlive all systems of tyranny ... no men ever entered earth more honorably than those who died in Spain.[64]

Notes

1. Stanley Payne, *The Collapse of the Spanish Republic, 1935–1936: Origins of the Civil War* (New Haven: Yale University Press, 2006), 359, 363–5.
2. Paul Preston, *The Spanish Holocaust: Inquisition and Extermination in Twentieth-Century Spain* (New York: W.W. Norton, 2012), xi, 665–71; Zara Steiner, *The Triumph of the Dark: European International History 1933–1939* (Oxford: Oxford University Press, 2011), 247; Herbert Matthews, *Half of Spain Died: A Reappraisal of the Spanish Civil War* (New York: Charles Scribner's Sons, 1973), 235.
3. Robert Merriman's Diary entries, 16 and 17 February 1937, Cary Nelson and Jefferson Hendricks, eds., *Madrid 1937: Letters of the Abraham Lincoln Brigade from the Spanish Civil War* (New York: Routledge, 1996), 84.
4. Eleanor Roosevelt to Gellhorn, 29 June 1938, Martha Gellhorn Papers, Boston University.
5. Richard Traina, *American Diplomacy and the Spanish Civil War* (Bloomington: Indiana University Press, 1968), 166; Dominic Tierney, *FDR and the Spanish Civil War: Neutrality and Commitment in the Struggle That Divided America* (Durham: Duke University Press, 2007), 58, 68, 89–90.
6. Adam Hochschild, *Spain in Our Hearts: Americans in the Spanish Civil War, 1936–1939* (Boston: Houghton Mifflin Harcourt, 2017), 171.
7. Tierney, *FDR and the Spanish Civil War: Neutrality and Commitment in the Struggle That Divided America*, 97, 104, 122.
8. Traina, *American Diplomacy and the Spanish Civil War*, 176–7; Tierney, *FDR and the Spanish Civil War: Neutrality and Commitment in the Struggle That Divided America*, 65–6.
9. John Diggins, *Mussolini and Fascism: The View from America* (Princeton: Princeton University Press, 1972), 329.
10. Claude Bowers, *My Mission to Spain* (New York: Simon and Schuster, 1954), 418; Robert Dallek, *Franklin D. Roosevelt and American Foreign Policy, 1932–1945* (New York: Oxford University Press, 1979), 180.
11. Matthews, *Half of Spain Died: A Reappraisal of the Spanish Civil War*, 198.

12   Nelson and Hendricks, *Madrid 1937: Letters of the Abraham Lincoln Brigade from the Spanish Civil War*, ix, 233; Edwin Rolfe, *The Lincoln Battalion: The Story of the Americans Who Fought in Spain in the International Brigades* (New York: Veterans of the Abraham Lincoln Brigade, 1939), 97; James Cortada, *Modern Warfare in Spain: American Military Observations on the Spanish Civil War, 1936–1939* (Washington: Potomac Books, 2012), 191; 'American Volunteers in Spain', *The Volunteer for Liberty*, 7 November 1938, 9; Ronald Radosh et al., *Spain Betrayed: The Soviet Union in the Spanish Civil War* (New Haven: Yale University Press, 2001), 49; Confidential Note on the situation of the International Brigades at the end of July 1937, 246.

13   Alvah Bessie, *Men in Battle: A Story of Americans in Spain* (New York: Veterans of the Abraham Lincoln Brigade, 1954), 153–4.

14   Oscar Hunter, '700 Calendar Days', in Alvah Bessie, *The Heart of Spain: Anthology of Fiction, Non-Fiction, and Poetry* (New York: Veterans of the Abraham Lincoln Brigade, 1952), 29.

15   https://www.brandeis.edu/cmjs/conferences/demographyconf/pdfs/Dashefsky_JewishPopulationUS2010.pdf; Peter Carroll 'Forward', in Hank Rubin, *Spain's Cause Was Mine: A Memoir of an American Medic in the Spanish Civil War* (Carbondale: Southern Illinois University Press, 1997), vxi.

16   Peter Carroll, *The Odyssey of the Abraham Lincoln Brigade: Americans in the Spanish Civil War* (Stanford: Stanford University Press, 1994), 14–19.

17   James Mellow, *Hemingway: A Life without Consequences* (Boston: Houghton Mifflin Company, 1992), 518; Robert Martin, "Hemingway's *For Whom the Bell Tolls*: Fact into Fiction" in *Blowing the Bridge: Essays on Hemingway and For Whom the Bell Tolls*, ed. Rena Sanderson (New York: Greenwood Press, 1992), 59–60; Cecil Eby, *Between the Bullet and the Lie: American Volunteers in the Spanish Civil War* (New York: Holt, Rinehart and Winston, 1969), 228 #14.

18   Hemingway to Dear Mike, 4 March 1937, OCO4-Series 2, Ernest Hemingway Papers, John F. Kennedy Presidential Library and Museum. Regarding Jordan and shooting of prisoners, see Hemingway's *For Whom the Bells Tolls*, 304.

19   Marion Merriman and Warren Lerude, *American Commander in Spain: Robert Hale Merriman and the Abraham Lincoln Brigade* (Reno: University of Nevada Press, 1986), 60.

20   Marion Merriman to Steve Nelson, 28 October 1985, Box 2, Steve Nelson Papers, Abraham Lincoln Brigade Archives, New York University (NYU).

21   Merriman and Lerude, *American Commander in Spain: Robert Hale Merriman and the Abraham Lincoln Brigade*, 12–13.

22   Marion Merriman Wachtel video interview re. herself, Brandeis University.

23   Hochschild, *Spain in Our Hearts: Americans in the Spanish Civil War, 1936–1939*, 5.

24   Merriman and Lerude, *American Commander in Spain: Robert Hale Merriman and the Abraham Lincoln Brigade*, 23; Marion Merriman Wachtel video interview re. Robert Merriman, Brandeis University; Marion Merriman, 'Tribute to Robert Merriman', nd January 1986, Carton 1, Robert Merriman Papers, University of California-Berkeley (UCB).

25   Hochschild, *Spain in Our Hearts: Americans in the Spanish Civil War, 1936–1939*, 7–9.

26   Merriman and Lerude, *American Commander in Spain: Robert Hale Merriman and the Abraham Lincoln Brigade*, 25, 27, 30.

27   Robert Merriman, 'Through the Ukraine to the Caucasus', *Pacific Weekly*, 16 September 1935; 'Recent Achievements of Collective Agriculture', *Pacific Weekly*, 30 September 1935, Carton 1, Robert Merriman Papers, UC-Berkeley.

28 Merriman and Lerude, *American Commander in Spain: Robert Hale Merriman and the Abraham Lincoln Brigade*, 56–7; Robert Merriman, 'Soviet Collective Farms', *Pacific Weekly*, 22 July 1935, 34–5, Carton 1, Robert Merriman Papers, UCB.

29 See Anne Applebaum, *Red Famine: Stalin's War on Ukraine* (New York: Random House, 2017) and Robert Conquest, *The Harvest of Sorrow: Soviet Collectivization and the Terror-Famine* (New York: Oxford University Press, 1986).

30 Robert Merriman, 'Soviet Collective Farms', *Pacific Weekly*, 22 July 1935, 34, Carton 1, Robert Merriman Papers, UCB.

31 Marion Merriman, who for a while worked as an assistant for Duranty, described him as 'knowledgeable' about the USSR and 'kind'. She also 'was amused by his blasé attitudes – particularly when there was little news and decided to file a "think piece"'. See Merriman and Lerude, *American Commander in Spain: Robert Hale Merriman and the Abraham Lincoln Brigade*, 53–8, 73; Marion Merriman, 'Tribute to Robert Merriman', nd 1986, Carton 1, Robert Merriman Papers, UCB.

    Anna Louise Strong did learn and worry about the famine crisis. But no evidence suggests that she discussed this matter with the Merrimans. She never publicly cast doubt on the official line that trumpeted the 'conquest of bread'. See Strong's *I Change Worlds: The Making of an American* (New York: Henry Holt and Company, 1935), 357–71.

32 Robert Merriman, 'Moscow the Soviet Capital', *Pacific Weekly*, 8 July 1935; 'Rest Homes in Soviet Russia', *Pacific Weekly*, 15 July 1935; 'Soviet Sports Parade', *Pacific Weekly*, 5 August 1935; 'A Trip to a Red Army Camp', *Pacific Weekly*, 26 August 1935, Carton 1, Robert Merriman Papers, UCB.

33 Robert Merriman, 'Letter from Soviet Russia', *Pacific Weekly*, 283, 18 May 1936, Carton 1, Robert Merriman Papers, UCB.

34 Merriman and Lerude, *American Commander in Spain: Robert Hale Merriman and the Abraham Lincoln Brigade*, 48–52; Anna Louise Strong, *The New Soviet Constitution: A Study in Socialist Democracy* (New York: Henry Holt and Company, 1937), v–vi, 91. Strong elsewhere hailed the Soviet document; see 'Soviet Constitution', January 1937, Accession 1309-001, Box 34, Anna Louise Strong Papers, University of Washington.

35 Joseph Davies, *Mission to Moscow* (New York: Simon and Schuster, 1941), 280; Kirschenbaum, *International Communism and the Spanish Civil War: Solidarity and Suspicion*, 136; David Mayers, *The Ambassadors and America's Soviet Policy* (New York: Oxford University Press, 1995), 118–20. Zinoviev and Kamenev were executed. Ninety-eight of 139 members of the central committee, as constituted in 1934, were also found guilty of capital crimes and shot.

36 Merriman's diary entry of 17 February 1937, Nelson and Hendricks, *Madrid 1937: Letters of the Abraham Lincoln Brigade from the Spanish Civil War*, 84.

37 Three-Day Visit to the Eastern Front, Valencia, 1 November 1937, Cortada, *Modern Warfare in Spain: American Military Observations on the Spanish Civil War, 1936–1939*, 185.

38 Eby, *Comrades and Commissars: The Lincoln Battalion in the Spanish Civil War*, 262; Hochschild, *Spain in Our Hearts: Americans in the Spanish Civil War, 1936–1939*, 246–7.

    Although Fuqua thought well of Merriman, the feeling was not reciprocated. The latter viewed the former with unease and had misgivings about his visiting/evaluating the American volunteers and then reporting to Washington. Diary entry, 27 October 1937, 57, Box 1, Robert Hale Merriman and Marion Merriman Papers, Abraham Lincoln Brigade Archives, NYU.

39 Michael Reynolds, *Hemingway: The 1930s* (New York: W.W. Norton, 1997), 277–8; Alex Vernon, *Hemingway's Second War: Bearing Witness to the Spanish Civil War* (Iowa City: University of Iowa Press, 2011), 33.
40 Merriman and Lerude, *American Commander in Spain: Robert Hale Merriman and the Abraham Lincoln Brigade*, 174.
41 Rolfe, *The Lincoln Battalion: The Story of the Americans Who Fought in Spain in the International Brigades*, 31; Vincent Brome, *The International Brigades: Spain 1936–1939* (London: Heinemann, 1965), 110.
42 Robert Merriman to Marion Merriman, 4 October 1937, Box 1; Robert Merriman to Marion Merriman, 24 April 1937, Box 8, Robert Hale and Marion Merriman Papers, Abraham Lincoln Brigade Papers, NYU.
43 Marion Merriman Wachtel video interview re. herself, Brandeis University.
44 Marion Merriman to Harriet and Myrt, 11 July 1937, Marion Notes, Box 8, Robert Hale Merriman and Marion Merriman Papers, Abraham Lincoln Brigade Papers, NYU; Merriman and Lerude, *American Commander in Spain: Robert Hale Merriman and the Abraham Lincoln Brigade*, 131.
45 Merriman and Lerude, *American Commander in Spain: Robert Hale Merriman and the Abraham Lincoln Brigade*, 148–9.
46 Rolfe, *The Lincoln Battalion: The Story of the Americans Who Fought in Spain in the International Brigades*, 141.
47 Robert Merriman to Marion Merriman, 28 March 1938, Box 1, Robert Hale Merriman and Marion Merriman Papers, Abraham Lincoln Brigade Archives, NYU; Eby, *Comrades and Commissars: The Lincoln Battalion in the Spanish Civil War*, 289–90, 321.
48 Eby, *Comrades and Commissars: The Lincoln Battalion in the Spanish Civil War*, 62, 71.
49 Robert Merriman diary, entry of 26 August 1937, Box 8, Robert Hale Merriman and Marion Merriman Papers, Abraham Lincoln Brigade Archives, NYU; Carroll, *The Odyssey of the Abraham Lincoln Brigade: Americans in the Spanish Civil War*, 112, 155–6.
50 Frank Ryan, ed., *The Book of the XV Brigade* (Madrid: Commissariat of War, XV Brigade, 1938), 223; Carroll, *The Odyssey of the Abraham Lincoln Brigade: Americans in the Spanish Civil War*, 164–5; Eby, *Comrades and Commissars: The Lincoln Battalion in the Spanish Civil War*, 244; Bessie, *Men in Battle: A Story of Americans in Spain*, 83, 85–6; Kirschenbaum, *International Communism and the Spanish Civil War: Solidarity and Suspicion*, 120.
51 Matthews, *Half of Spain Died: A Reappraisal of the Spanish Civil War*, 202–3.
52 Malcolm Cowley, 'Lament for the Abraham Lincoln Battalion', *Sewanee Review*, Summer 1984, 339; Notebook entry of 24 October 1938 in Bessie, *Alvah Bessie's Spanish Civil War Notebooks*, 130 Eby, *Comrades and Commissars: The Lincoln Battalion in the Spanish Civil War*, 262.
53 Kirschenbaum, *International Communism and the Spanish Civil War: Solidarity and Suspicion*, 188–9.
54 Marion Merriman to Luke Hinman, 28 July 1987, Box 2, Steve Nelson Papers, Abraham Lincoln Brigade Archives, NYU.
55 Marion Merriman Wachtel video interview re. herself, Brandeis University.
56 Merriman and Lerude, *American Commander in Spain: Robert Hale Merriman and the Abraham Lincoln Brigade*, 200.
57 Lee Kutnik video interview; Marion Merriman Wachtel video interview re. herself, Brandeis University.

58 Marion Merriman to Steve Nelson, 28 October 1985, Box 2, Steve Nelson Papers, Abraham Lincoln Brigade Archives, NYU.
59 George Huhn, 'Wrong Side in Spain Was the Right Side', *Philadelphia Daily News*, 10 January 1985.
60 Ellen Schrecker, *No Ivory Tower: McCarthyism and the Universities* (New York: Oxford University Press, 1983), 117–25.
61 Hemingway, *For Whom the Bell Tolls*, 244.
62 Merriman and Lerude, *American Commander in Spain: Robert Hale Merriman and the Abraham Lincoln Brigade*, 183; Marion Merriman Wachtel video interview re. herself, Brandeis University.
63 https://speakola.com/political/miguel-de-unamuno-last-lecture-1936.
64 Ernest Hemingway, "On the American Dead in Spain" in *The New Masses*, 3, 14 February 1939.

Chapter 4

JOHN BASSETT MOORE AND THE MODEST VIRTUES OF INTERNATIONAL LAW

David Clinton

Some seventy years ago, in the course of describing what he termed the 'legalistic-moralistic approach' to international affairs, which he decried as having had a harmful effect on United States foreign policy in the fifty years in which it had run 'like a red skein' through American thinking and actions, the distinguished diplomat George F. Kennan declared that it had in it

> something of the old emphasis on arbitration treaties, something of the Hague Conferences and schemes for universal disarmament, something of the more ambitious American concepts of the role of international law, something of the League of Nations and the United Nations, something of the Kellogg Pact, something of the idea of a universal 'Article 51' pact, something of the belief in World Law and World Government.[1]

Kennan discerned a kind of unfortunate unity in this conception of the purposes, responsibilities and aspirations of US foreign policy, which, as he saw it, had driven two generations of American policymakers and diplomats to march together in a direction harmful to the interests of their country and inimical to world order. With few and unheeded exceptions, Kennan told his listeners in the first of his lectures, this half-century had begun in 'a background of general torpor and smugness in American thinking about foreign affairs'. It ended, as did Kennan's series of lectures, with the dispiriting current events that marked American efforts to deal with a world the troubles of which were in some measure due to 'the deeper mistakes of understanding and attitude on the part of our society in general'.[2] There was, in short, a kind of malign unity in the 'legalistic-moralistic approach', in which all the elements identified by Kennan fitted together; simultaneously innocent and prideful, they were nevertheless consistent with one another and jointly misled Americans through the first half of the twentieth century.

Yet it is the contention of this chapter that the career of John Bassett Moore, which in some ways typified the attitude towards foreign affairs that Kennan was criticizing, demonstrated over these fifty years the progressive unravelling of the red skein, as Moore, the apostle of some of the elements of this approach, increasingly came into conflict with adherents of other elements, to such a degree that, by the end of the period, he found his greatest intellectual and policy adversaries among fellow subscribers to the legalistic-moralistic approach. This is a story of sundered relationships, disappointed hopes and collaboration replaced by acerbity. It is an account of discord overtaking the relations among those sincerely devoted to international cooperation.

Although less well known today than a century ago, John Bassett Moore had a remarkable career. Born in 1860 in Smyrna, Delaware, and having studied at the University of Virginia and read law in his native state, he was at the young age of twenty-six asked by Secretary of State (and former United States Senator from Delaware) Thomas Bayard to serve as third assistant Secretary of state, remaining at that post until 1891, when he became Hamilton Fish Professor of International Law and Diplomacy at Columbia Law School. Moore held the professorship until 1924, though he took several leaves of absence to serve in various diplomatic capacities – including assistant secretary of state in 1898 and later that same year counsel and secretary to the American commissioners negotiating the Treaty of Paris that ended the Spanish-American War. After his return from Paris, he worked closely with Secretary of State John Hay in dealing with the Boxer Rebellion in China and the siege of the American and other diplomatic missions in Peking. At the outset of the Wilson administration, he held the office of Counsellor in the Department of State. He was also recalled to government service in his representation of the United States in the Dominican Arbitration Tribunal, and at the Fourth International American Conference in Buenos Aires in 1910 and the International Commission of Jurists at Rio de Janeiro in 1912. Moore served on the Permanent Court of Arbitration at The Hague from 1912 to 1938, and on the Permanent Court of International Justice from 1920 to 1928. His career as a publicist and practising attorney, dealing particularly with cases in international law, lasted into the 1940s before ill health brought his withdrawal from public affairs and his death in 1947.

Although Moore's career thus stretched well back into the nineteenth century and almost to the mid-point of the twentieth, it is on the middle years, from the nineteen-teens through the nineteen-thirties, that this sketch will concentrate. Moore's disillusionment with Wilson's policies began his break with Wilsonianism and with some, though not all, tenets of Progressivism. From this time forward he would never again hold any position in the US government and he would increasingly become a voice of outside dissent, warning and opposition. Although hardly on the fringes of society – for during these years he remained a hugely successful and sought-after attorney and lived in financial comfort – he never again sat in the seats of power in the political life of his own country. He would instead be known through his voice as recorded in scores of articles, legal briefs and opinions, and speeches, along with several books.[3] In a way, he became the Cassandra of interwar American foreign policy.

The legalization of international politics

Moore's earliest and most consistently held prescription for international peace was arbitration. In an article published in 1891, some six years after he entered the State Department, he traced the history of the contributions of the United States to this 'substitution of reason for force in the adjustment of disputes among nations'. It was here that he first expressed in print his life-long conviction that the settlement of the Alabama claims and other disputes arising out of the American Civil War through arbitration conducted under the authority of the Treaty of Washington represented 'the noblest spectacle of modern times'. Here he characterized arbitration as an example of nations 'discussing and reasoning about their differences in a spirit of patience and forbearance' and declared that 'in view of the demonstrated efficacy of arbitration as a means of settling international disputes, the nation that seeks or recklessly invites a resort to arms must bear in the eyes of the civilized world a heavy responsibility'.[4]

In subsequent works leading up to the publication of Moore's two substantial documentary histories of the practice of arbitration, he laid down his general definition of the device as the resolution of disputes by one or more third parties basing their determination, not on compromise between the positions of the contending states, but on settled principles of international law.[5] In this emphasis on law lay the distinction between arbitration and mediation. 'Mediation is an advisory, arbitration a judicial, function', Moore declared in a formulation first enunciated in a 1903 address but repeated many times. 'Mediation recommends, arbitration decides.'[6]

It will be noted that this legal process rests on the assumption of an international society composed of sovereign states, each capable of undertaking commitments with other states, carrying out those commitments, and, through practice or treaty, embedding those commitments in international law. This body of law stood alongside, supplemented, and, at least to a degree, might ultimately replace diplomacy as the preferred method for dealing with conflicts among the states party to it. Pirates and other associations outside organized territorial states existed, but at the fringes of the society of states, and at the heart of that society and most important in determining and preserving its legitimate rules were 'civilized' states – a category itself resting on custom and practice.

Through painstaking negotiations, states could create and improve institutions that furthered this resort to law and reason rather than force and emotion. One of the outcomes of the Hague Conference of 1899 that caused Moore to term it a signal achievement of the society of states was the Convention for the Settlement of International Disputes, which laid the foundation for the Permanent Court of Arbitration. This body consisted of a list of international legal authorities designated by each signatory state, from which the parties to any dispute might choose to select a tribunal to decide the legal case created thereby. As valuable as Moore believed the practice of agreeing to arbitration of specific controversies to be, and as proud he was of his own country's record of submitting disputes to arbitration since the commencement of its independence, he still lauded the Permanent

Court as 'the highest achievement of the nineteenth century towards the creation of a permanent system for the peaceful disposition of international controversies'.[7]

Nevertheless, Moore recognized that this institution 'was not a court in the ordinary sense', while 'an actual trial court, with a fixed personnel, would afford greater certainty and continuity in the application of legal principles and contribute more to their systematic development'.[8] With that aim in mind, the second Hague Conference in 1907 laboured to negotiate such a tribunal, but failed to agree on a method for selecting the judges. It was therefore left to the powers in Paris in 1919 to include in the Covenant of the League of Nations a provision authorizing the League Council to propose and the League member states to adopt a Permanent Court of International Justice (PCIJ), a body that bore all the characteristics of institutional stability, sole reliance on principles of international law and fixed membership that constituted 'an actual trial court'. The progression from ordinary diplomacy – not to be despised, but still not a sufficient basis for replacing force with law – through mediation, to arbitration and its logical conclusion in an international tribunal, was for Moore an accomplishment of the highest order, and he was honoured to be selected himself to serve as a judge on the PCIJ, which he did from 1921 to 1928, despite the fact that the United States during those years did not ratify the treaty creating the Court.

This legalization of international politics could be taken quite far. At this early point in his career, Moore saw no justification in any limitations on the subjects on which states might bind themselves to employ arbitration, and he foresaw a bright, though long-term, future for 'international legislation'. In a remarkable essay published in 1906, as preparations went forward for the second Hague Conference, he contended that, with the establishment of the Permanent Court of Arbitration, a great step had been taken towards 'a permanent organization, always open for the exercise of judicial functions between nations'. Referring to proposals that the next Hague Conference 'be converted into a permanent body', he suggested that such a step would bring 'the same element of permanency in the domain of international legislation'. And, building on the first two suppositions, he declared 'the most striking imperfection in the international system today' to be 'the lack of a common agency for the enforcement of law' – 'the addition, in other words, to judicial and legislative power of what we call executive power'. Moore granted that 'this is a problem of the future, probably of the far-distant future', but he added, 'it is an idea and a goal toward which it is permissible to labor'.[9]

Of course, the Hague Conference of 1907 did not become a permanent legislative body, nor was an international executive agency equipped with power and authority to repress international lawbreakers ever established. In all likelihood, this essay constituted the high-water mark of Moore's willingness to contemplate the supersession of national sovereignty by an international body armed with something like the powers of a government. His proposals never again took the form of anything like a world state. For the next four decades of his life, Moore would find the most likely path to international peace leading through wholly different ideas and institutions.

Rather than making aggression or any other international dispute everyone's business through the creation and operation of a worldwide arbiter and enforcer of binding rules clearly distinguishing the author and the victim of aggression, Moore devoted much of his energy to the careful tracing of the legal status of neutrality through the ages and to its elucidation in contemporary times.[10] Far from involving the entire society of states in any given instance of aggression or war, either through the deterrent threat of a unified response by the international community that would assuredly overwhelm any potential illegal resort to force or through the employment of force to defeat such an action once taken, neutrality sought to create fire-breaks around international conflicts, limiting their destructive effect and allowing the rest of the members of international society to go about their collective lives as normally as the existence of a raging conflict between or among other members would allow.

Thus, by Moore's lifetime an elaborate set of rules and norms had developed defining the rights and responsibilities of neutral states, particularly in the matter of trade – those goods that could legally be sold and shipped to belligerents by neutrals and those that were considered contraband and might legally be stopped or seized by belligerents as un-neutral acts. Moore considered this evolving body of law to be one of the highest achievements of international diplomacy and throughout his career sought its extension and confirmation in every venue. He consistently advocated the greatest possible respect for ships and cargoes travelling from neutral ports and their protection from seizure by the naval forces of belligerent powers. Concurrently, he invariably warned neutral powers of the absolute necessity of their observing their neutral duties in not encouraging their nationals to engage in the shipment of goods clearly identified as contraband of war. His balancing of neutrals' rights and duties lay in the principle that neutral governments, while they had no legal obligation to prevent their citizens from engaging in international commerce of the type they chose, still fell under the duty of warning their nationals that, should their vessels attempt the hazardous practice of transporting contraband of war to a belligerent, their government would offer them no assistance if the ships and their cargoes should be stopped and confiscated by an opposing belligerent exercising its own rights under international law.

The supplanting of international law

The conviction that the actions of the Woodrow Wilson administration had largely abandoned this historic American stance formed an important part of Moore's critique of Wilson's presidency. Moore charged that Wilson had contributed to undermining the entire international structure of neutrality. Although Moore largely avoided public criticism of Wilson's actions at the time, his subsequent comments were scathing. Moore's recollection that 'Down to March, 1913, no government contributed more to the building up of the law of neutrality than did the United States' could not have been more pointed, and his conclusion that 'the confused notion ... that the United States became involved in the war through the defense of neutral rights' could not be more clear.[11] Moore's charge was that, in failing to defend its neutral rights against the Allies, and in developing novel doctrines on subjects such as the claimed right of neutral merchantmen to carry armaments, the US government had materially contributed to the idea, soon to arise in the post-war period, that the international law of neutrality had come to an end.

Moore's concern that in attempting to usher the practice of neutrality into a premature grave the United States was abandoning a route to limiting through legal means the scope and destructiveness of modern war did not stem from a personal dislike of Wilson, though he did record his opinion that 'of international law [the President] knew little, and of diplomatic history scarcely more'.[12] Nor was Moore driven by his nominal adherence to the Republican Party; as will be noted below, he had no praise for the League to Enforce Peace, with which many prominent Republicans were associated in the period leading up to and during the First World War, and he publicly and vociferously disagreed with Republican leaders such as Henry Stimson and Frank Kellogg. Rather, Moore believed that his variety of progressivism – grounded in the belief that the high road to peace lay, first, in promoting arbitration as an alternative to war in settling international disputes; second, in bringing under legal restraint the means of conducting war, as was attempted in the two Hague conferences; and third, in employing the rights and duties of neutrality to draw a ring around wars and isolate them as far as possible from the rest of international society – faced its greatest challenge in another form of progressivism, which, in his view, by demanding too much of an international community that in fact had very little substance, would end in making war more frequent and more destructive. From the 'Great War' to the end of his life, he would struggle against this contrary and, as he believed, wholly misguided view of war and peace.

Moore's doubts about collective security, which, as a means of deterring or defeating aggression, might have been thought to be consistent with his early advocacy of international legislation, began to appear as debate in the United States proceeded on plans for the reconstruction of international society, looking towards the conclusion of the First World War. In his analysis of 'The Peace Problem', delivered in April, 1916, for example, he recalled that similar plans had aroused misgivings about the size and potential use of any military force large enough to confront aggression anywhere, and suggested that 'the question who was the "first aggressor" [was] not so easy of determination that the parties to such an agreement would in the exercise of their independent individual judgments be likely to concur in their conclusions upon it'.[13] This issue of the capacity of the society of states to agree on the identity of the aggressor and the victim of aggression would increasingly weigh on Moore's mind in the following years. So would the incongruity, as he saw it, of preserving or restoring by peace through threats to wage increasingly comprehensive and destructive wars.

All of these obstacles convinced Moore that any 'League of Nations' or 'League to Enforce Peace', far from constituting a universally accepted institutional form representing a global consensus reflecting the views of all participants in the current conflict, would instead be largely a continuation of the alliance of the powers victorious in the war, lacking legitimacy in the eyes of their defeated opponents and productive of new controversies, the rights and wrongs of which would defy any international agreement.[14] In his 1919 article on 'Some Essentials of a League for Peace', he again attacked as 'extravagant and groundless' the 'assumption that nations in general could be expected to hold together in attacking a particular nation, on the mere allegation from some quarter that it had "begun" hostilities'.[15] The association of the new League with the Treaty of Versailles and the delay in admitting Germany to full membership in the League only increased Moore's apprehensions that the world's latest experiment in collective security represented a prescription for the expansion and production of armed conflict, in contrast to his preferred mechanisms for circumscribing any arena of war and preservation intact of a surrounding realm of peace.

Although Moore's duties as president of the Pan-American Society of the United States in the early 1920s and his service as a justice on the new PCIJ from 1920 to 1928 somewhat curtailed his public comments on other controversies of the day, he energetically entered into discussion of the 1928 agreement variously known as the Pact of Paris, the Kellogg-Briand Pact and (Moore's preferred formulation) the Kellogg Pact. This multilateral treaty, while it did not attempt to 'outlaw' war, as was often asserted, did represent a commitment by each of its signatories to renounce war as an instrument of its foreign policy. Moore's critique of the Pact stood on two grounds. First, under its terms and the understandings applied by various powers as a condition of their acceptance of it, the conditions under which signatories obligated themselves to avoid war as an instrument of policy were in fact so limited as to render the agreement nugatory. Leaving entirely up to each signatory the definition of self-defence and vital interests that would allow it to resort to force was to him of a piece with the increasing resort to the plea of vital interests and national honour that had in fact forced the cause of arbitration into retreat in the late nineteenth and early twentieth centuries, as states had limited the cases in which they bound themselves to judicial arbitration of their disputes.

If Moore's opinion of the handiwork of Secretary of State Frank B. Kellogg, who in his earlier post of senator from Minnesota had been a Progressive collaborator with Moore, was that the Pact was a nullity, Moore's later judgement when proposals came forth to give the Pact 'teeth' by empowering signatories to take economic and even military action against powers that, in their view, had violated their obligations under the Pact was even more hostile. For Moore, economic sanctions were inherently an act of war, and the addition of this unilateral or multilateral enforcement mechanism transformed the Pact from meaningless to menacing. It was, he argued, nonsensical to expect powers against which the warlike act of imposing sanctions was undertaken to do anything other than retaliate with their own economic or military coercive measures, and the resulting spiral of pain and hostility would make this supposed instrument for the renunciation of war into the engine of larger and more consuming wars.

Thus, when Moore was asked to comment on giving the Pact teeth by pairing it with the power of the League Council to identify states that had violated the territorial integrity or political independence of League member states, and further to encourage the United States to impose economic or other sanctions on states so identified, even though the United States was itself not a member of the League, Moore's reaction was thunderously opposed. When he was invited to comment on legislation proposed in early 1933, at the outset of the Franklin Roosevelt administration, to give the president authority to embargo the export of arms and munitions to one party to a foreign war but not the other, Moore replied at length, stating, first, that the international law of neutrality remained in full force, and nothing that occurred in the conduct of the war of 1914–18 or in the peace settlement that followed had altered this state of affairs; second, that, under the existing neutrality regime, a government that allowed the shipment of the means of war to one belligerent but not the other 'abandons its neutrality and is guilty of armed intervention' and 'virtually commits an act of war'; and, third, that any proposal that war could be rendered impossible by creating an unlimited right by third parties to undertake measures of war against one party or another of an existing conflict amounted to a faith that 'war can be abolished either by calling it peace or by refraining from calling it war'. The difficulty of identifying with certainty the aggressor again struck Moore as insoluble; he saw it as a 'wild and flimsy fantasy that, when nations fall out and fight, the question of the "aggressor," which still baffles students even of ancient wars, lies upon the surface of things, and may be readily, safely, and justly determined by outsiders, of whose freedom from individual interest or bias there is no guarantee'. Beyond securing their own interests and the wellbeing of their own citizens, the primary aim of neutral powers remained, in Moore's view, 'to limit the area, the destructiveness, or the duration of wars', and the replacement of the traditional doctrine of neutrality with what he viewed as the antithetical doctrine of collective security was, for him, precisely the wrong route to follow.[16]

There remained yet one further issue on which Moore parted company with his former allies in the Progressive movement as the international scene darkened through the 1930s. With well-publicized instances of alterations of international boundaries taking place through the threat or use of force, as with German demands on Czechoslovakia or the Italian attack on Abyssinia, and no effective collective security response appearing, leaders sought other means of preventing or defeating aggression without risking war. The earliest example of their solution was the announcement by Secretary of State Henry Stimson that the Hoover administration would adhere to a policy of 'non-recognition' of the legal legitimacy of any such conquests or cessions achieved by other than peaceful means, and the case in point was the Japanese absorption of much of Manchuria.

Recalling that his first encounter with what would come to be called the 'Stimson Doctrine' or the 'non-recognition doctrine' had taken place at the first Pan-American Conference in 1889–90, Moore bluntly declared that 'all systems of law recognize, by the doctrine of prescription and otherwise, that the recognition of accomplished facts plays, as a principle of certainty and peace, a large part in human affairs'. In international life, this recognition had often led the society of states to accept as new but settled law the transfer of territories from the defeated to the victorious state at the conclusion of a war (and as a counsellor to the American negotiators of the Treaty of Paris, which ended the Spanish-American War and brought under American sovereignty formerly Spanish territories in the Caribbean and the Philippines in 1898, Moore had seen this phenomenon first-hand). Despite his advocacy for the replacement of force and coercion with reason and law as means of settling international disputes, Moore saw no prospect that war could be eliminated from international life; his concern was with the amelioration of its effects and the reduction of its frequency. Asserting that 'the use of non-recognition as a coercive or deterrent measure has not as yet been attended with success, and, as a means of reforming foreign peoples, has signally failed', he brought the same charge against it than he had levied against collective security in general or the selective use of embargoes in particular: that 'those who employ it often must content themselves with futile words or must fight, while the adoption of the latter alternative would necessarily be a confession of failure'.[17]

In their different ways, all these attempted reforms of the international order seemed to Moore but variations on a single theme: a steady effort towards uniformity of statutes on particular matters such as rules of expatriation, which he always supported, was of a wholly different character than an insistence on uniformity of thought or regime. In their attempts to distinguish sharply between good international citizens and bad, aggressors and victims of aggression, or legitimate and illegitimate occupiers of territory, his former colleagues in the Progressive movement neglected to their peril what he consistently emphasized – what he called 'the right to be different'. By this phrase he meant a deep-seated respect for the diversity represented by the society of states and a consequent unwillingness to force a necessarily loose-jointed body of rules and norms into too tight a pattern or too demanding a set of expectations. What he styled a natural human 'passion for uniformity' ran headlong into an equally fundamental 'right to be different'.

Moore's reading in history and literature had convinced him that intrinsic to human nature was a conviction that one's own way, or the way of one's people, was the only true way, and one's possession of the truth carried with it a responsibility to spread that truth abroad, in recognition of its inherent validity and to the betterment of those required to relinquish inferior ways, even over their initial objections. This passion for uniformity could have constructive forms and desirable applications, among which Moore considered the gradual drawing together of certain legal codes and practices easing trade and bringing greater convenience and wealth to all. The general acceptance of a common rule according equal legal rights to all states was itself a measure of uniformity, though in the service of a deeper plurality, in its abjuring of the goal of universal monarchy and rendering of the states-system as normative. Nevertheless, uniformity could also have destructive and even tyrannical forms, leading to unnecessary conflict resulting from the effort to deprive peoples of their inherited modes of life, which they had evolved to meet their own circumstances, and to replace those rules of conduct with others drawn from wholly different times and places, unsuited to transplantation. Technological developments since the Industrial Revolution had on the whole, in Moore's estimation, increased the relative ability of formerly subject or laggard peoples to resist such impositions on their way of life, rendering such false applications of the passion for uniformity newly productive of strife and large-scale warfare.

While a trend towards uniformity had undoubtedly been a feature of American history domestically, Moore thought it one of the most evident strengths of American foreign policy that it had in general not only respected but even promoted legal acceptance of the differences that found their most evident expression in an international society composed of a multiplicity of independent states. Americans' own founding belief in the rightness of self-government inculcated an adherence to the principle of non-intervention in the domestic affairs of other states and a tradition of granting or withholding diplomatic recognition solely depending on the effective control by a claimant government of its territory and people. As early as 1905, in his book *American Diplomacy*, Moore had asserted, 'Among the rules of conduct prescribed for the United States by the [founding] statesmen who formulated its foreign policy, none was conceived to be more fundamental or more distinctively American that that which forbade intervention in the political affairs of other nations,' and, following from this grounding article of faith was the belief that 'the true test of a government's title to recognition is not the theoretical legitimacy of its origin, but the fact of its existence as the apparent exponent of the popular will'. From this principle, 'which is now [in 1905] universally accepted, it necessarily follows that recognition can regularly be accorded only when the new government has demonstrated its ability to exist'.[18] It was the gravamen of Moore's indictment of Wilson that, beginning in Mexico, but going on to other nations, American policy had succumbed to the destructive form of uniformity in adopting the 'theoretical legitimacy' of a government's origin and the approval of that origin by the American government as the test for American diplomatic recognition, whether of a government's admission into the society of states or of an alteration in the frontiers between two or more states. For Moore, this abandonment of the traditional American policy was productive of only confusion and strife, and he likewise opposed its application under the Stimson Doctrine.

Moore described interventions on behalf of freedom or what might latterly be called human rights as 'armed propagandism' or 'philosophical propagandism', and he universally opposed them. As abhorrent as he found its actions in its first two decades of power, he accorded even to the Bolshevik government of the new Soviet Union a right of non-intervention by outside powers, and he regularly endorsed including the USSR in all the institutions of international society, regardless of its adherence to a form of regime antithetical to all his convictions on individual liberty.[19] The ideological struggles of the twentieth century he found to be only the latest manifestation and test of the willingness of the international order to respect 'the right to be different'.[20]

Conclusion: The bifurcation of progressivism

Moore emphasized a progressive agenda for international life that relied on the cumulative attainment of an international society which, while it emphasized adherence to judicial and quasi-judicial institutions such as mandatory arbitration of all disputes ('all-in arbitration') and the application of international conventions on national conduct, including the laws of land and naval war negotiated at the two Hague conferences, the post-First World War effort to agree on similar regulations governing warfare in the air and the use of radio communications, and the international extradition of criminal suspects, nevertheless accepted warfare as a phenomenon that would remain part of this society so long as the consciences of statesmen and peoples did not banish intolerance, cupidity and pride from the human heart. It was therefore the purpose of this progressivism by stages to bring the conduct of war under stricter limitation and, when war could not be avoided altogether, to limit its disruption of international life within the smallest possible compass through the increasing reach of and respect for the principles of neutrality. Here was a view of war as something like a conflagration, which on (ideally) rare occasions might be required by prudent statesmen as a tool to protect their national communities, much as controlled burning might be needed to stop a forest fire. It was a view wholly at odds with that other branch of progressivism that conceived of war as a kind of international crime wave against which all law-abiding members of international society should in an anticipatory way declare their binding pledge to join a global posse dedicated to aiding the victim of aggression and defeating and bringing to justice the perpetrators of international lawlessness.

Moore also inveighed against efforts to carry out the asserted obligations of the 'new neutrality' through the legitimization of economic sanctions by third parties who claimed the right to impose commercial and financial penalties on those they deemed the authors of aggression while still also claiming all the rights of traditional neutrality to have their own freedom to conduct international trade and finance uninterrupted by any side. Moore believed that the party against which such sanctions had been imposed would never accept such discrimination and would inevitably retaliate against the sanctioning states, leading to escalation and drawing previously neutral states into the conflict. The effort to set up other states, which would undoubtedly have their own biases and self-interests, as the arbiters who would assign penalties and confer advantages among the participants in any international conflict would spread rather than contain the destructive inferno of war.

Not only was this way of conceiving international life mistaken, it constituted a standing invitation to the ideological takeover of international society and the undermining of the principle of national sovereignty. Moore, applying traditional standards of international law, contended that general adherence to that law required an international society of sovereign states, each possessing the solid loyalty of its people and the effective control of its territory and resources that made it competent to carry out the international obligations it undertook. Such a conception was incompatible with an asserted right to judge the legitimacy of the domestic regime of another state. Such a regime might commit acts that in a constitutional liberal democracy would be adjudged wholly illegitimate, but if it, through the sheer fact of continuing to exist and to have its domestic laws obeyed, fulfilled the requirements of international citizenship, it could not be denied the corresponding rights. Moore often cited Jefferson on this point, which he was willing to carry far enough to shield the Soviet government from official penalties or discrimination based on its form of domestic governance. Non-intervention in domestic affairs was his lodestar, and the advent of collective security in an era of ideological hostility his most feared nightmare. However repugnant the domestic behaviour of any government might be, the propagation of the tenets of liberalism by any method other than the power of its own example was for Moore the practice of 'international propagandism', which was fatal to stability and order in international life, and to liberty as he understood it – that is, the freedom of each people to choose its own way of life, subject only to its acceptance of its own correlative obligation to respect the choices made by other peoples.

All of the practices, beginning in the Wilson administration, that outraged Moore had as their response to the maladies of aggression and illegal conduct precisely the opposite prescription from what Moore advised. Where he wished to isolate disturbances to international life and quarantine their participants from the normal existence of the rest of international society, they sought to bring all of the international community into instances of palpable wrongdoing, so as to enlist the aid of third parties against the aggressor and on the side of the wronged party. Moore believed that the causes of most wars were far too complex and stemmed from motives far too mixed on all sides to allow a confident allocation of praise and blame among the parties. To attempt such a judgement was to invite the very self-righteousness and intolerance of differing opinions that, to him, already too much poisoned international co-existence.

Moore's last word

Moore's widening estrangement from the competing – and, as he saw it, antagonistic – strand of international progressivism left him profoundly concerned about the deterioration in the practices, and the conceptions, of international relations. He never lost faith in the moderate beneficent influence of international law on the conduct of international life, and he deeply regretted any zealotry that was willing to ignore or undermine legal practice in the pursuit of what were viewed as higher aims. His last works gave evidence of a certain withdrawal from the increasingly ominous world of the later 1930s; he never directly confronted the question of whether Nazi tyranny – at least as iniquitous as the Soviet practices that he criticized but did not favour confronting through intervention – justified bending or breaking the rules of neutrality in opposition to German expansion. 'Peace, Law, and Hysteria', not published until his *Collected Papers* appeared in 1944, made only passing references to the Second World War then raging, and consisted primarily of reaffirmations of positions he had taken over the years on subjects such as arbitration, public opinion and non-intervention.

To the extent that Moore's later contributions to public discourse had a theme, it was a raising of the gaze above even law, to the realm of attitudes and moral outlooks. Three examples will be given here, both to demonstrate that Moore's work had never ignored the subject of human nature and human thought, and to indicate that this long-time preoccupation appeared to grow stronger as the whole edifice of international law and cooperation to which he had devoted his career seemed to be collapsing around him. The first dates from a book he published in 1912, in which he concluded:

> Questions of war and of peace depend, and will continue to depend, not so much upon the size of military establishments as upon the cultivation of the spirit and habits of justice, of self-control, of reciprocal recognition of rights and of forbearance …. Outside the state, just as within the state, peace will be preserved only by carrying into our dealings one with another the sentiment of fraternity and the spirit of conciliation.[21]

It will be seen that balances of power and uses of military force apparently depend on something deeper – the habits of mind that are brought to the operation of regrettably necessary material means of self-defence, as to all aspects of international policy. The second example comes from the perhaps never fully completed 'Peace, Law, and Hysteria', in which Moore reaches for the most profound explanation for the fragility of peace, the frequent violation of law and the recurrent susceptibility to hysteria: 'the primal fact that it will not do to rely in fancied security upon any device for the avoidance of the use of force, unless we practise moderation and self-restraint, and see to it that we do not allow our feelings to carry us beyond the point where differences can be discussed in the light of reason'.[22] Here we see that Moore finds inadequate not only a reliance solely on military preponderance, which might not be surprising, given his lifelong advocacy of law, but also too great a faith in law itself, if law is not fortified by the prudence and reason that only distinguished statesmanship can supply. Finally, there is the warning in the pages of the last work published in Moore's lifetime other than three book reviews and the *Collected Papers*, the 1941 article 'What of the Night?' which breathes a realism that George Kennan, whose observation opened this chapter, might share:

> I assign, so far as concerns peace among nations, the chief place to what I call emotional hypocrisy, meaning the propensity to ascribe to those who differ with us some mental or moral obliquity. The world will never be at peace until men and women can, without regard to race, creed, color or nationality, or to political and social equality or inequality, cry out, with a whole heart and a united voice, in the language of the Litany, 'Lord, have mercy upon us miserable sinners!' And of this I see no prospect.[23]

In such an atmosphere of pervasive human fallenness and frailty, the modest virtues of international law may, until the millennium, be our surest refuge. Such seems to be the counsel of John Bassett Moore.

Notes

1. George Kennan, *American Diplomacy 1900–1950* (Chicago: University of Chicago Press, 1951), 82–3.
2. Ibid., pp. 12, 77.
3. Fortunately for any writer on Moore, his writings – aside from his monographs and several mammoth collections of documents – were compiled in bound form as *The Collected Papers of John Bassett Moore*, ed. Edwin Borchard, Joseph Chamberlain, and Stephen Duggan (New Haven: Yale University Press, 1944). Henceforward, all references to this work will be to *CP*, followed by volume and page number.
4. *CP*, I: 107, 113, 125, 126.
5. These two collections of documents on arbitration were *History and Digest of the International Arbitrations to which the United States Has Been a Party*, 6 vols. (Washington, DC: Government Printing Office, 1898) and *International Adjudications, Ancient and Modern, History and Documents*, 6 vols. (New York: Oxford University Press, 1929–36). The latter work was suspended in the disordered economic and political conditions of the later 1930s and was not completed in Moore's lifetime.
6. *CP*, III: 58.
7. 'The Permanent Court of International Justice', *CP*, VI: 80–1.
8. Ibid., p. 82.
9. 'An International Executive Power', *CP*, III: 265–6.
10. See Moore, 'Our System of Neutrality', *Harper's Magazine*, (May 1904), *CP*: CVIII: 837–48; 'The Meaning of Neutrality', *Annals of the American Academy of Political and Social Science*, (July 1915), *CP*: LX: 145–6; 'Neutrality, Peace Legislation, and Our Foreign Policy' (letter to Senator Hiram Johnson, 7 April 1939): Hearings before the Committee on Foreign Relations, 76th Congress, 1st Session, Part 21 (8 May 1939), Washington: Government Printing Office, 1939 (607–8), *CP*, VII: 168–169.
11. 'Fifty Years of International Law', *Harvard Law Review* I, no. 3 (1937), *CP*, VII: 131; review of *Neutrality for the United States*, *CP*, VII: 156.
12. '"What of the Night?"' *CP*, VII: 203.
13. *CP*, IV: 143–5.
14. See, for example, Moore's brief and largely unfavourable discussion of the platform of the League to Enforce Peace in his article on 'The International Situation', published in October 1918, only a month before the armistice ending the First World War, *CP*, V: 10–12.
15. *CP*, V: 72.
16. See 'Proposed Embargo on Exportation of Arms and Munitions of War', *CP*, VI: 401–8.
17. 'Fifty Years of International Law', *Harvard Law Review*, L, no. 3 (1937), *CP*, VII: 89–136 (124–5).
18. *American Diplomacy: Its Spirit and Achievements* (New York: Harper & Brothers Publishers, 1905), 130, 143.

19 See 'Post-War International Law', *Columbia Law Review* XXVII, no. 4 (April 1927), *CP*, VI: 302–3; 'Candor and Common Sense', Address before the Association of the Bar of the City of New York (4 December 1930), *CP*, VI: 346–9.
20 Ibid., p. 248; *The Principles of American Diplomacy* (New York: Harper & Brothers, 1918), 37.
21 *Four Phases of American Development: Federalism – Democracy – Imperialism – Expansion* (Baltimore: Johns Hopkins Press, 1912), 203.
22 *CP*, VII: 273–4.
23 Ibid., 213.

Chapter 5

ROCA-RUNCIMAN REVISITED: ANGLO-AMERICAN
RELATIONS AND ARGENTINA DURING THE
'INFAMOUS DECADE', 1933–43

Tony McCulloch

A few years ago, this writer had the pleasure of meeting the late Garry Runciman, the third Viscount Runciman of Doxford, for tea at the British Academy, of which Lord Runciman was then president. The main purpose of the meeting was to discuss the ill-fated mission to Prague in the summer of 1938 of his grandfather, Walter Runciman, to whom the government of Neville Chamberlain had given the forlorn task of trying to avert a European war over the German-speaking Sudetenland, in what was then Czechoslovakia. Runciman's mission to Prague came at the end of a long and distinguished career during which, amongst other things, he had served as president of the Board of Trade in the Liberal government of Herbert Asquith from 1914 to 1916 and again during the National government of Ramsay MacDonald and Stanley Baldwin from 1931 to 1937. At one point during our conversation, Lord Runciman remarked that his father, the second Viscount, Leslie Runciman, had told him that there were two places in the world where a Runciman might not be very welcome. One was the Czech Republic, in view of the fact that Walter Runciman's mission was followed by the notorious Munich agreement to dismember Czechoslovakia. The other was Argentina.¹

The 'Infamous Decade'

The Roca-Runciman agreement of May 1933 has a similar notoriety in Argentina to the Munich settlement in Europe owing to its association with the so-called 'Infamous Decade', a period located between two military coups – the first in September 1930 and the second in June 1943 – during which Argentina was ruled by a much-reviled Conservative-led coalition, the *Concordancia*. 'For thirteen years conservatives ruled Argentina,' Peter Bakewell has written. 'They did so by manipulating elections and relying on military backing,' he continued, echoing commonly held views amongst Argentine historians. 'Far from everything was negative', he added, but the 'conservative elite' suffered from growing political opposition, especially in the cities and above all in Buenos Aires. 'It was with the support of these urban workers that Colonel Peron rose to national prominence between 1943 and 1945, then to dominate Argentina as president from 1946 to 1955.'[2]

Another element of the 'Infamous Decade' was the accusation that Britain had taken advantage of its strong economic position in regard to Argentina to force the one-sided Roca-Runciman agreement upon that country. The agreement essentially guaranteed Argentina's largest market for the export of chilled beef in exchange for very favourable financial and commercial terms for British coal and manufactured goods. Whatever its economic effects, the Roca-Runciman agreement is generally seen as a powerful stimulant for the rise of Argentine nationalism in the 1930s, culminating in the military coup d'état of June 1943 and the subsequent rule of Juan Peron. While the agreement was defended by the Argentine government in 1933, and especially by Vice President Julio Roca who had led the delegation to London that negotiated it, Roca-Runciman was attacked by the opposition parties, especially supporters of former president Yrigoyen, overthrown in September 1930. They regarded the Roca-Runciman agreement as a corrupt sell-out to the British Empire that favoured British-owned businesses such as the Anglo Meatpacking Company or *Frigorifico Anglo del Uruguay*, owned by the very wealthy Vestey family, which sold large quantities of Argentine beef in Britain under its *Fray Bentos* brand.[3]

One of the main critics of the agreement was Senator Lissandro de la Torres who headed a Senate committee to investigate the meat trade and especially the meat-packing companies which he accused of making large and unjustified profits at the expense of the Argentine people. On 25 July 1935, at the end of a heated debate in the Senate chamber during which de la Torres bitterly attacked the Roca-Runciman agreement, he was struck by Luis Duhai, the minister of agriculture. Shots were fired from the gallery and although they missed de la Torres they hit another opposition Senator who died of his injuries later the same day. De la Torres was also challenged to a duel by the minister of finance, Federico Pinedo, which took place soon after but did not result in any further bloodshed. However, the fallout from the Roca-Runciman agreement continued to reverberate around Argentine politics for the rest of the 1930s and beyond, not least in the accusations by Peronists that it had made Argentina into a British colony.[4]

Alongside its significant role in relations between Britain and Argentina, the Roca-Runciman agreement also played an important part in Anglo-American relations during the 1930s and the Second World War. It was not well received in the United States and, in particular, it attracted the ire of Cordell Hull, FDR's secretary of state for most of his presidency, who was a zealous free trader and therefore an opponent of exclusive commercial and financial deals such as the Ottawa agreements of 1932 based on 'Imperial Preference' and the Roca-Runciman agreement in 1933. His criticism of British policy towards Argentina was compounded by his belief that the British government was undermining US policy in Latin America by encouraging the Argentine government in its uncooperative, not to say antagonistic, policy towards the United States and its 'Good Neighbour' initiatives. In his memoirs Hull argued that Britain's trade policy had put narrow self-interest before the larger goals that he had pursued. He further claimed that British policy had handicapped both his attempt to promote a more liberal international trade philosophy in Latin America in the 1930s and his campaign to pressure Argentina to abandon its links with the Axis powers during the Second World War.[5]

Taking Hull's criticisms as its starting point, this chapter aims to assess the extent to which the Roca-Runciman agreement influenced the broader Anglo-American relationship during Roosevelt's presidency, up to and including the United States joining the Second World War in December 1941. It tackles this question in three main parts. Firstly, it examines the origins of the agreement in the context of Anglo-Argentine relations after the First World War and the onset of the Great

Figure 5.1 The signing of the Roca-Runciman agreement, 1 May 1933. Julio Roca is in the foreground signing the document and Walter Runciman is sitting to his left.

Source: Getty Images.

Depression from 1930. Secondly, it discusses the nature of the agreement, the State Department's criticisms of it and the British response. Thirdly, it assesses the place of the agreement, and Britain's relationship with Argentina more generally, within Anglo-American relations during the period 1933–43, with particular reference to Runciman's subsequent visit to Washington in January 1937 and FDR's desire to cooperate with Britain to help counter the threat posed by Nazi Germany in the late 1930s.[6]

The historiography of the Roca-Runciman agreement

Before exploring the origins of the Roca-Runciman agreement it would be useful to examine the historiography of this event, which has been the subject of a great deal of academic and polemical writing in English, as well as Spanish, regarding its impact on the Argentine economy and its place in Argentine history. According to Gordon Bridger, 'In the demonology spread about colonialism and imperialism, this agreement was its culmination.' When the agreement was signed in 1933, he says, 'it was quite hysterically denounced by nationalists and the left as a betrayal by the cattle-owning oligarchy who were sacrificing local industry in order to secure their beef market in Britain'. David Rock argues that the negative impact of the Roca-Runciman agreement on Argentina's economy was exaggerated by its opponents. But 'affronted Argentines denounced the 1933 treaty as a rich cattlemen's charter devised by an unrepresentative regime in tow to British imperialists. They objected to being considered part of the British Empire whatever the advantages it gave them.' Winthop Wright has also raised doubts about the view that the Roca-Runciman agreement was bad for the Argentine economy – but there is little doubt that it contributed to the growth of Argentine nationalism and Anglophobia in the 1930s.[7]

In contrast to its importance in the history of Argentina in the 1930s, the Roca-Runciman agreement has received relatively little attention from historians of Anglo-American relations in this period. Rock's most detailed treatment of the agreement focuses very largely on its economic significance and says very little about its effect on Anglo-American relations more broadly. Benjamin Rowland's study of the commercial relations between Britain and the United States that culminated in the Anglo-American trade agreement of 1938 uses the Roca-Runciman agreement as a case study of the problems raised for Britain and the United States by the Ottawa agreements, but it does not assess the agreement's role in Anglo-American political relations. Similarly, Patricia Clavin's work on international economic diplomacy during the early 1930s points out the negative perception of the agreement in the United States, but it does not refer to its longer-term significance for US relations with Britain. Beyond these brief and largely economic treatments, there is no mention of the agreement in the main books on Anglo-American relations in the 1930s by historians such as David Reynolds and Brian McKercher. Nor is there much reference in works on US foreign policy and Argentina in the 1930s.[8]

The origins of the Roca-Runciman agreement

Relations between Britain and Argentina at the start of the 1930s were generally very good. Britain was a major market for Argentine agricultural produce, especially beef, amounting to £80 millions per year. Britain also exported various manufactured goods to Argentina, especially textiles, amounting to some £30 millions per year. The balance of trade was therefore very much in favour of Argentina, although earnings from 'invisible exports' such as interest on loans and shipping freights narrowed this deficit. The nature of the trading relationship meant that, in the words of the British Embassy in Buenos Aires, Argentina 'was, to some extent, an economic dependency of Great Britain', more akin in its commercial relationship with Britain to one of the Dominions than to a foreign country. Politically, the Argentine government was also quite favourable towards Britain at this time. President Yrigoyen, who had been re-elected to a second six-year term in 1928 despite being seventy-five years old, referred to the close relations between Argentina and Britain that he argued had helped to make Argentina a prosperous nation. He also regarded Britain as an important counterweight to US influence in Latin America, as he demonstrated by his warm welcome to the trade mission of Lord D'Abernon, a former British ambassador to Germany, in August 1929.[9]

This relationship was strengthened by the Hawley-Smoot tariff act of June 1930 which raised US tariffs to record-high levels. Nor was it seriously impaired by the revolution that overthrew President Yrigoyen in September 1930 and was later seen by its critics – especially supporters of the ousted president – as the start of Argentina's 'Infamous Decade'. Indeed, the British Embassy felt that the revolution 'may be said to have raised the prestige of the Argentine Government in the eyes of foreign nations, which had been impaired by Senor Irigoyen's neglect of foreign affairs and inaccessibility to foreign representatives'. The new government under General José Félix Uriburu was quickly recognized by the South American republics and, after a short delay, by Britain, the United States and the European powers. The new government also announced that it was abandoning the rather-aloof policy of President Yrigoyen towards Pan-American affairs and it was hoped in London that it would revive Argentina's dormant membership of the League and become more active in the League Assembly.[10]

These positive relations were confirmed by the success of the British Empire Industries Exhibition in Buenos Aires in February–March 1931, and the visit of Edward, Prince of Wales (and later Edward VIII), and Prince George, later Duke of Kent, to open the exhibition. Edward had previously visited Argentina in 1925 and he received a good reception from the government on his return, especially when he delivered part of his speech at the exhibition in Spanish. However, the growing impact of the Great Depression in 1931 led Uriburu's government to introduce exchange controls and a 10 per cent emergency tariff. The British Embassy in Buenos Aires maintained a generally positive attitude towards the new government despite these measures and its resort to dubious tactics to be in power, for example by vetoing the candidature of Dr Marcelo Alvear, a former president of the Republic and leader of the Radical Party in the general election of November

1931. The embassy was also pleased with the election of General Augustin Justo as president, who it described as 'a moderate and sensible man, who enjoys the support of the army and navy'. According to the embassy, Justo's election was 'undoubtedly the best thing that could have happened for the country'.[11]

However, the embassy reported that Anglo-Argentine relations 'suffered a distinct set-back during the latter part of 1932', mainly because of 'resentment felt towards British fiscal policy' and 'restrictions placed on Argentine exports to UK as a result of the Ottawa Conference' in August 1932. The onset of the economic depression had led to the formation of the National Government in Britain in August 1931 and the introduction of an Import Duties Act in March 1932 which imposed a 10 per cent *ad valorem* tax on imports into the UK. The main Argentine exports such as chilled meat, grain and wool were exempted from this tax and it was hoped in Buenos Aires that, despite pressure from the Dominions, the British government would not put any duties on Argentine chilled meat and wool and no major restrictions on Argentine wheat, maize, dairy products and frozen meat. When it became clear after the Ottawa Conference that there might be restrictions the Argentine government decided to send a mission to the UK led by Vice President Dr Julio Roca – to return the visits by Edward, the Prince of Wales, in 1925 and 1931 and to follow up trade talks begun by the Argentine ambassador in London, Dr Manuel Malbran.[12]

The Roca mission arrived in Britain on 7 February 1933 and was met by the Prince of Wales in person. The prince hosted Roca over the next few days before the opening of official negotiations on 15 February followed by the first meeting of the delegations, which was chaired by Walter Runciman as president of the Board of Trade. The negotiations proved difficult and complicated and there were frequent rumours that they were about to be broken off. There were various issues involved but, above all, there loomed the question of imports of Argentine meat, especially beef, following the onset of the depression and the Ottawa agreements. Roca and his mission required some kind of guarantee regarding the level of meat imports by Britain. From the British perspective, a major fear was that of being supplanted by the United States in the Argentine market for manufactured goods. Most of the detailed work in the negotiations was obviously undertaken by Board of Trade officials, led by Leslie Burgin, the Parliamentary undersecretary, but Runciman had a significant role to play in getting the agreement through its Cabinet discussions and the House of Commons.[13]

In fact, it was at Runciman's request that, on 15 March 1933, the British Cabinet discussed the Argentine negotiations. He said that the Board of Trade was asking for authority to meet the Roca Mission's concern regarding a possible reduction in the British import of chilled beef from Argentina over the following three years if there were to be a decrease in prices. Runciman wanted to be able to assure Roca that any such reduction would not be greater than 10 per cent in any one year. However, the minister of agriculture – Walter Elliott – objected to this on the grounds that it would adversely affect home producers of beef and could have political repercussions. He suggested 15 per cent instead and was supported by the secretary of state for Scotland, Sir Godfrey Collins, and the home secretary – a former secretary of state for agriculture – Sir John Gilmour. Runciman argued strongly that Britain needed an agreement as it had £450 million invested in Argentina, including railways, roads, docks and other public works. An agreement would also free up credits frozen by the Argentine government that were required for trade. The coal industry, especially in South Wales, was largely dependent on orders from Argentina, he continued, and an agreement would also aid British manufacturing and textiles.[14]

According to the Cabinet minutes, Runciman said that the desirability of an agreement with Argentina was evident during the Ottawa Conference. If the current negotiations failed, Britain would have missed a great opportunity to unfreeze credits and promote trade. It would also be more difficult to reach agreement with other countries. 'From the first he had considered the tariff policy of the National Government to be a pivot round which negotiations were to be opened up. If these negotiations were now to be abandoned, his usefulness would come to an end and he could not continue in such circumstances.' This thinly veiled threat by Runciman to resign if he was not allowed room to manoeuvre to make the agreement with Argentina was especially significant as he was a Liberal National and a key player in the government at this time. This may have been one reason why he received the powerful support of Neville Chamberlain, the chancellor of the Exchequer, who said that he 'could not put too strongly his sense of the disaster that would result from a breakdown in the Argentine negotiations' as this 'would put in question the whole of our foreign trade policy'.[15]

Runciman therefore got his way and this facilitated the second meeting of the delegations on 28 March chaired by his deputy, Leslie Burgin – also a Liberal National. But progress towards concluding an agreement remained slow as Roca had the habit of putting off negotiations from day to day so that time was running out before the mission was due to leave at Easter, in the middle of April. On 6 April 1933 the Foreign Office discovered that Runciman was apparently planning to go on a fortnight's holiday to the Mediterranean on 11 April, regardless of the state of the trade negotiations. Foreign Office officials expressed astonishment, with Vansittart minuting: 'I understand that the negotiations will come to a head on the 11th. It is surely impossible for the President of the Board of Trade to go away on that very day. In any case it would seem impossible for him to go away without saying anything to Dr Roca who is, after all, Vice President of a considerable country.' However, in the end, Runciman made only a brief trip to Scotland.[16]

Agreement in principle with the Roca mission was reached on 27 April and announced by Runciman in the House of Commons on the same day. The agreement was finally signed by Roca and Runciman on 1 May at the third and final meeting of the full delegations. Sir John Simon, the foreign secretary, was also due to sign but was indisposed. The agreement consisted of three main parts. Firstly, in Article 1 Britain agreed to maintain imports of Argentine beef at no less than 390,000 metric tonnes of refrigerated beef per year, which was the equivalent of the 1932 level. In addition, 85 per cent of the beef exports were to be made through foreign meat packers, thus maintaining the grip of the Vestey family on the meat-packing process. Secondly, in Article 2 the Argentine government agreed to reserve 12 million pesos for British holders of Argentine currency engaged in trade for which import or export permits had not been obtained. This freed up large sums frozen in Argentine banks by foreign exchange restrictions.[17]

Article 3 provided for the negotiation by August 1933 of a Supplementary Tariff Agreement. Negotiations took place in Buenos Aires from June and were very slow as the Argentine side was reluctant to agree to tariff requests made by Britain. Indeed, at a Cabinet meeting on 28 July Runciman sought permission to threaten to denounce the main agreement, signed on 1 May 1933, unless tariff concessions were finalized promptly. This request was granted but in the end the threat was not necessary. The deadline was extended and the Supplementary Agreement was eventually concluded on 26 September 1933 – just in time for approval by the Argentine Congress at the end of its session. The agreement provided for the reclassification or reduction of duties on 388 tariff items. Coal remained on the free list and was therefore untaxed and the Argentines agreed to buy 100 per cent of their coal needs in Britain. The Argentine government also declared its intention not to maintain its 10 per cent surcharge on imports except in the case of strong financial necessity and, even then, to give special consideration to British goods.[18]

The Roca-Runciman agreement and its critics

The Roca-Runciman agreement replaced the long-standing commercial treaty of 1825 and its 'most favoured nation' treatment of other trading partners, such as the United States. It had many critics at home in addition to the violent opposition that it encountered in Argentina. Some of these criticisms were voiced in a long debate in the House of Commons on 10 May 1933. The Argentine agreement was strongly defended by Runciman, who opened the debate, but it was attacked by the opposition parties, especially Sir Archibald Sinclair, the Liberal leader. Apart from concerns that the Roca-Runciman agreement might harm domestic agriculture and imperial preference for the Dominions it was also pointed out by Sinclair, amongst others, that the agreement could complicate the British position at the forthcoming London Economic Conference and that it might upset the Roosevelt administration as it was not in keeping with the spirit of the tariff truce favoured by Cordell Hull. He also questioned whether his former colleague, Runciman, previously an ardent free trader, really believed in the principles underlying the agreement with Argentina.[19]

The day after the Commons debate, Sir Ronald Lindsay, the British ambassador in Washington, sent a dispatch to London outlining the response of the US press to the Roca-Runciman agreement, which generally took the view that Britain had secured exclusive advantages from Argentina at the expense of the United States. The agreement had had 'a bad reception' in the United States, reported Lindsay, and had been 'assailed in headlines, news and leading articles'. No blame was attached to Argentina, said Lindsay. Rather, 'in the background of these press reactions has been the ancient suspicion that Great Britain, unless watched, will take some unfair advantage of the United States, combined with the peculiar sensitiveness to European rivalry with United States trading and other interests in South America'. Lindsay also noted: 'Criticism was undoubtedly more severe, and the prominence given to it was greater, owing to the concurrent United States-Argentina discussions in Washington on the World Economic Conference and the reports of delays in the Anglo-American discussions in London on the proposed tariff truce.'[20]

A detailed report by the British Information Office in New York elaborated upon American criticisms. 'The majority of the press cables from London have been provocative, and their tenor has been exaggerated by the headlines given them,' it said. In New York, the *Herald-Tribune* indicated that the United States 'unquestionably would retaliate' and called the agreement 'Great Britain's corner on Argentina's foreign exchange'. The *Wall Street Journal*'s headlines included 'Argentine Pact, British Victory' and 'Agreement leaves little Foreign Exchange for Trade with the Rest of the world', while the Hearst newspaper chain, a strong supporter of high tariffs, contrasted the agreement with the United States efforts to secure a tariff truce. Even the more liberal journals in the United States took a similar line, but there were some friendly comments. The *New York Times,* for example, said that, although American trade might be damaged by the Anglo-Argentine agreement, this would be the result of US policy. 'If the United States had followed England's example by buying heavily in Argentina, it could probably persuade the latter into a similar agreement, but the Hawley-Smoot tariff and artificial administrative restrictions had caused United States trade in the Argentine to fall off more than that of its competitors.'[21]

The British Foreign Office took a dim view of American complaints. 'All this adverse comment by the United States is really rather silly,' wrote one official. 'There is no question of our "cornering the peso": the exchange agreement merely promises us the value of our purchases (which is surely reasonable) less – and this has been conveniently overlooked – a deduction towards the payment of the foreign debt payable to other countries, including the US.' American alarm had arisen because the US policy of high tariffs had caused other countries to seek different markets. The Americans, he added, were beginning to realize that 'their tardy progress towards a better bargaining position has caused them to miss the Argentine bus which at one time – after Ottawa – was loitering temptingly past them. We on our side have no cause whatever to reproach ourselves or to make excuses.' Similar views were expressed by other officials. 'The agreement must be a great disappointment to the numerous Americans who confidently predicted that our days in South America were numbered,' noted one, while Robert Craigie, the head of the American Department, added: 'A lot of ill-informed and ill-natured criticism. We need not take all this very seriously, but it is interesting as showing how near to the surface all the old anti-British prejudices still lurk.'[22]

While Hull was restrained about the Roca-Runciman agreement in public, he expressed concern in private, for several reasons. Firstly, the Roca-Runciman agreement was signed in the lead up to the London Economic Conference which opened at the end of May 1933. Hull was in London as the head of the

US delegation and he was trying to negotiate a tariff truce with Britain and other participating countries. The Roca-Runciman agreement appeared to be against the spirit, if not the letter, of the tariff truce and did not augur well for his aim to promote trade liberalization during the conference. Secondly, he was keen for the United States to negotiate trade agreements with the countries of Latin America, including Argentina, as part of the administration's Good Neighbour policy, and this task would be made more difficult if the Roca-Runciman agreement played into the hands of domestic opponents, especially Republicans, who advocated a hard-headed trade policy rather than a more liberal one. Thirdly, he believed that the agreement was partly a result of the Ottawa accords and the system of imperial preference which he felt had the effect of 'greatly injuring our trade with the United Kingdom and the Dominions'. The trade agreement he most desired was an Anglo-American agreement and he deprecated any move by Britain that might make this more difficult.[23]

Apart from these broad considerations of policy Hull and the State Department were especially concerned about the exchange provisions of the Roca-Runciman agreement, and the advantages that they gave to Britain. Shortly after the agreement was announced Norman Davis – the American representative on the Organizing Committee for the London Economic Conference – received a message from Hull saying that 'this Government desires to express the judgment that the proposed treaty, certainly as a consequence of the exchange arrangements which are laid down and possibly as a consequence of its tariff features, contains elements of discrimination in favour of British trade which are inconsistent with the aims of world cooperation which alone can give meaning to the Economic Conference and to the preliminary conversations in which the American Government is engaged'. Hull expressed his fear that the agreement might undermine his attempts to secure a tariff truce during the conference and would encourage other countries, such as Nazi Germany, that were pursuing restrictive policies.[24]

The State Department also complained about the Roca-Runciman agreement to Argentina's ambassador in Washington who said that his government was helpless to prevent its exchange provisions as Britain was the main consumer of Argentine beef. A formal US protest was made to Argentina regarding the implementation of the exchange provisions of the Roca-Runciman agreement on 26 June, but the agreement was passed by both chambers on 1 August and this was followed by the Supplementary Tariff Agreement between Britain and Argentina in September. By this time the 'Roosevelt Bombshell' message to the London Economic Conference criticizing its preoccupation with currency stabilization had effectively brought it to an end, along with the dimming prospects of a tariff truce. But there were also other issues, apart from exchange controls, causing tensions between Washington and Buenos Aires, including the difficulties in the way of a US–Argentine trade agreement. A Congressional ban on the importation of meat from Argentina because of foot-and-mouth disease did not help relations, especially as livestock in the Patagonia region were entirely free from the disease. In fact, a US trade agreement with Argentina was not finally concluded until October 1941.[25]

The exchange issue continued to be a bone of contention between the United States and Argentina after the Roca-Runciman agreement and throughout FDR's first term, especially as the Argentine government was determined to negotiate a renewal of the agreement before the end of its expiry date in 1936. The US ambassador in Argentina, Alexander Weddell, reported in June 1936 that 'the Argentines are fully aware of their present advantage and are leaving no stone unturned to persuade us to come to a trade agreement with them. At the moment they are negotiating with the British for a renewal of the Roca-Runciman Agreement and will throw everything they can to the British to facilitate that end.' Indeed, the Argentine government had already agreed to the Anglo-Argentine Convention of 1935 that resulted in a 5 per cent decrease in Argentine chilled beef shipments to Britain and allowed the Dominions, especially Australia, to increase their exports of chilled beef to the mother country. On 26 November 1936 Runciman announced in the House of Commons that a new agreement had been reached with Argentina. This was signed on 1 December by Malbran, the Argentine ambassador, and Anthony Eden, the British foreign secretary. The Eden-Malbran agreement was even more favourable to Britain than its predecessor and in the words of one historian it became 'the cornerstone of relations between Britain and Argentina' until 1948.[26]

It was not only the economic aspects of Britain's relationship with Argentina that bothered Hull and the State Department. They also felt that it strengthened Argentina's determination to pursue a foreign policy that was ostentatiously independent of the United States and aimed at fortifying its self-identity as the preeminent state in South America. This approach was typified by Carlos Saavedra Lamas, the Argentine foreign minister from 1932 to 1938. While generally cooperative with Hull during the Montevideo conference in December 1933, when the Roosevelt administration consciously disavowed the Monroe Doctrine, he was much more combative during the Pan American Conference at Buenos Aires in December 1936. This behaviour outraged Hull, who led the US delegation, as Saavedra Lamas had just been awarded the Nobel Peace Prize, for which Hull had recommended him. The main issue of disagreement was the State Department's idea of a neutrality pact across the Americas. The US view was that this would support and strengthen the League of Nations, whereas Argentina took the view that it could potentially weaken the League by adopting a strict arms embargo modelled on recent US neutrality legislation rather than using discretion to favour the victims of aggression. Furthermore, according to the *New York Times*, there was some suspicion on the US side that Argentina had been encouraged to oppose the American plan by Britain.[27]

Runciman visit to Washington, January 1937

Given Hull's frustrations towards British trade policy during Roosevelt's first term, and not least his exasperation with the Roca-Runciman agreement, the visit of Walter Runciman to Washington in January 1937 at the personal invitation of the president was likely to provide a litmus test for Anglo-American relations at the start of FDR's second term. The visit was arranged by Arthur Murray, Lord Elibank, a British friend of the president's from his time as assistant secretary of the Navy during the First World War. Hull and the State Department inevitably saw Runciman's visit in terms of trade relations and a memorandum drawn up by the department presented the British minister in a rather unflattering light. 'He is at present extremely nationalistic, as has been evidenced by his promotion of and subscription to policies calculated to gain unfair advantage over American interests in many parts of the world,' read the State Department memo. 'His apparent unfriendliness to us may be due to indifference, supreme nationalism or, as his family have long been leaders in British shipping, he probably resents American aid to shipping lines.'[28]

This briefing paper, while rather overstated, did contain some truth. As one of the architects of the Ottawa agreements Runciman had abandoned his lifelong adherence to the Liberal doctrine of free trade, although he maintained that this had been necessary in the economic conditions of 1931–2. He also argued, not without justification, that he had moderated the high tariff aims of Tories like Neville Chamberlain in the National Government. Even the Roca-Runciman agreement, in the form of its Supplementary Tariff Agreement in September 1933, had resulted in tariff reductions. It must have been rather trying for Runciman, a disciple of Gladstonian liberalism – a creed that he was still advocating as late as 1931 – to have to listen to Cordell Hull's lectures on the virtues of free trade. Indeed, Hull's constant blandishments about free trade and his campaign for an Anglo-American trade agreement were referred to by officials in the Board of Trade as the 'Frothblower's Anthem', after a popular song of the time.[29]

Runciman arrived in Washington on 23 January and, accompanied by Lindsay, called on Hull at the State Department. 'Mr Hull was pleasant and genial, and he soon gave us to understand that his mind was centred on his liberalised trade policy,' recorded Runciman. The British minister referred to his own trade agreements since Ottawa as having broadened world trade. Hull, for his part, repeated the doctrines he had been preaching for several years. 'The peace of the world, he declared, could only be secured by obliterating the obstacles to international trade which at present gave rise to friction,' Runciman recorded. 'While not sharing his exaggerations, I told him that I thought his aspirations were well founded, even if expressed in language that went further than what I would use myself.' After dinner on 23, Runciman met Roosevelt and found him much less critical of British policy than Hull. According to Runciman, 'while describing Mr Hull's attitude and speaking warmly of his perseverance, he, the President, was more sympathetic towards our point of view and understood more clearly our difficulties than Mr Hull had done earlier in the day'.[30]

During his visit Runciman observed that Roosevelt was much less concerned about trade issues than Hull. 'Fiscal questions are not the chief interest of the President', he noted, 'and it is only in connection with their bearing on the maintenance of peace that he discussed these questions at all.' Runciman continued: 'The risks of war in Europe are present in his mind, and he returns repeatedly to his statement that the dictators are the danger. The only safe guardians of peace are the

Parliamentary countries.' While somewhat disappointed over his trade talks with Hull, Runciman regarded the visit as very worthwhile, and he now gave his full support to concluding a trade agreement with the United States. 'My impression is that for the next four years President Roosevelt's Government will be more than friendly, provided one or two points of friction are overcome,' Runciman wrote to Baldwin. 'The President is obviously anxious to maintain a degree of intimacy with the British Government … I hope that we shall lose no chance of collaborating with him promptly and candidly.'[31]

The Runciman visit showed that Roosevelt was primarily concerned at this time about the European crisis, which had dominated his conversations with the British minister. He also expressed his fears about Japanese aims but Latin America was less of an issue at this time. Runciman's visit proved to be the harbinger of a period of growing US involvement in international affairs that was highlighted by FDR's 'Quarantine speech' in October 1937. A central feature of US policy included Anglo-American financial and economic cooperation in terms of currency stabilization, trade negotiations and war debts – all areas that had bedevilled relations following the 'Roosevelt Bombshell' message to the London Economic Conference in July 1933. The Tripartite Currency Agreement of September 1936 with Britain and France was renewed several times until 1940, despite the growing weakness of the franc. The Anglo-American Trade Agreement pursued by Hull was eventually signed in November 1938 and the war debts issue was pushed into the background. For example, the regular war debt note to the British government that was due in June 1939 was sent earlier in the year so as not to coincide with the royal visit to the United States in that month.[32]

Mounting evidence of cooperation between the United States and Britain during Roosevelt's second term led the inveterate isolationist senator, William Borah, to accuse the administration of seeking a 'tacit alliance' with Britain against the 'dictator states' of Germany and Japan. As well as a speech in the House of Commons by the British foreign secretary that hinted at a closer relationship with the United States than was being publicly acknowledged, the revelation that secret naval talks had taken place in London in January 1938 greatly alarmed Borah and his fellow isolationists in the Senate. So too did the president's attempts to revise the neutrality laws in favour of Britain and France after Runciman's mission to Czechoslovakia was followed by the Munich crisis in September 1938. Borah was able to prevent the revision of the neutrality laws in July 1939 but once war had broken out the US arms embargo was replaced with a 'cash and carry' policy that greatly aided Britain as the strongest financial and naval power in Europe. Similarly, the Roosevelt administration successfully aided Britain with the Destroyer-Bases deal of September 1940 and the Lend Lease Act passed in March 1941, both prior to American entry into the war as a combatant in December 1941.[33]

Conclusions

Notwithstanding Hull's devotion to a more liberal trade policy and his trade agreements programme, not to mention what Sumner Welles termed his 'violent antipathy' towards Argentina, the Roca-Runciman agreement and its successors in 1936, 1939, 1942 and 1945 did not prove to be a major impediment in Anglo-American relations during FDR's presidency. Growing concern in Washington about Nazi ambitions in Europe, and increasingly in Latin America, and the need to support Britain, far outweighed the frustration felt by Hull about British policy towards Argentina, especially when the fall of France in 1940 left Britain as the main resistance to Germany and Italy in Europe. However, British trade with Argentina, especially beef imports, continued to be an irritant in Anglo-American relations, especially once the United States joined the war and Hull tried to force Argentina to abandon its status as a neutral – a status that contradicted American policy towards Latin America but that was very convenient for wartime Britain as it kept open Argentina's position as the main supplier of chilled beef and *Fray Bentos* products to the British armed forces and the general population.[34]

The colonial nature of the continuing trade relationship between Britain and Argentina was rather more than an irritant to Argentine nationalists, especially in the military, who regarded the Roca-Runciman agreement and its legacy as anathema and who helped to bring about the military coup of June 1943, thus ending what they regarded as an 'Infamous Decade' of corrupt conservative rule. The Anglo-Argentine trade agreement was renewed in 1945 but it ended in 1948 during the presidency of Juan Peron and was replaced by several successive short-lived and unsatisfactory agreements. The same era of growing nationalism also witnessed the sale of British-owned railways and tramways in Argentina as well as the rise of the Falklands issue in relations with Britain as the historic Argentine claim to 'the Malvinas' became a key symbol for critics of British colonialism, ultimately resulting in the Falklands War of 1982. As was the case some fifty years before, Argentina again became a major issue in Anglo-American relations and with a similar outcome – unease in Washington about the legacy of British colonialism but ultimately strong support for Britain resulting from more significant geopolitical and ideological considerations.[35]

Notes

1   For the Runciman Mission, see Paul Vysny, *The Runciman Mission to Czechoslovakia, 1938: Prelude to Munich* (London: Palgrave Macmillan, 2003); Tony McCulloch, 'Franklin Roosevelt and the Runciman Mission to Czechoslovakia, 1938: A New Perspective on Anglo-American Relations in the Era of Appeasement', *Journal of Transatlantic Studies* 1, no. 2 (Autumn 2003), 152–74. For the late Lord Runciman, see 'A Tribute to Viscount Runciman', 11 December 2020, https://www.thebritishacademy.ac.uk/news/a-tribute-to-viscount-runciman.

2   Peter Bakewell, *A History of Latin America*, 2nd ed. (Oxford: Blackwell Publishing, 2004), 526–7.

3   Gordon Bridger, *Britain and the Making of Argentina* (Southampton: WIT Press, 2012), 139–41; David Rock, *The British in Argentina: Commerce, Settlers and Power, 1800–2000* (London: Palgrave Macmillan, 2019), 282–6. See also David Rock,

Authoritarian Argentina: The Nationalist Movement, Its History and Its Impact (Berkeley and Los Angeles: University of California Press, 1993), 112–24.

4   For the Senate shooting, see David Rock, *The British in Argentina*, 283–4. See also reports in the *New York Times*, 24, 25, 26 and 27 July 1935.

5   Cordell Hull, *Memoirs*, Volumes I and II (London: Hodder and Stoughton, 1948), especially 352–6, 378–85, 519–26, 1409–22. See also Irwin Gellman, *Good Neighbour Diplomacy. United States Policies in Latin America, 1933–1945* (Baltimore, MD: Johns Hopkins University Press, 1979); Randall Bennett Woods. *The Roosevelt Foreign-Policy Establishment and the 'Good Neighbor': The United States and Argentina, 1941–1945* (Lawrence, KA: Regents Press of Kansas, 1979).

6   For detailed analysis of FDR's policy towards Nazi Germany at this time, see Tony McCulloch, *Tacit Alliance: Franklin Roosevelt and the Anglo-American 'Special Relationship' before Churchill, 1937–1939* (Edinburgh: Edinburgh University Press, 2021).

7   Gordon Bridger, *Britain and the Making of Argentina*, 139; David Rock, *The British in Argentina: Commerce, Settlers and Power, 1800–2000* (London: Palgrave Macmillan, 2019), 282; Winthrop Wright, *British-Owned Railways in Argentina: Their Effect on the Growth of Economic Nationalism, 1854–1948* (Austin, TX: University of Texas Press, 1974). See also Peter Smith, *Politics and Beef in Argentina: Patterns of Conflict and Change, 1900–1946* (New York: Columbia University Press, 1969); Daniel Drossdoff, *El Gobierno de las Vacas, 1933–1956. Tratado Roca-Runciman* (Buenos Aires, Ediciones la Bastilla, 1972); Edwin Frank Early, 'The Roca-Runciman Treaty and Its Significance for Argentina', University College London, PhD thesis, 1981; Roger Gravil, *The Anglo-American Connection, 1930–1939* (London and New York: Routledge, 2019).

8   Benjamin M Rowland, *Commercial Conflict and Foreign Policy: A Study in Anglo-American Relations, 1932–1938* (New York: Taylor and Francis, 1987), 68–93; Patricia Clavin, *The Failure of Economic Diplomacy: Britain, Germany, France and the United States* (London: Macmillan Press, 1996), 6, 112–14; David Reynolds, *The Creation of the Anglo-American Alliance, 1937–41: A Study in Competitive Co-operation* (London: Europa Publications, 1981); B. J. C. McKercher, *Transition of Power: Britain's Loss of Global Pre-eminence to the United States, 1930–1945* (Cambridge: Cambridge University Press, 1999; paperback, 2006). David Sheinin, *Argentina and the United States: An Alliance Constrained* (Athens, GA: University of Georgia Press 2006), mentions Roca-Runciman, 71–3.

9   UK National Archives (UKNA), Kew, FO/371/14196, A4727/4727/2, Eugen Millington-Drake (Counsellor) to Foreign Office, 24 May 1930: Annual Report on Argentina for 1929, 2–4. For D'Abernon's trade mission, see Gaynor Johnson, 'The D'Abernon Trade Mission to South America, 1929: Context and Reappraisal', in Thomas C. Mills and Rory M. Miller, *Britain and the Growth of US Hegemony in Twentieth-Century Latin America* (London: Palgrave Macmillan, 2020), 137–60.

10 UKNA, FO/371/15057, A2359/2359/2, Sir Ronald Macleay (Ambassador) to Foreign Office, 28 February 1931: Annual Report on Argentina for 1930, 2–6.

11 UKNA, FO/371/15799, A1156/1156/2, Sir Ronald Macleay to Foreign Office, 31 January 1932: Annual report on Argentina for 1931, 2–6.

12 UKNA, FO/371/17475, A1698/1698/2, John Leche (Counsellor) to Foreign Office, 6 February 1934: Annual Report on Argentina for 1933, 6–8.

13 For Roca and Prince of Wales, see reports in the *New York Times*, 7, 8, 11 and 13 February 1933. For report on Roca-Runciman negotiations, see UKNA, CAB/23, 18 (1933) item 3, 15 March 1933: statement by Runciman.

14 Ibid., contributions by Runciman, Elliot, Collins and Gilmour.
15 Ibid., contributions by Runciman and Chamberlain.
16 FO/371/16532, A/2812/48/2, Foreign Office minutes by P. Mason, 6 April 1933; R. C. Craigie, 6 April 1933; Sir R. Vansittart, 8 April 1933.
17 UKNA, FO/371/17475, A1698/1698/2, John Leche (Counsellor) to Foreign Office, 6 February 1934: Annual Report on Argentina for 1933, 6–8 (for details of articles 1 and 2 of the agreement).
18 Ibid., Annual report on Argentina for 1933, 8–9 (for details of article 3 and the Supplementary Trade Agreement).
19 *Hansard*, House of Commons debate, 10 May 1933: speeches by Runciman and Sinclair.
20 UKNA, FO/371/16532, A3945/48/2, despatch from Sir Ronald Lindsay to Sir John Simon, 11 May 1933.
21 Ibid. enclosure on 'Anglo-Argentine Trade Agreement: United States Press Comments', prepared by British Library of Information in New York.
22 Ibid. Foreign Office minutes by P. Mason, 24 May; D. V. Kelly, 24 May; R. C. Craigie, 26 May 1933.
23 Hull, *Memoirs*, I, 355. For Hull's general philosophy regarding international trade, see chapters 26 and 27, 352–77. For his desire for an Anglo-American agreement see Hull, *Memoirs*, I, 519–30.
24 *Foreign Relations of the United States* (*FRUS*), 1933, Volume IV, Doc 730, Secretary of State to the Chargé in Great Britain (Ray Atherton), 5 May 1933, for Norman Davis.
25 *FRUS*, 1933, IV, Doc 746, Acting Secretary of State (William Phillips) to Chargé in Argentina (John Campbell White), 13 June 1933, re discussion with Argentine ambassador; Doc 748, Phillips to White, 26 June 1933, re formal US protest to Argentina. See also Hull, *Memoirs*, I, 497–8 and *Memoirs*, II, 1140. For the 'Roosevelt Bombshell' message of 3 July 1933, see Clavin, *Failure of Economic Diplomacy*, 129–38. See also Herbert Feis, *1933: Characters in Crisis* (Boston, MA: Da Capo Press, 1976).
26 *FRUS*, 1936, V, Doc 170, Alexander Weddell (US ambassador) to Secretary of State (Hull), 1 June 1936; Doc 179, Weddell to Hull, 10 December 1936; *Hansard*, House of Commons, statement by Runciman, 26 November 1933; Drossdoff, *El Gobierno de las Vacas*, 92.
27 See Hull, *Memoirs*, I, 325–41 for relations with Saavedra Lamas at Montevideo conference; for Pan American conference at Buenos Aires, see Hull, *Memoirs*, I, 493–503; see also David Haglund, *Latin America and the Transformation of US Strategic Thought, 1936–1940* (Albuquerque, NM: University of New Mexico Press, 1984); *New York Times*, 13 December 1936.
28 US National Archives, State Department file 033.4111/13: memo on 'Right Honourable Walter Runciman', 22 January 1937; see also McCulloch, *Tacit Alliance*, 40–7; for a fuller account of the Runciman visit, see Tony McCulloch, 'Franklin Roosevelt and the Runciman Visit to Washington in 1937: Informal Diplomacy and Anglo-American Relations in the Era of Munich', *Journal of Transatlantic Studies* 4, no. 2 (Autumn 2006), 211–40; also Richard Harrison, 'The Runciman Visit to Washington DC in January 1937', *Canadian Journal of History* 19 (August 1984), 217–39.
29 University of Newcastle Library, Runciman Papers, Box 250, letter from Walter Runciman to his constituents, 29 September 1932; UKNA, PREM/1/291, Runciman to Baldwin, 8 February 1937. See also McCulloch, 'Franklin Roosevelt and the Runciman visit to Washington', 218–20.

30 UKNA, PREM/1/291, Runciman to Baldwin, 8 February 1937: Runciman memo; McCulloch, *Tacit Alliance*, 43.
31 UKNA, PREM/1/291, Runciman to Baldwin, 8 February 1937: Runciman memo; McCulloch, *Tacit Alliance*, 44–6.
32 McCulloch, *Tacit Alliance*, 281–99.
33 McCulloch, *Tacit Alliance*, 3–21 and 266–80.
34 For Welles quote, see Haglund, *Latin America and the Transformation of US Strategic Thought*, 37. See also Sumner Welles, *Seven Major Decisions* (London: Hamish Hamilton, 1951). For the Argentine meat issue in 1942–44, see Hull, *Memoirs*, II, 1409–19; see also Rock, *The British in Argentina*, 295–300.
35 For Anglo-Argentine relations during the Peron era and the Falklands war, see Rock, *The British in Argentina*, 303–38 and 358–66. For US policy see Christoph Bluth, 'Anglo-American Relations in the Falklands Conflict', in *International Perspectives on the Falklands Conflict*, ed. Alex Danchev (London: Macmillan, 1992), 203–23; Sally-Ann Treharne, *Reagan and Thatcher's Special Relationship: Latin America and Anglo-American Relations* (Edinburgh: Edinburgh University Press, 2015).

Chapter 6

THE OTHER ROYAL DIMENSION TO THE TRANSATLANTIC RELATIONSHIP: FDR AND THE DUTCH AND NORWEGIAN ROYAL FAMILIES DURING THE SECOND WORLD WAR

David B. Woolner

On Friday 28 April 1939, Crown Prince Olav and Crown Princess Martha of Norway disembarked from the Presidential Yacht, the *USS Potomac,* which had sailed up the Hudson River from Manhattan to transport the royal couple to Poughkeepsie, New York. The crown prince and princess had travelled to the United States at the invitation of US president, Franklin D. Roosevelt, who was there to greet Prince Olav and Princess Martha as the gangplank was lowered over the side of the vessel while a band of Royal Marines piped their arrival. The ostensible reason for their visit was to open the Norwegian Exhibition at the New York World's Fair, followed by an extensive tour of the United States. But there were other, less obvious reasons that FDR had for inviting the prince and princess to make their first visit to America; reasons that had as much to do with domestic politics, as they had to do with international relations.[1]

A mere six weeks before the royal couple arrived in New York, a stunned world learned that German forces had invaded Czechoslovakia. This marked a turning point in the long march towards the outbreak of the Second World War. Hitler's absorption of this territory made a mockery of his oft-stated claim that his chief aim in Europe was the unification of the German-speaking peoples. Moreover, his destruction of Czechoslovakia also made it clear that the British policy of appeasement – by which the Czech territory known as the Sudetenland was proffered to Germany as part of the September 1938 Munich settlement – was dead. There would be no 'peace for our time', as British prime minister Neville Chamberlain famously declared upon his return from his meetings with the German dictator. It now seemed obvious that Hitler was bent on further conquests and that it would only be a matter of time before war broke out again in Europe.

These ominous developments deeply alarmed Franklin Roosevelt, who from his first days in office viewed Hitler as 'a madman', and regarded the steady rise in German power in the late 1930s as a serious threat to American security.[2] In light of this, FDR remained convinced that should war break out the United States must do what it could to bolster the strength of the Western democracies. But Roosevelt's ability to offer aid to the European states was seriously hampered by the isolationist sentiment of the American people – who remained opposed to any US involvement in a European war – and by the equally strong isolationist sentiment in the US Congress, which passed a series of neutrality laws in the mid-1930s that prohibited the sale of US arms and munitions to either side in a conflict and severely limited the president's freedom of action in the conduct of US foreign policy.

Fearful that war might break out at any moment, FDR began a concerted effort in the spring of 1939 to get Congress to amend the neutrality legislation. His goal was to secure the authority to grant belligerent nations the right – at his discretion – to acquire arms from the United States on a 'cash and carry basis'. This would provide the president with a means to assist Great Britain and France in the event of war without direct US involvement in the conflict.[3] He also believed that securing a repeal of the arms embargo might help forestall the outbreak of war, as the ability of Great Britain and France to purchase such advanced weapons as aircraft in the United States might give Hitler pause.[4]

It may not have been obvious to most observers at the time, but FDR's decision to invite Prince Olav and Princess Martha to visit the United States represented another component of this strategy. Nor was this tactic confined to the Norwegian royal family. FDR also used the excuse of the 1939 World's Fair to issue invitations to the Crown Prince and Princess of Denmark, and most importantly, to King George VI and Queen Elizabeth of the United Kingdom – the first time that the reigning British Monarch ever visited American shores.

FDR's goal was to use the royal visits as a means to break down the isolationist attitudes of the American people by providing the public with an opportunity to witness what he called the 'essential democracy' of his royal visitors.[5] To this end he minimized official functions in Washington and insisted that his royal guests spend time with him at his family home in Hyde Park. A special feature of all three of these visits involved an informal picnic lunch complete with hot dogs on the grounds of Top Cottage, the unassuming hilltop retreat he built for himself as the place where he one day hoped to spend his retirement. He even went so far as to drive the royal couples to and from the hilltop picnic over the narrow farm roads that led to the cottage in his famous hand-controlled Ford roadster – an experience that Queen Elizabeth later reflected was far more nerve wracking than her experience in the London Blitz!

FDR made sure that there was extensive press coverage of these activities out of his belief that their 'simplicity and naturalness would produce a most excellent effect' that would not only showcase US support for the European regimes threatened by Hitler's designs, but also garner greater support for the repeal of the arms embargo among the American public. Nevertheless, it would not be until November 1939 – a full two months after the start of the war – that Congress would grant him the authority he requested.[6]

It was in the midst of all of these machinations that Prince Olav and Princess Martha journeyed to Hyde Park to spend the weekend with the president and Mrs.

Roosevelt. As FDR hoped, word of the royal couple's arrival was front page news across the county. It also coincided with a much-anticipated speech that Hitler gave in the German Reichstag in response to a recent appeal that FDR had issued to both Hitler and the Italian leader Benito Mussolini to pledge to ten years of peace – a request that both dictators rejected. As reported in the *New York Times*, the first thing that Princess Martha said to FDR as she took his hand was 'what did you think of Hitler's speech?' To which FDR's offhand reply was 'it left the door about an inch open'.[7] In fact, FDR fully expected that Hitler would reject his overture, but as he explained to Canadian prime minister Mackenzie King prior to issuing the appeal, 'If we are turned down the issue becomes clearer and public opinion in your country and mine will be helped.'[8]

Given the precarious situation in Norway and Denmark, it is perhaps not surprising that Princess Martha (who was born in Sweden to a Danish mother) was anxious to know how FDR felt about Hitler's scathing response to his appeal for peace. Moreover, the fact that she raised the issue provides one of the few pieces of evidence that the Crown Princess was not averse to discussing political issues with the president. But her comment also raises some important questions about the overall motivation of both the Norwegian and American governments in accepting the president's invitation for the royal couple to visit the United States at the very moment when the possibility of war in Europe had reached new heights.

Like FDR, the crown princesses' father, King Haakon VII, entertained serious doubts about the British policy of appeasement. Part of this may have stemmed from the views of his English wife, Queen Maud, who was the granddaughter of Queen Victoria and was known to be strongly anti-German. But whatever the case, Hitler's move into Prague certainly confirmed the king's view that Prime Minister Chamberlain's efforts would not produce satisfactory results.[9] King Haakon's reaction to these developments was quite different than FDR's, however. Whereas FDR viewed the collapse of appeasement as necessitating the pursuit of what might best be termed as an American policy of belligerent neutrality, the king doubled down on his view that a policy of strict neutrality 'is the only one compatible with the safeguarding of Norwegian interests'.[10]

In light of this, we should not necessarily interpret the timing or nature of Princess Martha's comments as an early indication of the softening of the king's or the Norwegian government's adherence to neutrality. If anything, the fact that the Norwegian government allowed the royal visit to go ahead confirms the fact that most of the world – and for that matter a good share of the American public – believed in the American commitment to neutrality. They also believed that FDR's efforts to secure peace in Europe in the spring of 1939 were sincere, when in fact FDR's missives to Hitler and Mussolini were but a small part of his overall and largely behind-the-scenes strategy to prepare the nation for war.

We do not know the extent to which FDR revealed this aspect of his thinking to the crown prince and princess, but there is little doubt that the president was quite taken with the couple, particularly Princess Martha, whose light-hearted elegant charm, and regal bearing, FDR found especially appealing. The weekend that the royal family spent with FDR in Hyde Park would mark the beginning of a warm friendship between the president and the princess that would continue for the next six years.

The basis for this longer-term friendship was the outbreak of the Second World War. Alarmed by the disintegration of events in Europe in the fall of 1939, FDR sent a letter to Crown Prince Olav in early January 1940 offering to shelter the royal couple's children at Hyde Park 'if by any unfortunate chance, things should go from bad to worse in Norway'. It was this overture that ultimately led Crown Prince Olav to reach out to FDR to take the president up on his offer.[11] In response, FDR would not only arrange for Princess Martha and her children to be evacuated from Norway via Finland in August 1940, he would also go on to host the family for a time at the White House, take the time to help her find a suitable residence for her family on the outskirts of Washington, DC, and would visit with Princess Martha on more than 100 occasions over the course of the war. This seeming dedication to the crown princess has led some observers to wonder if there was some sort of romantic attachment between FDR and Martha.[12]

That FDR was attracted to Martha and enjoyed her company there can be no doubt. But we should not read too much into their friendship. First, because FDR clearly relished being in the company of royalty. The diaries of his activities in both Washington and Hyde Park record numerous occasions when FDR played host to the crown heads of Europe. It was this penchant for royalty that not only led to FDR's close ties to Princess Martha – whom he referred to as his 'Godchild' – but the equally close relationship he established with the Dutch royal family. The president was quite proud of his Dutch ancestry, and in early November 1939, informed Queen Wilhelmina of the Netherlands – much as he would do with Crown Prince Olav two months later – that he would be quite happy to offer Crown Princess Juliana and her children refuge from the war in either Hyde Park or Washington where he and Eleanor would care for them 'as if they were members of our own family'. FDR sent a similar note to King Leopold II of Belgium, who had three children, and whom FDR regarded as an 'old friend' since their first meeting in 1918 during FDR's tour of England and the Western Front near the end of the First World War.[13]

King Leopold would remain in Europe but in June 1940 Princess Juliana and her children moved to Ottawa, Ontario, for the duration of the war. The reason the Dutch royal family decided Juliana should seek safety in Canada as opposed to the United States stemmed from the Queen's conviction that it was important for Juliana to take up residence in a country that was an ally of the Dutch government-in-exile in London (where Wilhelmina remained) so that, in the event of the Queen's death, Princess Juliana would be able to continue to exercise her royal powers.[14]

Given the relatively close proximity between Hyde Park and Ottawa, Princess Juliana and her children would also spend a good deal of time with FDR over the course of the war. Moreover, as was the case with Princess Martha, FDR established a warm bond with Princess Juliana, with whom he adopted the moniker 'your old uncle' and with which Juliana sometimes reciprocated by referring to herself as 'your little niece'. FDR also took it upon himself to try to find a summer residence for Princess Juliana (and the visiting queen) in western Massachusetts in the summer of 1942, while doing the same for Princess Martha. In the spring of 1943, FDR agreed to be named Godfather at the christening of Princess Juliana's fourth daughter, Princess Margriet, who was born in Ottawa in January.[15]

Princess Martha's proximity to the White House made it possible for FDR to see her far more often that he was able to see Princess Juliana and her family, however. She also had a personality that was quite compatible with the president's. As FDR's distant cousin, Margaret 'Daisy' Suckley recorded in her diary, Martha 'is gentle & sympathetic, has a sense of humor & is very responsive. He teases her all the time & she is very teasable & reacts with laughing and blushing.'[16] It was this aspect of Martha's temperament that FDR found so appealing; traits that in many respects mirrored his own nature and whose attraction becomes all the more understandable if we place their friendship in a broader context.

It is a well-known fact that FDR rarely confided his innermost thoughts to his family, friends and advisors. FDR's early life suggests that this reticence to show emotion or reveal his inner feelings stemmed from a practice that he and his mother adopted to deal with his father's weak heart. As James Roosevelt, who was fifty-four years old when FDR was born, became more and more of an invalid, mother and son conspired to always remain cheerful, and to avoid stress or public shows of emotion so as not to upset his delicate constitution. FDR carried this outward effervescence into adulthood, with the result that he often employed it – whether consciously or subconsciously – as a mask. This penchant for stoicism became all the more pronounced when FDR, at the age of thirty-nine, came down with infantile paralysis (polio), a development that left him without the ability to walk or stand without the assistance of others.[17]

For an individual in FDR's condition, who also had to bear the responsibility of high office, emotional impenetrability has its advantages. But it can also lead to a feeling of isolation and worse still, loneliness, even for a person surrounded by a large family and dozens of aides and assistants. It was also the case that by the time FDR had become president of the United States his relationship with Eleanor Roosevelt had evolved into more of a political partnership than a traditional marriage. FDR's alleged affair with Lucy Mercer, Eleanor's social secretary, during the period when FDR was serving as undersecretary of the Navy in the Wilson Administration, had led to their estrangement, which slowly healed over time, but which, as FDR's cousin Daisy reflected at the time of FDR's death, rendered it impossible for the two of them to relax together, a fact which she called 'the tragedy of their joint lives'.[18]

It is this private aspect of FDR's character that we must consider if we are to understand the nature of his relationship with Princess Martha. For there were very few people in FDR's life with whom he could relax and be himself, and even fewer with whom he would share his intimate feelings. Princess Martha fell within the circle of those with whom the president liked to relax – individuals whose relationship with the president was not based on a purely political or transactional basis.

Viewed from this perspective, the arrival of Princess Martha and her children at the start of the Second World War proved something of a blessing for FDR. For their visits with one another – whether at the White House, in Hyde Park, or at her estate in Bethesda Maryland – provided FDR with a much-needed respite from the war. Nevertheless, we must remember there were other individuals who fell into this category. It was also common practice for FDR to play host to foreign dignitaries with whom he liked nothing better than to get away from the confines of office by taking a country drive – his equivalent of going for a walk – or by engaging in chatty conversation over the president's cocktails before dinner, during what FDR called 'the children's hour'.

There was also a more serious side to FDR's relationship the Princess Martha. Norway's position within the context of the wartime alliance was certainly a subject of conversation between them, along with the condition of her countrymen under German occupation. As was the case with Princess Juliana and Queen Wilhelmina, it was not uncommon for FDR to provide Princess Martha with news on the progress of the war. FDR also corresponded with King Haakon VII, and was frequently in touch with Crown Prince Olav, either by letter, or in person during his many visits to the United States – some of which lasted three to four months.

Throughout these contacts, issues of special concern to Norway were often brought to the president's attention. These included the state of Norway's huge merchant marine fleet, which suffered heavy losses but rendered invaluable service to the Allied cause; the plight of Norwegian refugees in Sweden; the possibility of an Allied incursion into northern Norway; as well as the need to send food relief to the Norwegian people.[19] Given the centrality of Anglo-American relations, and the fact that Norway was but a relatively small part of a much larger alliance, it was not always possible for the president to act on these concerns or provide the Norwegian forces and merchant marine with all of the ships and/or war materiel they requested under the terms of the Lend-Lease programme (which allowed the president to provide arms and commodities to America's allies without the need for payment).

These exchanges also brought out the concerns of the president. In early 1941, for example – before the United States entered the war – FDR expressed an interest in having Princess Martha tour the Scandinavian regions of the United States 'to keep the names of the occupied nations constantly before our public'. Upon learning of this proposal in a conversation he had with Harry Hopkins in London, however, King Haakon voiced serious reservations, and in a note he sent to FDR shortly thereafter, expressed his fear that such a trip might give the impression in Norway 'that we are only having a good time out of the country' – a charge made worse by the German insistence that 'all of us have run away from duty'. He also worried about the strain such a tour might place on his daughter-in-law, who had already been through a great deal.[20]

In response, FDR reassured the king that he understood his apprehension, but he still felt that 'if, later on, the Scandinavians in the Northwest should ask your daughter-in-law to go there informally, as the Dutch have done in several instances ... [with] Princess Juliana, I think it would a good thing'. We must remember, he continued 'that your daughter-in-law represents a combination of Norway, Denmark, and Sweden, which symbolizes the independence of all three countries'.[21]

In spite of King Haakon's reservations, Princess Martha would go on to serve the war effort – delivering speeches about Norway's struggle for freedom, visiting Norwegian marine stations in the United States and Canada, and hosting official events at the Norwegian embassy, among other activities. Unaccustomed to speaking in public, FDR sometimes provided encouragement to Princess Martha, as on one occasion in the fall of 1943 when she telephoned him to express her anxiety about a forthcoming broadcast. FDR reassured her that she had nothing to worry about and immediately after listening to her speech returned her call to say that it was well done.[22] As the war dragged on, FDR would continue to do what he could to help Norway. But in spite of FDR's close relationship with Princess Martha and the Norwegian royal family, US support for the British, Russians and Chinese remained a priority. This left many members of the Norwegian government feeling as if they were not being treated as a full partner, particularly with respect to maritime policy.[23]

* * *

This same imbalance characterized the nature of the relationship between the United States and the Netherlands, in spite of the best efforts of the Dutch government and the House of Orange to elevate status of the Netherlands in Washington.

Here, we should remember, that unlike Norway, the Netherlands possessed an overseas empire that not only included the Dutch East Indies, but also important island possessions in the Caribbean. The Netherlands was also the third largest investor in the United States during the interwar period and US trade and investment with both the Netherlands and with colonial Indonesia during the 1920s and 30s was significant. Thanks to their commercial aplomb and colonial possessions, the Dutch had been able to cling to the notion that the Netherlands should be regarded as medium-sized or even major power that deserved to be treated as such.[24]

The inclusion of the Netherlands in the American-British-Dutch-Australian (ABDA) top-secret staff talks in February 1941 – where the four powers discussed military cooperation in response to the growing threat of Japan in the Pacific – certainly reinforced this view.[25] So too, did FDR's decision to allow the Dutch a seat on the Pacific War Council that was established in February 1942 in the wake of ABDA's demise following the Japanese sweep across the southwest Pacific in the spring of that year.

Yet it soon became apparent to the Dutch foreign Minister, Eeclo van Kleffens, that the Pacific War Council (which had no operational authority) was little more than a symbolic institution that offered his government little chance to influence Allied planning in the conduct of the war. Frustrated by what he perceived as a lack of respect for the Dutch position in the world, van Kleffens asked for a seat on the

Combined Chiefs of Staff (CCOS) – a request that FDR responded to by offering the Dutch participation only on issues directly pertaining to the Netherlands, such as the liberation of Dutch territory in Europe and Asia. In the end, these concessions proved to be of little significance, as, for all practical purposes, the CCOS remained closed to the Netherlands.[26]

In many respects, the inability if the Dutch government to make headway in Washington in the weeks and months following the Japanese attack in the Pacific should not come as a surprise. The average American knew little about the Netherlands while at the same time most Dutch – and their government – were much more concerned about their country's relationship with Great Britain – a fellow imperial power – than they were with Dutch relations with the United States.[27]

Part of what makes the Dutch royal family's wartime relationship with FDR so significant, therefore, is the opportunity it provided to place the Netherlands squarely in the minds of the American public. Van Kleffens (who was married to an American and firmly believed that the United States would emerge as the leading world power after the war) was well aware of this and in spite of these initial setbacks, continued to harbour hope that the close ties between the queen, Princess Juliana and FDR would lead to American recognition of the Netherlands as a leading middle power.

This effort reached a climax in the summer of 1942, when Queen Wilhelmina travelled to the United States at the invitation of the president. As noted, FDR arranged for the queen, Princess Juliana and her children to spend much of the summer in a rented cottage in Lee Massachusetts, not far from Hyde Park. In early August, the queen travelled to Washington for a three-day stay at the White House. The highpoint of her sojourn in Washington included an address to a joint session of Congress – the first ever by a reigning queen – where she reminded her listeners that the motto of the Dutch government-in-exile and of the Dutch people generally was 'no surrender'. She lamented the fact that the Netherlands and its peace-loving people were 'now in bondage to invaders who covered their wholesale systematic pillage with the firing squad [and] the concentration camp'. But the Dutch answer to this oppression, she insisted, was 'resistance until the end in every practicable shape or form'; a stand they adopted, she went on, because 'democracy is our most precious heritage'.[28]

The queen was also careful to remind her audience that she stood before them, not only as a spokesman of the nine million of her compatriots in Europe, but also of 'some seventy millions in Asia and in the Western Hemisphere whom I know to be at one with me in the spirit'. Well aware of the antipathy that FDR and a good share of the American populace harboured towards imperialism, the queen spent a good deal of time in her address detailing the efforts of her government to foster an atmosphere of mutual respect and tolerance among the Western and Asian inhabitants of the Netherlands East Indies. She insisted that throughout her entire reign 'the development of democracy and progress in the Netherlands Indies has been our constant aim' but that this movement towards self-government had been 'temporarily interrupted' by the Japanese invasion.

After pointing out the important contributions the Dutch armed forces and merchant marine were making to the war effort (like Norway, the Netherlands merchant marine fleet was one of the largest in the world), she closed her remarks with a reference to the long-standing friendship between the United States and the Netherlands. Indeed, this was not the first time, she remarked, that the United States and the Netherlands were associated in common warfare. The two countries were also 'comrades in arms', in the days of Washington – an 'ancient partnership we see revived today'. That is why, she said, that 'we considered the first Japanese bomb on Pearl Harbor as a bomb on ourselves. That is why we never wavered in our resolve to be with the United Nations until the end. United we stand and united we will achieve victory.'[29] By all accounts the Queen's 'militant address' was greeted with thunderous applause in Congress and was enthusiastically received by the thousands of Americans who listened to the address on the radio.[30] But this warm reception did little to alter the Netherlands status within the Grand Alliance or result in any major policy shift towards the Dutch government-in-exile in Washington.

The Netherlands, in short, was in many respects viewed in much the same way as Norway, as an important small power, whose strategic significance to the overall war effort remained relatively minor. That FDR shared this view can be seen in a memo he sent to his Naval aide, Captain John McRea, in June 1942, indicating his desire to gift, under Lend-Lease, a sub chaser vessel 'to Norway and to the Netherlands' with the suggestion that the gifting ceremonies take place on King Haakon's seventieth birthday and 'to further find out if there is any anniversary in Netherlands' history for turning over the "Queen Wilhelmina" to the Dutch' (both ships would be named for the respective monarchs). He also suggested that Princess Juliana be invited to the ceremony involving the ship named for the queen, and that an invitation should also be issued to Crown Princess Martha regarding the ceremonies involving the vessel named for the king.

Not surprisingly, FDR took advantage of the queen's presence in the capital to present her with the 173-foot vessel in a ceremony that took place at the Washington Naval Yard shortly after the queen delivered her address to Congress. In remarks that echoed the queen's, FDR took note of the Netherlands longstanding commitment to freedom, a commitment shared by the United States which made it 'natural and right' that the two countries have today 'joined hands in the common struggle'.[31]

Six weeks later, FDR presented exactly the same-sized vessel to Norway in a ceremony that not only reflected his empathy for Princess Martha, her family, and for the Norwegian people, but also reflected his determination to use his relationship with Norwegian royal family as a means to remind the American people about the fragility of democracy 'in a world where aggression spreads unchecked'.

Speaking with great determination, FDR said,

> If there is anyone who still wonders why this war is being fought, let him look to Norway. If there is anyone who has any delusions that this war could have been averted, let him look to Norway. And if there is anyone who doubts the

democratic will to win, again I say, let him look to Norway.

He will find in Norway, at once conquered and unconquerable, the answer to his questioning.

We all know how this most peaceful and innocent of countries was ruthlessly violated. The combination of treachery and brute force which conquered Norway will live in history as the blackest deed of a black era ...

But the story of Norway since the conquest shows that while a free democracy may be slow to realize its danger, it can be heroic when aroused. At home, the Norwegian people have silently resisted the invader's will with grim endurance. Abroad, Norwegian ships and Norwegian men have rallied to the cause of the United Nations. And their assistance to that cause has been out of all proportion to their small numbers.[32]

FDR then presented the ship – named for King Haakon VII – to Crown Princess Marta, as 'a token of the admiration and friendship of the American people'. He then closed with the hope that the day would soon come 'when she will carry the Norwegian flag into a home port in a free Norway!'[33]

* * *

As the tide of the war began to turn in the Allies' favour following the successful Allied landings in North Africa in November 1942 and the stunning Soviet victory in the battle for Stalingrad three months later, two issues became more and more prevalent within the context of US relations with Norway and the Netherlands: the first concerned humanitarian aid to the Dutch and Norwegian populations under occupation; the second concerned the shape of the post-war world.

Of these two issues, the one that was the most frequent topic in the correspondence and conversations that took place between FDR and the members of the Dutch and Norwegian royal families concerned food relief. FDR was deeply sympathetic to the needs of the Dutch and Norwegian populations, but his willingness to press for humanitarian aid ran into stiff opposition from his military advisors and especially from the British, who insisted that any move to relax the Allied blockade of the Continent would seriously weaken the war effort. After much discussion over how to provide relief to Norway, an agreement was finally reached in London at the end of 1943 that would allow 250 tonnes of food relief per month to be shipped into the country from neutral Sweden.[34]

The situation in the Netherlands proved to be far more difficult, however. Unlike Norway, there was no neutral state bordering the Netherlands from which to stockpile and ship supplies to the beleaguered population. The proximity of the Netherlands to Normandy also served as an impediment, as it rendered senior British and American military leaders even more reluctant to engage in any activity which might strengthen the German hold on northwest Europe. This situation became acute in the wake of the failure of Operation Market Garden in

September 1944 – the forlorn attempt to try to win the war in a single bold stroke that was supported by the willingness of 30,000 Dutch railway workers to go on strike in conjunction with the operation.

Incensed at this act of defiance, Hitler's regime decided to use the walkout as an excuse to exact revenge on the Dutch people. From this moment forward there would be no attempt on the part of German authorities to provide any transport or sustenance for the Dutch population. As a consequence, it was not long before food and fuel shortages became common occurrences in Holland. By December, the food shortage in the Netherlands had reached a critical point, and with the Allies reeling from Hitler's surprise offensive in the Ardennes, the prospects for Dutch liberation – and relief – all but vanished. By February 1945, the Netherlands found itself in the midst of a growing humanitarian disaster. Famine and malnutrition were now commonplace, particularly in large urban areas such as Amsterdam. As the weeks dragged on, and the day-to-day toll of deaths from starvation increased – especially among children and the elderly who had been reduced to eating ground tulip bulbs – the pressure on the British and American governments to do something became almost unbearable.[35]

Both Princess Juliana and Queen Wilhelmina reached out to FDR in the hope that the president could do something to alleviate the crisis. But the spectre of the famine facing the millions of Dutch citizens under German occupation placed FDR and the Allied military leadership in a moral dilemma. Maintaining the Allied offensive into Germany and thus ending the war as quickly as possible remained the first priority of the Allied military and political leaders. The need to maintain offensive operations required enormous quantities of food and fuel for the troops. On the other hand, the plight of the Dutch, and the proximity of the population to the Allied lines, made it extremely difficult for the Allied leaders to ignore what was happening in Holland. As FDR said in an urgent message he sent to the queen in early November 1944, the 'willful destruction be carried out by the Nazi barbarians in the Netherlands' had left him 'inexpressively shocked'.[36]

To help alleviate the crisis, FDR ordered General Eisenhower to arrange to have a certain portion of the supplies stockpiled for the Allied armies made available to the Dutch populace that had already been liberated.[37] At the same time, the Allied leadership also managed to secure the shipment of some relief supplies to the Netherlands by sea from neutral Sweden under the auspices of the Red Cross. These efforts turned out to be wholly inadequate, however, in part because the level of supplies on hand was too meagre to meet the enormity of the crisis, and in part because the German military leadership seized a portion of the material for their own use.[38]

As the crisis dragged on, FDR took the opportunity presented by a visit of Princess Juliana to Washington to attend his fortieth wedding anniversary on March 17 to publicly suggest a 10 per cent reduction in US domestic rations of certain commodities in support of relief operations. Such a move, he said during the course of his regularly scheduled news conference on March 16, could save the lives of large numbers of starving people, a trade-off he believed the vast majority of Americans would support as a matter of 'national decency'. Indeed, he could not bring himself to believe that the American people had suffered greatly in this war when compared to other countries – 'for instance Holland ... which is a very bad case'.[39]

This suggestion brought howls of protest from Congress on the charge that the Roosevelt Administration was 'depriving Americans of necessary nourishment to feed the world'. In light of this callous response, FDR could offer Princess Juliana – and Queen Wilhelmina whom he wrote to shortly after the princess left the White House – little more than a renewed promise to all he could to try to alleviate the emergency. 'You can be certain,' he assured the Queen, 'I shall not forget the country of my origin.'[40]

That this was the case is evident from the final exchange of the more than 3,100 messages that FDR exchanged with Winston Churchill during the course of the war. In early April, Churchill suggested that he and FDR send an ultimatum to the German commander in the Netherlands via the Swiss demanding that the International Red Cross be allowed to bring additional relief supplies into the country as soon as possible. If this entreaty should fail, the German command in Holland should be branded murderers and held 'responsible with their lives'.[41]

In what turned out to be the last cable the president sent to Churchill, FDR agreed. Shortly thereafter, General Eisenhower was given permission to begin negotiations with the Reich Commissioner in the Netherlands. As a result, over 10,000 tonnes of food and medical supplies were air-dropped into specified drop zones in the Netherlands between 29 April 29 and 7 May 1945.[42]

* * *

The pending victory of the Allied powers also led to increasing concerns about the makeup of the post-war world. On this question, one of the more delicate issues addressed in the conversations that took place between FDR and Queen Wilhelmina during her visit to the United States in the summer of 1942 involved the future of the Dutch Empire.[43] While FDR often publicly condemned colonialism as a dangerously anachronistic practice, he actually made sharp distinctions between the colonial practices of different European nations. He remained vehemently opposed to the re-establishment of French sovereignty in Indochina, for example, and although he harboured little sympathy for the restoration of the British Empire, America's ability to influence the British government on this question remained limited in light of the scale of the British contribution to the war.[44]

FDR adopted a much more benevolent attitude about the Dutch East Indies, however. Part of this stemmed from the long-standing tendency of the US State Department to view Dutch colonial practices in a more benign light than those of the French or the British. But it also stemmed from the understandings he achieved with Queen Wilhelmina, which reveal that although FDR agreed that once the Japanese had been driven back to their home islands, 'the Netherlands Indies must be restored,' he did so out of the belief that the public commitment she had made to self-government was genuine. As FDR noted in a conversation about the future of colonialism he had with the Australian minister in Washington in November 1944, 'he would support the Dutch … because he believed they were sincere in saying they would restore democracy in SE Asia'. He wished the British would do the same in Burma and Malaya, he said, but he held out little hope that they would do so.[45]

A far more important question involved the security of Europe once the war was over. As early as 1942, both the Dutch and Norwegian governments recognized that their future safety could only be achieved – as one Norwegian official put it – 'in cooperation with the great Atlantic powers'.[46] But by the end of 1943 it was clear that FDR had settled on the concept of world security being exercised through the 'four policemen' – the United States, Great Britain, China and the USSR – via the United Nations Organization. Given their disappointment over the performance of the League of Nations in the interwar years, as well as their apprehensions about the growth of Soviet power, both the Dutch and the Norwegian governments reacted somewhat warily to this proposal, expressing the view that they favoured the development of regional security organizations over the establishment of a single such entity. So too, in fact did Churchill and much of the British cabinet.

FDR refused to countenance such a notion, however, in part out his fear that the creation of a European security organization that included the United States would tie America's military assets to the Continent when they were committed elsewhere (i.e., in the Pacific). He also opposed the establishment of a regional European body that did *not* include the United States, as such an entity might resist US influence or evolve into an anti-Soviet combination.[47] Given FDR's view that the future peace of the world depended in large part in maintaining the Soviet commitment to what he called 'the family of nations' he maintained the view that on balance, regional bodies were a bad idea. In other words, stability and world order were only possible 'if the world powers are prepared to accept the responsibilities of leadership *within* the United Nations'.[48]

By the end 1945, both countries had become strong supporters of the United Nations, but this did not lesson their conviction that the United States had to play an active role in European security, a fact, somewhat ironically born out of the creation of the North Atlantic Treaty Organization (NATO) in 1949.

It would appear, then, that FDR opposition to regional security arrangements might be regarded as one of the first casualties of the Cold War. But his commitment to transatlantic relations was rock solid and one suspects that had he lived to see the end of the war he would have adjusted his views about the Soviet Union accordingly. Perhaps it is this aspect of FDR's relationship with the Dutch and Norwegian royal families that serves as its greatest legacy. For the close ties he developed with King Haakon, Crown Princess Martha and Crown Prince Olav, Princess Juliana and Queen Wilhelmina helped bolster the American public's commitment to FDR's internationalist agenda and solidify their belief that in spite of their regal status, the Dutch and Norwegian monarchs shared a common faith in democracy.

Sadly, FDR's would not live to see the day that the War ended in Europe. He died in Warm Springs, Georgia, of a massive cerebral haemorrhage on 12 April 1945 – less than three weeks after his departure from Washington for a well-deserved rest. Before leaving, FDR would enjoy one last dinner at the White House, joined by his wife Eleanor, and Crown Princess Martha and her husband.

Notes

1. Roosevelt Greets Royal Guests, *New York Times*, 29 April 1939, 4.
2. Paul Claudel to Paul – Boncour, 5 April 1933, *Documents Diplomatiques Français*, Series I, 3: 148–9.
3. In 1937, an amendment to the 1935 Neutrality Act allowed for the sale of commodities – not arms – to belligerent nations on a cash and carry basis. This amendment was set to expire in May 1939. FDR wanted to not only see this provision renewed, but also wanted to secure a lifting of the arms embargo in conjunction with this effort.
4. Indeed, FDR was a great believer in the advent of air power as a deterrent to war. Shortly after Prime Minister Chamberlain signed the Munich agreement FDR met with his top military advisors where he insisted that had the United States had the capacity to produce 10,000 warplanes per year, Hitler would have thought twice about moving into the Sudetenland. (Frank Friedel, *Franklin D. Roosevelt: A Rendezvous with Destiny* (New York: Little Brown, 1990)), 301–4.
5. FDR to Lord Tweedsmuir, Governor General of Canada, 3 November 1938, President's Secretary's File (PSF) Box 25, Franklin D. Roosevelt Presidential Library (FDRL); FDR to J. (Daisy) Borden Harriman, 7 July 1938, PSF Box 45; FDR to J. (Daisy) Borden Harriman, 27 December 1938, PSF Box 45, FDRL.
6. Frank Friedel, *Franklin D. Roosevelt: A Rendezvous with Destiny* (New York: Little Brown, 1990), 316–17.
7. President tells Norwegian Guest Hitler Leaves Door Open 'an Inch', *New York Times*, April 29, 139, 1.
8. FDR to William Lyons Mackenzie King, 18 April 1939, PSF, Box 25, FDRL.
9. Wayne S. Cole, *Norway and the United States, 1905–1955: Two Democracies in Peace and War* (Ames: Iowa State University Press, 1989), 76–7. For more on the Norwegian policy of neutrality see: Patrick Salmon, 'Norway', in *European Neutrals and Non-belligerents during the Second World War*, ed. Neville Wylie (Cambridge: Cambridge University Press, 2002), 53–68.
10. Ibid., and Harriman to Secretary of State, 1 September 1938, File 800, RG 84, Diplomatic Post Records, Oslo, National Archives, College Park, Washington.
11. FDR to Crown Prince Olav, 4 January 1940; Crown Prince Olav to FDR, 22 June 1940, PSF Box 45, Norway, 1940, FDRL.
12. The notion of a romantic relationship between FDR and Princess Martha was highlighted by the television series, *Atlantic Crossing* – a largely fictional account of the relationship between the president and the princess.
13. FDR, Memorandum for the Secretary of State, 11 November 1939, PSF, Box 44, FDRL.
14. H.R.H. Wilhelmina, Princess of The Netherlands, *Lonely but not Alone* (New York: McGraw-Hill, 1960), 156.
15. Princess Juliana, President's Personal File (PPF) 1382, FDRL.

16 Margaret 'Daisy' Suckley Diary, 7 May 1942 & 29 September 1943, FDRL.
17 David B. Woolner, *The Last 100 Days: FDR at War and at Peace* (New York: Basic Books, 2017), xi–xii.
18 Ibid., Suckley Diary, 12 April 1945, FDRL.
19 Cole, *Norway and the United States*, 104–6.
20 King Haakon VII to FDR, 2 February 1941, PSF Norway Box 45, FDRL.
21 FDR to King Haakon, 19 March 1941, PSF Norway Box 45, FDRL.
22 Suckley Diary, Tuesday, 5 October 1943, FDRL.
23 Cole, *Norway and the United States*, 106.
24 *Four Centuries of Dutch-American Relations*, ed. Hans Krabbendam, Cornelis A. van Minnen, and Giles Scott-Smith (New York: SUNY Press, 2009), 415.
25 Maurice Matloff and Edwin M. Snell, *Strategic Planning for Coalition Warfare, 1941–1942* (Washington: US Government Printing Office, 1952), 120–6; *Four Centuries of Dutch-American Relations*, 556.
26 van Kleffens to Sumner Welles, 5 February 1942, PSF The Netherlands, Box 42, FDRL; *Four Centuries of Dutch-American Relations*, 556.
27 Ibid., 524, 552, 560.
28 Address to Congress by Queen Wilhelmina of the Netherlands, 6 August 1942, (PPF) 1382, FDRL.
29 Ibid.
30 'Dutch Queen Vows Fight to the Finish', *Washington Post*, 7 August 1942, 1.
31 FDR Master Speech File, Address of Franklin Roosevelt on the Transfer of Ship, August 6, 1942.
32 FDR Master Speech File, 'Remarks of the President on the Transfer of Ship', 16 September 1942, Box 67, FDRL.
33 Ibid.
34 Cole, *Norway and the United States*, 106–7.
35 'Famine and Death Rampant in Holland', *Washington Post*, 10 March 1945, 3.
36 FDR to Queen Wilhelmina, 9 November 1944, Official File (OF) 246, FDRL.
37 FDR to Churchill, 28 February 1945, Map Room Files, Box 7, FDRL.
38 Henri A. van der Zee, *The Hunger Winter* (London: University of Nebraska Press, 1982), 170–5.
39 Presidential Press Conferences of Franklin D. Roosevelt, 16 March 1945, FDRL.
40 'Tighten Belts and Help Feed the World: F.D.R.', *Chicago Daily Tribune*, 17 March 1945, 1; FDR to Queen Wilhelmina, 21 March 1945, PSF The Netherlands, Box 45, FDRL.
41 Churchill to FDR, 9 April 1945, Map Room Papers, Box 7, FDRL.
42 FDR to Churchill, 11 April 1945, Map Room Papers, Box 7, FDRL.
43 Lloyd Gardner, 'FDR and the Colonial Question' in *FDR's World: War, Peace and Legacies*, ed. David B. Woolner, Warren F. Kimball, and David Reynolds (New York: Palgrave Macmillan, 2008), 128–9.
44 Robert J. McMahon, 'Anglo-American Diplomacy and the Reoccupation of the Netherlands East Indies', *Diplomatic History* 2, no. 1 (Winter 1978): 5.
45 William Roger Louis, *Imperialism at Bay: The United States and the Decolonization of the British Empire* (New York: Oxford University Press, 1986).
46 Cole, *Norway and the United States*, 117.
47 John Lamberton Harper, *American Visions of Europe* (New York: Cambridge University Press, 1994), 94–6.
48 Warren F. Kimball, 'The Sheriffs: FDR's Post-War World', in *FDR's World*, ed. Woolner, Kimball and Reynolds (New York: Palgrave Macmillan, 2008), 97.

Chapter 7

RE-ESTABLISHING THE HONOUR OF FRANCE IN THE AIR: FRANCOPHONE AVIATOR LITERARY FIGURES DURING THE SECOND WORLD WAR

Andrew Williams

Introduction: Why French airmen are of interest

The idea for this chapter arose from my long-standing interest in French history of the twentieth century and in particular the relations of France with the Anglo-Saxon nations, that is to say the United States and Great Britain.[1] One of the inspirations for this has a lot in common with Alan Dobson's lifelong obsession with subjects aeronautical. France has produced a significant number of writers of fiction and loosely disguised non-fiction about both the joys and despair of flight. It will be shown that France felt it has played a very significant, if not central, part in the story of flight, and that it has bought to that subject much of its cultural and artistic flair. Early French aerial exploits of note included the balloon flights of the Montgolfier brothers in the 1780s, ones that immediately drew the attention of the military authorities. Balloon warfare became an increasingly interesting topic, to the point where it was banned in the first Hague Convention of 1907, one of whose annexes declared 'the prohibition of the discharge of any kind of projectile or explosive from balloons or by similar means'.[2] So the military attractions of flight have been a central feature of the French imagination for several hundred years.

French aviators and writers from the First World War onwards are of particular interest to the student of contemporary international relations, and my focus here will be on a number of individuals who are as well known for their cultural production as for their fame as aircrew in war. Air warfare has often figured in books about key moments in international relations, figuratively as much as literally. This was particularly true during the Second World War when France had experienced arguably the most humiliating defeat in its history. The collaboration regime of Marshal Philippe Pétain after '*la débâcle* [retreat]', the French surrender

All translations from French to English are mine.

of 25 June 1940, was only countered, until the emergence of the French Resistance after 1941 within France, by the meagre French forces who had rallied to the exiled Charles de Gaulle in London. Prominent among those who were really able to fight back were aircrew that joined Royal Air Force squadrons, in the same way as the Poles of the famous 303 Squadron, which scored the most 'kills' (of German aircraft) during the Battle of Britain in 1940. There were many hundreds of French aircrews who did the same, often attacking targets in mainland France from bases in Britain in fighter bombers or flying out of North Africa in squadrons equipped by the US Air Force.

But there was also a literary fightback, one that figures in surprising places in the European, and especially French, literature of the wartime era and just after it. The British bombers that are pursuing fleeing German forces in *Les Mandarins*, Simone de Beauvoir's book about intellectual life in post-war Paris in April 1945 turn up in Heinz Rein's *Berlin Finale* in the same month, forming a liminal link across Europe. As de Beauvoir made clear in her description of the Paris of late 1944 and 1945 to write was to resist, and also to rebuild, in a world where everyone knew 'the Russians [were] in the process of sacking Berlin, the war was ending and another one beginning: how could a writer amuse himself with writing stories that never happened?'[3]

To attempt an answer to this question, I will examine the wartime writings of three French contemporaries of de Beauvoir: Antoine de Saint-Exupéry,[4] Romain Gary and Joseph Kessel.[5] All of these were writers who have achieved almost mythical status within the canon of French literature and beyond. One of them, Kessel, is even better known as a film writer in non-Francophone circles. Gary wrote his first book during the war, in between combat missions, but achieved real fame after the war. St-Exupéry was already famous and became more so after 1943 for his children's book *Le Petit Prince*. He was killed in action on 31 July 1944 over Marseilles while flying a US Air Force P-38 Lightning reconnaissance plane (F5B, No. 223). Kessel was a decorated fighter pilot in the First World War and flew in the same squadron as Gary in the Second. As writers all were recipients of major prizes (Gary even won the *Prix Goncourt* twice) and all are still popular and in print to the present day. So they all flew as combatant airmen during the Second World War. And all of them shared the interest of seeing a world in creation from '10,000 metres' in the air while flying a flimsy airplane, as St-Exupéry put it.[6]

The context in which they saw their visions was one dominated by war and by the much less visible planning of the new world order after 1945. As I have shown elsewhere, French input into what was known as 'Post-War Planning' (PWP) was patchy at best. Insofar as there were major inputs from French thinkers in exile into the PWP process they tended to be channelled in private conversations with prominent British and American politicians and policy makers, a process that I and others have described elsewhere.[7] De Beauvoir recounts that one of the characters in *Les Mandarins*, Henri Perron (possibly based on Albert Camus), goes to the *Quai d'Orsay* to ask the French diplomatic service to 'say something' about the situation in Portugal, where opponents of the fascist dictatorship of Antonio Salazar were trying to rally support from France, which they still saw as the premier beacon of democracy in Europe. The diplomat, 'Tournelle', an old Resistance friend, tells Henri bitterly that '[t]he truth is that we don't matter anymore [*La vérité c'est que nous ne comptons plus*]'. This was almost exactly the reproach made by the French Socialist (and subsequently *Président de la République*) Vincent Auriol to British deputy prime minister and Labour Party leader Clement Attlee in July 1944.[8] But the writers that figure here were important not only as writers but also as symbols of resistance. They were certainly public intellectuals of great importance and it can be argued that their thinking has marked public discourse far more than many a forgotten politician. They did not just talk about a new world, liberation and resistance, they acted it out in combat and a significant part of their influence resides in that commitment.

Applied modernity

We might even term the visions of our airmen as 'applied modernity', such was the importance of air flight to the modernist movement that emerged before, during and after the First World War. This was most clearly demonstrated by the Italian futurists, led by Filippo Marinetti, who started their Manifesto of 1909 with the declaration: 'We want to celebrate the love of danger, the habits of energy and fearlessness,' all emblematic of the very recent pioneers of the air.[9] It was also a key element of the Italian poet Gabriele d'Annunzio's dreaming of modernity and the 'new man'. D'Annunzio became a celebrated aviator himself dropping leaflets, and later bombs, on Vienna.[10] The machine-like warfare of the trenches seemed to confirm the arrival of a war that claimed to defend 'civilisation' but threatened to kill it. Emilio Gentile sees this as the worm in the heart of *La Belle Epoque*, nurtured by the collapse of bourgeois democracy and empire.[11] One of the undoubted attractions of aerial warfare was ironically that it was the *least* modern of the different methods of killing people in 1914–18, as the 'aces' were among the very few to regularly engage in one-on-one combat, usually to the death. They were latter-day knights, a feature lauded by D'Annunzio. Thus flying in general and air warfare had long dominated the discussion about modernity.

The war was followed by the failed peace of Versailles and then by a new series of atrocious modern wars in China, Abyssinia and Spain. This latter war can be seen as having been a dry run for the even worse horrors of the Second World War, both in its barbarity towards civilians and in its technological innovations, especially with the coming of age of armoured and aerial warfare. The literary and cultural result was usually one of despair. But it could be one of guarded hope. André Malraux, who had witnessed some of the horrors of the developing Chinese Civil War in the 1920s and given them literary immortality in *La Condition Humaine*, was also present in the first campaigns of the Spanish Civil War, as a journalist in Toledo where he observed the 1936–7 Battle of Teruel, later made into a film in 1945. Most interesting for our purposes was his commentary about the Franquist and Republican air forces,[12] and the emphasis put by him on the internationalization of the struggle against Franco.

International and national politics in the French literary imagination before 1939

Engagement[13]

We need first to understand the complex and rich literary and cultural background against which internationalists like Gary, Kessel and St-Exupéry were writing. The young generation of Francophone writers that either fought in the Second World War, like Gary and St-Exupéry, or were close observers of it were not in a sense typical writers of their time. Many prominent French writers were nationalists who nonetheless put themselves on the side of collaboration, often on the right of French politics, and allied themselves to Nazi Germany in a more or less enthusiastic way, like Pierre Drieu la Rochelle and Louis Ferdinand Céline.[14] In other words they saw their future as part of an 'internationalist' German empire, with a subordinate France. There is a strong, though not absolute, direct correlation between those who collaborated and those who were anti-Dreyfusards before 1910, especially the thinkers and activists who made up the nationalist party *Action Française*, led by Charles Maurras, who was tried as a collaborator after Liberation. He told the judge that it was 'the revenge of Dreyfus'.[15] All of them were 'committed [*engagé*]', but on a different side to Gary, Kessel and St-Exupéry. Most of them started from a perception of France that had failed but came up with different solutions to that failure.

Those that collaborated were, usually, of the generation of 1914, tortured by memories of the First World War.[16] Those who resisted were equally in revolt against the decadence of France. Kessel fought in the First World War as a fighter pilot, and even volunteered in 1918 to fight for France against the Germans in Russia, a devotion to the cause that even his fellow airmen thought excessive. His exploits, written up in a later semi-autobiographical book, *Les Temps Sauvages*, is an account of his observations in Siberia, to which we will return below.[17] Like Gary, Kessel was a devoted French patriot despite, or maybe because, he was from a family of refugees fleeing antisemitism in Russia (though born in Argentina where his family just happened to be at the time).

But other voices in France drew different conclusions about French ambitions to spread the word of France's emancipatory purpose after 1919, especially in the Third Republic's hopes for a new international order based on the League of Nations. That dream foundered on the refusal of the United States to adhere to the League and well-publicised disagreements with Britain, France's other ally of the war, dual developments which have often been seen as disabling the entire internationalist project. Before 1939 Robert Aron and Arnaud Dandieu, founders of *Ordre nouveau* [New Order], a loose coalition of cantankerous young intellectuals of the right and left of French politics, called for an end to parliamentary democracy, a return to revolutionary principles and a rejection of American capitalism, as well as harbouring a dismissive attitude to the League of Nations.[18] On the whole they had not fought in, or over, the trenches though they were dismissive of the world order created after 1918. Other writers like the future Vichy collaborationists Céline and Drieu had fought in the front line but held similar views. More non-conformist than anything else, they were part of a youth in revolt against the idiocies of bourgeois Europe that also published in *Esprit*, *La Nouvelle Revue Française* and other journals, and had an immense impact on French intellectual life before the war. Gary and Kessel took a different line, partly because as Jewish Frenchmen they abhorred the antisemitic policies of both the Nazis and Vichy, ones which Céline and Drieu embraced wholeheartedly, but also because they were natural French patriots.

Aviateurs et Politique

As discussed above, St-Exupéry as well as Gary and Kessel were aviators, all three fighting in Free French or other Allied aerial formations through at least some of the war, with St-Exupéry being killed in action in 1944.[19] Both Gary and Kessel flew with the Free French Lorraine 342 bomber squadron of the Royal Air Force. Together the three make up a substantial corpus of post-war literature that had a wide influence, certainly artistic and intellectual and, we would here argue, political. One reason for that is precisely their status as *résistants*, which gave them a popular standing similar to the (possibly) higher status of Albert Camus and Jean-Paul Sartre. Camus was certainly a *résistant*, editing the clandestine Resistance journal *Combat*, and Sartre had some claim to at least not being an obvious 'collaborator [*collabo*]'. Their self-proclaimed remit was different however. While Sartre and Camus spoke largely to an international politics outside Europe, these pilot-thinkers were imaginers of Europe itself. Gary, Kessel and St-Exupéry published books (see below for more exegesis) on their wartime experiences in 1945; Kessel and St-Exupéry were already well known as writers, Gary a complete unknown, but all were writing novels at a moment of a great need for a heroic French narrative.

Romain Gary

Gary was a pilot-instructor during the war, and an early *résistant* who went to join de Gaulle in London in 1940. He was to become one of post-war France's most celebrated novelists, as well as having a short but interesting diplomatic career, part of which took him to Los Angeles, after which he married the celebrated American actress, Jean Seberg.

Gary's autobiography, *La Promesse de l'aube*, a great deal of which describes his experiences during the war, is simultaneously amusing, depressing and illuminating about his struggle with what he calls the three Gods of 'stupidity' (*la bêtise*), 'the absolute truth' (*les vérités absolues*) and 'small mindedness' (*petitesse*), within which he included 'prejudice, disdain, hate'. Intellectually that led him, and his many followers, to reflect on the reality that these equivalents of the Horsemen of the Apocalypse had led to devastating war. In particular he hated racism 'a marvellous organizer of mass movements, wars, lynch parties, persecutions, [an] able dialectician, the father of all ideological formations, great Inquisitor and lover of holy wars, in spite of his mangy skin, his hyena head and his mangled feet still the most powerful and listened – to … [of our planet ….]'. Gary's primal scream, for as such it comes across in spite of his humour and delicate touch, is so moving because he was himself the victim of that particular God. But he also hated with a venom that cannot help but shock the other two Gods, and here of course his blows come at the expense of a much wider group than Nazis, which he subsumes as a 'cossack standing on a pile of corpses … [with] one half of humanity licking his boots ….' and their ilk. His most important blows land on the intelligentsia (with their heads so 'full of the love of abstraction'), the rich and powerful hypocrites who lend themselves to persuading the masses that horrors such as the atomic bomb are acceptable. Gary can be seen as the anti-Celine, in his love of humanity, linked with his despair for it.[20]

During the war, and while recovering from a severe wound in 1943, he wrote his first novel, considered one of his best, *Education européenne*. Interestingly he does not use his real experience as an aviator but writes an imaginary story of fighting on the Eastern Front, from where he originated as a young boy. The plot centres round a group of Polish partisans who are engaged in brutal combat with one of the SS's most feared and hated divisions, *Das Reich*, in the forests of the Ukraine. After 10 June 1944 the soldiers of *Das Reich* were known in France as the perpetrators of some of the worst Nazi massacres on French soil at Tulle and Oradour-sur-Glane. However, this was a skill they had perfected in the Ukraine. Ironically by 1944 many of the division were *Alsaciens*, Frenchmen who fought willingly or as conscripts (the '*malgrés nous*', 'against our will') for the SS. Gary's partisans hold different views on Germans, Russians and the difficulties of life and death, but they all agree that after the war Europe must change.

In a key exchange between Tadek Chmura, the doomed Polish poet partisan, and the hero of the book, Janek Twardowski, Tadek enumerates all the reasons for despair. But he says humankind needs a 'refuge … sometimes only a song, a poem, music, a book', but never 'despair … which [shows] only a lack of talent'. The talent needed is to re-imagine the future through art. So while they are in their current hellish situation the experience is a European education, a lesson in why the notions of liberty, human dignity and fraternity have made Europe what it is, or was. 'These are the darkest hours, they will pass [*C'est l'heure des ténèbres … Elle passera*].' One of the partisans, who becomes Janek's closest friend, Adam Dobranski, relates their mission of self-discovery by writing a novel (within the novel) with the same title as Gary's book, most of it based on a series of mythical tales of great power and savage humour. After a long and often-painful personal journey, Janek is the partisan that survives and cradles his dying comrade Adam as he promises to finally finish his book for him. He doesn't of course but Gary's most famous line sums up why: 'patriotism is the love of your own people. Nationalism is the hatred of others [*Le patriotisme, c'est l'amour des siens. Le nationalisme, c'est la haine des autres*]'. But what is often forgotten are the next words: 'All those Russians and Americans ... they are creating a great fraternity for the future, the Germans will have at least given us that [*Les Russes, les Américains, tout ça ... Il y a une grande fraternité qui se prepare au monde, les Allemands nous auront valu au moins ça*].' This is a book that was an important harbinger of a future united Europe, but also of an emerging world order, even if not exactly the one Gary envisaged in 1945.[21]

Antoine de St-Exupéry[22]

St-Exupéry was much older during the war, a celebrity pilot-author, a French version of Charles Lindbergh. He has been described recently as 'a man with the body of a stevedore, the mind of a pundit and the soul of a poet' and who saw himself as a mainspring within French thinking of the notion of 'solidarity', a term most associated with the important early twentieth-century French politician Léon Bourgeois, who was also a key architect of the Treaty of Versailles.[23] Bernard Lambert sees him as a man of great 'melancholy', whose wife on occasion found solace with other men, including his old friend the Franco-Swiss philosopher Denis de Rougemont.[24] He was certainly seen as a man of action who was also a great writer, if not uncontroversially so.

Some have accused him of hiding behind his prestige as a best-selling author and pilot. Long after his death Jean-François Revel and Pierre-Henri Simon engaged in a typically Parisian intellectual bar fight over St-Exupéry's reputation, the former snorting that '[l]e crétinisme sous cockpit prend des allures de sagesse', to which Simon replied, '[u]n idéalisme de carlingue vaut bien un existentialisme de bistrot'. This can be roughly translated as 'saying stupid things in a cockpit makes you look wise' and 'being an idealist in a fuselage is better than being a café existentialist'. But not many gentlemen scholars have had an airport named after them (at Lyon), or been described by Raymond Aron as one the '*deux consciences des Français de l'extérieur*', a theme I will return to shortly. He is eternally popular in France and beyond. He also left a substantial volume of wartime writings in the form of letters, political tracts and '*brouillons*' (which can be translated roughly as 'unpublished drafts'), with the most famous published piece being the autobiographical 'Flight over Arras', about the final days of May 1940, often referred to as *Pilote de Guerre*.

Pilote de Guerre is the most explicitly written of all the books considered here for an audience that likes to read about flying. St-Exupéry talks at length about the technical aspects of being a pilot and the problems of flying a rather slow reconnaissance aircraft against the numerous and deadly fighter planes of the *Luftwaffe*. He is told by his Commandant that his mission to Arras, to observe German troop and tank movements, is essentially doomed to failure as the Germans have total control of the air, and indeed the ground beneath it. The German forces were advancing faster than the French air force could assess, so it was likely, as they realized, that in the improbable event that any French plane survived to come back to its base, that base might no longer exist.

As he is told the mission is rather '*embêtante*' (annoying) he realizes that he is being sent on a '*mission sacrifiée*' (suicide mission) – the Commandant even suggests that he might be able to cancel it 'if you are not feeling well ….'. St-Exupéry refuses such a suggestion as unworthy ('*Voyons, mon Commandant!*'), even when the news is added that no less than six Messerschmitt ME109 fighters might meet him on the way to Arras (annoyingly flying at different heights) and takes off. His crew are not enthusiastic but off they go. And even though the six German planes see them, by some miracle they do not attack, whether due to pity or bravado, and the French crew are able to make it back to their base.[25]

This is not just an account of personal bravery, it is also a rumination about politics, and in particular about the fight for civilization that the war represents. In *Pilote de Guerre*, St-Exupéry claims that he does not think about the 'fight of the West against Nazism [*la lutte de l'Occident contre le nazisme*]. I think about the details of survival [*Je pense details immédiats*]'. But later in his account he admits that 'the fight of the West against Nazism is in fact analogous to questions of controls, levers and valves [*le combat de l'Occident et le Nazism … deviant … une action sur des manettes, des leviers et des robinets*]'. It is through the mechanism of flying that he is fighting an ideological battle. He goes on to elaborate that he has often been told repeatedly that 'France always finds a solution when all seems lost [*En France, quand tout semble perdu, un miracle sauve la France*]', but now he does not believe it.[26]

Once St-Exupéry was in exile, he became more politically committed. This can be seen in a later *oeuvre*, *Citadelle*, a curious, rambling (over 500 pages) and at times uplifting, semi-autobiographical essay, started in 1936 and worked on periodically throughout the war; there is no plot so it is not a novel in the normal sense of the word. A rumination on life, death and God, which he on occasion called his 'posthumous book' (indeed it was published in 1948), it was condemned at the time of its publication as 'biblical'. He never edited what was a series of drafts before being sent back into action in March 1943 (he was killed before he could re-write it in a more digestible form). Ironically he benefitted before 1940 from critiques of the growing manuscript from his then-friend the Nazi collaborator Drieu, with whom he shared a disavowal of 'any political system that has material welfare as its only aim [*tout système qui aurait le bien-être matériel comme seule fin*]'.[27] In that important sense he was as much a member of the Generation of 1914 as many of the collaborators, and indeed de Gaulle himself, all of whom decried French 'decadence' and its pursuit of American-style wealth. All of these thinkers had great respect for Germany, and saw the possibility, maybe even the necessity, of a better cooperation with France. Though their paths diverged after 1940, they all lived and died for this idea.[28]

After 1940 St-Exupéry also shared with his friend Raymond Aron a suspicion of de Gaulle's intentions as a leader of France, and that has tended to define him politically in the last period of his life, which ended over Marseille in July 1944. Aron portrays this crisis of conscience as a positive contribution, but Jacques

Maritain, who we have seen, was described by Aron as '[one of] the *deux consciences des Français de l'extérieur*' along with St Exupéry. Maritain, a confirmed and loyal Gaullist, condemned the latter for daring to suggest a 'union' with the United States in 1942, an idea which Maritain considered another 'tragic surrender of which the worst was the armistice of 1940 [*abandon tragique dont l'expression décisive a été l'armistice de 1940*]'. In many ways seeing France (and indeed Europe's) future as being linked, or not, to the Anglo-Saxon countries was a touchstone for many who resisted the German occupation. The French Socialist Party was split along similar lines, though many of them thought they could work most productively with the British Labour Party.[29] De Gaulle had decided by 1945 that he could not, and that was reflected in the views of Maritain and many others, Gaullist or otherwise.[30]

Of course Maritain must also have been aware that an Anglo-French union had been discussed in the last days before the Armistice (with de Gaulle himself representing then French prime minister Paul Reynaud at the talks in London). This was another union St-Exupéry would have agreed with – 'England is our conscience [*L'Angleterre, c'est notre conscience*]', and without which France would not still be at war. Maritain portrayed any obeisance to the Anglo-Saxons as a betrayal of France, and this while benefitting from US protection in New York. Aron had much more sympathy for St-Exupéry, who was 'in despair [*désespéré*]' at such statements, than for Maritain. Maritain says Aron 'thought politically, St-Exupéry wanted to ignore politics [*pensait à la politique, St-Exupéry … voulait ignorer la politique*]'.[31] But of course it depends which '*politique*' we want to emphasize, that of a cosmopolitan inter-Allied version (like Aron and St-Exupéry) or a French nationalist version (like Maritain). It was not St-Exupéry's only foray into appealing to the United States for help. His most significant, but apparently unpublished, appeal was in June 1940 when he was fighting with his squadron to hold back the German tide around Arras, in which he wrote to Lindbergh begging him to change his mind about the United States remaining out of the war.

St-Exupéry, in wishing to 'ignore politics', was in fact searching for a new way to formulate politics. As he commented when his doctor friend Pierre Lazareff was being positive about the effect Chamberlain had had on Hitler at Munich in August 1938, '*c'était bien prévisible. Tu mets en presence l'un et l'autre, Attila et Bergson. Pas de doute qu'Attila ne stupéfie Bergson. Quant à Bergson, il ne saurait produire aucun effet sur Attila*'.[32] Hitler had 'stupefied' the German population, now he was doing it to everyone else. And in this quest, said St-Exupéry, Hitler was a man of 'great sincerity [*bonne foi*]', as Attila might be said to have been when he confronted the dazzled Chamberlain/Bergson. The world must note that Nazi Germany was not the Germany of Goethe or Bach – this was a Germany intent on '*expansion … Cette tendance qui fait partie de toutes les espèces animales. Chaque race tend à pulluler et à exterminer les autres* … [this was a trait of all animal species, for each one tends to proliferate and exterminate the others]'.[33] This bleak and, we would now say, quasi-racist view was nonetheless still typical in a world where social Darwinism was more or less accepted and being played out on the battlefield and villages of Europe. Had he lived his voice might well have proved a moderating force over those in France after the war calling for revenge, but his words can be read in different ways. De Gaulle ensured that his books were banned in Algiers during the war, but that was due to St-Exupéry's obstinate refusal to endorse him as undisputed leader of France, and his support for the Anglo-Saxons.

Joseph Kessel

Joseph Kessel makes up the third of our French literary icons who took to the air in 1940–5. Like more than 2 million others of the period before 1914 who had fled the pogroms of the Czar, Kessel embraced his new homeland with a fierce affection as *'le petit Juif russe adopté par la France* [an insignificant Russian Jew adopted by France]' not least because France was for both himself and Gary the symbol of internationalist democracy, even if that dream was shattered during the Vichy regime of Philippe Pétain.[34] Without indulging too much in amateur psychology, we can suggest that for both Kessel and Gary France became a substitute for the parents they either never knew (Gary was never sure who his father was) or who came to replace them. This was very clear in Kessel's case when as a very young airman (in a biplane) in 1918 he had lost the squadron leader he idolized. In his fictional account of the time, he had been the 'beating heart ... whom it was a joy to obey [*il était l'esprit, le Coeur, le foyer vital ... le chef auquel obéir était une joie*]' of a group of aviators.[35]

But Kessel clearly based this on real life, and he also discovered he loved war itself, part of a devil-may-care approach to life, love and risk that continued throughout his life. It can be seen in his many books and films, not least of which was *Belle de Jour,* starring Catherine Deneuve (1967, directed by Luis Buñuel, and based on Kessel's novel of 1928) about a woman who sells her body to alleviate the boredom when her husband is at work. As for war, in 1918 Kessel had signed up to continue the fight against Germany for his adopted country in Siberia, in the far east of Russia, when most of his comrades were just happy to have survived. He was embarked at Cherbourg just as the Armistice was signed but was ordered to go anyway. After other adventures in Vladivostok he fell madly in love with a young White Russian woman and discovered a very unfortunate second love for alcohol.[36] The interwar years saw both tendencies consolidate, as well as a flourishing career as a journalist (for *Le Figaro* and *Mercure de France,* among other publications) and author with the very prestigious publishing house Gallimard. Kessel had become an instant national treasure (if of the right as much of his early writing harboured a virulent anti-Sovietism) and instantly recognizable to a growing audience.[37]

From early on in his life as an author, Kessel evoked the drama of aerial warfare. Even before the events recounted in *Les Temps Sauvages* (actually a much later publication) he had described in great detail the life of his squadron and its charismatic leader Thélis Vachon, in his novel, *L'Equipage,* published in 1923. His vivid descriptions bought the realities of combat to life before Saint Exupéry, whose first 'air' novels in the late 1920s were those of a commercial pilot, even if a pioneer.[38] So the French public was already primed for his novels in the genre. But France itself was not primed for another global conflict, as Kessel observed when he spent some days in Britain as a reporter for *Paris-soir* as war was about to be declared. In Britain he was impressed with the appointment by Neville Chamberlain of his old opponent Winston Churchill and the atmosphere of resigned acceptance of the need to stop Hitler; when he got home he mostly noticed those who refused to 'die for Danzig [*mourir pour Dantzig*]'. Increasingly he was convinced that France needed new leaders, but he could not see who that might be. His disarray was enhanced when he was called up at the age of forty-one and put into a motorized cavalry regiment, when he had ended the previous war as a *sous-lieutenant* in the French air force. The deception was reinforced by then being given a job as a '*journalier*' and not a '*journaliste*', so a 'day labourer' rather than a 'journalist', digging trenches with two famous actors in made-up uniforms from the local department store. Kessel realized that a disorganized France would be no match for the armoured forces of the *Wehrmacht* and airpower of the *Luftwaffe*, at that moment destroying the Polish army.[39]

This was a feeling that both persisted and was confirmed by events. After seeing for himself (by then promoted to be an intelligence officer) the situation at the Front near Reims in mid-May 1940, and having also seen that at least the troops of General de Lattre de Tassigny were resisting the German advance, Kessel returned to Paris where he told the Prime Minister Paul Reynaud, and his mistress Hélène de Portes, the latter in the presence of her hairdresser and her manicurist, what he had witnessed. Given that de Portes was of dubious loyalty, Kessel received further confirmation that France was probably going to be defeated, but his instinct as a writer pushed him to see what was going on in Dunkirk, where he found himself exposed to the same dangers as all the other soldiers escaping the beaches; he confessed it was the most terrifying experience of his life, even if '*d'une beauté hallucinante*'. This was at the same moment that Saint-Exupéry was watching the German advance over Arras. Kessel returned to Paris via Folkestone to deliver his story to *Paris-soir* and, after finding time to bury a member of his family in the Montparnasse Cemetery, he left Paris with the rest of his newspaper's staff on 13 June for Clermont-Ferrand. But by the end of June France had surrendered and Kessel realized that as a famous Jewish Frenchman he had to leave.

But where to go? His preference was the United States, especially after he learned of the sinking by the Royal Navy of the French fleet in the harbour of Mers-el-Kébir on 3 July 1940, an act which infuriated him.[40] He realized that going to London might extinguish his popularity with his essentially French public. Kessel was thus not initially repelled by the regime of Marshal Pétain, under whom he had served and from whom he had received a decoration. Like many other French Jews (of whom there were over 225,000), as well as a large number of Jews who had fled Germany like Léon Werth, he felt he had nothing to worry about from the Vichy government. That was disabused by the Vichy antisemitism laws of 16 July 1940 (which deprived French people who were born elsewhere, especially Jews, of their citizenship) and the German 'Otto List' on 28 September of books that were now to be banned in France. Charles de Gaulle figured on this, as did Kessel.[41] But what is bizarre is that Kessel continued to believe that these laws were only intended to divert the attention of the Germans, already experiencing mild acts of resistance by late 1940, especially in Paris. Kessel went to Anthéor, near Saint-Raphaël on the Côte d'Azur where he wrote what his biographer has called 'the first novel to glorify the growing Resistance'.[42]

Kessel's *Les Maudru* was only published as a limited edition in 1945, mainly due to the paper shortage of that year in France. However the manuscript is dated 16 February 1941, so from a very early period of the war as described above. But the novel then had a strange journey, as Kessel was exfiltrated with some assistance from the British Intelligence Service (MI6) and a high-ranking and very brave British officer he knew in MI6, 'Richard' Bodington, whom he had helped in the 'CARTE' Resistance network in 1942. He escaped to Spain at the end of that year. The novel itself, of which there were only two manuscript copies, nearly never saw the light of day. One copy was burnt by Kessel himself and the other ended up in the well of a friend of his then-girlfriend Germaine Sablon. Kessel made it to Britain and joined the same squadron as Gary, whom he met for the first time in March 1943 while the latter was recuperating from wounds he had received in action. Kessel only managed to fly for a Free French squadron in late May 1944, flying in Mitchell bombers.[43]

Les Maudru is the story of a French peasant family from the *Pas de Calais*, and traces that family's feelings about the first year of the war. The son, Désiré Maudru, is a pilot member of a bomber crew, much as Kessel was to become later in the war. The text reads like the film scripts at which Kessel excelled and has all the physical and erotic charge of his other work, like *Belle de Jour*. Désiré's plane is shot down by German fighters over Bruges, presumably in the same battle of 1940 that St-Exupéry experienced over Arras on the other side of the French border. Meanwhile his father, Tancrède, and his mother, Margot, try and get on with their lives in the *Pas de Calais* in spite of the war. Désiré initially feels '*en dehors de tout cela* [distanced from all that]', even in the middle of the battle and seeing his crew killed. The Germans, the whole family has decided, are 'too strong', unlike the 'last time' and Tancrède has decided the war is over – why fight on for the '*beaux yeux des Anglais*', whom he dislikes?[44]

It transpires that Margot had slept with a passing English boy ten years previously and had never been allowed to fully forget her trespass, while the thought of it had continued to torture Tancrède. The English were literally in their heads and whenever they had cropped up in a conversation Tancrède had gone to the local bar and drunk far too much rum, not that he ever lost his temper or became violent, just morose. Now he had a son who was presumably a prisoner of the Germans and his drinking companion Pierre, who had lost a leg in 1914–18, and several young men were talking about going over the Channel and joining the Free French. But in his Anglophobe bitterness Tancrède decided to collaborate by standing a round for two German motor bike troops who entered the bar.

All that changes in the story when two of the young men, Simon and François (nickname 'l'Innocent'), discover Désiré Maudru hiding in a barn, while Tancrède is drinking with the German soldiers. Désiré has escaped German capture and made his way back to France where he now wants to fight on with the English. But one of the two naïve young men takes him to the bar to see his father, now in the company of German soldiers, who immediately suspect something unusual in the apparition of the down at heel Désiré. His father immediately whisks him home, where his son bursts into floods of tears for his massacred comrades, for he is no longer 'distanced from all that'.[45] He dislikes the English as much as his father and likes only 'his pay, women, wine and newspapers', except when a Spitfire had removed a Messerschmitt from his plane's tail that had been about to shoot him down. Now he spends his spare time on the coast watching the German planes speeding towards England, while occasionally making love to the serving girl at the local inn on the same cliffs. On one such occasion he discovers she is wearing a small swastika emblem, which ends their relationship.[46]

Then Désiré tells his father he has heard a French pilot talking from London on the radio. His father replies that if his son was to join the exiles it 'would not be the first possession [*bien*] of mine they stole', a clear reference to Margot's fling, though it is a reference which Désiré does not understand. Désiré decides to flee to England taking as much information as he can to guide the English bombers, when he is told about the sinking of the French fleet at Mers-el-Kébir – 'nothing less than that my friend' the barman tells him. It gets worse when he hears that his brother Jacquot's warship, the *Bretagne*, has been lost with all hands in that battle. His father tells him that if he is still of a mind to go to England he will hand him over to the Germans or beat him to a pulp. The old soldier of the previous war, Pierre, laments the turn of events, for he had fought with the English and liked them, while Simon and François tell Desiré they have actually been persuaded to go to England by the news, that only the English have understood that they have to target the 'Germans, they are really fighting them [*Boche. Ils font la guerre*]'. But Desiré is still torn by his desire to fight and his unwillingness to bring more pain to his family, and it is his mother that finally persuades him to leave.

After setting off in a small boat across the Channel, they are strafed by a Messerschmitt, François is wounded and they are finally picked up by a Royal Navy patrol boat and transported to Kent. Pierre and François enlist as merchant seamen. Maudru, now called *Mauodriou* by his fellow English airmen (who cannot pronounce his name properly), wears a blue RAF uniform and is (very slowly) learning the most useful English words, including 'Lets have a drink'. But he is unhappy not be sent into action straight away, and is seriously home sick, to which the constant refrain from his Squadron Leader is 'Don't think too much Mauodriou'. He persuades his superior officer to let him fly a special mission over the area he came from in Northern France where a strange triangle of smoking fires had been seen. From his bomber he finds it is next to his family's farmhouse, but he is hit by a massive amount of anti-aircraft fire and lands on the sea. He saves his rear gunner, who is wounded, and manages to swim to shore where he recognizes the beach he had left from with Simon and François. He first goes to the home of the veteran *poilu* Pierre and changes his clothes and looks after his gunner. He cannot admit why he went to see Pierre before his parents. He needn't have worried, as it turns out his father had lit the bonfires to show the RAF where to bomb a German munitions depot. While Desiré had been away the Germans had shot one of his father's friends who had a radio, forced those with fishing boats to help with invasion planning, and successfully encouraged collaboration by selectively releasing POWs. The 'war had been over. I was in agreement and I showed it ... [Now] I am going to make war on them in my own way ... [As for Desiré] ... you are to go back and come back and bomb the hell out of them [*foutre le feu*]'.[47]

This very moving tale is the most realist of all the texts mentioned here, and the most accessible to an ordinary audience. It is a tale of a humiliated *France profonde* collaborating and finally waking up to the necessity of resistance. The anti-English sentiment of the beginning is never dispelled, except by Pierre, who regrets that the French and English had drifted apart since the battles he fought at the Dardenelles in 1915. But the tone changes as events do, and with no concessions to liberal sentimentality. It is a small and perfectly formed *vignette* of the transformation from acceptance of defeat to resistance and a form of inner liberation.

Conclusions (en guise de ...)

So can we really say that these writers solve the problem of their credibility as both authors and aviators? Do they answer de Beauvoir's question: ' ... how could a writer amuse himself with writing stories that never happened?'[48] Equally can we counter the jibe thrown at St-Exupéry that he was a better writer than an airman for his aviator friends and a better aviator than a writer by his writing acquaintances? Rightly or wrongly these authors believed that to act *and* to write avoided this dilemma; the act of resistance 'in the air' was not the same as resisting while sitting scribbling in a garret. Moreover, these writers followed the same journey as their countrymen and women. They started in the same despair and terror as did the rest of France in 1940, and through their actions *and* writing gave rise to substantial hope among the French population, the very basis of restoring self-belief and self-respect. Thus at its best aerial warfare acted as a personal impetus for many French (and other) writers to transform what can only be described as existential moments of terror and self-doubt into significant reflections on not only personal dilemmas but also on topics of political importance. They became the individual consciences of a collective tragedy.

They all equally present a very coherent view of the world they wish to see, but not as historians or politicians in terms of categories, but in terms of allegories, metaphors and imaginary discourses. These discourses are based on personal experience or immanent observations of the world around them. As St-Exupéry put it in *Vol sur Arras* they had all seen their country burning 'from 10,000 metres', seen 'in ten minutes ... three hundred years of patience and sunshine [burn]'[49] and they show the impact of that on the inhabitants and those who are fighting on the ground and in the air better than any historian could do.

Do they add anything to the world of 1940–5 as it is understood by historians and other more real-world commentators? In some ways they seem, from our perspective, to describe what we think we know about the period and its dilemmas. But we could say that they have given a 'soundtrack', as Kessel would probably have put it, to an epoch. Very few ordinary French people of today know much about this period from reading historical tomes, and even less from those of political scientists. But these fictional writers have been constantly read since 1945, their discourses have become part of a national conversation in France and beyond. They do not therefore lack verisimilitude, and they have become part of the writing of the new mythology of the West. If only for that reason they merit examination, which we have done here of necessity in a very cursory way.

But we could also add that any of the themes that are evoked have clear parallels with 'history' as it is understood by historians. France did collapse in 1940, most of the population did conclude that the war was over; the sinking of the French fleet at Mers-el-Kébir persuaded many that England was as bad as Germany; collaboration was widespread, etc. The arguments among the Free French about de Gaulle were every bit as intense as Aron's description of St-Exupéry, and all the more real given that the writer was indeed formulating his ideas 'at 10,000 metres'. There are of course exceptions to this rule, as Gary was not on the Eastern Front, though his descriptions of it and of the depredations of the *Das Reich* division have more than stood the test of time; his views on nationalism are part of the very best of the French language on the topic: '*Le patriotisme, c'est l'amour des siens. Le nationalisme, c'est la haine des autres.*'⁵⁰ The story told in *Les Maudru* by Kessel is possibly imaginary, including its accounts of RAF banter on Kent airfields (where Kessel nonetheless spent some of the war), but it has more than the ring of truth. It certainly fulfils the need to express the 'typical', which the Marxist critic Georg Lukacs saw as the exemplification of the 'authentic', a word that has been hijacked by Sartre, whose reputation has ridden on the back of real resistance fighters.

Their key and lasting appeal is that the earthy realism of all of these writers goes to the heart of the concerns of most inhabitants of France, a country where there has always been an obsessional combination of patriotic fervour and the problems and benefits of physical and spiritual love. Both of these are in constant juxtaposition with their reflections on everyday politics.

Notes

1   Among my publications to date on the subject are: Andrew Williams, *France, Britain and the United States, Volume 1, 1900–1940: A Reappraisal* (London: Palgrave Macmillan, 2014); Andrew Williams, *France, Britain and the United States, Volume 2, 1940–1961: A Reappraisal* (London: Palgrave Macmillan, 2020).
2   International Committee of the Red Cross, *Declaration (XIV) Prohibiting the Discharge of Projectiles and Explosives from Balloons* (The Hague, 18 October 1907). Regrettably this was only ratified by Britain and the United States although it is still in force today: https://ihl-databases.icrc.org/ihl/INTRO/245 (accessed 14 January 2021).
3   Simone de Beauvoir, *Les Mandarins* (Paris: Gallimard, 1954); Heinz Rein, *Berlin Finale* (London: Penguin, 2019), first published (Berlin: Dietz Verlag, 1947). The quote is from *Les Mandarins*, 157.

4   Hereafter 'St-Exupéry', though 'Saint-Ex' was the acronym favoured by Raymond Aron: Antoine de St-Exupéry, *Ecrits de Guerre, 1939–1944* (Paris: Gallimard, 1994), *Préface* by Raymond Aron, 12. I have used this edition. In English: *Wartime Writings, 1939–1944* (New York: Harcourt, 1986). I will also use his: *Pilote de Guerre: Mission sur Arras* (New York: Editions de la Maison Française, 1942; Paris: Gallimard, 1972). For biographies see: Dominique Lablanche, Stacy de La Bruyère, and Françoise Bouillot, *Saint-Exupéry: Une vie à contre-courant* (Paris: Albin Michel, 1994); In English: Stacy Schiff, *Saint-Exupéry: A Biography* (New York: Alfred A. Knopf, 1994); Paul Webster, *Antoine de St-Exupéry: The Life and Death of the Little Prince* (London: Pan Macmillan, 1993). On Aron (in English) see, Olivier Schmitt, ed., *Raymond Aron and International Relations* (Abingdon: Routledge, 2018).

5   Gary was born in Vilnius in Lithuania; Kessel was from Russia, though he was born in Argentina to Lithuanian parents. Both were naturalized French citizens.

6   St-Exupéry, *Ecrits de Guerre*, 'lettre à X', December 1939, 43.

7   Williams, *France, Britain and the United States, Volume 2, 1940–1961*, esp. chapter 3.

8   De *Beauvoir, Les Mandarins*, 151–2; Auriol to London, 13 July 1944 – the letters had been written on 12 May – Auriol AN, AU10 Dr 5. Auriol became *Président du Conseil* (prime minister) in 1946 and *Président de la République* between 1947 and 1954, thus a key politician of the Fourth Republic; Andrew Williams, 'France and the Origins of the United Nations, 1944–45: "Si La France ne compte plus, qu'on nous le dise"', *Diplomacy and Statecraft*, June 2017, 223.

9   Emilio Gentile, *L'Apocalypse de la modernité* (Paris: Flammarion, 2011), 55.

10 The 'Pike', as D'Annunzio was termed, as much for his sexually predatory behaviour as anything else, organized the occupation of Fiume after the First World War to protest against Italy's treatment at the Treaty of Versailles. He was a key inspiration for Italian fascism: Lucy Hughes-Hallett, *The Pike: Gabriele d'Annunzio – poet, Seducer and Preacher of War* (London: Fourth Estate, 2013).

11 Gentile, *L'Apocalypse de la modernité*, 34–5.

12 André Malraux, *L'espoir* (Paris: Gallimard, 1937); English version: *Man's Hope*, (New York: Modern Library, 1941); the film was called *Espoir: Sierra de Teruel*, in black and white, not released in France until 1945.

13 Denis de Rougemont, 'Contribution à une recherche éventuelle sur les sources de la notion d'engagement de l'écrivain', 17–25, *in* 'L'Ecrivain et la Politique: Les problèmes de l'engagement', *Cadmos*, Spring 1978.

14 Notably: Pierre Drieu La Rochelle, *La Comedie de Charleroi* (Paris: Gallimard, 1934) and *Socialisme fasciste* (Paris: Gallimard, 1934); Louis-Ferdinand Céline, *Voyage au bout de la nuit* (Paris: Editions Denoël, 1932).

15 For the context, see Williams, *France, Britain and the United States, Volume 2, 1940–1961*, 17.

16 Robert Wohl, *The Generation of 1914* (London: Weidenfeld and Nicolson, 1980). This term refers to those who fought in the Great War.

17 Joseph Kessel, *Les Temps Sauvages* (Paris: Gallimard, 1975). It might be noted that by the time he arrived in Russia in 1919 the war was over, but his observations of the Vladivostok area are remarkable. Most of his time getting there, in place, and returning to France was spent under the influence of alcohol.

18 Robert Aron and Arnaud Dandieu, *Décadence de la nation française* (Paris: Editions Rieder, 1931) and *La revolution nécessaire* (Paris: Editions Rieder, 1933).

19 Antoine de St-Exupéry, *Wind, Sand and Stars* (New York: Reynal and Hitchcock, 1939); in French: *Terre des Hommes*, 1939. See also, by the same author, *Pilote de*

Guerre (Paris: Gallimard, 1972), first published 1942, *op.cit supra*., and *Le petit prince* (Paris: Gallimard, 2007), first published 1943.

20   Romain Gary, *La Promesse de l'aube* (Paris: Gallimard, 1960). Here quotes are from the 1980 'definitive' edition.

21   Romain Gary, *Education européenne* (Paris: Calmann-Levy, 1945, later Paris: Gallimard, 1960). It was first published, in English, as *Forest of Anger* (London: Cresset Press, 1944), 76–7, 89 and 246.

22   For some of the academic analysis of St Exupéry as an aviator and author, see Claude Carlier, '1939–1940, L'armée de l'air française dans la tourmente: capitaine Antoine de Saint-Exupéry, pilote de guerre', *Guerres Mondiales et Conflits Contemporains*, no. 249 (2013): 129–46; Richard Rumbold and Margaret Stewart, *The Winged Life: A Portrait of Antoine de St Exupéry, Poet and Airman* (London: Weidenfeld and Nicolson, 1953); Benyon John, *St Exupéry, 'Vol de nuit' and 'Terre des hommes'* (London: Grant and Cutler, 1990).

23   Orville D. Menard, 'Léon Bourgeois, Antoine de St Exupéry and *Solidarité*', *International Social Science Review* 68, no. 1 (2001): 5–6.

24   Bernard Lambert, 'La Mélancholie d'Antoine de St-Exupéry', *Revue des Deux Mondes*, October 1994, 154–62. These ridiculous debates arguably reached rock bottom when another French intellectual remarked that he was 'plus pilote qu'écrivain aux yeux des intellectuels, plus écrivain que pilote aux yeux de ses camarades de vol' ['a better pilot than a writer when judged by intellectuals, and more of a writer than a pilot when judged by other aircrew.']: Lambert, 156.

25   St-Exupéry, *Pilote de Guerre*, 15–18, 25–30.

26   St-Exupéry, *Pilote de Guerre*, 25, 39 and 77.

27   Antoine de St-exupéry, *Citadelle* (Paris: Gallimard, 1948), 7–8; *Ecrits de Guerre, 1939–1944, op.cit*.

28   Andrew Williams, 'Charles De Gaulle: The Warrior as Statesman', *Global Society: Journal of Interdisciplinary International Relations* 32, no. 2 (April 2018): 162–75.

29   For more on this, see Andrew Williams, 'The Labour Party and Its Relations with the SFIO in London, 1940–44', in *European Socialist Networks and the Remaking of European International Policy after 1945*, ed. Melanie Torrent and Andrew Williams (London: University of London Press, *forthcoming*).

30   See: Emmanuelle Loyer, *Paris à New York: Intellectuels et artistes français en exil (1940–1947)* (Paris: Grasset et Fasquelle, 2005).

31   Aron, quoting Maritain, in: St-Exupéry, *Ecrits de Guerre, 1939–1944*, 11–13. On England: 'lettre à X', end December 1939, 49.

32   St-Exupéry, *Ecrits de Guerre*, '1939', 17.

33   St-Exupéry, *Ecrits de Guerre*, radio broadcast of 18 October 1939, 25.

34   Yves Courrière, *Joseph Kessel ou Sur la piste du lion* (Paris: Plon, 1985), 92.

35   Kessel, *Les Temps Sauvages* (Paris: Gallimard, 1975), 13. In real life the French pilot he so admired was called Thélis Vachon, but he also lost most of his comrades in the last battle of the war (Courrière, *Joseph Kessel*, 127–8).

36   Kessel, *Les Temps Sauvages*, Section 3, '*Aime-moi noire*' The literal translation of this is 'love me like a black woman' as the subsequent part of the quote ['*Aime-moi noire, disait-elle à un homme. Blanche, tout le monde m'aimerait*'], seems to indicate.

37   For a summary, see Courrière, *Joseph Kessel*, Second and Third Section.

38   Joseph Kessel, *L'Equipage* (Paris: Gallimard, 1923); Antoine de Saint-Exupéry, *Terre des Hommes* (Paris: Gallimard, 1939), in English: *Wind, Sand and Stars* (London: Penguin, 1995). His other most notable 'air' books, before *Pilote de Guerre*, were

Courrier Sud (Paris: Gallimard, 1929) and *Vol de Nuit* (Paris: Gallimard, 1931), both about his life in South America as a mail pilot.
39 Courrière, *Joseph Kessel*, 517-19.
40 Courrière, *Joseph Kessel*, 528-38; Joseph Kessel, *Témoin parmi les hommes: L'Heure des châtiments: Reportages, 1938-1945* (Paris: Tallandier, 1956).
41 Léon Werth, *Deposition, 1940-1944: A Secret Diary of Life in Vichy France* (Oxford: Oxford University Press, 2018); Courrière, *Joseph Kessel*, 542-3.
42 Courrière, *Joseph Kessel*, 548-9.
43 Courrière, *Joseph Kessel*, 562-72 and 599. Courrière and Kessel get quite a lot wrong about Nicolas Bodington, whom they wrongly call Richard (or Dick), previously a reporter on the *Daily Express*. He knew Kessel from an earlier part of the war.
44 Joseph Kessel, *Les Maudru* (Paris: Julliard, 1945), 8, 17, 19.
45 Kessel, *Les Maudru*, 39-47.
46 Kessel, *Les Maudru*, 49, 62.
47 Kessel, *Les Maudru*, 72-80, 99-121.
48 Simone de Beauvoir, *Les Mandarins*, 157.
49 St-Exupéry, *Pilote de Guerre*, 81.
50 Gary, *Education européenne*, 246.

Chapter 8

THE BRITISH ROYAL AIR FORCE: OPERATIONS OVER LAOS AGAINST THE HO CHI MINH TRAIL, 1962

Priscilla Roberts

Inconclusive rumours that the British Royal Air Force (RAF) flew occasional covert missions in the Vietnam War have circulated for decades, but so far evidence that British aircraft provided anything more than humanitarian relief services, notably by delivering supplies earmarked for refugees, has proved elusive.[1] It seems, however, that in the second half of 1962, in great secrecy a series of such flights took place. These missions were intended to assist with newly initiated US attempts to interdict and shut down the increasingly effective Ho Chi Minh Trail logistical network of roads, paths and bunkers that transported supplies from communist North Vietnam via Cambodia and Laos to supporters in South Vietnam.

Notes taken in March 2013 from the logbook of the navigator on these operations, Flight Lieutenant Donald Roberts (1929–2014) of 48 Squadron, then based at RAF Station Changi in Singapore, together with his personal recollections, provide some insights into both the extent and limits of British support for the United States in Indochina, at a time when the situation in the region was still decidedly fluid.[2]

Background

The 1954 Geneva Accords, the product of the international conference held in Switzerland in mid-1954 to resolve the conflicts in Indochina, recognized Cambodia and Laos as independent nations. Vietnam was left divided at the 17th Parallel, with a communist government headed by Ho Chi Minh controlling the north, while a non-communist administration led by President Ngo Dinh Diem held power in the south. The southern state became in effect a US client, heavily dependent upon American aid and assistance. Fearing that the communists would win nationwide elections, scheduled for 1956, and so take over all of Vietnam, US officials advised the Diem administration to refuse to allow the South to participate in these. The Northern Viet Minh government embarked on plans to mount a guerrilla campaign with the objective of reuniting Vietnam. From 1958 onward, military supplies were funnelled southward to National Liberation Front (Viet Cong) insurgents from the north along a gradually expanded complex of mountain trails and pathways that traversed border territories in neighbouring Cambodia and Laos. In 1958–9, North Vietnam invaded Laos to facilitate the construction of this network. Viet Cong fighters also sought sanctuary by crossing the boundaries into these ostensibly neutral countries.[3]

Within Laos – and ultimately in Cambodia, too – these activities and efforts to counter them proved immensely destabilizing. By the early 1960s, the situation within Laos was fragile in the extreme. Would-be neutralist governments headed by Prince Souvanna Phouma encountered not merely external pressures, but also challenges from both the right-wing military, which staged a coup in 1961, bringing General Phoumi Novasan to power, and the leftist Pathet Lao, which offered significant communist opposition. From May 1961 to July 1962, a second Geneva Conference was held, co-chaired by Great Britain and India, that included representatives from fourteen countries, including all three major powers, the Soviet Union, China and the United States, together with France, Canada, Poland, and Burma, as well as Laos, Cambodia and both Vietnams. After more than a year of negotiations, in which US assistant secretary of state for Far Eastern affairs W. Averell Harriman played a leading role, as did British diplomats, all agreed that Laos should be neutralized, and once more have a tripartite coalition government headed by Souvanna Phouma, in which the pro-American, pro-communist and neutralist factions were all represented. The powers that signed the declaration on 23 July 1962, the date it entered into force, all pledged themselves to respect the neutrality of Laos.[4]

Even at the time, it was apparent that for at least some of the signatories, this proclamation meant primarily that they would discreetly restrain and camouflage rather than halt their activities within Laos. To a degree that its communist patrons, China and the Soviet Union, probably did not fully appreciate until later, North Vietnam was determined to continue the struggle to unite both Vietnams until victory was attained. In terms of infiltrating supplies and personnel into South Vietnam, quietly upgrading the Ho Chi Minh Trail infrastructure in the Laos borderlands remained a top priority. Viet Cong representatives were, for the most part, far less interested in enabling a Pathet Lao victory, and were prepared to work with any Lao government that tolerated or turned a blind eye to their activities.

On the US side, the administration of President John F. Kennedy engaged in something of a love affair with the concept of counterinsurgency, especially the idea of dispatching irregular units to work with indigenous anti-communist forces. In Laos, a country with a population of approximately 3 million that the French had cobbled together in the post-1945 years out of disparate and ill-assorted elements, the Meo (Hmong) hill tribes concentrated in the mountainous areas traversed by the Ho Chi Minh Trail offered an alternative anti-communist grouping that might well prove more effective than the official Royal Lao Army military forces. The Meo, together with other hill tribes, constituted more than half the country's population. By late 1961, 11,000 Meo were receiving US support, while US training teams were working with both the Meo and the Royal

Lao Army.[5] Sir John Addis, the British ambassador to Laos, expressed doubts over the impact of this strategy on Laos, 'a country which has never known real unity', on the grounds that it would undercut 'essential' moves towards integration involving efforts to ensure 'that the minority tribes should be drawn into the Laotian community and given a share of national consciousness and responsibility'.[6] But with Kennedy, Harriman and Roger Hilsman, the director of the State Department's Bureau of Intelligence and Research and a former Office of Strategic Services guerrilla fighter with Merrill's Marauders during the Second World War, all committed to using the Laotian hill tribes to close down the Ho Chi Minh Trail, the British government was not prepared to express any reservations. Whatever misgivings they might privately harbour, British officials would, indeed, facilitate the US approach.

The signature of the Laos agreement went in tandem with initiatives by the United States to strengthen and reinforce its position in Southeast Asia. In South Vietnam, Kennedy boosted counterinsurgency efforts and increased the number of US advisers in the country from 700 to 12,000. Following a successful Pathet Lao and Viet Cong attack on the northern provincial Lao capital of Nam Tha in early May 1962, the United States persuaded the nervous government of neighbouring Thailand, a member – together with the Philippines, Pakistan, Australia, New Zealand, France, Britain, and the United States – of the US-backed Southeast Asian Treaty Organization (SEATO), to request assistance from its alliance partners, as evidence of their support. Since 1961 the Thais, who had backed Phoumi's military government, had argued that as it stood SEATO, lacking any formal military forces or guarantees, was inadequate – to quote Thai foreign minister Thanat Khoman, an 'ineffective and unreliable' security arrangement.[7]

In May 1962, around 1,000 US troops who had just participated in joint SEATO 'Cobra' military exercises were already present in northern Thailand. In mid-May 1962, the United States deployed an additional Marine Battalion Landing Team and two air squadrons, one from the Air Force and one attached to the Marines, an extra 1,800 men in all. By the end of the month, total US forces in Thailand had risen to between 5,000 and 6,000, located in areas close to those regions of Laos where Pathet Lao units were operating. The United States asked other SEATO nations, including Australia, New Zealand and the United Kingdom, to send token forces as a tangible display of solidarity that would boost Thai morale. Kennedy wished to see 'as many SEATO flags in Thailand as possible'. Ironically, when the British offered to send back a Hunter fighter squadron that had taken part in the Cobra exercises, the Thais were unenthusiastic, and it took US pressure to make them accept.[8]

The aftermath of the Geneva Accords

Following the signing of the Neutralization Agreement on 23 July 1962, the United States withdrew the 1,200 American and third-country personnel of its Military Advisory Assistance Group from Laos, an exercise completed in early October

1962. US officials, including President Kennedy, Harriman and Hilsman, wished to ensure that, should the Laos agreement collapse, the blame would not fall on the United States.[9] In practice, this did not mean the cessation of all US-backed operations in Laos, especially its efforts to mobilize the hill tribes against the Pathet Lao and the Viet Minh. In July 1962, Harriman permitted the US Central Intelligence Agency (CIA) to retain a mere two paramilitary officers in Laos. He made it clear to William Colby, head of the CIA's Far East Division, that he expected full weekly briefings on CIA activities in Laos and Southeast Asia. As the reports of a continuing active North Vietnamese military presence in Laos became more ominous and convincing, Harriman relented and permitted Air America to resupply the Hmong with food and ammunition, albeit in secret. Military training operations for the Hmong in Thailand were also quietly continued.[10] In late July 1962, during a Souvanna Phouma visit to Washington, Kennedy also authorised extensive economic aid to the new Lao government, which received 85 per cent of its total revenues from US assistance programmes.[11]

US reconnaissance operations to discover whether North Vietnamese forces were genuinely complying with the Geneva agreement and leaving Laos became more problematic, after a supersonic F-101 Voodoo fighter flying a low-level surveillance mission at eight thousand feet over the Plaine des Jarres was hit by Pathet Lao anti-aircraft fire on 14 August 1962. Although the pilot managed to avoid crashing the jet and made an emergency landing at Don Muang Air Base in Thailand, US Ambassador to Laos Leonard Unger wished to cease all such overflights of Laos, unless the Lao government gave specific permission for these. Harriman duly recommended that the United States should end 'all covert flights over Laos'. Since they continued at the rate of two or three per day, albeit at high altitudes, until at least November 1962, it seems that in this case, his advice was disregarded.[12]

The use of British aircraft to fly missions over Laos – including what may have been the delivery of New Zealand SAS personnel – suggests that, in the interests of maintaining good relations with the United States, their country's ally, partner and patron, top British officials were equally willing quietly to contravene the recent Neutralization Agreement. As Nicholas Tarling and Matthew Jones have pointed out, despite differences over some specifics of policy, on a wide range of issues the British sought to maintain a special relationship with the United States; to ensure that their partner and ally had a continuing commitment to Southeast Asia; and to influence and sometimes moderate the US approach to that area. From the prime minister down, British officials were conscious that their country did not possess unlimited resources for defence, constraints that likewise led them to place a high value on the encouragement of regional stability.[13] In mid-August 1962, Kennedy bluntly suggested to some of his top advisers, including Harriman and Michael V. Forrestal of the National Security Council, plus several economic officials, that Britain and France, as the countries that had pushed hardest for neutralization, should provide substantially more financial aid to Laos, since 'Souvanna is their protégé'.[14] Providing a delivery service in hazardous conditions was one way of blunting such demands.

The British also had their own interests in Asia to consider, particularly the status of Hong Kong, a territory that they would continue to administer until 1997, but where their position depended in large part on the tacit acquiescence of the People's Republic of China, and to some extent on implicit support from the United States.[15] Well before Henry Kissinger developed the concept of linkage, the British were perfectly familiar with the pragmatic reality. To satisfy the demands and expectations of their far more powerful partner, where possible, British officials would make conciliatory gestures to the United States, offering relatively minor concessions to demonstrate good will, even if they believed these likely to have little practical effect. In July 1961, for example, Prime Minister Harold Macmillan and his cabinet authorized the dispatch to beleaguered South Vietnam of a small British Advisory Mission, headed by Sir Robert Thompson, renowned for his successful use of counterinsurgency tactics to defeat communist rebels during the Malayan Insurgency of the late 1940s and 1950s. Unfortunately for the United States, the 'strategic hamlets' programme introduced in South Vietnam, at least partly on Thompson's advice, proved far less effective than similar measures had in Malaya.[16]

The British were far less eager to undertake more substantial operations in Indochina. Interestingly, by September 1961, American officials, notably W. Averell Harriman, were advancing proposals to British defence leaders that, should the ongoing Geneva negotiations fail to result in an agreement, the existing SEATO Plan 5 calling for limited counterinsurgency measures in Laos in an emergency situation should be upgraded into a much larger military operation, one that would involve sealing off the Thai border, and the formal occupation of all of southern Laos up to the 17th parallel. The Harriman proposals envisaged the deployment in Laos of 10,000 Thai troops and 5,000 South Vietnamese soldiers, as well as Western forces. The Americans were reluctant to raise these suggestions with Asian members of SEATO or South Vietnam, as they feared doing so might compromise prospects that the Geneva negotiations would succeed, but they did put the British, Australians and New Zealanders in the picture. British military officials were decidedly dubious as to the strategic and logistical feasibility of any such intervention. They also feared that these operations might spark full-scale intervention by Viet Minh and Chinese forces.[17] The Australian chiefs of staff were equally sceptical.[18] Britain still maintained large military bases in both Singapore – then still a British colony – and Malaya, which had recently gained independence. The British chiefs of staff feared that, by stoking anti-colonial sentiment and boosting anti-British political groups in Malaya and Singapore, large-scale SEATO intervention in Laos might jeopardize both the existing UK defence agreement with Malaya and negotiations then in progress for the creation of a Greater Malaysia incorporating Singapore.[19]

Limited British air supply operations into Laos, however embarrassing it might have been, had knowledge that they were in progress become public, were a far less hazardous and costly means of satisfying US demands for support. The missions that British aircraft flew on behalf of the United States in the second half of 1962 were probably part of the overall British effort to facilitate the conclusion and if feasible the successful implementation of the Laos Neutralization Agreement, while promoting good relations with the United States. They may also have constituted part of the overall show of strength by SEATO, to demonstrate its commitment to the defence of neighbouring Thailand.

British missions over Laos, July–November 1962

By the early 1960s, the fact that the CIA was running its own airline flying supposedly covert missions in Southeast Asia was pretty much an open secret, at least among air crew active in the region. Then and later, purportedly neutral Laos was a particular focus of interest for such ventures.[20] For some months from March to August 1961, US Marine airplanes and personnel were temporarily deployed at Udorn Thani air base in Thailand, to provide support and maintain Air America helicopters involved in anti-Viet Cong and anti-Pathet Lao campaigns in Laos. While these undertakings were not strictly secret, those involved were strongly discouraged from publicizing information about them and instructed by superiors that the only information they could offer was 'No comment'.[21]

British missions over Laos would have been equally sensitive, and perhaps even more so, since they took place after the signing of the Laos neutralization accords, to which the United Kingdom was a party. According to my father's recollection, the reason that American officials requested the British to undertake these flights was that, at this juncture, the fleet run by Air America and the CIA included helicopters and single- and twin-engine aircraft but no four-engine airplanes. Flying missions over the rugged mountains of Laos would be particularly hazardous in twin-engine airplanes, because if one engine should develop problems, the other would lack the power to maintain the necessary altitude, and all on board were in danger of a crash in which they might well be killed. The hazards were real. On an early US-backed covert mission intended to insert into North Vietnam a team of guerrilla operatives christened 'Atlas', the aircraft – apparently an Air America helicopter – involved crashed on 12 March 1962, probably hit by anti-aircraft fire, with some of those on board captured and eventually put on trial in North Vietnam.[22] Losing an aircraft in these circumstances carried the further risk of compromising the Laos Neutralization Agreement, should other parties involved wish to make an issue of these flights. The US government therefore decided to ask the British, who had a number of four-engine Handley Page Hastings transport aircraft in RAF Squadron 48, based at RAF Changi in Singapore, to fly several missions over Laos from Thailand, delivering military personnel and matériel to assist the hill tribes in the secret war then already in progress. From a purely self-interested perspective, should a British military aircraft be lost over Laos, the onus of explaining why it was there in the first place would fall upon the government of the United Kingdom rather than that of the United States.

This was a relatively brief episode in Western air operations over Laos. According to my father, towards the end of 1962 Air America took over these missions on behalf of the United States. In one respect, his recollections were apparently inaccurate. According to his account, by late 1962 Air America had acquired some four-engined aircraft, which meant that they no longer needed to rely on the British Handley Page Hastings. The historian John Prados, by contrast, told me that in Laos, Air America always relied entirely upon single- and twin-engine planes for all its flights, including those into the Lao uplands. Prados suggested that, if the United States did employ British aircraft and crews for these particular missions, there must have been some other reason for this, such as 'hauling capacity, or specifically the British nationality'.[23] It is possible, of course, that the Americans were not completely truthful with their British counterparts as to the reasons why they first requested British assistance. More documentary evidence would be very useful. When these missions ceased, the British fliers were apparently further told that the Americans had eventually decided to handle these flights themselves, partly because they fundamentally preferred running these operations independently, thereby remaining fully in charge of them, and partly because the British military needed all their Singapore-based aircraft to deal with the Brunei Revolt, which blew up in December 1962. The US government reportedly wished to award all the British aviators involved the Distinguished Flying Cross, but the British government vetoed the suggestion, since awkward questions might be asked as to just what these fliers had done to deserve an American medal.

The British aviators involved were ordered to maintain complete secrecy about these missions and warned against divulging information on these activities or their whereabouts even to their wives. To ensure deniability, they were also instructed to refrain from entering details of the flights in their flying logbooks, though they were permitted to include data on their journeys between Singapore and Thailand.

My father was apparently selected to participate in these missions because he was a particularly highly qualified navigator, cleared to fly VVIPs (Very Very Important People) such as the queen of England and the marshal of the RAF. He was particularly valued for his ability to provide accurate guidance for flying an aircraft using traditional dead reckoning methods employing only calculations using his sextant, charts and other data, without any reliance on electronic instruments. He could plot a flight plan that would deliver an aircraft to its intended destination with an exceptionally low margin of error, of just a few feet or yards. (In later life, as computers became more prevalent in flying, he would say that he was probably one of the few people left in the world who still knew how to direct an aircraft using old-fashioned methods.) He told me that one of the pilots on the squadron, as I recall the squadron leader, to whom he was not particularly close, but whose flying abilities he came to admire greatly after undertaking these trips with him, specifically asked for him as a navigator on these missions, because he was known for his excellent navigational skills.

In the second half of 1962, my father flew on a total of six secret missions over Laos, flying out of either Chiang Mai airfield in Northern Thailand or Don Muang airport near Bangkok. Although he and his colleagues were forbidden to enter the flights over Laos in their logbooks, he entered details in his flying logbook of the flights to, from, and within Thailand, as follows (these are copies of the original entries):

Hastings TG 612, pilot Squadron Leader Douglas Wood
July 25, 11.30 a.m., Changi-Dong Muang
July 26, 13.15, Dong Muang-Changi

Hastings TG 526, pilot Squadron Leader Douglas Wood
August 2, 09.30, Changi-Chiang Mai (Radio Compass Malfunction! R Comp L/D)
August 2, 17.00, Chiang Mai-Don Muang (Radio Compass Malfunction! R Comp L/D)
August 3, 08.00, Dong Muang-Changi

Hastings TG 531, pilot Flight Lieutenant Grafham
August 14, 05.00, Changi-Don Muang
August 14, 10.00, Don Muang-Chiang Mai
August 14, 14.30, Chiang Mai-Don Muang
August 15, 07.00, Don Muang-Chiang Mai
August 15, 09.30, Chiang Mai-Dong Muang
August 15, 12.10, Don Muang-Changi

Hastings TG 523, pilot Flying Officer Huntington
October 13, 05.00, Changi-Chiang Mai
October 13, 13.30, Chiang Mai-Don Muang
October 14, 08.00, Dong Muang-Changi

Hastings TG 536, pilot Flight Lieutenant Dickinson
November 28, 06.00, Changi-Chiang Mai
November 29, 09.00, Chiang Mai-Don Muang
November 29, 11.20, Don Muang-Changi

According to my father, the first of these trips – flown two or three days after the signature of the Geneva Agreements – was a dummy run, to test their ability to fly these missions: he was asked to get the plane to a certain destination within one minute's accuracy, flying without radar or electronic instruments and using only traditional navigation methods.

On at least one of the subsequent trips, they transported what they were told was a New Zealand SAS team of fifteen to twenty members, who parachuted in, to work with the hill tribes. By the early 1960s, links in Southeast Asia between the British and New Zealand militaries were already rather close. The British already had a significant history of working with New Zealand SAS (NZSAS) forces, who played a significant role in eliminating rebel elements in the later years of the Malayan Emergency, from November 1955 to December 1957. From late 1957 onward, New Zealand regular forces remained deployed in Malaya and Singapore, representing New Zealand's commitment to the SEATO alliance. From at least late 1964 to the end of 1966, the NZSAS worked closely with British and Australian SAS teams in eradicating pro-communist insurgents in Borneo who supported Indonesia in the ongoing Indonesian Confrontation (Konfrontasi) efforts to seize Brunei and annex Sabah and Sarawak (East Malaysia) from the Malaysian Federation. In the later 1960s, NZSAS units were deployed in Vietnam from 1968 to 1971, undertaking a range of hazardous reconnaissance missions and mounting ambushes of communist forces. All these operations have been covered in some detail in histories official and unofficial.[24]

According to Ian McGibbon: 'In 1962, as part of a precautionary build-up in the vicinity of the trouble [in Laos], the [New Zealand] army's Special Air Service (SAS) squadron was sent to Thailand for seven weeks, and three of 41 Squadron's Bristol Freighters were also committed.'[25] This has been described as New Zealand's somewhat 'token' contribution to early US operations in Indochina, after Kennedy requested 'as many SEATO flags in Thailand as possible'. Historians of the NZSAS, including Christopher Pugsley, Rhys Ball and Ron Crosby, provide further details on this deployment, which apparently consisted of a detachment of thirty SAS personnel, who were stationed in Thailand from 2 June to 16 September 1962. It was headed by Major Mal Velvin, who – though he himself lacked any previous NZSAS experience – enjoyed good relations with his opposite numbers among the 6,000-strong US military forces then based in Thailand. The NZSAS unit, in Ball's words 'a group of highly trained, jungle-warfare and counterinsurgency instructors and advisers', worked closely with US Marines and Special Forces units in Thailand, training in jungle warfare and sharing expertise. New Zealand Troop Sergeant Peter Rutledge later recalled that when the deployment began in June 1962, it was believed that 'a major North Vietnamese concentration' had infiltrated from Laos into north-eastern Thailand, and it was anticipated that the New Zealand arrivals would be deployed to that region to assist in counter operations and blocking further infiltration points. Both Ball and Crosby state, however, that during this deployment, members of the NZSAS unit were restricted to training exercises, and never took part in actual counterinsurgency operations within Thailand or beyond its borders. By the end of their time in Thailand, whatever North Vietnamese concentration of forces might have been present in north-eastern Thailand was believed to be dispersing.

It is perhaps worth noting that from 17 July 1962 the NZSAS group apparently split into two contingents. The first group, 1 Troop was deployed in the Ban Chanthuk area of central Thailand, working closely with the 'Wolf Hounds' of E Company 1 Battle Group of the 27th U.S. Infantry, engaged in what the official report on this operation described as 'jungle immediate action drills, ambushes, cordoning and searching a local village, live firing and recreational training'. In late August it moved to Chiang Mai in northwest Thailand, an 800-kilometre journey by road. The NZSAS detachments arrived equipped with a mere two landrovers, which only sufficed to transport one of these two troops, so were compelled to rely upon their American allies for additional vehicles. The second group, the less experienced 3 Troop, a unit that included '[a]bout ten' operatives, initially trained with US Green Beret Special Forces Team 312A at Udorn in north-eastern Thailand. After 1 Troop moved on to Chiang Mai, in late August 3 Troop replaced it, to undergo further training with the 'Wolf Hounds' in Ban Chanthuk. Finally, in early September, 3 Troop moved to southeast Thailand, undertaking border patrols, apparently joined at some point by the personnel of 1 Troop. At this point, in early September, some SAS members were given training in the use of a new model of American parachutes, which involved groups making practice drops within Thailand.[26]

According to historian Christopher Pugsley, the NZSAS detachment in Thailand 'lacked tactical cohesion … [and] its command elements were equally untidy and confusing'.[27] These features may have facilitated or even been the result of a covert operation that, unlike many such undertakings, apparently went unremarked or at least unchronicled then and later. One NZSAS officer, Brigadier Ian Burrows, later recalled that, though, he was not personally involved in the NZSAS secondment to Thailand and 'had only heard stories … it must have been a fairly gung-ho really cowboy-ish stuff'.[28] If one-half to two-thirds of the NZSAS group were in fact able to disappear into Laos for an extended period of time in August 1962, this characterization was perhaps even more accurate than Burrows realized. One suspects that this particular mission may well have been the second trip (2 August 1962) in my father's logbook, when the pilot was once again Squadron Leader Douglas Wood. It is worth noting that this was the only such trip on which the logbook contained an annotation that on this flight there had been a 'Radio Compass Malfunction!' My father confirmed to me that nothing of the sort had occurred. Given the particular sensitivity of this flight, with a British airplane ferrying covert operatives on a mission into supposedly neutralized Laos, this entry may have been a precaution, just in case word of this flight did eventually leak out. In the interests of plausible deniability, this would have allowed the British government to cite navigational difficulties as the reason for intruding into Laotian airspace. Tight security was evident in other aspects. My father recalled that as this group of men were waiting on the tarmac to board the aircraft, he attempted to chat with the team members, introducing himself and asking who they were. Those who replied all laconically informed him that their name was 'Smith'.

If these passengers were indeed NZSAS men, a relatively minor British and New Zealand intervention in Laos in the second half of 1962 seems to have been conducted so efficiently off record as to escape all scrutiny. Another possibility is that, despite what the British aircrew were told, some or all of these operatives were not in fact NZSAS personnel. In February 2019, after an earlier version of this chapter was published as a Cold War International History Project working paper, the historian Rhys Ball very generously undertook some follow-up inquiries in New Zealand, including interviews with surviving veterans from the deployment in Thailand. Two gave detailed accounts of their activities during this episode, in which they stated that they knew of no one in either NZSAS group who were involved in RAF parachute drops beyond the Thai border. One NZSAS veteran even speculated that these passengers might have been 'US advisors deployed with the Laotian Forces [who] were using helicopters, light aircraft and transporters, they were getting shot at'. Rhys Ball suggests that 'if New Zealanders were involved, it would have been only a couple-handful at the most, joining up with a group of British/American soldiers. It would not have been authorised'.[29] Whatever the truth of the matter, it seems that those organizing these flights wished the British aircrew involved to believe that they were delivering NZSAS personnel to Laos.

The subsequent trips involved dropping supplies to operatives down below. Whether these were munitions, food or medical equipment I do not know, as my father never specified. On at least one trip to Thailand (and beyond), from 14 to 15 August 1962, the aircraft seems to have flown two sorties over Laos. Possibly it first brought in supplies from Singapore, made an initial delivery run over Laos, and then picked up extra supplies at Don Muang, ferrying these up to Chiang Mai and then onward to Laos, before finally returning home to RAF Changi in Singapore. As described above, over these two days, on 14 August, a US reconnaissance fighter narrowly escaped being shot down over Laos and limped back to Don Muang.[30] With the future of all Western overflights of Laos now politically problematic, undertaking immediate additional supply drops to those on the ground would have been a logical response. Following one trip, though I am not sure which, the ground crew servicing one British Hastings that flew these missions discovered a bullet hole in the plane after it returned to Thailand, but that was the only hostile fire or response they encountered during these operations. The NZSAS group – with or without any 'Mr. Smiths' who might at some point have gone to Laos – were officially withdrawn from Thailand on 16 September, but these secret flights continued until late November. It is quite possible that they were delivering supplies intended to support other pro-American elements in the Laotian mountains.

If my father was the only 48 Squadron navigator involved, about which I am not clear, there also seems to have been a hiatus in these missions during the second half of October, which coincided with the Cuban Missile Crisis. I know that at the time news of the crisis became public and for several days thereafter, due to a mechanical failure, my father and the entire crew of the Hastings he was flying at that time were trapped in South Korea, waiting for the arrival of an essential spare part for the aircraft. Given the sensitivity of the Cuban situation, it seems possible that the Kennedy administration (and the British) wished to avoid any additional provocative measures with the potential to spark unrelated crises that might escalate existing problems. My father recalled that at this juncture the South Korean military was itching to invade North Korea, leading US officials in Seoul to insist on grounding the South Korean air force, while US troops stationed at the Demilitarized Zone turned their artillery southward, to deter any over-enthusiastic South Korean military units from attacking the North. With restraint the order of the day, the United States may have also temporarily suspended British covert missions over Laos.

My father suspected that a secret operation with significant diplomatic implications for British and US policy must have been agreed at the highest level, between British premier Harold Macmillan and John F. Kennedy. The two men did indeed meet earlier that year, when Macmillan visited the United States, to be hosted by Kennedy in Washington from 27 to 29 April 1962. Laos was definitely on the agenda, though the record of their discussions included in the *Foreign Relations of the United States* series makes no mention of any potential covert use of British aircraft.[31]

According to the CIA database, Marshal Sir Thomas Pike of the RAF, the British Chief of Air Staff, visited the United States from 13 to 19 April 1962, with meetings in Washington with Curtis LeMay, chief of staff of the US Air Force, and CIA director John McCone tentatively scheduled for the early part of his visit. It is possible that those involved may have provisionally set up this arrangement at that time, to be cleared by Kennedy and Macmillan at the end of the month.[32] Sir Thomas and his entourage were scheduled to travel onward to Britain's Pacific military base on Christmas Island (Kiritimati), to observe the first in a series of thirty-one US tests of nuclear explosive devices conducted on and around the island between April 25 and 30 October 1962. In another example of Britain's desire to win US goodwill through timely and useful favours, the Macmillan government permitted the Kennedy administration to mount these tests from the British facilities on the island, which had also hosted Britain's tests of atomic and hydrogen bombs in 1957 and 1958.[33] (As it happened, my father was on Christmas Island at this time, flying in one of the aircraft that observed the first US explosion. He and other crew members surreptitiously and against instructions shot cine film of the explosion, which was later developed in Singapore, and which I have watched.)

Sir Thomas and his wife and entourage then continued their thirty-one-day round-the-world tour of the United States and of RAF stations and installations, which up to that time had included Canada, Christmas Island, Fiji, the Solomon Islands, Papua and North Borneo, arriving from Hong Kong at RAF Changi on 3 May 1962. In Singapore, they spent a relatively restful three days as the guests of Sir Nigel Poett, commander-in-chief of Britain's Far East Land Forces, even relaxing for two hours on a boat tour of Singapore harbour, before continuing on to the remote Maldive Islands airbase of Gan, in the Indian Ocean.[34] This visit would have given Sir Thomas – who arrived a few days after Macmillan visited President Kennedy in Washington, on a visit during which the two men discussed a range of subjects, including Laos – the opportunity to brief Sir Nigel and other prominent military officers in Singapore on the proposed arrangement, including the need for complete confidentiality. At present, however, this is an entirely hypothetical scenario. If it is correct, it would mean that even before the May 1962 Nam Tha crisis and the conclusion of the Geneva Accords, top-level British and American officials were contemplating the possibility of covert British military assistance in Laos. Interestingly, moreover, on 3 May 1962, the date of Pike's arrival in Singapore, the British chiefs back in London held a meeting, the entire record of which still remains classified.[35]

Without more concrete evidence, of course, such guesswork remains only speculative. Captain John Sullivan, a pilot from the same squadron who often flew with my father, said that though he had not been aware of these particular flights, from time to time the unit did undertake secret missions. 'It's quite possible. We did occasionally do things like that,' he recalled. Consulted by a journalist from the London *Times*, Air Chief Marshal Sir Michael Graydon, chief of the British Air Staff from 1992 to 1997, likewise thought this story might be well-founded, stating: 'I cannot be sure that the flights described took place but the evidence is convincing; moreover, 48 Squadron was based at Changi up until 1967 and equipped at that time with the Hastings aircraft which, being four-engined, would have been better for operations in the rugged terrain of Laos than twin-engine aircraft.'[36]

Rumours notwithstanding, information on this episode seems to have remained classified for well over fifty years. British military aircraft and personnel were effectively functioning as an upmarket delivery or taxi service for the United States, albeit one of a highly specialized and skilled nature. It is worth remembering that at this point, the hostilities in Vietnam had not yet metastasized into the all-consuming conflict that they were to become, at least for the United States, nor was potential involvement in Vietnam or Laos anywhere close to as politically sensitive an issue domestically as it would subsequently become in Britain. Yet within Singapore, the fact that British aircraft based on the island were undertaking flights over Laos in defiance of the newly signed Geneva Accords might have had undesirable political and diplomatic ramifications for the position of the United Kingdom in what was then still a major British defence outpost in Asia. All involved, it seems, went to great lengths to keep these operations secret, with greater success than is often the case with covert missions. To date, even specialized histories of the war and negotiations over Laos by scholars and journalists who have been exceptionally diligent in tracking down sources and exploring elusive leads have failed to unearth tangible evidence of the involvement of British aviators. Or, indeed, of the NZSAS, if they were indeed represented among the Western military personnel who parachuted into Laos.

An undertaking of this nature must have left some kind of paper trail in its wake: in the United Kingdom, the United States, New Zealand and Thailand, and perhaps elsewhere. On the British side, Harold Macmillan and the top echelons of the Foreign and Commonwealth Office, the Ministry of Defence, and the RAF must have been consulted. Although their numbers must by this date be dwindling rapidly, the higher-level military officers at RAF Changi would undoubtedly have been aware that aircraft and aviators under their command were flying these missions. It is certainly intriguing that the minutes of at least one meeting of the British chiefs of Defence on what would seem to be a particularly salient date are still classified. To date, the impact of the Covid-19 pandemic has made it impossible to sift through all the potentially relevant files in the UK National Archives, if only to note what still remains closed to researchers.

In the United States, John F. Kennedy, W. Averell Harriman, Roger Hilsman, John McCone and William Colby were all likely to have known of these operations. Even though his extensive papers in the Library of Congress offer no clues on the subject, Harriman, who insisted on receiving weekly CIA briefings on operations in and over Laos and personally approved each CIA mission, was probably aware of the details. With or without authorization, some NZSAS personnel may have taken part in these operations, though how much if anything the New Zealand government knew about this is another intriguing question. And one may wonder whether the Thai authorities were officially informed – or even wished to know – where the British transport aircraft that collected men and supplies from military bases in Thailand were delivering these. Yet, however insistent all those involved were upon total secrecy, some kind of written record must have been made, and in all probability survived. Arrangements involving the use of official military aircraft to undertake covert operations at another nation's behest are not negotiated and implemented out of thin air. One has to hope that eventually, perhaps hidden away in files that are still currently closed, quite possibly on the grounds that opening them would reveal confidential diplomatic information that might still adversely affect one country's relations with another ally, additional solid information on this intriguing and obscure little episode will emerge.

Notes

1. The most comprehensive effort to explore the precise ramifications of British involvement is that of freelance journalist Gerald Prenderghast, *Britain and the Wars in Vietnam: The Supply of Troops, Arms and Intelligence, 1945–1975* (Jefferson, NC: McFarland, 2015). See also https://www.arrse.co.uk/community/threads/did-any-british-forces-serve-in-vietnam.
2. My father had spoken to me of these operations several times in the past. On a visit to Britain in March 2013, just over a year before his death, I took detailed notes from his flying logbook on these particular flights.
3. For an in-depth history of the Ho Chi Minh Trail, see John Prados, *The Blood Road: The Ho Chi Minh Trail and the Vietnam War* (New York: John Wiley, 1999).
4. Nicholas Tarling, *Britain and the Neutralisation of Laos* (Singapore: National University of Singapore Press, 2011); William J. Rust, *So Much to Lose: John F. Kennedy and American Policy in Laos* (Lexington: University Press of Kentucky, 2014), chs. 1–7; Nigel Ashton, *Kennedy, Macmillan, and the Cold War: The Irony of Interdependence* (Houndmills: Palgrave Macmillan, 2002), 1–5, 28–47; Laurent Cesari, *Les grandes puissances et le Laos, 1954–1964* (Artois: Artois Presses Université, 2007), 212–74.
5. Tarling, *Britain and the Neutralisation of Laos*, 269–70; Cesari, *Les grandes puissances et le Laos*, 219; Prados, *Blood Road*, 51–2; Rust, *So Much to Lose*, 138–9, 158–71.
6. Sir John Addis to Denis Warner, 19 June 1962, quoted in Tarling, *Britain and the Neutralisation of Laos*, 448. On Addis' opposition to the last-ditch efforts of right-wing Lao politicians, especially Phoumi Novasan, to prevent the conclusion of the Geneva Accords, which Addis countered by pressuring the American Embassy in Laos to cut off its financial subsidies to the Lao government, see also Dennis Warner, *The Last Confucian* (New York: Macmillan, 1963), 216–17.
7. Tarling, *Britain and the Neutralisation of Laos*, 364–400, 407–13, quotation from 379.
8. Tarling, *Britain and the Neutralisation of Laos*, 407–13, quotation from 412, 415; Rust, *So Much to Lose*, 118–22.

9   Timothy N. Castle, *At War in the Shadow of Vietnam: U.S. Military Aid to the Royal Lao Government 1955–1975*, rev ed. (New York: Columbia University Press, 1993), 47–9.
10 Castle, *At War in the Shadow of Vietnam*, 49–52; William Colby and Peter Forbath, *Honorable Men: My Life in the CIA* (New York: Simon and Schuster, 1978), 193–5; Cesari, *Les grandes puissances et le Laos*, 282–5; Rust, *So Much to Lose*, 165; Randall B. Woods, *Shadow Warrior: William Egan Colby and the CIA* (New York: Basic Books, 2013), 225–30.
11 Rust, *So Much to Lose*, 154–6.
12 Rust, *So Much to Lose*, 157–8.
13 Tarling, *Britain and the Neutralisation of Laos*, esp. 1–5; Prenderghast, *Britain and the Wars in Vietnam*, 108–9; Matthew Jones, *Conflict and Confrontation in Southeast Asia, 1961–1965: Britain, the United States, and the Creation of Malaysia* (Cambridge: Cambridge University Press, 2002), 22–6.
14 Rust, *So Much to Lose*, 155–6, quotation from 156; the full text of this meeting is given in 'Meeting on Laos', 15 August 1962, in Timothy Naftali, ed., *The Presidential Recordings: John F. Kennedy 1–3: The Great Crises*, 3 vols. (New York: Norton, 2001), 1:418–38, quotation from 425.
15 See esp. the chapters by Priscilla Roberts, Tracy Steele, Lu Xun, Glen Peterson, and Chi-Kwan Mark, in *Hong Kong in the Cold War*, ed. Priscilla Roberts and John M. Carroll (Hong Kong: Hong Kong University Press, 2016).
16 Prenderghast, *Britain and the Wars in Vietnam*, 50, 53–8, 103; Peter Busch, *All the Way with JFK? Britain, the US, and the Vietnam War* (Oxford: Clarendon Press, 2003), 6, 66–134, 202–3.
17 C.O.S. (61) 325, G. S. Cole, 'Current Plans for Intervention in Laos–Harriman Proposals', 14 September 1961, and Annexes I and II, DEFE/5/117, UK National Archives (UKNA); also C.O.S. (61) 336, G. S. Cole, 'Brief for Anzam Defence Committee Meeting – Agenda Item 6. Current Military Planning for Laos', 18 September 1961, and Annexes I and II, ibid. For further details of the talks between British and US officials at this time, see 'Plan for Southeast Asia', n.d., 'Analysis of U.S.-U.K. Talks on Contingency Plans for Laos', 26 August 1961, enclosing 'Last Version (British) of Terms of Reference, With U.S. Comments', and 'Report of Tripartite Officials Talks on Laos', Paris, 6 August 1961, Folder 1961–2: Laos Conf: Plans for Southeast Asia, Box 534, Series: Special Files: Public Service: JFK/LBJ Admin: Trips & Missions, W. Averell Harriman Papers, Manuscripts Division, Library of Congress, Washington, DC.
18 C.O.S. (61) 365, Chiefs of Staff Committee, 'Possible Military Intervention in Laos: Military Planning Discussions between the United States and United Kingdom Military Advisers and the United States and Australian military Advisers: Report by the Australian Chiefs of Staff Committee', 6 October 1961, DEFE/5/118, UKNA.
19 C.O.S. (61) 379, Chief of Staff Committee, 'The Implications for the United Kingdom in South East Asia of Participation in SEATO Operations in Laos', 16 October 1961, DEFE/5/118, UKNA. On the rather fluid situation in Malaya and Singapore at this time, with political leaders including Tunku Abdul Rahman of Malaya and Lee Kuan Yew of Singapore privately backing US operations in Indochina but for political reasons remaining publicly neutral, see Wen-Qing Ngoei, *Arc of Containment: Britain, the United States, and Anticommunism in Southeast Asia* (Ithaca, NY: Cornell University Press, 2019), ch. 4; Geoffrey C. Gunn, *Singapore and the Asian Revolutions*

(Macau: Geoffrey Gunn, 2008), 217–58; Jones, *Conflict and Confrontation in Southeast Asia*.

20 See Joshua Kurlantzick, *A Great Place to Have a War: America in Laos and the Birth of a Military CIA* (New York: Simon and Schuster, 2017); Roger Warner, *Back Fire: The CIA's Secret War in Laos and Its Link to the War in Vietnam* (New York: Simon and Schuster, 1995); James E. Parker Jr., *Codename Mule: Fighting the Secret War in Laos for the CIA* (Annapolis, MD: Naval Institute Press, 1995); Jane Hamilton-Merritt, *Tragic Mountains: The Hmong, the Americans, and the Secret Wars for Laos, 1942–1992* (Bloomington: Indiana University Press, 1993); Kenneth Conboy with James Morrison, *Shadow War: The CIA's Secret War in Laos* (Boulder, CO: Paladin Press, 1995); Castle, *At War in the Shadow of Vietnam*; Christopher Robbins, *Air America: The Explosive True Story of the CIA's Secret Airline*, 2nd ed. (London: Weidenfeld and Nicolson, 2012); Christopher Robbins, *The Ravens: The Men Who Flew in America's Secret War in Laos* (New York: Crown, 1987); Thomas Leo Briggs, *Cash on Delivery: CIA Secret Operations during the Secret War in Laos* (Rockville, MD: Rosebank Press, 2009); Allen Cates, *Honor Denied: The Truth about Air America and the CIA* (Bloomington, IN: iUniverse, 2011); Karl L. Polifka, *Meeting Steve Canyon . . . and Flying with the CIA in Laos* (Scotts Valley, CA: CreateSpace Independent Publishing Platform, 2013); Craig W. Duehring, *The Lair of Raven* (Scotts Valley, CA: CreateSpace Independent Publishing Platform, 2014); William E. Platt, *Low and Slow: Fly and Fight Laos* (Seattle, WA: WEP11345Books, 2015); Gerald Naekel, *Mohawks Lost: Flying in the CIA's Secret War* (Scotts Valley, CA: CreateSpace Independent Publishing Platform, 2016); John H. Fuller and Helen Murphy, eds., *The Raven Chronicles In Our Own Words: From the Secret War in Laos* (Lexington, KY: Chronicles Project, 2016); Reginald Hathorn, *Here There are Tigers: The Secret Air War in Laos, 1968–69* (Mechanicsburg, PA: Stackpole Books, 2008).

21 History Division, US Marine Corps, *Operation Millpond: U.S. Marines in Thailand 1961* (Quantico, VA: US Marine Corps, 2009).

22 The details of this operation are somewhat hazy, with different accounts offering varying versions. See John Prados, *William Colby and the CIA: The Secret Wars of a Controversial Spymaster* (Lawrence: University Press of Kansas, 2009), 350, n. 13; also Kenneth Conboy and Dale Andradé, *Spies and Commandos: How America Lost the Secret War in Vietnam* (Lawrence: University Press of Kansas, 2000), 46–7; Woods, *Shadow Warrior*, 148; John L. Plaster, *SOG: The Secret Wars of America's Commandos in Vietnam* (New York: Simon and Schuster, 1977), 22; John L. Plaster, *SOG: A Photo History* (Boulder, CO: Paladin Press, 2000), 10.

23 Personal communication, John Prados to Priscilla Roberts, 2 March 2018.

24 See the works by McGibbon, Rabel, Pugsley, Crosby and Ball cited in previous notes.

25 Ian McGibbon, *New Zealand's Vietnam War: A History of Combat, Commitment, and Controversy* (Dunedin, New Zealand: Exisle Publishing, 2013), 30. On the various calculations driving New Zealand policy towards Southeast Asia at this time, foremost among which were the desire to accommodate the United States, in order to justify the US security guarantee to New Zealand under the 1951 ANZUS Pact, see also Roberto Rabel, *New Zealand and the Vietnam War: Politics and Diplomacy* (Auckland: Auckland University Press, 2005), 44–5.

26 Christopher Pugsley, *From Emergency to Confrontation: The New Zealand Armed Forces in Malaya and Borneo 1949–1966* (Oxford: Oxford University Press, 2003), 185–8; Ron Crosby, *NZSAS: The First Fifty Years* (New York: Viking Penguin, 2009), 129–35; and Rhys Ball, 'The Platforms: An Examination of New Zealand Special Air

Service Campaigns from Borneo "Confrontation" to the Vietnam War, 1965-1971' (Ph.D. thesis, Massey University, New Zealand, 2009), 26-9, quotation from 28. Rutledge's recollections are quoted in Crosby, *NZSAS*, 130, and the official report in Crosby, *NZSAS*, 131-3.

27 Pugsley, *From Emergency to Confrontation*, 185.
28 Christopher Pugsley, Interview of Brigadier Ian Burrow, 23 October 1991, copy in New Zealand Defence Force Malayan Oral History Project, NZSAS Association Archive, Wellington, New Zealand, cited in Ball, 'The Platforms', 28.
29 Rhys Ball to Priscilla Roberts, 3 February 2019.
30 Rust, *So Much to Lose*, 157-8.
31 Memorandum of Conversation, Washington, April 28, 1962, Document 336, US Department of State, *Foreign Relations of the United States, 1961-1963*, Vol. 24: *Laos Crisis* (Washington, DC: Government Printing Office, 1994), 707-8.
32 Memorandum for Chief, FI Staff, DD/P, 'Visit of the Chief of the Royal Air Force, to the United States, 13 to 19 April', 16 March 1962, CIA Crest Database, https://www.cia.gov/library/readingroom/docs/CIA-RDP33-02415A000300090050-3.pdf.
33 Christopher Sandford, *Harold and Jack: The Remarkable Friendship of Prime Minister Macmillan and President Kennedy* (Amherst, NY: Prometheus Books, 2014), 152-3; Ashton, *Kennedy, Macmillan, and the Cold War*, 23, 201-6.
34 'S'pore Stop for RAF Chief on World Trip', *Straits Times*, 28 April 1962, http://eresources.nlb.gov.sg/newspapers/Digitised/Article/straitstimes19620428-1.2.113?ST=1&AT=search&k=sir%20thomas%20pike&QT=sir,thomas,pike&oref=article; 'RAF Chief Flies In', *Straits Times*, 4 May 1962; http://eresources.nlb.gov.sg/newspapers/Digitised/Article/straitstimes19620504-1.2.4; 'RAF Chief on Boat Ride', *Straits Times*, 6 May 1962, http://eresources.nlb.gov.sg/newspapers/Digitised/Article/straitstimes19620506-1.2.102.
35 The minutes of this meeting are missing from DEFE/4/145, UKNA.
36 Quoted in Lucy Fisher, 'Britain's secret Vietnam missions', *The Times*, 2 February 2019, 21.

Chapter 9

BRITAIN, THE US BICENTENNIAL AND THE
STATE VISIT OF QUEEN ELIZABETH II TO THE
UNITED STATES, 1976

Jonathan Colman

The 'special' Anglo-American relationship had lost some of its lustre within a few decades of its birth in the Second World War, largely because of diminishing memories of wartime cooperation, changing national priorities and Britain's declining ability to maintain a global defence presence alongside the United States.[1] In the 1960s, against a background of public hostility to the war in Vietnam, the government of Harold Wilson declined to send even a token number of troops to support the United States there and it reduced British military commitments in Asia. At the beginning of the next decade, Richard M. Nixon and National Security Adviser (later Secretary of State) Henry Kissinger focused on triangular *détente* with the Soviet Union and the People's Republic of China. Meanwhile, the government of Edward Heath was more concerned with joining the European Community (achieved in 1973) than in conspicuously close relations with the United States. Although Heath backed even the more controversial aspects of American efforts to secure favourable terms in Vietnam, his refusal in October 1973 to allow US aircraft to use British air space for resupplying Israel during the Yom Kippur War angered Washington, prompting Kissinger to ask an aide to compile a list of punitive measures that might be imposed on the British government. The suggestions ranged from delivering an oral reprimand to Ambassador Lord Cromer, through to dismantling the institutional pillars – nuclear and intelligence collaboration – of the Cold War 'special relationship'.[2] Upon resuming power in 1974, Harold Wilson sought to improve relations with the United States, but the effort was at odds with further cuts to Britain's global military presence.[3] The cuts reflected economic problems and, in the view of a White House adviser, a 'grasping little Englandism and a not-so-splendid isolationism' at large in the country.[4] Lord Cromer's successor, Peter Ramsbotham, reflected in his review of 1975 that 'our economic troubles, and particular the rapid growth of inflation, caused a deep shock here' and meant that British image took 'a considerable beating in the hands of the American media'.[5] Generally, there was a sense among the managers of US foreign policy that the alliance with Britain was a declining asset.

Winston Churchill, in constructing the 'special relationship' during the war, had emphasized the 'fraternal association of the English-speaking peoples' rooted in long-standing historical and cultural connections. Historians, such as H.G. Nicholas, tended to follow suit.[6] At least since the 1970s, though, scholars have taken generally a more critical approach to the Anglo-American relationship, attaching much greater importance to the influence of national interests than to sentiment and culture. Christopher Thorne, for example, wrote that the wartime alliance against Japan saw 'widespread suspicions on both sides of the Atlantic', with the Americans, for example, believing that Churchill 'and his smoothly-operating advisers were manipulating [...] America's military strategy and political intentions'. Britain and the United States' respective national interests 'could and did differ and conflict as well as coincide'.[7] However, there has been a renewed emphasis on the cultural dimension of the relationship, with John Dumbrell contending in a survey of the 1960s to the 2000s that 'shared culture has been an important and sustaining influence in the "special relationship" [...] as a practical and quotidian bolster to cooperation rooted in interests'.[8] Robert M. Hendershot has suggested boldly that 'sentimentality', in the form of 'shared memories of alliance and combat, shared democratic and historical heritage, shared language and literary traditions, shared cultural references, shared popular culture, and shared familial ties', has been 'key to the durability of the special relationship since 1945'.[9]

This chapter explores how in 1976 the British government participated in the US bicentennial celebrations as a way of reinvigorating the ties with the United States, through the invocation of Anglo-American heritage and values on a grand scale. The high point of British involvement, a state visit to the United States from the Queen Elizabeth and Prince Philip the Duke of Edinburgh, generated great acclaim but lasting benefits are harder to discern.[10] American policymakers were still inclined to look disparagingly upon British policies, as was evident in connection with Britain's continued economic problems. The chapter contributes to the literature about the impact of history, sentiment and values, and about the generally overlooked role of the monarchy, in the Anglo-American relationship.

The Americans as well as the British had reason to celebrate in 1976 beyond the bare fact that it was the United States' 200th birthday. Nixon's resignation over the Watergate affair in 1974 and the collapse of South Vietnam the following year had left the United States 'a confused and disillusioned society', according to Ramsbotham. There was a need to 'brighten the grey atmosphere, unify the country and concentrate the minds of Americans on older and more permanent values'.[11] For President Gerald Ford, the bicentennial celebrations would help to recapture the national pride and unity that existed (or were said to exist) 'before Vietnam', and would enhance the international image of the United States (Britain was not the only country with an image problem).[12]

Chaired by Lord Lothian and containing 'many people distinguished in Anglo-American relations', the British Bicentennial Liaison Committee (BBLC) was responsible for managing Britain's participation in the celebrations. It operated under the aegis of the Foreign and Commonwealth Office (FCO) with a healthy budget of £500,000.[13] The BBLC recommended that the funds for British participation in the bicentennial should be divided into three areas: a 'centre-piece' gift to the American government and people; an arts exchange fellowship programme; and various other projects. In response to an American proposal for something 'relating to the foundation of the United States as a democracy',[14] the BBLC conceived the idea of an original copy of Magna Carta. The British Museum, Lincoln Cathedral and Laycock Abbey each held originals, but the proposal met with opposition. John Killick of the FCO complained that it was not 'very original. One of the copies [...] was on loan to the US Public Archives for a year in the 1960s!'[15] The British Library, which was responsible for the British Museum's two copies of Magna Carta, rejected the BBLC's idea of making an outright gift, or a loan in perpetuity, of one of the manuscripts. Chairman of the British Library Board, Lord Eccles, maintained that providing 'the one good copy we possess' of the manuscript would generate 'a storm of protest' in Britain, and would give rise to 'immense pressure from other countries for the return of books, manuscripts and museum objects which would be claimed to be part of their national heritage. How would the Elgin Marbles and the Benin Bronzes fare if the policy advocated by your Committee was adopted?'[16] It was decided therefore to loan the copy of Magna Carta to the United States for a year, rather than surrendering it permanently.

Americans relished the historical significance – as generally perceived – of Magna Carta, with the State Department commenting that it was 'a milestone in providing guarantees against arbitrary power'.[17] A journalist for the *New York Times* believed that Magna Carta showed that the values behind the Declaration of Independence 'did after all owe a great deal to the people from whom independence was declared'.[18] The gift resonated too in the light of liberal concerns about the accretion of power to the executive branch. Historian and former John F. Kennedy adviser, Arthur M. Schlesinger, wrote in 1973 that the post-war presidents – above all Truman, Johnson and Nixon – 'almost came to see the sharing of power with Congress in foreign policy as a derogation of the Presidency. [...] The image of the President acting by himself in foreign affairs, imposing his own sense of reality and necessity on a waiting government and people' had become 'the new orthodoxy'.[19] Watergate compounded the sense of a presidency that rode roughshod over propriety.

While Magna Carta is regarded generally as a canonical text in the cause of liberty, it is fair to suggest that there was (and no doubt remains) widespread ignorance of the *actual* Magna Carta and its context. Christopher Greenwood has noted that in 1215 the barons

> had just invited a French invasion in support of their claims against King John. It was not the liberties of Englishmen against foreigners that was their priority, and the idea that they were early champions of human rights would have struck them as ludicrous. Most of them wanted to be left alone by the king so they could get on with persecuting and exploiting their tenants and serfs in peace.[20]

Greenwood added that 'Jefferson, Madison and the others' who wrote the Declaration of Independence and the US Constitution merely thought or at least 'pretended' that 'they were building on Magna Carta'. It is 'hardly surprising' that 'most people' have never read it: 'it is not one of those texts that trips off the tongue. There is nothing like the resounding words of the American Declaration of Independence'.[21]

Although the loan of Magna Carta to the United States in 1976 was intended to reflect the establishment of the United States as a democracy, the 'Founding Fathers' were by no means democrats; according to James Madison (1787), 'democracies have ever been spectacles of turbulence and contention; have ever been found incompatible with personal security or the rights of property; and have in general been as short in their lives as they have been violent in their deaths'.[22] Madison and the other framers of the Constitution established not a democracy but a republic, with the introduction of the universal franchise in the United States only after the First World War. Moreover, the newly fledged nation was not just a republic, but a slave-owning one. What matters, though, in the context of the bicentennial is that the popular perception of Magna Carta is an example of 'collective memory' or 'collective beliefs', which, according to Kathrin Bachleitner, are 'not concerned with history itself but only with its legacy as it is remembered and interpreted'.[23] Thus, the loan of Magna Carta, with its democratic associations, was an apt gift to a people who were well invested in the legend. At the presentation ceremony in Congress in June, with the US Air Force orchestra performing Kurt Weil's 'Ballad of Magna Carta', Lord Chancellor Elwyn Jones gave a speech extolling Magna Carta's importance for British and American democracy.[24]

There was another British gift for the bicentennial, a replica of the Liberty Bell cast by the same foundry in London that had made the original in the mid-1700s. Once more, legend prevailed over reality. What was first known as the Old State House Bell hung in the Pennsylvania State House in Philadelphia and was used for matters such as marking the death of prominent citizens and celebrating patriotic holidays. It became associated with American independence and gained its title only at the end of the 1830s, when abolitionists adopted it as a symbol.[25] Later, the bell's abolitionist and civil rights associations were largely forgotten.

British participation in the bicentennial celebrations could be taken for granted, but a state visit from the Queen could not. There were worries in the British government early in 1974 about her visiting the United States with Nixon, under the shadow of Watergate, still in office.[26] His resignation later that year solved that worry. There were further British reservations about the Queen visiting in a presidential election year. The electoral dimension was evident in the comments of J.G. Moreton at the Washington Embassy, who after taking soundings in the White House commented that in the light of the 'virtual certainty' that Jimmy Carter would win the Democratic Party nomination, Ford did not want 'Governor Carter to be present at any official function'.[27] More fundamentally, there were questions about whether Her Majesty should have anything at all to do with the bicentennial, because the Declaration of Independence was an explicit rejection not just of British rule in general but of the Crown in particular, with the charge that King George III had inflicted 'repeated injuries and usurpations' on the Americans. Moreover, the ensuing war was a major setback for Britain. In 1975 Chancellor of the Exchequer Denis Healey suggested in connection with a proposed bicentennial coin that 'there could be some public criticism of the introduction into the British coinage of a perpetual reminder of an event which [...] must be regarded as a defeat for British arms and prestige'. He even suggested, 'We might be accused of toadying' to the Americans.[28] Yet concerns along these lines did not prevent the Queen from participating in the bicentennial in the most prominent way, that is, by visiting the United States.

The exact timing of the visit touched on further sensitivities. In 1975 Ramsbotham raised the question of 'a bilateral Anglo-American occasion' on Independence Day, a suggestion which went down well with Ford and Kissinger, but it turned out not to be viable because 'we are being consistently told at lower levels that this would not be appropriate, either because the American people would not wish to share that day, or because President Ford will certainly be obliged, on 4 July, to attend American celebrations [...] and not be able to pay due attention to the Queen if she came' – not least because of the presence of other visiting heads of state and government.[29] It would never do to allow the Queen to be side-lined, even if it meant her arriving after the main day of celebration, so it was decided that she should visit the United States from 6 to 11 of July. Then there was the question of exactly where she should go. In 1975 Foreign Secretary James Callaghan recommended visiting 'the Mid-West, Deep South or even California. After all, the USA is more than the Eastern Seaboard'.[30] However, the latter had, as the FCO noted, 'great symbolical and historical significance with regard to the events of 1776'.[31] The final itinerary covered Washington, Philadelphia, New Haven and New York, with Boston being added under pressure from Massachusetts senator Edward Kennedy through the US ambassador in London, and a fellow Bostonian, Elliot Richardson.[32] Boston had been the main centre of resistance to the Crown in the run-up to 1776, and now there were worries about how the city's substantial Irish-American minority, which saw British rule in Northern Ireland as a form of colonial oppression, might respond to the Queen's presence.

There were those, especially in the British government's Department of Industry, who wanted the Queen to travel to the United States by Concorde, the Anglo-French supersonic passenger aircraft which was the subject of negotiations about establishing routine transatlantic flights. While Concorde offered the chance to show that Britain was capable of advanced technology (albeit in partnership with France), it also threatened to generate controversy. The consul-general in Philadelphia noted that while the city authorities there would support the Queen's arrival in Concorde, Governor [Milton] Shapp of Pennsylvania, 'an old and bitter enemy of Mayor [Frank] Rizzo of Philadelphia, is attempting' to have the landings of supersonic passenger aircraft 'banned throughout Pennsylvania'. It was feared that the Queen's arrival in Concorde might cause a public dispute between Shapp and Rizzo.[33] As Michael Palliser of the FCO explained to the Department of Industry's Sir Anthony Part, a storm over Concorde would undermine the purpose of the state visit, which was to 'to reassure Americans about our future'.[34]

Another British official suggested, in the light of plans for France's President Giscard D'Estaing to travel to the United States by Concorde for the bicentennial, that it would be 'gimmicky and contrived' if the Queen did the same.[35] France had provided decisive support for the 'Patriot' cause in the Revolutionary War, and, unlike Britain, had never fought against the United States, making it all the more desirable for the Queen to stay out of President D'Estaing's shadow. Thus, the royal party travelled in an exclusively British mode of transport, the royal yacht *Britannia*. The FCO explained to a member of the public who had complained about the decision to forego the use of Concorde that: 'The use of *Britannia* is an appropriate and imaginative way of visiting the bicentennial cities, three of which, New York, New Haven, and Boston ... lie on the seaboard.'[36]

As John W. Young has commented, 'today, monarchs, except in the few cases where they hold executive power, no longer travel abroad to engage in diplomatic negotiations or gather intelligence, but they can have a real impact on diplomatic life'. In the British case, foreign journeys by members of the royal family 'have become more frequent occurrences, helping to support diplomatic ends'.[37] The FCO noted that a state visit from the Queen is 'a big gun in the armoury of our external diplomacy'. It represented an important aspect of the bilateral relationship and 'says something important to the rest of the world about Britain. More than most other Heads of State, the Queen symbolises the continuity and stability of national life, persisting through changes of government'.[38] Her great interest in the business of state and the Palace's access to a wide range of official documents made her very knowledgeable about domestic and international affairs – perhaps more so than many ministers and politicians. Writing in 2013, Philip Murphy commented that the Queen 'has been privy to the inner workings of government for longer than any other contemporary public figure in the UK'.[39]

As Princess Elizabeth, she and Prince Philip had visited Washington in 1951 at the invitation of President Truman soon before the death of her father, George VI, in 1952. She returned there in October 1957 for a state visit. There is evidence that she saw this visit as a way of easing the post-Suez Crisis strains in Anglo-American relations. Worried about the damage to the international relationship that he had done so much to foster, Winston Churchill had written to President Eisenhower in November 1956, prompting the American leader to express his grave concerns about the ill-conceived Anglo-French-Israeli military operation which was then unfolding in Egypt. Churchill showed the reply to the Queen. Although her response was somewhat elliptical, she appeared to recognize that there was scope for her to help repair the damage to Anglo-American relations: 'It is most interesting to learn [of Eisenhower's] appreciation of the situation, and I hope it means that the present feeling that this country and America are not seeing eye-to-eye will soon be speedily replaced by even stronger ties between us.'[40] Prime Minister Harold Macmillan did not want the visit to follow too obviously and closely on the heels of the Suez crisis, but he was confident all the same about 'the value to the alliance of a visit to the United States by the Queen'.[41] With the aid of Macmillan's emollient efforts and against a background of Soviet advances in the arms race, the state visit of late 1957 created a climate of goodwill that helped put

9. *Britain, the US Bicentennial and the State Visit* 159

the difficulties over Suez to one side. As the British consul in Detroit, Michigan (a traditionally anti-British state), explained shortly afterwards, the visit

> has done a great deal by implication to re-emphasise the special relationship of Britain in relation to the United States and the differences between her position and that of other Allied countries. In this respect it has contributed directly towards redressing the effect of the Suez crisis, which reduced Britain's status and strengthened the tendency to put her on a level with any other country.[42]

It was no coincidence that Macmillan followed up the state visit with his own trip to Washington to sign a Declaration of Common Purpose with President Eisenhower. Perhaps with the 1957 precedent in mind, Peter Ramsbotham (who was based at the UN in New York that year) anticipated in 1975 that the next state visit would have a special role in strengthening 'the Anglo-American connection'.[43]

The British were deeply committed to the success of the Queen's bicentennial trip to the United States. According to a presidential aide, 'tremendous emphasis is being placed on this visit [...] with no doubt considerable interest on the part of the Queen. [...] the British want it to be as effective as possible'.[44] The Washington Embassy carried out detailed planning in coordination with the Protocol Department of the State Department. Working with the Protocol staff was straightforward but dealing with the White House was a different matter, as Ramsbotham noted: 'Its somewhat cumbrous bureaucratic machine seemed incapable of focusing attention on the visit until very late in the day, partly, no doubt, because of preoccupations with electoral matters and earlier State visits.' Fortunately, once Mrs Ford 'and her staff gave their full attention' to the Queen's 'visit, it was obvious that they would spare nothing to make it a success'. The organizational demands were substantial, underlining just how much time and effort the British invested in the visit. As Ramsbotham noted in relation to the Washington programme, there was 'the logistical nightmare [...] with the Embassy itself, in the space of just over twenty-four hours, being the site of a Press Reception for 120, a Staff Reception for 1200, a Heads of Mission Reception for 300, a State Dinner for 86, and a post-Dinner reception for 1400'.[45]

As if to consolidate 'collective beliefs', the Queen put an expedient 'spin' on the American Revolution. In her speech in Philadelphia (where she presented the copy of the Liberty Bell), for example, she depicted the War of Independence as a victory for both Britain and the United States on the grounds that it taught the British a much-needed lesson in statesmanship which enabled the later development of 'special' transatlantic bonds. Overlooking the periods of war and tension that punctuated the next hundred years or so, she maintained that lasting Anglo-American friendship was soon in place and emphasized how the two countries had lined up with one another in the world wars of the twentieth century 'in defence of our common heritage of freedom'.[46]

The main set-piece event was the White House dinner on 7 July, with over 200 guests, and which was televised live to a wide audience. The after-dinner entertainment included Bob Hope and Telly Savalas, both known favourites of

Her Majesty. In Ramsbotham's words, 'It is perhaps kind to draw a veil over the other part of the entertainment by a group of pop singers', who performed 'a vivid electronic tone-poem' called 'Muskrat Love', about the courtship of these animals.[47] Later in the visit, in a seeming acknowledgement of Britain's relative decline, and in a nod – or perhaps a tip of the crown – to presidential power, the Queen showed deference to her hosts. A journalist noted that 'At Newport, Rhode Island, where the President and Mrs Ford were tendered a second dinner by the Queen, Mr Ford was formally piped aboard' *Britannia*, an honour usually reserved for the Queen and other sovereigns in uniform.[48] The Queen herself was said to have initiated the precedent, which was intended 'to highlight the respect for the position of the President of the United States by the United Kingdom'.[49]

Her Majesty's impressive grasp of current events allowed her to excel in the behind-the-scenes discussions. The recently appointed ambassador to the United Kingdom, Anne Armstrong, commented that when Her Majesty spoke with Ford and Kissinger in the *Britannia*, it was clear just 'how knowledgeable she is in foreign affairs [...] They were talking about the complexities of Cypriot politics, which, of course, is Byzantine; all sorts of subjects, and the Queen was an expert on all those subjects'.[50] The 1976 visit facilitated further exchanges among politicians and diplomats on such matters. Callaghan's successor as foreign secretary, Anthony Crosland, lunched with Kissinger at the State Department 'and had a useful exchange with him', which they resumed the next day.[51]

In contrast to some of the sentimentality, there was a hard-headed commercial dimension to the visit, in the form of a 'Sea Day' in *Britannia*, which took place while the Queen was on shore in Washington. Reflecting the growing priority the British government had attached to commercial diplomacy in recent years, the goal was to use '*Britannia* to contribute towards Anglo-American relations in the area of direct exports, invisibles, and inward investment',[52] by hosting an event for numerous American 'decision-makers' in economic and financial fields.[53] The impact of the sea day is hard to measure, but it was a worthy attempt to boost Anglo-American trade and economic links, and to improve US perceptions of the British economy. The only dark spots in the otherwise-bright picture of the state visit were a couple of public protests, but they amounted to little. In Philadelphia, 'a hellfire preacher and a band of followers [...] objected to the omission of a Biblical phrase' on the copy of the Liberty Bell.[54] Worries about Irish-American demonstrations in Boston led Governor Michael Dukakis (perhaps with British prompting) to call out the National Guard, but, in the words of a reporter, 'the protests were peaceful and limited to a few banners and Irish green, white and orange tricolours'.[55]

While the Queen was always been reticent about expressing her personal views,[56] she had every reason to be happy about her visit to the United States in 1976, given how the American public and politicians alike greeted her with enthusiasm and respect. According to Anne Armstrong, the Queen's presence during the bicentennial celebrations was 'the most successful visit of a head of state to our country ever [...] I've never seen such crowds greet any visitor to America'.[57] Ramsbotham quoted Elliot Richardson: 'There is something here of great value and strength, not measurable in terms of GDP or units of power ... something which you, through the Queen, can give to the world.' Ramsbotham, the main organizer, waxed lyrical: the visit was 'a triumph. Its impact on the most senior Americans and on the general public alike was extraordinary.' The fact that Americans were 'flattered and impressed that the Queen should come to join with them in celebrating the loss of the American colonies', and the 'mystique of the monarchy', helped to explain the large crowds who turned out to see the royal couple. The state visit 'will long be remembered as the high point of foreign participation and can only be of the greatest value in reaffirming and strengthening British ties with the United States and in enhancing our standing in American eyes'.[58]

The state visit made its mark on American domestic politics. A White House analyst noted soon after that although Jimmy Carter had criticized President Ford on various foreign policy topics, 'bicentennial visits by political leaders of the Western Alliance and by Queen Elizabeth' had largely eliminated criticisms of Ford's handling of intra-alliance questions.[59] The visit by the Queen, who had a popular appeal that none of the other bicentennial guests could equal, therefore boosted Ford's prospects of victory in the presidential election in November – although it was not enough to deny Carter success.

There were some British observers who took a dim view of their country's participation in the bicentennial. The writer of a letter to *The Telegraph* was 'bored to distraction by the American bicentennial junketing and, reflecting upon the ineptitude and bungling of our present-day politicians, it is a source of mystery to me why we in England should choose to celebrate the equal idiocy and incompetence of George III and Lord North'.[60] A proposed Early Day Motion in Parliament reflected concern about the neglect of the role of the United Empire Loyalists, who had maintained their allegiance to the Crown during the War of Independence and in settling Canada and the Caribbean afterwards.[61] The FCO responded that 'we have forgotten neither the victors nor the vanquished' in the Revolutionary War, 'but rather have celebrated the birthday of one of our closest allies'. The FCO also had to address the argument that the American rebellion in 1776 paralleled Rhodesia's illegal declaration of independence in 1965 under a white minority government, which had since resisted British and Commonwealth pressure to adopt black majority rule.[62] But according to the FCO, there were distinct differences 'between the America of 200 years ago and the situation in Rhodesia today'. The 'Queen's message to the people of the United States and the British Government's policy on Rhodesia' were perfectly consistent because:

> Her Majesty stated that Britain had lost the American colonies because we lacked the statesmanship [...] 'to know the right time and the manner of yielding what is impossible to keep'. That is the lesson we are trying to impress on the white minority in Rhodesia.[63]

Critics may not have found this persuasive. There were those within the FCO who also had reservations about the state visit. Writing in August, E.N. Larmour dismissed the idea of royal 'mystique' by suggesting that while the Queen 'does a highly competent and professional job with great skill', the monarchy did not possess 'supernatural qualities'. The impact of even the most successful royal state visit was strictly limited: 'The goodwill is largely personal, and I doubt that it has any lasting political, still less commercial, effect. I do not believe that the Queen's bicentennial visit to the United States, which was obviously a great personal success,' would improve American perceptions of Britain.[64] Indeed, the warmth of the shared bicentennial celebrations and the 'mystique of the monarchy' did not stop American policymakers from taking a cold and realistic stance in September when Britain had to turn to the US-dominated International Monetary Fund (IMF) for rescue. As Kathleen Burk has commented, 'Britain was humiliated [...] this was the first case of a modern industrial country turning to the IMF for this type of loan [...] she was treated the same as any other indigent country'.[65] While the IMF's willingness to provide support showed at least some confidence in Britain's future, perceptions of a declining ally were not easily banished. Early in 1977, the FCO's Ramsay Melhuish suggested that 'our current public image throughout the United States remains poor', in large part due to economic problems.[66] Furthermore, as we have seen, Britain was not the only foreign country to celebrate the American bicentennial; a Washington official expressed particular satisfaction at 'the overwhelming German celebration' of the event.[67] This was an era in which the US government was inclined to look to the prosperous Federal Republic as the most important European ally, which meant that ritualistic British references to the World Wars were not always going to strike the right note.

In sum, the success of Britain's contribution to the US bicentennial celebrations relied in large part on admiration for the Queen, and on the binding effect of historical legend, in a context in which feelings mattered more than facts. The visit suggests that if heritage and history are to be invoked as a means of strengthening the Anglo-American relationship, they need to have a rather loose relationship with the *actual* past, which has been as much about clashing interests as hands-across-the-sea cordiality. History, culture and shared values may well, as some scholars have claimed, hold a significant background importance for relations between Britain and the United States, but the 1976 jamboree in which the British exploited these factors vigorously brought only a short-lived euphoria that appeared to have little or no lasting influence on the general relationship.

Anglo-American bonds have had their ups and downs since 1976, and so too has the British monarchy because of various controversies and scandals. A London newspaper suggested in 2021 that 'A distinction has to be made between the liberal elites who clearly have a disdain for the monarchy for ideological reasons' and most 'ordinary Americans who like the Queen'. A poll in the United States rated the Queen's favourability at 68 per cent, a level not recorded for a US president since support peaked for George W. Bush in the aftermath of the 9/11 attacks.[68] However, royal visits are likely to be of less value as a means of furthering the Anglo-American relationship, because much of the affection and respect for the monarchy has centred on Elizabeth in particular, and because the proportion of Americans who can trace a British or even European background has long been diminishing. It does not help in an era of heightened sensitivity to injustice against minorities that the royal family is a historical beneficiary of colonialism and slavery.[69] Unfortunately for Britain on occasions when the Anglo-American relationship might need a shot in the arm, future monarchs are unlikely to generate as much enthusiasm in the United States as did Queen Elizabeth II in 1976.

Notes

1 The author would like to thank Lubna Qureshi and Jack Southern for their helpful comments on a draft of this chapter.
   On Anglo-American difficulties in the late 1960s and the 1970s, see e.g. Jonathan Colman, A 'Special Relationship'? Harold Wilson, Lyndon B. Johnson and Anglo-American Relations 'at the Summit', 1964–68 (Manchester: Manchester University Press, 2004); Saki Dockrill, Britain's Retreat from East of Suez: The Choice between Europe and the World? (Basingstoke: Palgrave, 2002); Sylvia Ellis, Britain, America, and the Vietnam War (Westport: Praeger, 2004); Catherine Hynes, Heath, Nixon and the Year of Europe: The Year That Never Was (Dublin: University College Dublin Press, 2009); Klaus Larres, Uncertain Allies: Nixon, Kissinger, and the Threat of a United Europe (New Haven: Yale University Press, 2021); Thomas Robb, A Strained Partnership? US–UK Relations in the Era of Détente, 1969–77 (Manchester: Manchester University Press, 2011); and Andrew Scott, Allies Apart: Heath, Nixon and the Anglo-American Relationship (Basingstoke: Palgrave, 2011).
2 Springsteen to Kissinger, 'Possible Pressure Points on the UK', 30 October 1973, Foreign Relations of the United States (hereafter FRUS) 1969–1976, Volume E-15, Part 2 Documents on Western Europe, 1973–1976, document 226. https://history.state.gov/historicaldocuments/frus1969-76ve15p2/d226. The Heath government strove for neutrality in the conflict. The US government did not implement any of the suggested punishments – perhaps because the British, although struggling internationally, were still an important ally. See Scott, Allies Apart, 166–95. See also Jonathan Colman, '"What Now for Britain?" The State Department's Intelligence Assessment of the "Special Relationship", 7 February 1968', Diplomacy and Statecraft 19 (June 2008): 350–60, for a detailed and positive US assessment of the British contributions to the partnership by the late 60s.
3 Kissinger to Ford, 15 November 1974, FRUS 1969–1976 Vol E-15, Part 2, document 233. https://history.state.gov/historicaldocuments/frus1969-76ve15p2/d233 See also Thomas Robb, 'The "Limit of What Is Tolerable": British Defence Cuts and the "Special Relationship," 1974–1976', Diplomacy & Statecraft 22, no. 2 (2011): 321–37.
4 Lord to Kissinger, 29 January 1975, FRUS 1969-1976 Vol E-15, Part 2, document 236. https://history.state.gov/historicaldocuments/frus1969-76ve15p2/d236.
5 Ramsbotham to Callaghan, 'Annual Review for 1975', 31 December 1975, FCO 82/652, National Archives, Kew. Unless otherwise noted, all documentary evidence cited is from this archive.
6 H.G. Nicholas, Britain and the United States (London: Chatto and Windus, 1963).
7 Christopher Thorne, Allies of a Kind: The United States, Britain and the War against Japan, 1941–1945 (Oxford: Oxford University Press, 1978), 700, 701.

8   John Dumbrell, *A Special Relationship: Anglo-American Relations in the Cold War and After* (Basingstoke: Hampshire, 2001), 2.

9   Robert M. Hendershot, *Family Spats: Perception, Illusion and Sentimentality in the Anglo-American Special Relationship, 1950–1976* (VDM Verlag Dr Muller, 2008), 3. See also idem and Steve Marsh, eds., *Culture Matters: Anglo-American Relations and the Intangibles of 'Specialness'* (Manchester: Manchester University Press, 2020).

10 On the international role of monarchy, including state visits, see Gaynor Johnson, 'Royal Diplomacy: British Preparations for the State Visit of King George VI and Queen Elizabeth to the United States, June 1939', *Diplomacy and Statecraft* 32, no. 2 (2021): 330–50; Philip Murphy, *Monarchy and the End of Empire: The House of Windsor, the British Government and the Postwar Commonwealth* (Oxford: Oxford University Press, 2013); idem, 'State Visits Made and Received by the British and other European Monarchical Heads of State' in *The Role of Monarchy in Modern Democracy: European Monarchies Compared*, ed. Robert Hazell and Bob Morris (London: Hart Publishing, 2020), 133–48; Frank Prozascha, *Eagle and the Crown: Americans and the British Monarchy* (New Haven: Yale University Press, 2016); John W. Young, *Twentieth Century British Diplomacy: A Case Study of Diplomatic Practice, 1963–1965* (Cambridge: Cambridge University Press, 2008), 170–95.

11 Ramsbotham to Crosland, 30 July 1976, FCO 82/681.

12 Address by President Ford in New Orleans, 23 April 1975, *Foreign Relations of the United States* (hereafter *FRUS*) *1969–1976, Volume XXXVIII, Part 1, Foundations of Foreign Policy, 1973–1976* (2012), document 57. https://history.state.gov/historicaldocuments/frus1969-76v38p1/d57. See also Hallvard Notaker, Giles Scott-Smith, and David J. Snyder, eds., *Reasserting America in the 1970s: US Public Diplomacy and the Rebuilding of America's Image Abroad* (Manchester: Manchester University Press, 2016), and M. Todd Bennett, 'The Spirits of '76: Diplomacy Commemorating the US Bicentennial in 1976', *Diplomatic History* 40, no. 4 (September 2016): 695–721.

13 Dales to Rucker, 11 November 1974, FCO 26/1729.

14 Meeting on 8 January 1975 to discuss American bicentennial activities, FCO 26/1735.

15 Killick minute, 18 February 1975, FCO 26/1735.

16 British Library Board to Marquess of Lothian, 6 March 1975, FCO 26/1729. The Elgin Marbles – now known as the Parthenon Sculptures – is a collection of ancient Greek sculptures and architectural details. The 'Benin Bronzes' (made of brass and bronze) are a group of sculptures which include elaborately decorated cast plaques, commemorative heads, animal and human figures, items of royal regalia, and personal ornaments. See https://www.britishmuseum.org/. On the controversy over the former collection, See Christopher Hitchens, Robert Browning, and Graham Binns, *The Elgin Marbles* (London: Chatto and Windus, 1987). See also Christine Sylvester, *Art/Museums: International Relations Where We Least Expect It* (London: Routledge, 2009).

17 Kissinger to Ford, undated, Briefing Books 1958–80, Executive Secretariat, Entry A1-5037, RG 59, NARA II, College Park, Maryland.

18 Robert B. Semple Jr., 'Britain and Bicentennial: Old Ties and New Tours', *New York Times*, 27 May 1976.

19 Arthur M. Schlesinger, *The Imperial Presidency* (Boston: Houghton Mifflin, 1973), 206.

20 Christopher Greenwood, 'Magna Carta and the Development of Modern International Law', *Israel Law Review* 49, no. 3 (2016): 437.

21 Greenwood, 'Magna Carta', 436. See also David Starkey, *Magna Carta: The True Story behind the Charter* (London: Hodder and Stoughton, 2015).
22 James Madison, 'The Same Subject Continued: The Union as a Safeguard against Domestic Faction and Insurrection', Federalist No 10 (23 November 1787).
23 Kathrin Bachleitner, 'Diplomacy with Memory: How the Past Is Employed for Future Foreign Policy', *Foreign Policy Analysis* 15 (2019): 493. David Reynolds points out that the 'term "collective memory" has not gone unchallenged; some argue that it involves a misleading metaphorical transfer from individual consciousness to public attitudes'. The terms 'myth or, more neutrally, "collective beliefs" … seem more effective than 'memory' in conveying the constructedness of such communal attitudes'. See David Reynolds, 'International History, the Cultural Turn and the Diplomatic Twitch', *Cultural and Social History* 3, no. 1 (2006): 84.
24 Ramsbotham to Crosland, 'Magna Carta: The British Parliament's Bicentennial Gift to Congress', 1 July 1976, FCO 82/677.
25 Eric Foner, *Give Me Liberty: An American History*, 5th ed. (New York: Norton, 2017), 458–9.
26 Ramsbotham to Crosland, 30 July 1976, FCO 82/681.
27 Moreton (Embassy Washington) to Moore (Buckingham Palace), 17 June 1976, FCO 82/680.
28 Healey to Wilson, 17 October 1975, PREM 16/1153.
29 Ramsbotham to FCO, undated, FCO 26/1738; Young, *Twentieth Century Diplomacy*, 191.
30 Ferguson to Curle, 8 December 1975, FCO 73/237.
31 Curle to Private Secretary, 9 December 1975, FCO 73/237.
32 R.W.H du Boulay to Private Secretary, 16 December 1975, FCO 73/237. On the ambassadorships of Richardson and his successor (March 1976) Anne Armstrong, see Alex Spelling, 'Ambassadors Richardson, Armstrong and Brewer, 1975–81', in *The Embassy in Grosvenor Square: American Embassies to the United Kingdom, 1938–2008*, ed. Alison R. Holmes and J. Simon Rofe (Basingstoke: Palgrave Macmillan, 2012), 189–214.
33 Washington (Ramsbotham) to FCO, undated, FCO 73/237.
34 Palliser to Part, 14 April 1976, FCO 73/237.
35 Smith to Thomas, 9 January 1976, FCO 82/678.
36 Hughes to Wheble, 9 June 1976, FCO 82/680.
37 Young, *Twentieth Century Diplomacy*, 170.
38 Memorandum, 'Value of State Visits', undated, FCO 49/701.
39 Murphy, *Monarchy and the End of Empire*, 11–12. She also 'knows more state secrets than any living person', as Richard J. Aldrich and Rory Cormac point out in *The Secret Royals: Spying and the Crown, from Victoria to Diana* (London: Atlantic Books, 2021), 2.
40 Peter Boyle, ed., *The Churchill-Eisenhower Correspondence, 1953–1955* (Chapel Hill and London: University of North Carolina, 1990), 213; Montague Browne, *Long Sunset: Memoirs of Winston Churchill's Last Private Secretary* (London: Cassell, 1995), 213–14; Murphy, *Monarchy and the End of Empire*, 68. See also Aldrich and Cormac, *The Secret Royals*, 419–26.
41 *FRUS 1955–1957 Western Europe and Canada XXVII* (1992), https://history.state.gov/historicaldocuments/frus1955-57v27/d252 Note 3.
42 Moss (British Consul in Detroit) to Caccia (Washington Embassy), 25 October 1957, FCO 372/7469.

43 Peter Ramsbotham, Annual review for 1975, 31 December 1975, FCO 82/652.
44 Jack Marsh, 'Memorandum for the Record', 13 June 1975, Gerald R. Ford Presidential Library and Museum, https://www.fordlibrarymuseum.gov/library/document/0067/1563326.pdf.
45 Ramsbotham to Crosland, 30 July 1976, FCO 82/681.
46 'The Queen Says 1776 Taught Britain a Lesson', *The Times*, 7 July 1976, 5.
47 Ramsbotham to Crosland, 30 July 1976, FCO 82/681.
48 'The Grand and the Simple', *The Economist*, 17 July 1976, 36, 39.
49 'The Queen Breaks with Tradition', *The Telegraph*, 12 July 1976, 10.
50 Interview of Anne Legendre Armstrong by Ann Miller Morin, 7 October 1987, Association for Diplomatic Studies and Training, Arlington, Virginia. The Cyprus issue pitted NATO members Greece against Turkey, and the Turkish invasion of the island had led to Cyprus' partition in 1974. https://www.adst.org/OH%20TOCs/Armstrong,%20Anne%20Legendre.toc.pdf?_ga=2.148046578.458154844.1628876845-949063370.1628876845.
51 Ramsbotham to Crosland, 30 July 1976, FCO 82/681.
52 Booth to Statham, 13 February 1976, FCO 82/678. On commercial diplomacy, see John Fisher, Effie G. H. Pedaliu, and Richard Smith, eds., *The Foreign Office, Commerce and British Foreign Policy in the Twentieth Century* (Basingstoke: Palgrave, 2016).
53 Booth to Consul-General, 30 March 1976, FCO 82/678.
54 George Gordon, 'A City Goes Wild to See the Queen', *Daily Mail*, 7 July 1976.
55 Nicholas Comfort, 'The Queen Hears Boston Attack on Race "Cowards"', *Daily Telegraph*, 12 July 1976, 11.
56 The Queen's reticence about expressing her own views might be seen as the personal counterpart to the institutional secrecy surrounding the British monarchy; the Freedom of Information Act (2000) 'exempts information if it relates to communications with or on behalf of the Sovereign'. See Murphy, *Monarchy and the End of Empire*, xi–xiii.
57 Brian Connell, 'Mrs Anne Armstrong: From the Nixon Crash to the Court of St James', *The Times*, 27 September 1976.
58 Ramsbotham to Crosland, 30 July 1976, FCO 82/681.
59 Janney and Ahern to Eagleburger, 'Foreign Policy Issues for Election Year 1976', 21 July 1976, *FRUS 1969–1976 XXXVIII, Part 1, Foundations of Foreign Policy, 1973–1976* (2012), document 81. https://history.state.gov/historicaldocuments/frus1969-76v38p1/d81.
60 Letters to the Editor, 'Celebration', John M. Gwynne Hughes, *The Telegraph*, 12 July 1976, 10.
61 The United Empire Loyalists were those settlers who remained loyal to the Crown during the Revolutionary War and left the thirteen colonies afterwards. Some settled in the Caribbean but most (50,000 or so) went to Canada where they helped to settle what later became the provinces of Quebec, Ontario and New Brunswick.
62 See Carl P. Watts, *Rhodesia's Unilateral Declaration of Independence: An International History* (Basingstoke: Palgrave, 2012).
63 Hughes to Thomas and Price, 'Loyalty: Early Day Motion No. 504', 13 July 1976, FCO 82/677. On the British monarchy's involvement with the Rhodesian/Zimbabwean question, see Murphy, *Monarchy and the End of Empire*, 100–6, 137–42.
64 E.N. Larmour, 'Value of State Visits', 16 August 1976, FCO 49/701.

65 Kathleen Burk, *Old World, New World: The Story of Britain and America* (London: Little, Brown, 2007), 629. See Also Kathleen Burk and Alec Cairncross, *Goodbye, Great Britain: The 1976 IMF Crisis* (New Haven: Yale University Press, 1992), and Richard Roberts, *When Britain Went Bust: The 1976 IMF Crisis* (London: OMFIF, 2016).
66 Melhuish to Edmonds, 20 January 1977, FCO 82/725.
67 Tuchman to Brzezinski, 23 November 1977, *FRUS 1977–1980 XXX Public Diplomacy* (2016), document 107, https://history.state.gov/historicaldocuments/frus1977-80v30/d107 (emphasis in the original). See also *A Final Report to the People Volume 1. The Bicentennial of the United States of America* (Washington, DC: USGPO, 1977), 227.
68 David Charter, 'Royals Still at Heart of Special Relationship', *The Times*, 13 March 2021, 41.
69 See Laura Clancy, *Running the Family Firm: How the Monarchy Manages Its Image and Our Money* (Manchester: Manchester University Press, 2021), especially Chapter 7, 'Megxitting the Firm: Race, Postcolonialism and Diversity Capital', 194–221.

Chapter 10

REAGAN'S INCOHERENCE: NICARAGUA IN THE REAGAN DOCTRINE AND THE END OF THE COLD WAR

David Ryan

The Reagan administration persisted in its demonization of the Sandinistas until the transition to George H.W. Bush, who quickly sought to remove the controversial issue from the top agenda.[1] In the apogee of Reagan's vision, the Sandinistas were depicted in extreme terms. On 1 May 1985, he signed an executive order finding 'that the policies and actions of the Government of Nicaragua constitute an unusual and extraordinary threat to the national security and foreign policy of the United States and hereby declare a national emergency to deal with that threat'.[2] How such a small country of Central America acquired a mythological status as a threat to the United States emerged through a 'credibility trap'. Once the threat had been defined in Reagan's rhetoric, once the administration had made its commitment to support the *contras,* counterrevolutionaries seeking to overthrow the Sandinistas, once the rhetoric was embellished to such an extent and delivered in august public settings, it was difficult to back away, especially after defeat in Vietnam, breaking commitments to the South Vietnamese regime. US credibility relied on demonstrable *resolve.*[3] The neoconservatives sought to reverse the 'Vietnam syndrome' and its inhibitions on US power. Moreover, Alexander Haig, the first secretary of state, thought, in Wilentz's words, 'a splendid little war in El Salvador ... would end the Soviet's adventurism and reverse the Vietnam syndrome'.[4] Reagan too thought that 'El Salvador is a good starting point. A victory there could set an example.' [5] The rationale was that the Sandinistas persisted in supplying the Salvadoran rebels, *Frente Farabundo Marti para la Liberacion Nacional* (FMLN), with aid from Cuba, in turn backed by the Soviet Union. In their minds, the 'domino theory' was alive and well.

Domestic politics also affected Reagan's Nicaragua policy. For the neoconservatives, in Westad's words, the region 'became the preferred domestic battleground for imposing a new and more offensive approach to the Cold War'.[6] A victory there, against a small and relatively easy target, could demonstrate US resolve. As the national security advisor, Robert McFarlane, testified to Congress:

We had just witnessed a five year period where the Soviet Union tried out a stratagem of sponsoring guerrilla movements that would topple moderate regimes, and install their own totalitarian successor, and they had phenomenal success … in Angola, Ethiopia, South Yemen, Cambodia, Afghanistan, Mozambique, [and] Nicaragua. … If we could not muster an effective counter to Cuban-Sandinista strategy in our own backyard, it was far less likely that we could do so in the years ahead in more distant locations … We had to win this one.[7]

Yet on a broader canvas, Reagan had promised to confine Marxism-Leninism to the 'ash heap of history' in an address to the British House of Commons in 1982, and he had labelled the Soviet Union the 'evil empire' in an address to Evangelists in 1983.[8] The 'triumphalist' turn in the Reagan historiography worked within the framework advanced by Francis Fukuyama on the end of History.[9] Reagan's strategy was purportedly pivotal to that end. There were prominent celebrants of the US role at the end of the Cold War, even as it took them by surprise. The 'triumphalist' and 'vindicationalist' interpretations either directly attributed the strategic narrative to Reagan's vision, the application of pressure through a military build-up and the Reagan Doctrine on the 'periphery', which added to the costs of an already faltering Soviet system.[10] Yet, as Alan Dobson pointed out in his analysis of NSDD 75, the document 'does not seem to meet even the criteria for prevailing over, never mind defeating, the Soviets'. It was ultimately a strategy for change, a renewed relationship and *accommodation*.[11] NSDD 75 outlined a strategy of pressure and accommodation with the Soviet Union from as early as 1983, concluding, that officials should avoid making statements to encourage expectations, and 'the U.S. must demonstrate credibly that its policy is not a blueprint for an open-ended, sterile confrontation with Moscow, but a serious search for a stable and constructive long-term basis for U.S.-Soviet relations'.[12] The Reagan 'reversal' pre-dated Gorbachev, yet the 'strategy' was one of engagement not triumph or vindication.[13]

Nevertheless, as the communist regimes of Eastern Europe collapsed and the Berlin Wall fell, events that were unanticipated and unpredicted, Cumings writes, 'with it came a further, more general collapse in the critical function'. There were many ways to understand the events, but 'in the U.S. the dominant tendency was to turn these events into a celebration of ourselves'. Despite all the costs, and US support for authoritarian regimes throughout the world, the narrative was filtered through the Cold War paradigm, and largely forgotten.[14] The popular accounts, and here Judt takes aim at Gaddis's *The Cold War*, were stories, 'as seen from America, as experienced in America, and told in a way most agreeable to many American readers'.[15]

The traditional narrative welded the Reagan 'strategy' on the Soviet Union to the Reagan Doctrine in the Third World, primarily focused on Afghanistan and Nicaragua.[16] Yet, Soviet engagement frequently involved more costs than benefits. The Soviets were in a desperate occupation of Afghanistan, seeking ways out from an early stage.[17] Yet bogging them down in Afghanistan also provided another opportunity to make that territory 'their Vietnam' as Zbigniew Brzezinski, President Carter's national security advisor, suggested;[18] that strategy of attrition and the costs of war associated with the *Mujahedin* resistance contributed to Moscow's difficulties and demise. There is little doubt on this as even Gorbachev recognized the Afghan 'bleeding wound' in 1985.[19]

The Soviet commitment to Nicaragua was at a very different scale. It largely contributed to the regime's defence, but aid was totally inadequate in terms of any Sandinista offensive capacity, in the region or against the United States. The Soviet supply, primarily of HIND helicopters and T-55 tanks, post-dated the origins of the *contra* and CIA/NSC-directed efforts against Managua. US Lieutenant-Colonel John Buchanan testified to a congressional committee in September 1982, that he had enough military experience, 'to see that a smoke screen was being laid'. Soviet supplied weapons to Nicaragua were wholly inadequate for offensive purposes; the T-55 tanks were severely constrained by local topography. He concluded 'that the Reagan administration is distorting the facts in order to justify covert operations aimed at overthrowing the Sandinistas'.[20] Wayne Smith, the ranking US diplomat in Havana, equivalent to ambassador, established that the Cubans had suspended shipments to Nicaragua to facilitate diplomatic solutions. Smith later wrote two books casting severe doubt on administration claims on Cuba and the Soviet Union: *The Closest of Enemies* and *The Russians Aren't Coming*.[21] In a report commissioned by the State Department, Carl Jacobsen noted, 'all too many US claims proved open to question'. Moreover, 'the counterweights to Soviet influence are also more far-reaching and varied than sometimes appreciated'. West European aid, UN agencies, Japanese and Latin American support and trade rose as Washington withdrew.[22]

Despite the convolutions of the Iran-Contra affairs, the state of emergency declared in 1985 remained in place, and support for the *contras* persisted, even after Mikhail Gorbachev signalled a retreat from the region[23] in particular and from Soviet support for revolution abroad, essentially, a reversal of the Brezhnev Doctrine of 1968. A cartoon depicted Gorbachev sailing away from Cuba waving a handkerchief, leaving 'Robinson Castro' stranded on the island.

There was an incoherence in the Reagan search for 'accommodation' and a 'constructive long-term' relationship with Moscow while simultaneously supporting the ineffective *contras* at a high political cost. The commitment to the *contras*, outside of any traditional 'Cold War' framework, also provided a foil against the conservatives and neoconservatives[24] accusations of 'appeasement' as Reagan pursued engagement with Moscow – a far cry from 'evil empires' and historical embers. Engagement with the United States assisted Gorbachev in his internal struggles.

In a way Reagan's conservatism represented a rebuff to the 'Sixties', yet he was also a product of that decade and its culture. As Moser writes, he represented 'the triumph of Andy Warhol: famously unable to distinguish between image and reality, metaphor and object, experience filmed and experience lived'.[25] Reagan's lack of engagement was legendary. His presidency was largely a scripted one – advisors feared leaving him alone with the press. He shied away from settling internal disputes, sometimes, especially on Nicaragua, allowing contradictory agendas to work in tandem. His grasp of detail was widely disparaged. Moser extends: 'His presidency was defined by this notion of politics as role-playing, as camp: "the farthest extension, in its sensibility, of the metaphor of life as theatre." For Reagan, Joan Didion wrote, "rhetoric was soon understood to be interchangeable with action."'[26] But action to what end?

Though 'covert' operations had been ongoing since 1981, and earlier, the Reagan Doctrine[27] was not publicly defined till 1985, sometime after the Reagan 'reversal'. Comfortably re-elected Reagan's 1985 State of the Union identified its purpose: 'We must stand by all our democratic allies. And we must not break faith with those who are risking their lives – on every continent, from Afghanistan to Nicaragua – to defy Soviet-supported aggression and secure rights which have been ours from birth.'[28] The term 'Reagan Doctrine' is attributed to Charles Krauthammer writing in *Time* magazine in April 1985.[29]

This depiction was in line with Reagan's earlier geopolitical illusion, that 'The Soviet Union underlies all the unrest that is going on. If they weren't engaged in this game of dominoes, there wouldn't be any hot spots in the world.'[30] Beyond Afghanistan the suggestion that US policy on Nicaragua impacted Soviet demise is difficult to accept. While US operations were directly pertinent in Afghanistan where the costs to the Soviet Union were considerable, by comparison the Soviet expenditure on Nicaragua was meagre. There was support, but of negligible quantity. Nevertheless, Gorbachev was also keen to cut that bill in 1987. Moscow derived little from the commitment. Soviet 'New Thinking' wanted to minimize the costs of Third World engagement. In 1987 Gorbachev wrote that it was preposterous to think that the Sandinista revolution was the 'work of Moscow and Cuba'. He referred to the US line as a 'standard, hackneyed ideological substantiation for an undeclared war against a small country'. He found it 'preposterous' to think that Nicaragua '"threatens" US security', and that Soviet bases were to be built there, 'bases which the Americans supposedly know about but which I … have never heard of'.[31]

Shortly after the end of the Cold War, the editor of *Diplomatic History*, Michael Hogan, commissioned a range of historians to reflect on the transition. Walter LaFeber asked the question: 'An End to *Which* Cold War?' In his essay he suggested that the conflation of several different objectives into *the Cold War* masked US motivations. He advanced the notion of four separate but concurrent cold wars: the conventional clash between the United States and Soviet Union, another between the United States and recalcitrant Third World regimes, another Transatlantic *cold* war on the future shape of Europe, and finally a cold war within the United States, centred on its identity, and the tensions between a more democratic, open and individualistic country or one driven by the 'national security state' with its limits on domestic liberty.[32] While Reagan placed Nicaragua in the conventional Cold War, it was also pertinent to the US struggle with the 'periphery' and domestic politics, especially for those disgruntled with Reagan's 'reversal' on Moscow.

After the Vietnam War it was imperative to reassert US leadership and credibility. A key 1982 National Security Strategy paper, NSDD 32, spoke of bringing about 'a fundamentally different East-West relationship by the end of the decade'. It sought to 'contain and reverse the expansion of Soviet control and military presence throughout the world'. Yet it noted that direct confrontation with the Soviets was unlikely, even if they were more confident because 'they may expect that the burden of avoiding such a confrontation is shifting to the U.S'. NSDD 32 combined elements of the Nixon Doctrine and the Reagan Doctrine: 'In contingencies not involving direct Soviet aggression our strategy is to rely on regional states to the extent possible.' And 'the U.S. will rely primarily upon indigenous forces to protect mutual interests, with U.S. assistance as appropriate'. The Sandinistas were at once an *extraordinary* threat, *and* one that could be addressed through proxy forces. 'Where quick termination of conflict cannot be assured, the U.S. must confront adversaries with the prospect of a prolonged, costly, and ultimately unwinnable war.'[33] The *remedy* fell far short of the *prescription*.

In 1983 NSDD 75 developed the strategy further. Dobson reached the following conclusion:

> Reagan intended to negotiate with the Soviets from a position of strength. He expected his overall strategy, including the array of economic tactics deployed, to bring the Soviets to constructive agreements rather than to vanquish them and their system. He neither intended nor expected the early demise of the Soviet Union to be the direct consequence of his actions.[34]

Despite the Reagan administration conflation of Nicaragua with the 'central' Cold War, Soviet interests and objectives were relatively limited.[35] The US assertions on Soviet policy in Nicaragua frequently caused tensions even as Washington sought to improve relations. Ironically, the Bush administration maintained the line, even as it relegated the importance of Nicaragua. When Bush, James Baker, Brent Scowcroft and Robert Gates met Eduard Shevardnadze, amongst others, in September 1989, the Soviet foreign minister made it clear they supported the Nicaraguan elections and that they were not sending weapons. Bush responded that they were 'troubled by the flow of substantial arms shipments into Nicaragua'.[36] The issue persisted into the December 1989 Malta summit. Bush alleged that arms still flowed to Nicaragua, that there was little evidence of 'New Thinking' in the region, that Moscow had not pressed Managua. They noted that the Soviets 'claim to have suspended arms shipments to Nicaragua' but they noted they remained deeply troubled by the continued shipments from the Soviet bloc, Cuban and Nicaraguan support for the FMLN. At the first plenary session Gorbachev told Bush that there were more political parties in Nicaragua than the United States, there was pluralism, that the Sandinistas were not real Marxists, in fact he thought it 'laughable' to characterize them as such. The core problems were socio-economic. Moscow supported the elections and would abide by the UN-monitored results. Finally, Gorbachev stated, 'I want to emphasize again: we are not pursuing any goals in Central America. We do not want to acquire bases or strongholds there.'[37] Despite this, the Bush administration also sought normalization with the Sandinistas on the assumption that they would win the 1990 elections.[38]

Back in 1983, NSDD 75 concluded that United States should 'avoid generating unrealizable expectations for the near-term progress in U.S.-Soviet relations. At the same time, the U.S. must demonstrate credibly that its policy is not a blueprint for an open-ended, sterile confrontation with Moscow but a serious search for a stable and constructive long-term basis for U.S.-Soviet relations.'[39] The strategy included a three-pronged approach of containment and 'over time revers[ing] Soviet expansionism' through competition; to diminish the power of the ruling elite, and 'to engage the Soviet Union in negotiation to attempt to reach agreements which protect and enhance U.S. interests' consistent with reciprocity. Hence, it had to be clear that 'unacceptable behavior' would incur costs to the Soviets, but that 'genuine restraint in their behavior would create the possibility of an East-West relationship that might bring important benefits for the Soviet Union'. They identified an opportunity to advance the strategy at the point of transition from Brezhnev to his successors,[40] even though things moved slowly till Gorbachev's arrival. Crucially, on the Third World, the document stated, 'The U.S. must rebuild the credibility of its commitment to resist Soviet encroachment on U.S. interests and those of its Allies and friends' by effectively supporting those willing to resist Soviet pressure or initiatives. In Central America aid would be provided to offset 'Cuban destabilizing activities'.[41]

They would contain and reverse Soviet expansion and to promote evolutionary change, though they realized it could not be accomplished quickly. 'The coming 5–10 years will be a period of considerable uncertainty in which the Soviets may test U.S. resolve by continuing the kind of aggressive international behavior which the U.S. finds unacceptable.' Finally, contrary to the triumphalist seam in the historiography, NSDD 75 clearly sought improved relations, not the demise or defeat of Moscow. The United States would not adjust its policies to the 'Soviet internal conflict', *but* 'rather try to create incentives (positive and negative) for the new leadership to adopt policies less detrimental to U.S. interests'. And 'The U.S. will remain ready for improved U.S.-Soviet relations if the Soviet Union makes significant changes in policies of concern to it.'[42]

But therein lies the predicament between illusion and reality, between rhetoric and action. Nicaragua was crucial to Reagan's credibility. Within a short period after the production of NSDD 75, Reagan delivered his famous speech to a joint session of Congress in an increasingly desperate attempt to extract *contra* funding. The problem was that in 1982 Congress had passed the Boland amendment, basically cutting off funding to the *contras* for the 'purpose of overthrowing' the Sandinistas, 'or provoking a military exchange between Nicaragua and Honduras'. The amendment attached to the Defense Appropriations Act for 1983 was accepted 411-0, largely because a more restrictive proposal by Representative Tom Harkin would have cut aid entirely.[43] While the *contras* wanted to overthrow the Sandinistas, the administration maintained the pretence that their primary purpose was to 'interdict' the flow of weapons from Cuba through Nicaragua to the FMLN, who sought to overthrow the US-supported, brutally atrocious regime. By 1986 the International Court of Justice found against Washington in a case brought by Nicaragua, concluding that any arms transfers were not 'on a scale of any significance, since the early months of 1981, or that the Government of Nicaragua was responsible for any flow of arms at either period'.[44] US intelligence analyst, David McMichael, testified to the International Court of Justice that there had been no detection of arms shipments during his employment at the CIA starting in March 1981. US Ambassador to Nicaragua, Lawrence Pezzullo and Wayne Smith in Cuba, as well as US Ambassador to El Salvador, Robert White, all questioned administration claims.[45] Subsequently, Congress was divided on *contra* aid, US public opinion was consistently sceptical of Reagan's characterization of the problem[46] most Latin American countries and most European allies were wary of the elevated rhetoric depicting a dire threat to the United States. Nevertheless, playing a role, with an earnest delivery, Reagan made preposterous assertions. On 27 April 1983, he informed a joint session of Congress, that NATO could not trust the United States if it could not prevail against the Sandinistas. He stated, 'If we cannot defend ourselves there, we cannot expect to prevail elsewhere. Our credibility would collapse, our alliances would crumble ... We have a vital interest, a moral duty, and a solemn responsibility.'[47] Yet to placate fears of direct US intervention, he assured the representatives, 'let me say to those who invoke the memory of Vietnam: There is no thought of sending American combat troops to Central America'.[48] He went on to claim that if the Nazis had placed importance on the Caribbean – so should the United States. The Democratic Party response painted a very different picture. Senator Christopher Dodd acknowledged that Reagan had bought his audience 'to their feet', but he had not 'brought them to their senses'. He rejected Reagan's portrayal of the situation, affirming:

> If Central America were not racked by poverty, there would be no revolution. If Central America were not racked with hunger, there would be no revolution. If Central America were not racked with injustices, there would be no revolution. In short, there would be nothing for the Soviets to exploit. But unless those oppressive conditions change, that region will continue to seethe with revolution – with or without the Soviets.[49]

Reagan's position on Nicaragua and the Soviet Union was incoherent. He sought improved relations with the Soviets, but certainly not its demise, simply a transformation from the stale Cold War. As Dobson argues, despite his vehement criticism of détente, he ended up practising something very similar;[50] accommodation, negotiation, aid and integration. Yet none of this characterised the US–Sandinista relationship.

Even before Gorbachev there were considerable differences on Sandinista identity, objectives and its links to Moscow. The administration made extravagant assertions, there was extensive propaganda[51] that advanced images of Soviet-supported *dominos*. As though the differences and tensions between Havana and Moscow over Central America were unimportant, the 'axis' stretched from Moscow, through Cuba, to Sandinista Nicaragua. El Salvador was usually the end of the domino row, but some documents produced by administration extremists included a threat to the Panama Canal, and the oil fields of Mexico.[52] Reagan traded on geographic proximity reminding audiences that 'El Salvador is nearer to Texas than Texas is to Massachusetts. Nicaragua is just as close to Miami, San Antonio, San Diego and Tucson as those cities are to Washington, where we are gathered tonight.'[53]

If Sandinista intentions divided Washington, there were still questions on 'capability' with their limited supply of weapons, no doubt effective for domestic operations, they were hardly a match for the US-supplied states, El Salvador, Honduras, Guatemala. The Sandinistas did not launch any offensives on other countries; their export of weapons ceased early in the Reagan period. Yet Reagan's rhetoric persisted, undiminished through the decade. But he was working against the tide of US opinion.[54]

That public scepticism fed into congressional politics to interrupt Reagan's objectives. The voting pattern on *contra* aid was inconsistent, swayed by 'swing voters'. Depending on the year, aid was advanced and then cut off or restricted. The inconsistency caused considerable trouble for the *contras* largely stationed on the Honduran side of Nicaragua's northern border. Hence, the administration turned to 'third' countries and individuals to provide aid, setting off the Iran-Contra affair.[55]

Simultaneously, Gorbachev took the initiatives centred on domestic transformation through *glasnost* and *perestroika*, and foreign policy innovation through 'New Thinking'. In Archie Brown's *The Human Factor* on the end of the Cold War, his first paragraph takes us from Reagan's 'evil empire' speech to him strolling around Red Square with Gorbachev. Asked, if he still believed the Soviet Union was an evil empire, he replied, 'No. That was another time, another era.'[56] But Reagan's mindset had not changed on Nicaragua. Ironically, the Iran-Contra investigations left Reagan a lame-duck president. In his final two years 1987 and 1988, superpower summitry and accommodation with the Soviets provided a salve for his reputation. The president was protected from the direct brunt of Iran-Contra, but many in his administration were indicted on criminal charges, later pardoned by George H.W. Bush.[57]

Brown argues that many believe the Cold War came to an end through Soviet capitulation after the economic and military pressures applied by the Reagan administration. Despite Soviet expansion in the early Cold War, the military gap was clearly in favour of the United States. By the 1980s a rough parity had set in; both powers could destroy the other. Given this position, Brown argues based on Soviet documents that Soviet leaders and officials like Yuri Andropov, Konstantin Chernenko, Andrei Gromyko or Dmitry Ustinov saw no need for domestic reform or concession to the United States or NATO on defence issues; 'the notion that the Reagan administration left the Kremlin leaders no option but to change the system and seek accommodation with the US and its allies is as questionable as it is popular'.[58]

The earlier era of détente was strained by Soviet and Cuban operations in Angola, Reagan's charged rhetoric on accommodation and appeasement in his run against President Gerald R. Ford in 1976, amongst other issues. The Soviet invasion of Afghanistan in 1979 signalled transformation. The 'second cold war'[59] brought considerable tension and fear to the proverbial streets of many a European city. Yet Reagan's hard-line of rhetorical confrontation also brought relative isolation. After 1983, and especially evident in NSDD 75, a rhetorical turn on the Soviet Union, paved the way for summitry and negotiation on a range of issues, not least arms control. But to necessarily attribute the collapse of the Soviet Union to Reagan's initiatives is to enter into a problem of causality, just because X precedes Y, it does not mean that X caused Y.[60] Certainly, there were significant changes introduced by Gorbachev by the end of the decade; but they were also conducted in the context of economic decline and domestic difficulties. Conservative Soviet rearguard resistance to reform accentuated Gorbachev's predicament. Garthoff argues, 'During the first half of the 1980s, Reagan's political stance was the dominating factor in the relationship between the two countries. In most of the second half of the decade, Gorbachev's initiatives were of primary importance.'[61] Still, it does not follow that Reagan caused the Gorbachev revolution, or that Reagan caused the Soviet demise.

Gorbachev advanced initiatives centred on reform and reduced foreign policy costs. He read the European anxiety well and advanced numerous arms proposals, routinely rejected by the Pentagon. The columnist, Andrew J. Glass, was worried that the United States could not assure Moscow of its good will, 'the national security apparatus in the White House remains thoroughly fractionated. With so many hawks and pseudo-hawks flapping about in the Reagan aviary, it will muster all the administration's ability in diplomatic falconry merely to fashion a cogent response to the latest Soviet initiative'. Simultaneously, Gorbachev's popularity soared across Europe, while Reagan was mired in Iran-Contra.[62] In that regard Graebner and colleagues argue, 'Gorbachev rescued Reagan from the near-disaster of the Iran-contra affair.' Gorbachev took the diplomatic initiatives; he was less politically and ideologically constrained than Reagan; 'the Third World issues that troubled Washington were not his concern.'[63] Ultimately, as Shultz out-manoeuvred administration ideologues, a hard-line Nicaragua policy could appease.[64]

The Reagan military build-up and its soaring costs extended US difficulties. Gorbachev realized that Moscow gained little from military expansion in the Cold War; Afghanistan was not an exception. Invasion, intervention in Angola, or military support for the Sandinistas did not pay Moscow with tangible benefits. Conversely, the Reagan build-up did not pressure the Soviets to retract or withdraw, that came with the realization of the costs of over-extension. Gorbachev extracted ideology from Soviet foreign policy, imbuing it with realism. He later wrote, 'it seemed that our aged leaders were not especially worried about our undeniable lower living standards, our unsatisfactory way of life, and our falling behind in the field of advanced technologies'.[65] On the US side, the military build-up not only distorted the priorities of the domestic economy, accelerating the 'speculative boom', generating 'unprecedented federal deficits', economic stagnation and a relative decline in productivity, even as Japan and Germany advanced productivity generated through research and domestic electronic production. The costs of the US build-up deeply impacted its economy and relative position in the world, exacerbating US relative decline, which began in the late 1950s or early 1960s.[66]

Ironically too, when Secretary of Defense, Caspar Weinberger, delivered his famous speech in November 1984,[67] laying out criteria for the use of and deployment of US military forces, Shultz characterized it as a form of appeasement.[68] Weinberger realized that the costs of intervention or engagement of the 'Soviets' far outstripped the benefits; moreover, the criteria were advanced to stay the hands of those who wanted to take the war to Nicaragua.[69] The phenomenal US military power could not, did not and subsequently would not lead to transformations on the ground in Nicaragua.

To a large extent, the memory of the Vietnam War, perhaps epitomized in Weinberger's speech but echoed throughout US media, culture and opinion polls, contained Reagan on Nicaragua.[70] Henry Kissinger, the former secretary of state and national security advisor for Presidents Nixon and Ford, captured Reagan's essential incoherence on Nicaragua. On the assumption he was talking off the record, he stated that the policy made no sense – it could not be that Nicaragua posed such a vital threat to the United States while simultaneously peanuts were thrown at the problem: covert aid in small amounts, CIA operations to mine the harbours of the country, economic pressures and isolation, diplomatic intransigence. Kissinger wondered, 'when you meet the President … you ask yourself, how did it ever occur to anybody that he should be governor, much less president?' *Contra* aid was inadequate to the supposed threat. Kissinger observed, 'Either the analysis is wrong, or the solution is wrong. It cannot be that it is such a vital interest and it can be solved with $100 million.'[71] NSDD 75 created linkage in the US strategy; concessions and accommodation would be contingent on Soviet behaviour, especially in regional conflicts. It was customary, in speech after speech, to enumerate and itemize Soviet-supported troop numbers and military levels in a range of countries.[72] Despite the linkage of NSDD 75, ultimately the Reagan administration did not condition the superpower summitry on Soviet international operations, which contradicted their earlier position.[73] Instead, regional issues were brought up as a stick to beat Gorbachev and Shevardnadze with, repeatedly. Gorbachev set the timetable for Soviet withdrawal from Afghanistan and extended the thought that they could 'untie' the Afghan knot and 'use it as a basis of untying other regional knots'. Reagan and his people were not willing to go there. Gorbachev clearly signalled a desire to act with Washington on these issues, but observed, 'the US seemed uninterested or unwilling to work cooperatively'.[74] This, despite the 'Reagan reversal' and the option to focus on shared interests.[75]

For Beth Fischer the seeming intransigence is explicable. Even though Reagan had reversed his position on the Soviet Union, he persisted with the Reagan Doctrine. The United States, largely through the CIA, continued to dole out aid to the *contras* and the *mujahedin* and to those resisting 'communism' in other peripheral conflicts. While it might appear contradictory, she argues that Reagan's 'logic' was frequently contradictory. Driven by the fear of nuclear war he changed his views on the Kremlin, 'but he did not revise his assessment of communism'. Reagan downplayed the notion that Gorbachev and his associates were communists because he held a shared interest with them on international security and nuclear war.[76] Engagement with Gorbachev, or for that matter Deng Xiaoping, did not seem to trouble him; they were *now* more pragmatic communists. Yet the Sandinistas continued to animate his animosity. Extraordinary, if you think about it. First, much assessment would suggest that the Sandinistas included a wide-ranging set of ideological positions and if anything were at that stage, nationalist above all.[77] Second, Reagan had spent so much time and political effort creating what would become the 'rhetorical trap' by insisting that the Sandinistas, the FMLN, the Cubans, were all part of the Soviet grand designs.

Eventually Gorbachev took the stratagem to the global stage. Western Europe was central to his reforms and economic revival. Diplomatic engagement and trade would produce a more profitable relationship. His intention was to work against the divisions created by Winston Churchill at Fulton, Missouri with the 'Iron Curtain' speech of 1946.[78] At the United Nations in 1988, making a virtue out of necessity, he advanced further initiatives on arms reduction but also advanced a message clearly critical of the Reagan Doctrine. He had also recognized the futility of excessive defence expenditures and ongoing Soviet support for revolutions abroad.[79] In his *Memoirs,* Gorbachev wrote, 'the speech to the UN must [be] a "Fulton in Reverse", "anti-Fulton"'.[80] Just as the Iron Curtain had helped to solidify the image of the Cold War, in 1988 Gorbachev sought to transform global perceptions, transcending the '1946 model'.[81] He berated the Stalinist assumptions on global socialism, but also noted the US assumptions 'about the probability of open Soviet military aggression was unrealistic and dangerous'. War was unlikely, Stalin did not want it and 'the country was exhausted and destroyed; it had lost tens of millions of people, and the public hated war'.[82]

Gorbachev was more far-sighted than his adversarial comrades. Perhaps the warning on the future was in part aimed at a less secure Bush. Bush and his advisors were less convinced of the transformation in the Soviet Union. Both Robert Gates and Brent Scowcroft cast doubt on the depth of real change; Scowcroft indicated that the Cold War was not over. Bush had been reaching out to the hard-liners in the Republican Party during his 1988 campaign; he could say little on accommodation for risk it might be cast as appeasement. Hence, Georgy Arbatov advised Gorbachev to simply act unilaterally – inconvenient for some in the United States, it would grip world attention.[83] George Shultz, observed, 'if anybody declared the end of the Cold War, he did it in that speech. It was over'. Dramatic cuts, thousands of tanks, 500,000 personnel and withdrawals from East European countries were announced. As Gorbachev insisted on the 'deideologization' of interstate relations,[84] Reagan was open to it in the case of Moscow, but not for Nicaragua. The speech was received with a 'storm of applause' more than mere courtesy.[85] The *New York Times* lined up his speech with those of Woodrow Wilson's Fourteen Points in 1918, and with Roosevelt and Churchill's 'Atlantic Charter' of 1941, not since then, they opined 'has a world figure demonstrated the vision Mikhail Gorbachev displayed yesterday at the United Nations'.[86]

Reagan's ideologues had jumped ship. Richard Pearle, Fred Ikle and then Weinberger left the administration in 1987. The more moderate principals, led by Shultz, joined by Colin Powell as national security advisor ushered in a new tone of cooperative engagement. Eduard Shevardnadze reciprocated. Graebner and colleagues observed that the 'pragmatists who dominated the foreign policy establishment understood that the United States not only had no choice but to coexist on the planet with the U.S.S.R. but also wielded no authority to change the Soviet system'. They saw Gorbachev as a durable leader who recognized the costs of the arms race.[87]

Fischer, Leffler and others have clearly argued that Reagan's desire to engage the Soviet leadership preceded Geneva 1985 or the arrival of Gorbachev. When Andropov died on 9 February and Chernenko took over Reagan began a correspondence to facilitate relations 'characterized by constructive cooperation' the letter two days into Chernenko's ill-fated term related. Reagan concluded, 'we do not seek to challenge the security of the Soviet Union and its people'. He added that neither he nor the American people held offensive intentions towards the Soviets. He concluded, 'Our constant and urgent purpose must be … a lasting reduction of tensions between us. I pledge to you my profound commitment to that end'.[88]

Reagan did not necessarily want to end the Cold War in so far as his understanding of it was global, but he did want better relations with the Soviets. While there were plans and initiatives, often contradicted by others in the incoherent administration, to improve relations, as stated in NSDD 32 and 75, there were no plans for the disintegration of the Soviet Union. The events of 1989 were entirely unimaginable. Not uncontested, but with growing vigour the message was to improve relations. Gorbachev fought hard to revive the Soviet Union and the communist system, yet the patient he sought to resuscitate on the operating table failed to regain consciousness.[89] Fischer concludes, 'Gorbachev's role in bringing about the end of the cold war cannot be overstated. The manner in which he revolutionized Soviet politics, particularly Soviet foreign policy, was pivotal.'[90]

Despite Gorbachev setting Castro and Ortega adrift, US animosity towards the Sandinistas remained undiminished, curbed only by the illegal and incompetent adventures of the administration, public opinion, some congressional scepticism and international opprobrium. Reagan's hostility towards the Sandinista revolution rested on his imagination of them and their impact on his credibility. Despite the exaggerated claims emanating from the White House, Nicaragua was marginally important to the Soviets in the early 1980s and more of a political liability in the late 1980s.

Notes

1   William M. LeoGrande, 'From Reagan to Bush: The Transition in US Policy towards Central America', *Journal of Latin American Studies* 22, no. 3 (October 1990): 595–621; David Ryan, 'The Peripheral Center: Nicaragua in US Policy and the US Imagination at the End of the Cold War', in *Foreign Policy at the Periphery: The Shifting Margins off US International Relations since World War II*, ed. Bevan Sewell and Maria Ryan (Lexington: University of Kentucky, 2017).

2   Ronald Reagan, 'Executive Order 12513 – Prohibiting Trade and Certain Other Transactions Involving Nicaragua', 1 May 1985, Ronald Reagan Presidential Library, https://www.reaganlibrary.gov/research/speeches/50185a.
3   William M. LeoGrande, *Our Own Backyard: The United States in Central America, 1977–1992* (Chapel Hill: University of North Carolina Press, 1998).
4   Sean Wilentz, *The Age of Reagan: A History, 1974–2008* (New York: HarperCollins, 2008), 153–6.
5   Hal Brands, *What Good Is Grand Strategy? Power and Purpose in American Statecraft from Harry S. Truman to George W. Bush* (Ithaca: Cornell University Press, 2014), 113.
6   Odd Arne Westad, *The Global Cold War: Third World Interventions and the Making of Our Times* (Cambridge: Cambridge University Press, 2005), 344.
7   Peter Kornbluh, 'The U.S. Role in the Counterrevolution', in *Revolution and Counterrevolution in Nicaragua*, ed. Thomas W. Walker (Boulder: Westview, 1991), 325.
8   Ronald Reagan, 'Address to Members of the British Parliament' (Public Papers of the President, 8 June 1982), Ronald Reagan Presidential Library, https://www.reaganlibrary.gov/research/speeches/60882a; Ronald Reagan, 'Remarks at the Annual Convention of the National Association of Evangelicals in Orlando, FL', 8 March 1983, Ronald Reagan Presidential Library, https://www.reaganlibrary.gov/archives/speech/remarks-annual-convention-national-association-evangelicals-orlando-fl.
9   Francis Fukuyama, 'The End of History?', *The National Interest*, no. 16 (Summer 1989); Ellen Schrecker, 'Cold War Triumphalism and the Real Cold War', in *Cold War Triumphalism: The Misuse of History after the Fall of Communism* (New York: The New Press, 2004); Bruce Cumings, 'Time of Illusion: Post-Cold War Visions of the World', in *Cold War Triumphalism: The Misuse of History after the Fall of Communism*, ed. Ellen Schrecker (New York: The New Press, 2004), 71–99.
10 John Lewis Gaddis, *The United States and the End of the Cold War: Implications, Reconsiderations, Provocations* (New York: Oxford University Press, 1992), 119–32; John Lewis Gaddis, *We Now Know: Rethinking Cold War History* (Oxford: Clarendon, 1997); Tony Smith, *America's Mission: The United States and the Worldwide Struggle for Democracy in the Twentieth Century* (Princeton: Princeton University Press, 1994), 304–7; John Patrick Diggins, *Ronald Reagan: Fate, Freedom, and the Making of History* (New York: W.W. Norton, 2007); Brands, What Good Is Grand Strategy? 142–3.
11 Alan P. Dobson, 'The Reagan Administration, Economic Warfare, and Starting to Close Down the Cold War', *Diplomatic History* 29, no. 3 (June 2005): 532; Alan Dobson, 'Ronald Reagan's Strategies and Policies: Of Ideology, Pragmatism, Loyalties, and Management Style', *Diplomacy and Statecraft* 27, no. 4 (2016): 746–65.
12 Ronald Reagan, 'U.S. Relations with the USSR, National Security Decision Directive 75, The White House', 17 January 1983, Ronald Reagan Presidential Library, https://www.reaganlibrary.gov/public/archives/reference/scanned-nsdds/nsdd75.pdf.
13 Beth A. Fischer, *The Reagan Reversal: Foreign Policy and the End of the Cold War* (Columbia: University of Missouri Press, 1997).
14 Cumings, 'Time of Illusion: Post-Cold War Visions of the World', 74–7; Schrecker, 'Cold War Triumphalism and the Real Cold War', 1–26; Allen Hunter, 'The Limits of Vindicationist Scholarship', in *Rethinking the Cold War*, ed. Allen Hunter (Philadelphia: Temple University Press, 1998), 1–3; Michael Cox, 'The End of the Cold War and Why We Failed to Predict It', in *Rethinking the Cold War*, ed. Allen Hunter (Philadelphia: Temple University Press, 1998), 159–61.

15 Tony Judt, 'Whose Story Is It? The Cold War in Retrospect', in *Reappraisals: Reflections on the Forgotten Twentieth Century* (London: Vintage, 2008), 371.
16 For analysis of the beliefs, see: James M. Scott, *Deciding to Intervene: The Reagan Doctrine and American Foreign Policy* (Durham: Duke University Press, 1996); Chester Pach, 'The Reagan Doctrine: Principle, Pragmatism and Policy', *Presidential Studies Quarterly* 36, no. 1 (March 2006): 75–88.
17 'Westad, *The Global Cold War*, 348.
18 Zbigniew Brzezinski, 'Memorandum to the President, Reflections on Soviet Intervention in Afghanistan', 26 December 1979, Jimmy Carter Presidential Library.
19 Svetlana Savranskaya and Thomas Blanton, 'Afghanistan and the Soviet Withdrawal 1989 20 Years Later, National Security Archive Briefing Book, 272', National Security Archive, 15 February 2009, https://nsarchive2.gwu.edu/NSAEBB/NSAEBB272/index.htm.
20 John H. Buchanan (Lt. Col) USMC retired, 'Statement before the Subcommittee on Inter-American Affairs, Committee on Foreign Affairs, US House of Representatives on US Aid to Honduras, Washington D.C.', 21 September 1982.
21 David Ryan, *US-Sandinista Diplomatic Relations: Voice of Intolerance* (London: Macmillan, 1995), 29; Ryan, 'Peripheral Center'; Wayne S. Smith, *The Closest of Enemies: A Personal and Diplomatic Account of U.S.-Cuban Relations since 1957* (New York: W.W. Norton, 1987); Wayne S. Smith, *The Russians Aren't Coming: New Soviet Policy in Latin America* (Boulder: Lynne Reinner, 1992).
22 Jacobsen, 'Soviet Attitudes towards, Aid to, and Contacts with Central American Revolutionaries' (US Department of State, June 1984), 15, 17, 31; Nicola Miller, *Soviet Relations with Latin America 1959–1987* (Cambridge: Cambridge University Press, 1989).
23 Brands, *What Good Is Grand Strategy?* 135.
24 Michael Schaller, *Right Turn: American Life in the Reagan-Bush Era* (New York: Oxford University Press, 2007).
25 Benjamin Moser, *Sontag: Her Life* (London: Allen Lane, 2019), 423.
26 Ibid., 424.
27 Scott, *Deciding to Intervene*.
28 Ronald Reagan, 'Address before a Joint Session of the Congress on the State of the Union' (6 February 1985), Ronald Reagan Presidential Library, https://www.reaganlibrary.gov/archives/speech/address-joint-session-congress-state-union-february-1985.
29 Chester Pach, 'The Reagan Doctrine: Principle, Pragmatism and Policy', *Presidential Studies Quarterly* 36, no. 1 (March 2006): 76.
30 Walter LaFeber, *America, Russia, and the Cold War 1945–2006* (Boston: McGraw Hill, 2008), 302.
31 Mikhail Gorbachev, *Perestroika: New Thinking for Our Country and the World* (London: Fontana, 1987), 175.
32 Walter LaFeber, 'An End to Which Cold War?', in *The End of the Cold War: Its Meaning and Implications*, ed. Michael Hogan (Cambridge: Cambridge University Press, 1992), 13–19.
33 'U.S. National Security Strategy, and Accompanying Papers, April 1982, Document 8290283 (NSDD 32) System II, NSC Records, the Reagan Presidential Library', April 1982, Ronald Reagan Presidential Library.
34 Dobson, 'Reagan Cold War'; Dobson, 'Reagan's Strategies'.
35 Cole Blasier, 'The Soviet Union', in *Confronting Revolution: Security through Diplomacy in Central America*, ed. Morris J. Blachman, William M. LeoGrande, and Kenneth Sharpe (New York: Pantheon Books, 1986), 269.

36 George H.W. Bush and Eduard Shevardnadze, 'Meeting with Eduard Shevardnadze, Foreign Minister of the Soviet Union, Memorandum of Conversation, 21 September 1989, The Shevardnadze File, Briefing Book 481' (National Security Archive, 24 July 2014), National Security Archive, Washington, DC.
37 George H.W. Bush, 'The President's Meeting with Soviet President Gorbachev, Malta, Briefing Book 2', 2 December 1989, George H. W. Bush Presidential Library; Jan S. Adams, *A Foreign Policy in Transition: Moscow's Retreat from Central America and the Caribbean 1985–1992* (Durham: Duke University Press, 1992), 110.
38 LeoGrande, 'Reagan to Bush'.
39 Reagan, 'NSDD 75'.
40 Ibid.
41 Ibid.
42 Ibid.
43 Ryan, *US-Sandinista*, 38–9; Cynthia Arnson, *Crossroads: Congress, The Reagan Administration, and Central America* (New York: Pantheon Books, 1989), 106; Rasmus Sinding Sondergaard, *Reagan, Congress, and Human Rights: Contesting Morality in US Foreign Policy* (Cambridge: Cambridge University Press, 2020), 222–32.
44 International Commission of Jurists, 'International Court of Justice, Nicaragua v. The United States of America, The Hague' (ICJ, 27 June 1986), 93, 109–10, 112.
45 Lawrence Pezzullo, 'Letter to Author, Baltimore, Maryland', 18 September 1990; International Commission of Jurists, 'Nicaragua v. US', 63, 75; Smith, *Closest of Enemies,* 244; Ryan, *US-Sandinista*, 15.
46 Richard Sobel, *The Impact of Public Opinion on U.S. Foreign Policy since Vietnam* (New York: Oxford University Press, 2001), 99–139; William M. LeoGrande, 'Central America and the Polls: A Study of US Public Opinion Polls and US Foreign Policy towards El Salvador and Nicaragua under the Reagan Administration', Special Report (Washington, DC: Washington Office on Latin America, March 1987).
47 Ronald Reagan, 'Central America: Defending Our Vital Interests, Address to a Joint Session of Congress, 27 April 1983', *Department of State Bulletin* 83, no. 2075 (June 1983): 1–5.
48 Ibid.
49 Christopher J. Dodd, 'Senator, Text of Democratic Response to Reagan Speech to Congress, 27 April 1983', *Congressional Quarterly Weekly Report* 41, no. 17 (30 April 1983): 856–7.
50 Dobson, 'Reagan's Strategies', 760.
51 Eldon Kenworthy, 'Selling the Policy', in *Reagan versus the Sandinistas: The Undeclared War on Nicaragua*, ed. Thomas W. Walker (Boulder: Westview, 1987), 159–81.
52 L. Francis Bouchey et al., *The Committee of Santa Fe, A New Inter-American Policy for the Eighties* (Washington, DC: Council for Inter-American Security, 1980).
53 Reagan, 'Central America'; Reagan, Ronald, 'President Reagan's Address on Central America to Joint Session of Congress', *New York Times*, 28 April 1983.
54 LeoGrande, 'Polls'; Sobel, *Impact of Public Opinion.*
55 US Senate Select Committee on Secret Military Assistance to Iran and the Nicaraguan Opposition, 'US Senate Select Committee On Secret Military Assistance to Iran and the Nicaraguan Opposition, US House of Representatives, Select Committee to Investigate Covert Arms Transactions with Iran, Iran-Contra Affair', 100th Cong., 1st Sess., S. Rept. No. 100–216 / H. Rept. No. 100–433 Washington, DC: GPO, 17 November 1987' (Washington, DC: GPO, 17 November 1987).

56 Archie Brown, *The Human Factor: Gorbachev, Reagan, and Thatcher, and the End of the Cold War* (Oxford: Oxford University Press, 2020), 1.
57 Lawrence E. Walsh, *Final Report of the Independent Counsel for Iran/Contra Matters, (3 Vols.)* (Washington, DC: Court of Appeals, 4 August 1993).
58 Brown, *The Human Factor*, 2.
59 Fred Halliday, *The Making of the Second Cold War* (London: Verso, 1983).
60 David Hackett Fischer, *Historians' Fallacies: Toward a Logic of Historical Thought* (New York: Harper and Row, 1970), 166.
61 Raymond L. Garthoff, *The Great Transition: American-Soviet Relations and the End of the Cold War* (Washington, DC : Brookings Institution Press, 1994), 2–3.
62 Norman A. Graebner, Richard Dean Burns, and Joseph Siracusa, *Reagan, Bush, Gorbachev: Revisiting the End of the Cold War* (Westport: Praeger Security International, 2008), 92.
63 Graebner, Burns, and Siracusa, 89.
64 Beth A. Fischer, *The Reagan Reversal: Foreign Policy and the End of the Cold War* (Columbia: University of Missouri Press, 1997), 73–5.
65 Odd Arne Westad, *The Cold War: A World History* (London: Allen Lane, 2017), 535.
66 Graebner, Burns, and Siracusa, 105; John Kenneth Galbraith, *The Culture of Contentment* (London: Sinclair-Stevenson, 1992).
67 Caspar Weinberger, 'The Uses of Military Power, Secretary of Defense, to the National Press Club, Washington D.C' (PBS Frontline, 28 November 1984), http://insidethecoldwar.org/sites/default/files/documents/Statement%20by%20Secretary%20of%20Defense%20Weinberger%20at%20National%20Press%20Club,%20November%2028,%201984.pdf.
68 George P. Shultz, *Turmoil and Triumph: My Years as Secretary of State* (New York: Charles Scribner's Sons, 1993), 649–51.
69 Graebner, Burns, and Siracusa, *Reagan, Bush, Gorbachev*, 107.
70 David Ryan, '"With One Hand Tied behind Our Back": Collective Memory, the Media and US Intervention: From the Gulf War to Afghanistan', in *The Uncertain Superpower: Domestic Dimensions of U.S. Foreign Policy after the Cold War*, ed. Bernhard May and Michaela Honicke Moore (Opladen: Leske and Budrich, 2003).
71 AP, '"Off Record" Kissinger Talk Isn't', *New York Times*, 20 April 1986; Agence France-Presse, 'Kissinger Takes Poke at President Reagan', 21 April 1986.
72 Beth A. Fischer, *The Reagan Reversal: Foreign Policy and the End of the Cold War* (Columbia: University of Missouri Press, 1997), 30–5.
73 Ibid., 35.
74 Westad, *The Cold War*, 549.
75 Fischer, *Reagan Reversal*, 40.
76 Ibid., 148–9.
77 Elizabeth Dore and John Weeks, *The Red and the Black: The Sandinistas and the Nicaraguan Revolution*, vol. 28, Institute of Latin American Studies, University of London (London: Institute of Latin American Studies, 1992), 21–8; Dennis Gilbert, *Sandinistas: The Party and the Revolution* (Cambridge: Basil Blackwell, 1988), 19–40; James Dunkerley, *The Pacification of Central America* (London: Verso, 1994).
78 David Ryan, 'Curtains, Culture and Collective Memory', *Journal of Transatlantic Studies* 14, no. 4 (December 2016).
79 Mikhail Gorbachev, *Address to the United Nations General Assembly, 43rd Session*, Digital Archive (The Wilson Center, 7 December 1988, https://digitalarchive.wilsoncenter.org/document/address-mikhail-gorbachev-un-general-assembly-

session-excerpts); Brown, *Human Factor*, 229–46; William Taubman, *Gorbachev: His Life and Times* (London: Simon & Schuster, 2017), 419–26.
80 Geoff Roberts translation, Mikhail Gorbachev, *Zhizn'I Reformy [Life and Reforms]*, vol. 2, Moscow: Novosti, 1995, 131–2. Email to David Ryan 22 June 2015.
81 Mikhail Gorbachev, *Zhizn'I Reformy [Life and Reforms], Vol. 2* (Moscow: Novosti, 1995).
82 Ibid.
83 William Taubman, *Gorbachev: His Life and Times* (London: Simon & Schuster, 2017), 419.
84 Brown, *Human Factor*, 241–3.
85 Taubman, *Gorbachev*, 422.
86 Graebner, Burns, and Siracusa, *Reagan, Bush, Gorbachev*, 110.
87 Graebner, Burns, and Siracusa, 110–11.
88 Melvyn P. Leffler, *For the Soul of Mankind: The United States, The Soviet Union, and the Cold War* (New York: Hill and Wang, 2007), 360–1.
89 Robert V. Daniels, *The End of the Communist Revolution* (London: Routledge, 1993), 1–4.
90 Fischer, *Reagan Reversal*, 145–6.

Chapter 11

NORTH GEORGIA, THE AMERICAN SOUTH, AND TRANSATLANTIC CULTURE AND HISTORY

T. Christopher Jespersen

The geographical area of North Georgia is not normally associated with transatlantic history and culture. It is commonly thought to be too remote from the coastal region, which is certainly true. North Georgia is generally defined as being located at longitude 33.86 degrees north. Atlanta, by way of comparison, is longitude 33.74 degrees north. There is, in short, not much difference between the two, and for the purposes of this chapter, Atlanta will be considered part of the larger region. The locale is demarcated by the mountainous region in the northern part of the state and runs from the state capitol of Atlanta to the northern border with Tennessee and North Carolina. North Georgia is a distinct part of the state and has more in common with its northern neighbours because of the mountains than it does with the coastal or southern parts of the state like Savannah, Brunswick, Valdosta or Albany. North Georgia is located well north of what is colloquially called 'the gnat line', or the longitude above which gnats, those pesky little flying insects, can live. Additionally, Atlanta is much farther west than most people realize. It is, for example, as far west as Lexington, Kentucky and Cincinnati, Ohio. Atlanta is thus not an east-coast city so much as it is a metropolis in the northern part of the state very close to the Appalachian Mountains.

Geography aside, for the moment, what do people think of when they hear the word Georgia? Often times it involves the 1939 movie *Gone with the Wind*. Producer David O' Selznick's rendering of the best-selling novel by Margaret Mitchell has earned nearly $400 million during its long history of release and re-release, making it one of the highest grossing films ever. And, interestingly enough, the film has a transatlantic aspect to it since one of the main characters, Rhett Butler, famously played by Clark Gable, was a gunrunner during the American Civil War from 1861 to 1865, importing arms from England across the Atlantic to the American South.

And what do people think of when they hear the more regionally specific words of North Georgia? Staying with the theme of famous Hollywood films, things then

Originally presented at the 2018 Transatlantic Studies Association Annual Meeting.

move from *Gone with the Wind* to *Deliverance*, which was filmed in Rabun County and on the Chattooga River, both very much a part of the region. John Boorman's 1972 film starring Burt Reynolds, Jon Voight, Ned Beatty and Ronny Cox depicts four friends from Atlanta who go to North Georgia for a weekend of canoeing and camping and, along the way, encounter the local folks, an experience that begins with the famous music scene of the banjo and guitar duet but quickly turns tragic and deadly in somewhat shockingly graphic ways. With a $2 million budget and a $46 million box office take, the film was a commercial as well as a critical success, and for many decades thereafter, it came to define the region in stark and unsettling terms.

For the purposes of this chapter, however, it is worthwhile to think about a more expansive view of the region and consider that North Georgia and the state of Georgia are very much part of the American South, the Confederacy that tried to secede from the Union in 1861 over the issue of slavery, and, failing that, later instituted a rigid system of racial segregation known as Jim Crow. However much that may be true, and all that said, the question arises: what does any of that have to do with transatlantic history?

The work of John Burrison provides a first clue. His article, 'Transported Traditions: Transatlantic Foundations of Southern Folk Culture', quoted Emily Ellis, a North Georgian, who, in 1970, said: 'some of the oldest folk tales found in the South are English', and she gave, by way of example, a tale that is traceable to fifteenth-century England:

> One night two tramps were walkin', and they had to pass a cemetery. And they heard voices, so they stopped and listened. And they heard this voice saying, 'You take this one an' I'll take that one, you take this one an' I'll take that one.' And what they didn't know was that two men had come along earlier and shook a walnut tree, and they were dividin' up the walnuts. And they set there listenin' to 'You take this one, I'll take that one.'
>
> And they said, 'What is that?' And one of them said, 'Well, I think it's the Devil and the Lord dividin' up the people in the cemetery.'
>
> And just as they had reached this conclusion one of the men said [loudly]: 'And I'll take the two on the outside.' An' nobody saw the tramps anymore!'[1]

A second example, or clue, to the transatlantic connection, is broom jumping, or jumping a broom at weddings, which is often thought to be of African origin since it was practised by slaves, and in recent decades has been revived in the African American community. The practice, however, would not be strange to anyone from Wales, where it is known as a 'besom wedding'. In addition, in Great Britain, there are numerous nineteenth-century references to broomstick marriages, including the 1836 Marriage Act, which, because it introduced the notion of civil marriages (i.e. not church weddings), was known by its critics as the Broomstick Marriage Act. And yet, during the 1840s and 1850s, the act of jumping a broom became common in weddings between slaves in the American

South, a practice that was revived after the publication (and television series based on the book) of Arthur Haley's mega-sensation, *Roots,* in the late 1970s.

A third example highlighting the transatlantic connection involves alcohol, that universally hailed and consumed commodity on both sides of the Atlantic Ocean. The North Georgia region is well known for its backwoods distilling techniques, creating what is called moonshine or hooch. As much as moonshine is considered a southern act of rebellion against federal authority, its roots are transatlantic. The distilling techniques that so many locals used were originally perfected in places like Ulster and elsewhere and were brought to the Appalachian Mountains of North Georgia and used on the local crop, corn, to produce that local alcohol product, moonshine. Distilling was not indigenous to the region; it was brought by immigrants from across the Atlantic and adapted to local conditions.

A fourth, and somewhat interesting, example comes in the form of food: specifically, barbeque. As Andrew Warnes has asserted in his book, *Savage Barbeque: Race, Culture, and the Invention of America's First Food,* 'barbecue does little more than naturalize to America an idea of barbarism that European explorers carried with them as part of their transatlantic cargo'.[2] Warnes' work is an aggressive interpretation, based more in literary theory than history, one grounded in inferences drawn more so than what the evidence indicates. Just the same, his work is thought-provoking and speaks to the style in which European ways of cooking were transported across the Atlantic, and from there, how they were changed in unforeseen manners.

In quoting a journalist named David Dudley, Warnes insists that 'by installing barbeque as just about the most macho [food] imaginable, [it] reminds us that transatlantic English cultures have long bent and warped the food into shapes altogether more malignant than the roadside sign BBQ'. Warnes avers that the key was understanding just how European barbecue was, and, again, in referring to Dudley, he asserts 'that barbeque, as it is understood today and as it has been understood for centuries in the west, evokes a stereotype of savagery that has nothing to do with Native culture and everything to do with white European need'. Warnes ties together the term 'barbarian' in its original meaning with barbeque:

> *Savage Barbeque* shows that transatlantic literary culture has placed in circulation an invented paradigm that has seized on a Native Caribbean term for a cooking frame, *barbacoa,* apprehended its affinity with the Latin for those beyond Rome's jurisdiction, and duly insinuated that all *barbarians* must *barbeque* and all who *barbeque* must be *barbaric*.[3]

On the word 'barbeque', Warnes offers an aggressive connection: '*Barbacoa* ... acquired its savage and bloody connotations because of its entry into emerging European racial discourses. Only after its transatlantic encounter with the European idea of barbarism did it begin to outpace its banal and practical origins and acquire the bloody meanings even today associated with it.'[4]

That may all seem a bit much, but perhaps the most interesting point Warnes makes is one offered by someone else: He quotes the writer John Shelton Reed, who once said, 'Southern barbeque is the closest thing we have in the U.S. to Europe's wines or cheeses; drive a hundred miles and the barbeque changes.'[5]

Reed makes a fair point as the American South is replete with different types of barbecue, almost all regionally or even locally based. Vinegar or tomato based, sweet, spicy, or smoky, the possibilities are nearly endless, and from North Carolina to Texas, the varieties of barbeque boggle the mind. Food and fermented libations thus provide some evidence of the transatlantic connections between North Georgia, the South and the other side of the Atlantic. Indeed, and well beyond barbecue, Charles Joyner once observed, 'Every southerner, regardless of race, shares both African and European traditions …. The central theme of southern folk history might well be described as the achievement of cultural integration.'[6]

There's more to connect the South with the other side of the Atlantic, particularly on the literary front. Charles Dickens offered some important insights into southern culture after visiting the United States in 1842. As Charles Wells wrote, 'Dickens's visit to America is an iconic moment in the broader history of transatlantic literary, cultural and economic exchange that has sparked exciting studies of the Atlantic world by historians such as David Armitage, Bernard Bailyn, Rebecca Scott and Jack Greene.'

Dickens's literary output focusing on his travels across the country, and after having visited Richmond, Virginia, was not universally acclaimed on either side of the Atlantic. Southerners found his criticism of slavery inappropriate. Others found the criticisms and observations mundane. And yet, as Wells points out, 'That rich fabric comprising countless intellectual and cultural threads created what Paul Giles has called the "transatlantic imaginary", a fictive but powerful creation that shaped the identity of peoples throughout the Atlantic world.'[7]

Wells asserts that there was more to the matter than what Dickens may have initially offered, and certainly more than what his audience considered. 'Perhaps even more importantly, analyzing the evolution of Dickens' relationship to slavery and the American South demonstrates the power of transatlantic debates in domestic politics, particularly the debate over the virtues and vices of bondage and free labor.'[8]

In another example from the literary world, in a 2012 article in the *Journal of Transatlantic Studies*, Sophie Croisy explored the transatlantic cultural collisions in Barbara Kingsolver's novel *The Poisonwood Bible*. 'Kingsolver's text is thus a place of transatlantic encounter; it is a contact zone, a place of constant collision and collusion between the "authentic" Old White South qua closed geographical and political space, and the other, the dark subject and its dark land of origin – Africa. It is a place where the modern, transcultural aspect of the South and its potential for productive cultural sharing are revealed.'[9]

While exploring various types of transatlantic literary connections, Southern Gothic, a subset of gothic literature, got a makeover complete with sex and soap opera sensibilities. Beginning in 2008, Bram Stoker's *Dracula* came to life in the American South as the HBO mini-series *True Blood*, which lasted for seven seasons and ran to eighty episodes. The first gothic novel was Horace Walpole's 1764 novel *The Castle of Otranto*. And with *True Blood*, the character Manfred, the lord of the castle in Walpole's novel, becomes Sookie Stackhouse, the semi-clothed halfling who serves customers at a local restaurant. She becomes romantically enmeshed with a nearly 200-year-old vampire named Bill Compton. Sookie became the Mina Harker of the twenty-first century.[10]

While on the topic of supernatural creatures, zombies should certainly be part of the mix, especially considering that not only is the AMC hit series *The Walking Dead* filmed in Georgia, it turns out that zombies have distinctly transatlantic associations, or so writes Sarah Juliet Lauro in her 2015 book, *The Transatlantic Zombie: Slavery, Rebellion, and Living Death*. 'A history of the zombie myth would chart its journey across the globe, as it was borne on the slave ships across the Atlantic and sprouted among the sugarcane plantations of the Caribbean, as it was carried to Europe in the incendiary reports of missionaries, settlers, journalists, and anthropologists.' Lauro does concede that piecing together the full story is problematic given fragmentary evidence:

> Staring into aporias, we can only wonder whether the creature may have migrated to the American South during the Haitian Revolution, tied up in the kerchiefs of those unfortunates who were swept by their masters to climes kinder to the slaveholder. In places the zombie's history is irrecoverable, and we must admit our own limitations, confined as we are to one side of the story, that which was written down by Europeans, who usually were not objective ethnographers but had vested interests in representing the slave population as superstitious and savage.[11]

The zombie, Lauro asserts, is a figure of resistance to enslavement: 'How could one people have had complete ownership and dominance over another group if not by means of sorcery?'[12] Indeed, the question raises the spectre of resistance and revenge since zombies feast on the human brains of the living. As Lauro concludes, 'The zombie most clearly translates the experience of the African slave into a folkloric figure – biologically alive but "socially dead," as the subjectless agent of another's bidding.'[13]

Having thus far made the general case for the connections between the American South, and North Georgia as part of the region, and how those two figure in transatlantic history and culture, a few specific cases allow for further consideration about the nature of the relationship. The first example involves President Jimmy Carter, the former governor of Georgia, president of the United States from 1977 to 1981, and West German chancellor Helmut Schmidt, who served in that capacity from 1974 to 1982. Problems between the two began in October 1976 when Schmidt, who had developed a close personal relationship with then President Gerald Ford, spoke publicly to *Newsweek* about how much he liked Ford, all the while insisting that he did not want to interfere with the American presidential election. 'I have to abstain from any interference in your campaign, but I really like your President, and I think he has done quite a bit to help in these past two years. But on the other hand, I am not going to say anything about Mr. Carter, neither positive nor negative, I have met him for one hour only.'

Carter's team was incensed. And although Schmidt's staff tried to explain it as some inelegant phrasing during an early morning interview, Schmidt told British prime minister James Callaghan he was uncertain about what would happen if 'a very much unknown farmer governor' got into the White House.[14] Transatlantic relations did not improve between the two leaders subsequently.

Long after both men had left office, in a 12 October 2010 article in *Der Spiegel* Carter laid out his objections to Schmidt, whom he considered to be a 'mercurial grouch' and who then, in turn, lectured Americans about global economics and vanished when Carter wanted Germany's assistance with something. In early 1978, Carter wrote: '"Schmidt seems to go up and down in his psychological attitude. I guess women are not the only ones that have periods."'[15]

The problem, as is often the case, was that Carter offered a singular, and most definitively American, perspective on the relationship. 'But right after moving into the White House, Carter started asking West Germany's government – then led by Schmidt – to change its economic policies and, to a lesser extent, its foreign and energy polices, as well. Even if Carter did have some valid arguments on certain points, no head of state is ever happy to get those kinds of requests.' Carter labelled Schmidt 'quite volatile' and was concerned about his 'irrationality'.

Schmidt, for his part, was reluctant to give up leader of the Free World, a position he had assumed during Gerald Ford's brief presidency. Carter was not willing to follow Schmidt's lead, and Schmidt resented the newcomer. Acrimony ensued. In short, tensions in transatlantic relations are by no means a recent or an exclusively twenty-first-century phenomenon.

The second, and certainly seemingly more culturally agreeable, example specific to North Georgia came on 18 August 1965, when the Beatles played at Atlanta Fulton County stadium. Tickets were priced between $4.50 and $5.50. Their set was twelve songs and lasted a little over thirty minutes. 'It was mass hysteria,' said ten-year-old Lance Jones of North Augusta, as recounted by Ed Turner in 2010 for the *Augusta Chronicle*.[16] 'Normal-looking, church-going Southern girls were going absolutely nuts.' That quote is worth reviewing one more time: 'Normal-looking, church-going Southern girls were going absolutely nuts.' Lance Jones was referencing white Southern girls. And because the Beatles refused to perform before a segregated audience, this presented a threat to the existing segregated Southern society. The group insisted that tickets be available to any and all patrons, regardless of race, a seismic matter in Georgia at the time, but one that the locality acquiesced to in order to have the Fab Four perform. That the Beatles insisted on racial equality in terms of audience, combined with the fact that churchgoing, white, Southern-teenage-girls were 'going absolutely nuts' at the Beatles' arrival and performance, threatened to upend the existing societal norms and expectations. This was 1965, and the Civil Rights Movement was in full force, and the most popular rock band in the world was performing in the South created a situation: transatlantic cultural transmissions had come home to take root, and that was a problem. Many Southerners objected in the strongest terms, and yet, their protests were futile. Change was happening, and the Beatles were the most obvious symbol of that.

11. North Georgia, the American South

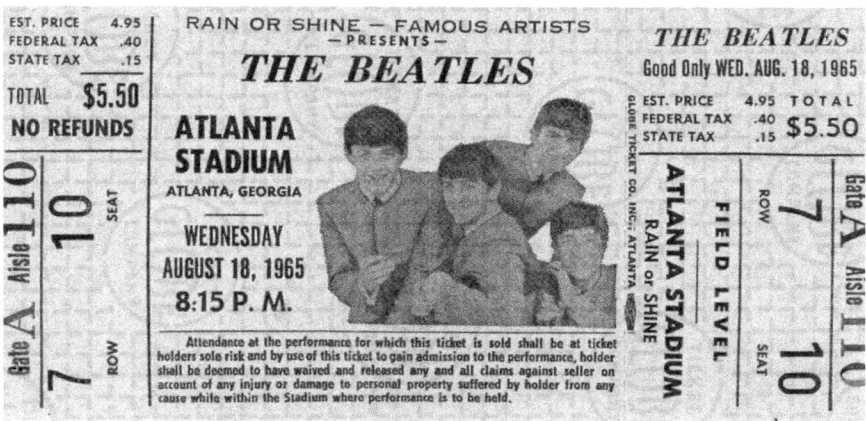

Figures 11.1a and 11.1b The Beatles in Atlanta, 1965. 18 August 1965; Atlanta, GA, USA; Beatles' only Georgia show took place half a century ago in Atlanta. © Augusta Chronicle – USA TODAY NETWORK.

The *Atlanta Journal Constitution (AJC)*, an often-progressive media for societal change, was, in the case of the Beatles, concerned, writing the next day, 'hearing a Beatles concert is the most amazing and entertaining headache that a person can get'. The *AJC*'s snarky comments aside, it is important to recognize that the major newspaper of the city, state, and South needed to write about the visit of the most famous rock-n-roll band of its era. Some forms of cross-cultural transmission are not as readily welcomed as others, depending on the audience. But that did not mean the Beatles were not influential in the South. Quite the contrary: as Tommy Verran told the *AJC* in a fiftieth anniversary reflection on the Beatles' visit: 'We all dressed alike in matching turtleneck shirts, denim coats, blue jeans and Beatle boots.' And Tommy Verran was from Cairo, Georgia.[17]

The final example of the cross-cultural connection between Georgia and the transatlantic community comes in the form of the Reverend Martin Luther King, Jr. and his winning the Nobel Peace Prize on 10 October 1964. In his speech, King asked the question as to why the movement he represented had won at that time: 'why is this prize awarded to a movement which is beleaguered and committed to unrelenting struggle; to a movement which has not won the very peace and brotherhood which is the essence of the Nobel Prize'. Beleaguered – that sounds familiar many decades later in terms of the nature of transatlantic relations. But committed to an unrelenting struggle – well, that sounds familiar too. King answered the question he posed by stating: 'following the people of India', the movement he represented had 'demonstrated that nonviolence is not sterile passivity, but a powerful moral force which makes for social transformation'. He was tracing, of course, the line from the British colonization of India, Gandhi's policy of non-violent resistance, to the American South and the Civil Rights Movement and right back to Europe at Oslo.

Sarah Lauro had a point: 'how could one people have had complete ownership and dominance over another group if not by means of sorcery? If the zombie most clearly translates the experience of the African slave into a folkloric figure – biologically alive but "socially dead," as the subjectless agent of another's bidding,' then King's actions and his movement challenged the status quo.[18] And the Nobel Committee's decision to recognize his work brought international attention to Civil Rights in the American South. From Oslo to Atlanta, the transatlantic connection could not have been clearer.

More than a half century after speaking in Oslo, King's words continue to speak to transatlantic relations. King insisted, 'Sooner or later all the people of the world will have to discover a way to live together in peace, and thereby transform this pending cosmic elegy into a creative psalm of brotherhood. If this is to be achieved, man must evolve for all human conflict a method which rejects revenge, aggression and retaliation. The foundation of such a method is love.'

King's call for love is a consistent theme in transatlantic relations. After all, the Beatles sang, 'All you need is love.' It is no less desperately needed today than it was in King's time. Transatlantic relations are, on occasion, depending on governmental leaders and international circumstances, no less strained today than they ever have been. King's recognition by the Nobel committee was an act of transatlantic cultural affirmation for King and his movement. It set Americans on notice that the struggle for racial equality was drawing international attention. And at that moment, it reinforced the movement's direction.

From the broader connections between the North Georgia region and the other side of the Atlantic through the diffusion of food and drink, literature and visual media, to the specific examples of politics and diplomacy between state leaders and a musical performance by the most famous rock-n-roll band in history, transatlantic influences reached all the way to the mountains of North Georgia. John Shelton Reed was onto something when he compared the very local nature of barbeque in the southern United States with wine and cheese manufacturing in Europe. And yet, whatever difference or peculiarities there may be 100 miles apart, the broader connections made across the Atlantic are undeniable. North Georgia is part of the dynamic transatlantic world. It is impossible to understand the region without appreciating those sinewy connective tissues that tie North Georgia and influence its makeup.

Notes

1   John A. Burrison, 'Transported Traditions: Transatlantic Foundations of Southern Folk Culture', *Studies in Literary Imaginations* 36 (Fall 2003): 8.
2   Andrew Warnes, *Savage Barbeque: Race, Culture, and the Invention of America's First Food* (Athens: University of Georgia Press, 2008).
3   Ibid., 7.
4   Ibid., 31.
5   Ibid., 90.
6   Burrison, 'Transported Traditions', 13.
7   Jonathan Daniel Wells, 'Charles Dickens, the American South, and the Transatlantic Debate over Slavery', *Slavery & Abolition* 36 (2015): 2.
8   Wells, 'Charles Dickens, the American South, and the Transatlantic Debate over Slavery', 2–3.
9   Sophie Croisy, 'Re-visioning Southern Identity: Transatlantic Cultural Collisions in Barbara Kingsolver's *The Poisonwood Bible*', *Journal of Transatlantic Studies* 10 (September 2012): 224.
10 For additional sources on the gothic connection, see Stephen M. Park, 'Haunting the Plantation: The Global Southern Gothic in Eric Walrond's *Tropic Death*', *The Southern Quarterly* 55, no.4 (Summer 2018): 70–90 and Raphael Hoermann, '"A Very Hell of Horrors"? The Haitian Revolution and the Early Transatlantic Haitian Gothic', *Slavery & Abolition* 37, no. 1 (March 2016): 183–205.
11 Sarah Juliet Lauro, *The Transatlantic Zombie: Slavery, Rebellion, and Living Death* (New Brunswick: Rutgers University Press, 2015): 8.
12 Ibid., 16.
13 Ibid., 17.
14 Kristina Spohr, 'A Prickly Pair: Helmut Schmidt and Jimmy Carter', 26 April 2016, https://blog.oup.com/2016/04/helmut-schmidt-jimmy-carter/.
15 http://www.spiegel.de/international/world/no-love-lost-carter-diary-reveals-rocky-relationship-with-german-chancellor-schmidt-a-721449.html.

16 Ed Turner, 'Beatles Made a Big Impression in Atlanta', *The Augusta Chronicle*, 18 August 2010.
17 17 August 2015, *Atlanta Journal Constitution*, by Yvonne Zusel.
18 Lauro, *The Transatlantic Zombie*, 16.

Chapter 12

PERSONALITIES AND POWER WITHIN THE SPECIAL RELATIONSHIP AT THE COLD WAR'S END

Jeffrey A. Engel

She was his first. Also his last. During the eight years in-between the two state dinners held at the White House in her honour, no foreign leader influenced President Ronald Reagan so much as British prime minister, Margaret Thatcher. Together Britain's 'Iron Lady' and 'Great Communicator' from the United States formed one of the Anglo-American alliance's most enduring couples, second in importance and intimacy only to the progenitors of the special relationship itself: Franklin D. Roosevelt and Winston Churchill. Just as no history of the Second World War can fail to mention the president of Pearl Harbor and the prime minister of the Blitz, any full retelling of the diplomacy and international politics that contributed to the Cold War's end must note their successors. Neither caused the Cold War to end (no matter what their most rabid supporters fatuously claim). Yet neither would the story have played out as it did, and so relatively and remarkably peacefully, without the personal trust that underlay their conjoined great power diplomacy.

Reagan and Thatcher had each been youthful admirers of their respective political leaders, and the diplomatic relations their own relationship produced two generations later also revealed, especially when compared to their own successors, some fundamental truths about that much-celebrated special relationship between the two great English-speaking nations on far sides of the Atlantic Ocean. Most especially, the close dynamics, and tensions too, between the occupants of the White House and Downing Street at the tail end of the Cold War demonstrated yet again Thucydides indisputable logic: strong nations do what they want; weaker ones, what they may.

The pair were ideological compatriots, and political contemporaries. Each led long-ascendant conservative waves to the top of their respective political universes. Reagan's victory came in 1980, with a resounding Electoral College drubbing of outgoing President Jimmy Carter, whose defeat many on the right interpreted not just as a triumph of their own political philosophy, but additionally a blow against a dangerously pervasive pessimism that considered America's best days resigned to the past. The 1970s had given plenty of cause for concern.

Defeat in Vietnam, political disenchantment over Watergate and repeated embarrassments in the Middle East all coupled with persistent stagflation – the troubling new combination of economic stagnation and unbridled inflation – to produce the worst persistent economic retreat in the generation-plus since the Great Depression. Real wages were down, while prices across the board soared. The country's international trade account dipped into the red in 1973 for the first time in multiple generations. It rebounded a year later, but by the close of the decade never again would Americans sell more overseas than they'd consumed. There was, Carter said – accurately, though not politically prudently – in 1979, a 'crisis of confidence' throughout American society. 'It's clear that the true problems of our nation are much deeper – deeper than gasoline lines or energy shortages, deeper even than inflation or recession,' he told his fellow citizens in a prime-time television address. 'The erosion of our confidence in the future is threatening to destroy the social and political fabric of America.' Salvation, he argued in a manner befitting his status as the nation's first evangelical Christian to hold his office, lay through doing more, with less. 'There are no short-term solutions to our long-range problems,' he preached. 'There is simply no way to avoid sacrifice.'[1]

Reagan preached optimism instead. America's best days lay ahead, he routinely declared from the campaign trail, promising to 'make America great again' and revitalize its power and prosperity without sacrificing anything more than the burdensome welfare-state initiated with Franklin Roosevelt's New Deal – something he supported – but then expanded too far by FDR's Democratic successors. Roosevelt saved his family, Reagan said on more than one occasion, providing assistance and employment for the troubled family of his youth during a particularly troubling time. He voted for the man four times, and once president himself, told aides 'I am still for the New Deal.'[2]

However, he continued, 'It is the great society I object to.'[3] Voters only needed to recommit to traditional values, most especially in his mind, to constraining and ideally reducing a bloated state whose too-frequent interventions in their daily routines weakened their native work-ethic, sapped their natural confidence and needlessly complicated their lives. 'These United States are confronted with an economic affliction of great proportions,' he said in his first inaugural, mere moments after taking his oath of office.[4]

Agreeing with Carter's starting point that pervasive pessimism prevented American greatness, Reagan offered a far different solution. 'We suffer from the longest and one of the worst sustained inflations in our national history,' the newly sworn-in president continued. 'It distorts our economic decisions, penalizes thrift, and crushes the struggling young and the fixed – income elderly alike. It threatens to shatter the lives of millions of our people.' Ultimately, Reagan asked, building to his speech's climax, 'can we solve the problems confronting us?' History replied yes, Reagan said, though its voice carried a particularly un-American accent. 'To paraphrase Winston Churchill, I did not take the oath I have just taken with the intention of presiding over the dissolution of the world's strongest economy.'[5]

Thatcher held Churchill's old post, not just as Great Britain's prime minister, but also as leader of its Conservative Party. An impressionable youth during Churchill's wartime leadership, and an unabashed supporter then and after, she too considered government's growth endemic, and dangerous, championing a political crusade not only against the era's economic and diplomatic travails piled up throughout the 1970s by an overreaching state, but also the broader consequences of imperial decline. 'It is not given to his generation of our countrymen to create a great Empire,' she explained on the eve of taking power in 1979. 'But it is given to us to demand an end to decline and to make a stand against what Churchill described as the long dismal drawling tides of drift and surrender, of wrong measures and feeble impulses.'[6]

Like it or not, however, the empire Churchill refused to dissolve had largely done so without his consent by the time Thatcher rose to party prominence. London ruled more than seventy overseas possessions when Queen Elizabeth took the crown during Churchill's second turn as prime minister. A mere handful remained by 1979, and the steady reduction of British flags around the world epitomized the country's economic and geopolitical standing. Edward Heath ruled Britain's Conservatives, and held Downing Street as well, during the first years of the 1970s, but left office in 1974 beset by rising unemployment, industrial inefficiency, energy crises and a second miner's strike in two years. In other words, the same economic headwinds Americans faced across the ocean as well. Labour's Harold Wilson reduced unemployment in Heath's stead, but only at the cost of rampant inflation and an embarrassing financial bailout from international lenders. Only pessimism appeared in abundant supply. 'Our place in the world is shrinking,' Labour politician and future prime minister, Jim Callaghan, confessed mid-decade. 'Our economic comparisons grow worse, long term political influence depends on economic strength, and that is running out.' Better opportunities abounded elsewhere. 'If I were a young man,' he bluntly stated, 'I should emigrate.'[7]

Thatcher meanwhile was ascendant in opposition. Head of the Conservatives from 1975 on, her party pounced once Callaghan called a general election in 1979. 'Labour isn't working,' their campaign posters read in 1979, and like Reagan on the far side of the Atlantic would a year later, Thatcher promised to rebuild through retrenchment. 'Our country's relative decline is not inevitable,' she said at the start of 1979 general election. 'We in the Conservative Party think we can reverse it, not because we think we have all the answers but because we think we have the one answer that matters most. We want to work with the grain of human nature.'[8]

Ideological compatibility, coupled of course with the new administration's desire to nod approvingly towards the special nature of the Anglo-American relationship, therefore led Reagan's White House to make Thatcher their first guest of honour at a state dinner. They'd met a few years before, and Reagan pointedly visited Downing Street in 1979 while on a pre-presidential tour designed to shore up his otherwise-limited diplomatic credentials. Each considered the other a kindred spirit, and more importantly, perceived in the other a partner in struggles that long pre-dated their turns in office. 'Great Britain and the United States are kindred nations of like-minded people and must face their tests together,' Reagan said in his welcoming remarks for Thatcher's February 1981 visit. 'We are bound by common language and linked in history. We share laws and literature, blood, and moral fibre. The responsibility for freedom is ours to share.'[9]

Thatcher replied in turn, linking the nation's bilateral relations to their own personal connection. 'Mr. President, the natural bond of interest between our two countries is strengthened by the common approach which you and I have to our national problems,' she declared. 'If we are to succeed in the battle of ideas, if we are to hold fast and extend the frontiers of freedom, we must first proclaim the truth that makes men free. We must have the courage to reassert our traditional values and the resolve to prevail against those who deny our ideals and threaten our way of life.'[10]

Enemies abounded, at home and abroad, but one in particular interested both leaders most: the Soviet Union. An ally of each during the Second World War, it did not take even a year following the close of hostilities for new tensions to rise between the undisputed leaders of the capitalist and communist worlds. The Cold War ensued, pitting each ideology against each other in a multi-generational battle for global dominance. That sentence is no exaggeration. There was scarcely a spot on earth, and certainly no nation, untouched by the superpower conflict. That is only fitting, since the consequences of a Cold War turned hot – and the ensuing deployment of the more than 40,000 nuclear weapons the two sides collectively commanded – could, indeed would, extinguish all human life on earth.

Reagan took office hoping not merely to survive the Cold War, but to win. 'Communism is neither an economic or political system,' he told audiences throughout the 1970s and into his presidency. 'It is a form of insanity ... contrary to human nature.'[11] Together, he told Thatcher during their first White House meeting in 1981, their countries might hasten its demise. 'Prime Minister, everywhere one looks these days the cult of the state is dying, and I wonder if you and I and other leaders of the West should not now be looking toward bright sunlit uplands and begin planning for a world where our adversaries are remembered only for their role in a sad and rather bizarre chapter in human history.'[12] He repeated the point a year later, this time in London, though once more with Thatcher approvingly looking on. 'The march of freedom and democracy which will leave Marxism-Leninism on the ash heap of history as it has left other tyrannies which stifle the freedom and muzzle the self-expression of the people.'[13]

Reagan did not know precisely how, or when, communism would collapse; only that it would. The same vague sense of inevitability infuses much of the literature exploring how the conflict arose as well. Historians have difficulty pinpointing precisely when the Cold War began. Some see its roots in the Anglo-Soviet-American summits conducted between 1943 and 1945. Others think the brewing conflict could no longer be denied by 1948, once Soviet-led forces blockaded the parts of Berlin still occupied by Western forces (the United States, the United Kingdom and France) as a result of deals worked out years before, at the aforementioned great power summits. President Harry Truman's declaration, known to history as his 'doctrine', a year before offers a potential starting point as well. The United States would support 'free peoples who are resisting attempted subjugation by armed minorities or by outside pressures' – in other words, communists – Truman told Congress and the wider world in 1947, and particularly in strategic hotspots such as Greece and Turkey in which a cash-strapped British government could no longer afford to buttress.[14] Within the handover of responsibility from one English-speaking empire to another, proponents of a uniquely powerful Anglo-American bond find ample evidence for the relationship being not merely strong, but special. 'There has been no overt action in the immediate past by the USSR which serves as an adequate pretext for an "all-out" speech,' Truman's aide, George Elsey, acknowledged at the time.[15] But the public needed to understand, or at least frightened into accepting, the responsibility of global peacekeeper that had already passed from London to Washington.

The Berlin airlift or the Truman Doctrine offers potential Cold War starting points, but I prefer to date the Cold War's formal start from a different moment, albeit one with a critical Anglo-American flair of its own. A year before Truman announced his doctrine of support against communist aggression worldwide, it was Winston Churchill who sounded the most clarion call to arms against their shared rapacious foe. 'From Stettin in the Baltic, to Trieste in the Adriatic, an iron curtain has descended across the continent,' the recently ousted former prime minister declared.[16] Any serious student of the Cold War can no doubt complete his ensuing anti-Soviet diatribe. So too does any serious student of the Cold War know that seated next to Churchill, smiling not merely as a warm Midwestern host in his home state but the enthusiastic smile of a man who wholeheartedly agreed, was Harry Truman himself.

The Cold War formally began, if there is a formal date to be bound, with words offered by a leading British statesman to an American audience that included an approving American president. This is how it might well have ended, too, when Thatcher reappeared in Washington in late November, 1988, for what would be Reagan's last state dinner in the White House. The drizzle and fog outside seemed almost a homage to London. Indoors, movie stars mingled with politicians one last time for a president with Hollywood roots. 'We set out to change a nation,' Reagan toasted his guest, 'instead, we changed the world.'[17] Even suffering from fatigue and the early signs of the dementia that would within a few short years cost Reagan his life, the old actor could still deliver at the mic. It was Thatcher, however, who stole the show. 'Together we could get our countries back on their feet, restore their values,' she said, 'and create a better yet safer world.'[18]

Precisely how safe she detailed the next day. She'd spent the morning with the president-elect, publicly reaffirming even before Reagan's successor was sworn into office that the special relationship would continue to thrive even if one of the principal actors retired. Whatever she said, therefore, carried an air of coordination, just as when Churchill had spoken with Truman in advance of his epic 1946 speech, or similarly in 1982 when Reagan condemned Soviet communism to the 'ash heap of history', while Thatcher approvingly looked on.[19] Bound by their common language and purpose, her timing and setting implied, the new administration and her own government would continue to speak with one voice. What she said, therefore, mattered, and what she said made headlines around the world. 'We are not in a Cold War now,' she told reporters before her departure back across the Atlantic. East and West instead enjoyed 'a new relationship much wider than the Cold War ever was'.[20]

Historians now and into the future will inevitably debate when to date the Cold War's end, undergoing much the same exercise as when attempting to pinpoint its start, and Thatcher's November 1988 words in the White House will make a good claim for the title. If nothing else they show a clear change over time, as something fundamental must have occurred between 1981 and 1988 to convince both Reagan and Thatcher, two unabashed Cold Warriors, that the conflict had entered a new and presumably final phase. Two things in particular. First, Mikhail Gorbachev came to power in Moscow in 1985, promising political reform (*perestroika*) and social openness (*glasnost*) as intertwined solutions to the Soviet Union's glaringly apparent woes. Soviet communism wasn't working, being incapable of providing the economic or spiritual needs of its own people or its broader empire. This was apparent to most honest observers by the late 1970s, though the ensuing collapse of global petroleum prices in the early 1980s reduced the Soviet Union's most significant financial asset and its last bulwark against overall collapse. Selected general secretary in 1985 after a long career rocketing up the Communist Party's hierarchy (in the Soviet Union, a rise across three decades was considered shocking speed), Gorbachev came to power seeking not to eliminate the Soviet state – though that was the ultimate unplanned result of his policies – but to rebuild and thus save the state and its communist ideals he held dear. 'We can't go on living like this', he told his wife upon assuming power. 'The system was dying away, its sluggish senile blood no longer contained any vital juices.'[21]

Salvation required solvency, however, and thus among Gorbachev's first moves once ensconced in the Kremlin was to signal his desire for reduced East–West tensions, less because they had become too dangerous, but mostly because they'd become far too expensive for Moscow to maintain while simultaneously re-investing in its domestic reforms. Put simply, being unable to afford both guns and butter for some time, and having chosen the former for decades, Gorbachev's cadre believed peace, or at least its appearance, a necessary prerequisite for renewed prosperity. To survive, he said, required savings found in the most obvious, but also the most ominous, place: by reducing the cost of the Cold War itself, which could only come by reducing the tension that had built for decades across that Iron Curtain Churchill described years before. As one of Gorbachev's principal foreign policy advisers explained, successful restructuring on such scale demanded they reformulate not just the 'arithmetic' of Superpower tensions, meaning how much was spent on defence, but also the basic 'algebra' of spending priorities.[22]

Unilaterally reducing tensions is hard, however, and dangerous. Peace requires partners, and Gorbachev was fortunate to find in Thatcher not merely a willing participant in discussion of a new East–West dynamic, but also an advocate for persuading Reagan to try the same. Gorbachev was someone 'with whom we can do business', she said after dealing with the new Soviet leader. He appeared to be 'an unusual Russian in that he was much less constrained, more charming, more open to discussion and debate, and did not stick to prepared notes', she wrote, advising the president to give the new man at least the opportunity to state his case. Even as she cautioned 'the more charming the adversary, the more dangerous', she implored Reagan to meet Gorbachev, and more importantly, to listen earnestly to him.[23]

Reagan agreed, but in doing so revealed to subsequent historians the inherent nature of the Anglo-American special relationship at this time. More specifically, its inherent power dynamic. Head of the weaker partner, Thatcher could advise and cajole her American counterpart, with counsel warmed by years of their personal trust. She could not ultimately convince Reagan to do something he did not already desire to try, nor in fact was her own willingness to treat with the new Soviet leader sufficient to prompt any significant reduction in superpower tensions. Only the American president could do that, and Reagan had plenty of reasons of his own for seeking reduced tensions by the start of his second term.

One in particular stands out: he was scared. Bellicose language from both sides during his first years in office had produced by 1983 hair-trigger tensions, leading to multiple near nuclear exchanges based upon faulty data interpreted by frightened policymakers and military leaders in the most pessimistic light. The Soviets 'are so defense minded, so paranoid about being attacked that without being in any way soft on them we ought to tell them no one here has any intention of doing anything like that', Reagan confided to his diary that year.[24] At the same time, he conceded that Soviet leaders had good reason to view American strategy, and in particular American strategists, with alarm. Briefed yet again on the Pentagon's overall strategy for nuclear war, Reagan wrote that the presentation left him only able to think about the recently aired movie, *The Day After*, which portrayed the devastating even hopeless aftermath of a nuclear exchange through the prism of one small Kansas town. He was not the only one unable to put memories of the movie aside. More Americans tuned in to watch the film than that year's Super Bowl, and its depressing message left its mark not only on the overall politics of the day, but on the president as well. 'Yet there were still some people at the Pentagon who claimed a nuclear war was "winnable,"' Reagan observed. 'I thought they were crazy.'[25]

Reagan thus had his own reasons for hoping Gorbachev's reforms presented an opportunity and was undoubtedly pressed by Thatcher to greet the new Soviet leader with an open mind. He'd wanted to meet with Gorbachev's predecessors, believing both in the power of personal diplomacy and in his own persuasive aura, but the timing never seemed right. More than timing, in fact, 'they keep dying on me,' he told one aide during his first term, as three Soviet leaders in a row succumbed to age and poor health.[26] He was thus an eager convert to Thatcher's endorsement that Gorbachev was different, not only because he trusted her opinion, but because he already wanted to believe she was right. 'I want you to know, I think there's something to this man,' she told Reagan in December of 1984, mere weeks after he'd won a second term in landslide fashion. 'He's got a vision. He [Gorbachev] wants to see the world change and I think the two of you might be able to begin that process. You should think about this, Mr. President. There is something there with him.' A witness to their conversation later explained, 'she had a big impact … she told him that at Camp David'.[27]

But, was he persuaded? In truth Reagan listened to Thatcher but also wanted to believe Gorbachev was indeed a new brand of Soviet leader, because he too hoped by the start of his second term for reduced superpower tensions. More to the point, he hoped for broad nuclear disarmament, having become thoroughly disillusioned in their utility, and even their morality. 'He periodically would say, "Let's get rid of them [nuclear weapons],"' one of Reagan's national security advisers during his second term recalled, and no amount of bureaucratic pushback could persuade him otherwise. 'When you win forty-eight out of fifty states, you, too, can talk about eliminating nuclear weapons,' Secretary of State George Schutz explained to frustrated colleagues.[28] They thought Reagan's dream of a nuclear-free world delusional, naive and dangerous. Yet Reagan tried. Persuaded to meet with Gorbachev in 1985, it was only a year later that the two men nearly – so very nearly – concluded an accord designed to eliminate all nuclear weapons by the year 2000. Disarmament hadn't even been on the agenda when the two leaders met in Reykjavik in 1986, but the opportunity to turn the momentum of reduced East–West tensions into a non-nuclear nirvana proved too tempting to avoid, but then ultimately too politically difficult to achieve. Their accord crumbled in the eleventh hour, neither man willing nor able to risk the ire of their own less-idealistic bureaucracies back home.

Note, however, that Reykjavik occurred after Reagan and Gorbachev met in Geneva, which in turn took place after Thatcher's suggestion that the time had come for a bilateral Soviet-American summit. The power dynamics on display in that sentence should not be overlooked lightly. Thatcher could suggest, but only Reagan could decide. Thatcher could prompt, but Reagan was not convinced of Gorbachev's possibility, let alone his sincerity, until the two men had met (in her absence). Put in its simplest yet most profound terms, Thatcher could desire better East–West relations; she could embrace or at least endorse Gorbachev's reforms; she could even call for a more stable and peaceful Europe; but she could not do anything of substance to bring those changes about on her own. She was not invited to the meetings that mattered most. The president had all the power, because the United States was, unquestionably, the more powerful partner in their unequal special relationship.

The same was true after Reagan left office. Thatcher made headlines by declaring the Cold War effectively over following her morning of meetings with President-Elect George H.W. Bush in late November of 1988, but she could only hope her powers of persuasion proved as potent with the new president as with the last. Indeed, this is why her statement that the Cold War was no more made headlines in the first place: because Bush and those around him were not yet convinced. More accurately, they disagreed, and perceived Thatcher's public statements designed not only to prod the new administration into a more amenable line towards Gorbachev, but also to reassert her own position as the American president's principal overseas adviser. 'Gorbachev badly needs a period of stability,' incoming National Security Adviser Brent Scowcroft explained to journalists mere hours after taking up his new West Wing office in January of 1989, 'if not definite improvement in the [superpower] relationship so he can face the awesome problem he has at home of trying to restructure his economy.' More menacingly, Scowcroft continued, Gorbachev seemed 'interested in making trouble within the Western Alliance', in particular by convincing Washington's NATO allies – including, Great Britain – through 'a peace offensive' that the Soviets were no longer to be feared. Anyone who thought otherwise, he argued, was merely naive. As he put it mere weeks after Thatcher's declaration, no matter what Gorbachev promised, or European leaders like Thatcher desired, 'The Cold War is not over.'[29]

Thatcher did not let up once Bush took office. Speed was of the essence lest 'the euphoria' surrounding Gorbachev's promises swell beyond control, she said, urging Bush to meet with the Soviet leader at his first opportunity. Painfully aware that Bush did not share her enthusiasm, or her sense that the Cold War was waning if not already in a new final phase, she praised Bush's 'past statements for dealing with the Soviets' which were 'right on the mark', even though they directly contradicted her own public and private remarks. 'I don't want to be cast as the person stalling better East–West relations,' Bush told Thatcher, though in saying so he made plain that his concern was less for the substance of the charge than of its potential origin.[30] European leaders could advise, he explained; but even Thatcher had to understand that the decision of whether and when to meet Gorbachev in person, and more fundamentally of how next to meet the Soviet challenge, would be made not on Bonn, Paris, or even Whitehall, but instead in the White House alone.

The dynamic repeated over the ensuing years. Thatcher advised, cajoled and supported. Bush took credit for her presence when he desired, using her to demonstrate international support for uncomfortable positions, but never finding her recommendations or opinion decisive. So obvious was the power disparity between them, a close reading of his words demonstrates that Bush clearly revelled in having Thatcher by his side as a political prop, not as a puppet master. No better example exists of this dynamic than Bush's remarks mere days after Saddam Hussein's invasion of Kuwait in August 1990. Purely by coincidence, Bush and Thatcher were scheduled to meet – more accurately, to both attend – at the Aspen Institute in Colorado only a few days later. Reporters clamoured to hear more of his developing response to the crisis, and Bush wasted no time including her both in his welcoming introductions and in noting the significance of her presence:

> And of course, I've saved the piece de resistance to the very end, our very special guest, our friend, the distinguished world leader, Margaret Thatcher. It was very, very comforting to me today when I went out to try to represent you, the people of the United States, in expressing our views on the current emergency, I would say, in the Persian Gulf – naked aggression by the State of Iraq. I felt very comforted by the fact that as I spoke Prime Minister Thatcher was there with me answering the tougher questions and standing shoulder to shoulder with the United States. Madame Prime Minister, let me say that for more than a decade now America has known no better friend of freedom anywhere in the world than you, and it's an honor to join you today.[31]

No American president would suggest foreign interference in their decision-making was the decisive factor. The country has too long an isolationist, even xenophobic, streak for that. Thatcher's voters share a similar independent streak, but also a clear understanding of the great power pecking order at the Cold War's end. Hence, when addressing European diplomats on the subject of a new European security structure in late August 1990, she could offer with no fear of domestic backlash the reminder that 'Not for the first time in Europe's history we have to give thanks for the United States and its President, for giving leadership and moving rapidly and decisively to defend not only America's own interests but those of Europe as well. We owe a great debt of gratitude to President Bush for his courage and steadiness.'[32]

Subtle word choices can be revealing. In this case, they reveal that Bush drew strength from Thatcher's presence, but at no time suggested anyone but he would lead whatever ensuing coalition or international response formed against Hussein. Thatcher, meanwhile, even while making a case for European leadership, casually and reflexively noted that Bush's 'leadership' proved decisive in the current crisis. One might well say that a close reading of the subtlety of two speeches out of the hundreds each gave annually does not offer conclusive evidence of the imbalance of power inherent in the Anglo-American special relationship in 1990, nor would that be a novel observation. Yet even as it is hard to argue that the United States was not the dominant partner, there is ample evidence that even Reagan, Thatcher's great friend, made decisions affecting his country without her consent, even on matters of particular national pride. 'She was very adamant and continued to insist that we cancel our landings on Granada,' Reagan recalled of the 1983 American invasion of the British Commonwealth Nation increasingly under Cuba's influence. 'I couldn't tell her that it had already begun.'[33]

The same demonstration of power was revealed in Bush's response to an issue Thatcher cared for deeply: Germany's unification. This too offers another candidate for the moment the Cold War concluded, as many historians consider Germany's fate a crucial factor in the post-1945 East–West split. Thatcher clearly hoped for continued political division even in the wake of the Berlin Wall's surprising fall in November 1990, and the East German regime's ensuing unsurprising collapse. She feared renewed German nationalism, and indeed militarism, an inevitable consequence of German unification, and was not shy about saying so publicly, or more bluntly behind closed doors. 'I've read my history,' she lectured aides.[34] She'd been bombed by Germans in the last war, and had no interest in enabling them another go in the future.

Bush had other plans, however. Working primarily with Kohl, he negotiated an international accord which gave Germans not only one government, but a whole place in the North Atlantic Treaty Organization (NATO). This, frankly, Bush cared about far more than any rise of German nationalism, because he believed to his core that European peace itself could only be maintained with an on-site American presence, which itself required a viable NATO of which Germany could not be successfully divorced. So long as the United States stayed in Europe, he reasoned, American policymakers could keep the pattern of European violence from repeating, and keep Germany under wraps, especially. 'Our European allies want us there,' he told reporters, 'because they know that the United States is there as a stabilizing factor' against unknown threats and uncertainty, 'and we will be there for a long time to come.' Cutting to the heart of the matter, Bush answered not only the central question underlying Germany's diplomatic fate, but also a question no reporter had yet asked. 'I'm not contemplating a neutralized Germany,' he said. Just as words matter for what they reveal, pronouns matter most of all.[35]

Bush decided, negotiated with Kohl, and only then turned to assuaging Thatcher's fears, and similar concerns for revitalized German nationalism raised by France's Francois Mitterrand and Gorbachev. Each of the four powers would need to agree to rewrite the accords for Germany's governance still in effect from the Second World War, and each ultimately required American support more than a divided Germany. Once Bush decided, in other words, the international course was set. All that was left was gaining allied agreement, which Bush did not by persuading Thatcher so much as by listening to her. The remarkable weekend of February 24–6, 1990 in which Bush and Kohl negotiated Germany's future at Camp David – a place Thatcher knew well – reveals this dynamic in full. Kohl was on site. Thatcher a voice from afar the American president need only manage. 'Unification was coming fast,' she told Bush mere hours before Kohl's arrival, and 'all are worried about the consequences.' Indeed, she continued, 'if we are not too careful, the Germans will get in peace [European dominance] what Hitler couldn't get in war.'[36]

'This is very helpful, timely, and interesting,' the president replied, never suggesting her concerns were in any way convincing. He'd called so Thatcher could vent her spleen and feel heard, even if the ultimate decision of Europe's future geography would be decided by a German and an American in the snowy mountains outside Washington, DC. 'I can't do anything about her,' Kohl complained. 'I can't understand her. The Empire declined fighting Germany – she thinks the UK paid this enormous price, and here comes Germany again.'[37]

'We don't look at it that way,' Bush assured his guest, and ultimately Thatcher could be a bump, but not an insurmountable obstacle, on the road to German unification. 'You and I must take care to consult' their British counterpart, he said. 'I called Margaret today just to listen to her, which I did for an hour.'[38] So convinced was Bush of the procedural formality of the call, in fact, at the close of the weekend he and Kohl read statements to the press announcing their conclusions – statements that had been written by White House aides not only before the German Chancellor's visit, but before his conversation with Thatcher. He would hear her words, in other words, not heed. She was, after all, 'a good friend of the States', he'd earlier told his diary, 'but she talks all the time when she's in a conversation'.[39]

Her advice mattered. Her friendship buoyed. Her presence demonstrated international support and allied solidarity. Yet ultimately her words, no matter how capable of changing newspaper headlines, only changed Cold War dynamics when the president allowed. It had been that way since Truman's time. Churchill's declaration of Cold War, his aforementioned 'Iron Curtain' address, meant all the more because the president of the United States publicly agreed. Britain's prime minister declared the Cold War on, and for all intents and purposes it was, because the more powerful partner within the special relationship consented. Forty-three years later, another British prime minister travelled across the Atlantic and declared the Cold War had ended, and it didn't, because the incoming American president disagreed. In the final analysis, that is all one needs to know about the imbalance of power embedded within Anglo-American relations from the Cold War's start to its end. So too which nation could act as it liked, and which required permission.

Notes

1. Public Papers of the Presidency (University of California-Santa Barbara American Presidency Project), 'Address to the Nation on Energy and National Goals', 15 July 1979. https://www.presidency.ucsb.edu/documents/address-the-nation-energy-and-national-goals-the-malaise-speech. Hereafter PPP UCSB.
2. William E. Leuchtenburg, *In the Shadow of FDR* (Ithaca: Cornell University Press, 1993), 361.
3. Ibid.
4. PPP UCSB, 'Inaugural Address', 20 January 1981, https://www.presidency.ucsb.edu/documents/inaugural-address-11.
5. Ibid.
6. Philip Abbott, 'Leadership by Exemplar: Reagan's FDR and Thatcher's Churchill', *Presidential Studies Quarterly* 27, no. 2 (Spring 1997): 199.
7. Tim Harford, 'Echoes of a Bygone Age Show Britain Losing Its Sense of Direction', *The Financial Times*, 14 September 2017.
8. Papers of Margaret Thatcher, Margaret Thatcher Foundation, 'Conservative Party General Election Manifesto', 11 April 1979, https://www.margaretthatcher.org/document/110858. For Thatcher's expression of the same point in her own words, see also, Thatcher Papers, 'Speech to Conservative Central Council', 24 March 1979, https://www.margaretthatcher.org/document/103980.
9. 'Texts of Statements of Greeting Exchanged by President Reagan and Prime Minister Thatcher', 26 February 1981, UPI Archive, https://www.upi.com/Archives/1981/02/26/Text-of-statements-of-greeting-exchanged-by-President-Reagan/5675352011600/.
10. Ibid.
11. Annelise Anderson, 'Remarks on Ronald Reagan, Intelligence, and the End of the Cold War', 11 November 2011. The Hoover Institution Archive, https://www.hoover.org/research/remarks-ronald-reagan-intelligence-and-end-cold-war.
12. 'Texts of Statements of Greeting Exchanged by President Reagan and Prime Minister Thatcher', 26 February 1981, UPI Archive, https://www.upi.com/Archives/1981/02/26/Text-of-statements-of-greeting-exchanged-by-President-Reagan/5675352011600/.
13. 'Text of Reagan's Address to Parliament on Promoting Democracy', *New York Times*, 9 June 1982.
14. PPP UCSB, 'Special Message to the Congress on Greece and Turkey', 12 March 1947, https://www.presidency.ucsb.edu/documents/special-message-the-congress-greece-and-turkey-the-truman-doctrine.

15. Thomas J. McCormick, *America's Half-Century* (Baltimore: Johns Hopkins University Press, 1995), 77.
16. Winston Churchill, 'Sinews of Peace', 5 March 1946, The National Archives, 'Iron Curtain' Speech, https://www.nationalarchives.gov.uk/education/resources/cold-war-on-file/iron-curtain-speech/.
17. Jeffrey A. Engel, *When the World Seemed New: George H.W. Bush and the End of the Cold War* (New York: Houghton-Mifflin Harcourt, 2017), 20.
18. Donnie Radcliffe and Joseph McLellan, 'Fond Farewells at the White House', *The Washington Post*, 17 November 1989.
19. 'Texts of Statements of Greeting Exchanged by President Reagan and Prime Minister Thatcher', 26 February 1981, UPI Archive, https://www.upi.com/Archives/1981/02/26/Text-of-statements-of-greeting-exchanged-by-President-Reagan/5675352011600/.
20. Engel, *When the World Seemed New*, 20.
21. Robert G. Kaiser, 'Taking His Place in History', *The Washington Post*, 10 November 1996.
22. Engel, *When the World Seemed New*, 52.
23. Thatcher Archives, 'Thatcher-Reagan Meeting at Camp David', 24 December 1984.
24. James Mann, *The Rebellion of Ronald Reagan* (New York: Viking, 2009), 42.
25. David Hoffmann, *The Dead Hand: The Untold Story of the Cold War Arms Race and Its Dangerous Legacy* (New York: Anchor, 2010), 92.
26. James Graham Wilson, 'Did Reagan Make Gorbachev Possible', *Presidential Studies Quarterly* 38, no. 3 (September 2008): 457.
27. Miller Center for Public Affairs Ronald Reagan Oral History Project, 'Interview with James F. Kuhn', 71.
28. Mann, *The Rebellion of Ronald Reagan*, 43.
29. Engel, *When the World Seemed New*, 85.
30. George Bush Presidential Library, 'Telcon with Prime Minister Margaret Thatcher', 23 January 1989.
31. PPP UCSB, 'Remarks at the Aspen Institute Symposium', 2 August 1990.
32. Thatcher MSS, 'Speech to European Democrat Union Conference', 30 August 1990.
33. Ronald Reagan, *An American Life* (New York: Threshold, 1990), 454–5.
34. G.R. Urban, *Diplomacy and Disillusion at the Court of Margaret Thatcher* (London: I.B. Taurus, 1996), 112.
35. Engel, *When the World Seemed New*, 343.
36. George Bush Presidential Library, Papers of Condoleezza Rice, Subject Files, File: 2+4 Germany No. 3 (2), 'Bush-Thatcher Telcon', 24 February 1990.
37. Svetlana Savranskaya et al, eds., *The Last Superpower Summits* (Budapest: Central European University Press, 2016), 603.
38. Ibid.
39. Jon Meacham, *Destiny and Power: The American Odyssey of George H.W. Bush* (New York: Random House, 2016), 371.

Chapter 13

THE ANGLO-AMERICAN SPECIAL RELATIONSHIP: PAST, PRESENT, FUTURE

Steve Marsh

The Anglo-American special relationship has been a core feature of international relations (IR) since the Second World War and has naturally attracted significant scholarly interest. Traditionally this scholarship has been dominated by IR theorists and diplomatic historians. The former have investigated the special relationship conceptually by examining the conduct of Anglo-American relations comparatively with other international relationships and set against the patterns of behaviour predicted by IR theories, especially realism.[1] Diplomatic historians have provided detailed archive-derived accounts of Anglo-American cooperation and conflict set predominantly within a frame of power and mutual utility.[2] More recently understanding of the Anglo-American relationship has been broadened by scholars examining the impact of cultural connections between the United Kingdom (UK) and United States (US).[3]

This chapter examines how the modern special relationship has evolved from its inception in the Second World War through to the present. In doing so it traces the changing nature of Anglo-American relations and offers reasons why the special relationship has, contrary to numerous predictions, survived both systemic change upon the end of the Cold War and the transition from a partnership of equals to a highly asymmetric relationship. Finally, it offers some tentative suggestions as to why the special relationship will likely continue to confound its doomsayers in the foreseeable future.

Origins of the special relationship

In March 1946 former British prime minister Winston Churchill, now leader of the opposition in the House of Commons, travelled to Fulton, Missouri, to deliver what he regarded as one of the most important speeches of his career. Remembered foremost for its articulation of East–West tensions that eventuated in the Cold War,

---

This chapter was completed in mid-2021. However, subsequent events including conclusion of AUKUS and reaction to the Russia-Ukraine war tend to support the claim made that UK-US relations are likely to remain close in the foreseeable future.

the so-called Iron Curtain speech also implanted the term 'special relationship' into the lexicon of Anglo-American relations.[4] Churchill was little concerned for the conceptual accuracy of this nomenclature; political scientists and IR theorists could have responsibility for that. His primary objective was to bind Britain and America together as a counter to Soviet power and to continue the intimate and wide-ranging UK–US cooperation that had developed during the Second World War. Never before, or since, had two Great Powers integrated their efforts as these did in their fight against the Axis powers. The US–UK combined chiefs of staff jointly devised and directed strategy. American and British servicemen were commanded by each other's officers. Five Combined Boards provided coordinated access to raw materials and the production and distribution of munitions, goods and services. The Lend-Lease programme delivered to the UK $27 billion worth of US goods without payment and the UK reciprocated $6 billion worth.[5] And there was widespread sharing of intelligence and technology, including the Manhattan project that developed the atomic bomb.

In hindsight the Second World War clearly brought forth the modern special relationship, albeit that its antecedents can be traced far further back in Anglo-American history.[6] Yet when the war ended there was no certainty that close US–UK wartime cooperation would extend into peacetime. The United States emerged with its homeland unscathed by the conflict and possessing enormous self-sufficiency, a monopoly over the atomic bomb, the world's most advanced industrial-military complex and a dominant global economic position. It held $20 billion of the world's $33 billion of gold reserves, manufactured over half of the world's goods and controlled over half of the world's shipping. In contrast, Britain's infrastructure was badly war-torn, basic life essentials were in short supply, and the economy was exhausted by the war effort and dislocated by its dependence on overseas trade and investment. By 1945 its exports were 30 per cent of the 1939 total, import prices had risen 50 per cent, its gold and dollar reserves had more than halved, and it had liquidated substantial overseas assets and incurred the largest external debt in history.[7]

The stark reality in 1945 was that the Second World War had accelerated shifts in power such that Britain needed cooperation with the United States more than the United States needed cooperation with Britain. In March 1944 British officials concluded that their principal objective should be to harness American power to British ends, steering 'this great unwieldy barge, the United States of America, into the right harbour'.[8] Yet the United States gave little indication of such pliancy. It ended lend-lease abruptly and subsequent negotiation of the 1946 US loan to Britain was an acrimonious affair.[9] The Combined Boards were dismantled rapidly. The US Congress passed the McMahon Act that terminated Anglo-American nuclear cooperation. American commitment to European security became uncertain as the US demobilization programme gathered such speed that even Secretary of Defence Forrestal expressed concern.[10] US determination to drive a multilateral free trade system contributed heavily to the disaster of sterling convertibility in 1947. And battle re-joined within the American body politique between internationalism and isolationism; mixed American reactions to Churchill's Iron Curtain speech spoke clearly to this. A State Department-sponsored opinion poll in February 1947 found 70 per cent to be against a hard-line policy towards the Soviets.[11]

That the special relationship took root in the post-war world owed in part to assiduous British diplomacy. Churchill, for instance, tirelessly advocated close Anglo-American cooperation and in developing a practice of prime minister-president summit meetings established one of the enduring symbols of the special relationship.[12] Much more significant, though, was gradual US acceptance that the Soviet Union and communism more broadly threatened American interests. George Kennan's famous Long Telegram in 1946 provided both an ideological and a *realpolitik* basis for a US policy of containing communist expansionism.[13] This thinking, as evidenced by the subsequent Truman Doctrine, European Recovery Programme (Marshall Aid) and Senate passage of the Vandenberg Resolution, progressively gained political traction to a point that in 1950 National Security Council Resolution 68 effectively shifted containment policy from a primarily European to a global level. These new American priorities restored to Anglo-American relations a common enemy and renewed Britain's value as an ally to the United States.

In 1950 American officials concluded that of US international relationships Britain was 'in a special or preferred position – the facts of the world situation require it'.[14] Britain was politically stable, had recovered many losses incurred to its empire during the initial stages of the Second World War, retained significant military assets and had government committed to its being a leading world power.[15] Hence the Attlee government re-introduced conscription in 1947, diverted resources away from much-needed exports to rearmament programmes and maintained rationing whilst concomitantly devoting a greater proportion of national income to defence expenditure than did the United States. Additionally, Britain's decline was disguised by the wartime destruction suffered by other countries. Thus, for example, in 1950 Britain accounted for 25.5 per cent of world exports of manufactured goods, a market share that was up from 21.3 per cent in 1937 and equivalent to more than two and half times that of France and three times that of West Germany.[16] In short, Britain was the strongest ally available to the United States in waging global containment and a renewed sense of common purpose consequently dispelled the post-Second World War malaise in Anglo-American relations. In May 1950 British representatives at the London Conferences noted of the Americans, 'It is the first time since the war that they have approached us as a partner on the most general issues of policy.'[17]

The notion of a special relationship gained ground as Anglo-American functional cooperation widened and deepened. As an American military report concluded in April 1950, 'there is and should be a special U.S.–U.K. relationship … Accordingly an examination of the relationship is necessary, not to see whether it can be retained but to see how it can be strengthened.'[18] Anglo-American economic power underpinned the liberal international economic system that was established at Bretton Woods in 1944 and which became vital to economic recovery and prosperity within the Western Alliance. The BRUSA Agreement that in March 1946 marked the reaffirmation of the vital Second World War intelligence cooperation between the United Kingdom and United States was progressively expanded to become the so-called five-eyes with the inclusion of Canada, New

Zealand and Australia. The UK and US military power gave NATO credibility from its formation in 1949 and British and Commonwealth troops were soon fighting alongside their American counterparts in the Korean War. Anglo-American naval power was key to protecting vital sea lanes and Britain afforded key strategic bases for American conventional and nuclear forces. Furthermore, the provisions of the McMahon Act were progressively worked around until agreement in 1958 of the Mutual Defence Agreement re-enabled unprecedented sharing of Anglo-American nuclear research and weaponry.

None of this meant frictionless Anglo-American relations; far from it. The British feared consequences of the virulence of American anti-communism, resented the spread of American influence into areas hitherto of their control and fought against US–Soviet bilateralism that would force Britain from the top table of international powers. Conversely, the Americans were suspicious of British socialism, feared that Britain placed protecting its economic interests ahead of anti-communism and were sensitive to the British tactic of using American power to support Britain's overseas interests. Nevertheless, such differences were generally negotiated within boundaries expected of the Anglo-American alliance and the evolution of exceptionally close diplomatic and functional cooperation infused the deepening special relationship with resilience such that it could weather temporary high-level political differences and even serious ruptures such as the 1956 Suez crisis.

Years of transition[19]

In 1967 US Ambassador to the Court of Saint James, David Bruce, wrote, 'The so-called Anglo-American special relationship is now little more than sentimental terminology, although the underground waters of it will flow with a deep current.'[20] What had happened to warrant Bruce's conclusion? And why ultimately was he proven wrong?

At the highest political levels, there had been a progressive changing of the guard. The resurrection of Anglo-American relations had been overseen by officials who had forged relationships during the Second World War and experienced first-hand the exceptionally close UK–US cooperation that had been so important to victory. By the 1960s a new generation of political leaders and officials were in power. They were less influenced by the wartime experience and sometimes ambivalent about Anglo-American relations. This made tensions within Anglo-American relations more difficult to manage, such as those over British refusal to commit militarily to the Vietnam War and in 1973 over the Yom Kippur War, the latter even leading to temporary US suspension of UK–US intelligence cooperation in protest of British policies.[21] It also meant that the consideration of Anglo-American relations came secondary to other objectives more often. For instance, in the early 1960s US under-secretary of state George Ball championed a Multilateral Force solution to tensions within NATO over nuclear defence that would as a by-product have compromised Britain's national deterrent and jeopardized wider UK–US nuclear cooperation. Similarly, in the early 1970s Prime Minister Edward Heath downplayed the special relationship to secure British membership of the European Communities (EC) – so much so that US secretary of state Kissinger privately accused him of being 'Gaullist in his outlook, and the only anti-American UK Prime Minister in many years'.[22]

However, much more influential than the changing of the political guard were shifts in power and strategic focus that even officials sympathetic to Anglo-American relations could not ignore when assessing the utility of UK–US cooperation. The coincidence of Anglo-American strategic priorities weakened. Britain became focused increasingly on Europe whilst Vietnam, the Indo-Pakistan War and Nixon's opening to China all drew US attention to Asia. These differences were fed further by diverging interpretations of the Cold War. The United States viewed the world primarily through a prism of superpower balance and anti-communism. Britain, and many other West European governments, was suspicious of US–USSR bilateralism and less convinced of the Soviet threat given an established East–West balance in Europe and the emergence of détente.

It was Britain's relative decline, though, that most moved Bruce to pronounce the special relationship to be over. Even as Anglo-American relations deepened in the early 1950s, it became increasingly obvious that Britain could not maintain its overseas capabilities and obligations. Prime Minister Macmillan's Wind of Change speech signalled the inevitability of independence sweeping through the British Empire. Lack of confidence in Britain's economy weakened sterling and its eventual devaluation in 1967 also drew pressure upon the Bretton Woods system. And in January 1968 Prime Minister Harold Wilson acknowledged British overstretch by announcing Britain would withdraw from East of Suez. Furthermore, this contraction in Britain's global footprint and capabilities accelerated into the early 1970s. Over the period 1950–73 Britain's GNP slipped from second largest to sixth, its share of world trade declined from 11 to under 6 per cent, and its military manpower contracted from fourth position to fifteenth in 1973.[23] Its overseas dependent territories also diminished hugely. In 1973, excepting southern Rhodesia, they totalled *c*.700,000 square miles and some 5 million people; in 1945 they had accounted for 6.4 million square miles and 500 million people – excluding Canada, Australia, New Zealand and South Africa.[24] In October 1974 Kissinger bluntly advised President Ford that the United States had to 'operate on the assumption that Britain is through'.[25]

Why, then, did the special relationship not fade away as Bruce predicted? The answer lies partly in an unforeseen transformation in American fortunes that shook US confidence and made working with allies ever more important. The American economy faltered. In 1968 inflation ran at 4 per cent and the Federal Reserve increased US interest rates to 5.5 per cent – their highest level since 1929 and the onset of the Great Depression. In 1971 the United States ran a trade deficit for the first time in the twentieth century and the Nixon administration signalled the end of the Bretton Woods system when in August that year it unilaterally announced a series of measures to support the American economy, including a 10 per cent import surcharge, devaluation of the dollar and cancellation of the direct international convertibility of the dollar into gold. From November 1973 to March 1975 the American economy remained in recession, unemployment peaked in May 1975 at 9 per cent and wage-price controls encouraged stagflation. Concomitantly, domestic and international confidence in American leadership weakened. The heavily televised Tet offensive in January 1968 further inflamed anti-Vietnam War sentiment within America and the assassination of Martin Luther King brought civil rights tensions to a head. The emergence of detente exposed transatlantic differences over how to handle the USSR. And the unravelling of the Watergate saga drained credibility from the presidency. A poll in 1972 indicated that 38 per cent of Americans felt their leaders had 'consistently lied' to them over the past ten years. In 1975 that figure had mushroomed to 69 per cent.[44]

The other key development that helped the special relationship at this time was the rise in the relative utility of soft power. In the 1950s and early 1960s Europe was the key Cold War battleground and the calculus of war, peace, and national survival rested primarily with military strength, technological innovation and economic coercion.[45] However, construction of the Berlin Wall symbolized an uneasy status quo in Europe and a progressive shift in the geographic focus of the Cold War towards the periphery. The Cuban Missile Crisis and advent of Mutually Assured Destruction moved East–West relations towards arms control – something reflected in the 1968 Nuclear Non-proliferation Treaty, the 1972 Anti-Ballistic Missile Treaty and the development of detente.[46] In addition, the structures and distribution of power in the post-Second World War international system were shifting as the world became more interdependent and new influential international actors emerged – including MNCs, TNCs, OPEC and the supranational EC. Economic power became increasingly dispersed as Japan recovered, West Germany experienced its 'economic miracle' and the EC expanded. International organizations became more difficult to manage in the face of decolonization and developing world nationalism. And OPEC action during the Yom Kippur War demonstrated new vulnerabilities in advanced industrial societies arising from commodity dependence.

Cumulatively these changes encouraged a relative decline in the utility of hard power, especially military power, promoted a much more complex international system and left the United States in need of restoring confidence in its leadership at home and abroad. Crucially for the special relationship, this meant in turn that the United States needed to re-engage allies, shift the balance of its policy style towards multilateralism and seek to shape in suitable ways a growing number of international organizations, institutions and regimes. Britain once again stood first amongst US allies, being blessed with soft power resources disproportionate to its size and military strength. English was the lingua franca of international business and British culture was consumed globally. Britain held privileged positions within the institutions created in the aftermath of the Second World War, especially its permanent UN Security Council status. It was also a key Atlanticist member of NATO and had become a member of the EC in 1973, transformed empire into Commonwealth and established itself in the exclusive club of official nuclear powers.

Just as importantly to the Americans, Britain was inclined to leverage its soft power in ways complementary to US objectives. For a start, British as well as American principles and power flowed through the international institutions and organizations created after the Second World War and it was therefore in UK interests to see these preserved through judicious reform and adaptation. British officials noted this confluence of interest in April 1974 when concluding, 'The President and his key advisers are committed to policies which identify US self-interest with positions on major issues which are favourable to British interests e.g. the pursuit of liberal trade policies, the revitalisation of transatlantic relations and a continuing commitment to the defence of Europe.'[26] More generally, policymakers found that the combination of shared English language and historic cultural, political and economic ties induced similar Anglo-American perspectives on world affairs. As Prime Minister Wilson noted of talks with President Ford in January 1975, 'We don't have, you know, to spend about fifty minutes in every hour arguing about first principles, arguing about trying to convince one another. They are thoroughly practical and that's why you get six times as much results out of an hour of discussions such of the kind we've had.'[27] Furthermore, these long-standing ties and reciprocal cultural consumption nurtured affinity between British and American peoples that was both important in sustaining Anglo-American cooperation and, especially after the Vietnam War, politically valuable to successive US presidencies in demonstrating to the American people that the United States did not stand alone in its leadership of the Free World. In November 1974, the US State Department noted poignantly, 'Without identifying hypothetical situations, it seems prudent to assume that at some time in the next 5–10 years we may want to have a British flag alongside our own for both political and military reasons.'[28]

The contemporary special relationship

The end of the Cold War was thought by some to portend the denouement of the special relationship. Anglo-American strategic interests would diverge once the Soviet threat vanished, the dominant rationale for close functional cooperation would be removed and Britain would likely be drawn into a European rather than global vocation.[29] Instead, dissolution of the USSR demonstrated that the special relationship had evolved beyond a strategic alliance; it had become reflexive, patterned behaviour. As former US secretary of state, Henry Kissinger, once recalled, the wartime habit of intimate, informal collaboration became a permanent practice.[30]

Nevertheless, for reflexive cooperation and affiliative sentiment to be maintained the special relationship needed to remain relevant. From the British perspective, this was never seriously questioned; Prime Minister Johnson emphasized in January 2021 that building good relations with the White House was 'an important part of any UK prime minister's mission'.[31] British security and prosperity remained entwined with US leadership of the liberal international order that had been established after the Second World War and survived the Cold War with only limited evolution. Immediately after the Cold War, with much talk of the American unipolar moment and the triumph of democracy, it seemed Britain's role would be to support the global expansion of this liberal democratic order. Later, following 9/11, chastening wars in the Middle East and the rise of China, that role would instead be to help the United States defend the rules-based international order against a growing array of threats.

The importance of Anglo-American cooperation to the UK was underscored by two key continuities in British foreign policy. The first was unwavering belief that Britain remained a global actor with global responsibilities, albeit the presentation of this vision varied: medium-sized power punching above its weight, pivotal power and most recently 'Global Britain'. Second, the key contours of post-Cold War British foreign policy supporting this objective changed little. Consider in this respect Prime Minister Blair's articulation of Britain as a pivotal power in November 1999:

> We have got over our Imperial past – and the withdrawal symptoms [...] We have a new role [...] It is to use the strengths of our history to build our future not as a superpower but as a pivotal power, as a power that is at the crux of the alliances and international politics which shape the world and its future.[32]

This couching of British foreign policy in post-Churchillian rhetoric scarcely veiled continued preferences for the traditional three circles, albeit with a substantial re-balancing. The weight of British history flowed through the Commonwealth, Europe hosted key organizations, the United States was the most important partner in international politics and Britain's transatlantic intermediary role remained intact – albeit later badly strained by the 2003 Iraq War and much diminished by Brexit.

The US perspective on Anglo-American relations and wider world affairs would thus most determine the health of the post-Cold War special relationship. US strategic priorities were both more extensive and overlapped less with Britain's than during the Cold War. European inability to deal with civil war in the Balkans following the dissolution of Yugoslavia held US attention upon Europe longer than initially seemed likely. Nevertheless, American priorities progressively shifted towards the Middle East and Asia. Also, US relative power was so great that American policymakers had choices between taking unilateral action and working through alliances and multilateral institutions. At the same time, this global leadership should not enable others to freeride or overstretch US resources – a consideration evidenced in burden-sharing debates and President Trump's America First programme. Furthermore, how the United States identified strategic threats and sought to respond would help determine Anglo-American interaction opportunity.

In practice post-Cold War US handling of the special relationship was somewhat mixed. President George H. Bush upset Prime Minister Thatcher by emphasizing

Germany as a partner in leadership.³³ President Clinton allegedly had to be reminded to mention the special relationship at a time when his relations with Prime Minister Major were on a 'grin and bear it' basis.³⁴ The Obama administration reportedly regarded the special relationship as a joke.³⁵ And President Trump broke norms of Anglo-American policy consultation and coordination and publicly criticized senior British government officials on numerous occasions, even forcing the replacement of the British ambassador to Washington, Sir Kim Darroch. Nevertheless, George H. Bush appreciated deeply Major's support during the First Gulf War and good personal relationships developed between Clinton and Blair, George W. Bush and Blair and Barack Obama and David Cameron. Similarly President Biden affirmed the special relationship ahead of a G7 meeting in the UK in June 2021. Indeed, all post-Cold War US presidents publicly affirmed the special relationship and indulged its trappings and ceremony; even Trump declared the UK–US relationship to be 'the highest level of special'.³⁶

This American mixed messaging reflected less ambivalence about Anglo-American relations than it did the difficulties of managing a truly global foreign policy where all allies wish to feel 'special', domestic politics intrude and energy gets drawn towards problematic actors and issues. Still, though, it had consequences for Anglo-American cooperation and impression management of the special relationship. With the asymmetry of Anglo-American relations greater than ever, US neglect of British opinion, actual or perceived, drew much angst. Images of Prime Minister Gordon Brown seemingly chasing Obama for a meeting in the kitchens of the United Nations were hardly congruous with Anglo-American partnership. It questioned, too, whether the age-old assumption held good that Britain's stalwart support for the United States, sometimes costly and controversial, yielded the access, consultation and influence within American decision-making hoped for. As Danchev argued, 'Without reciprocity, the special relationship is a thing of rags and tatters, a facsimile of its former self, a performance, increasingly hollow.'³⁷ A YouGov poll in May 2010 revealed that 85 per cent of respondents thought the UK had little or no influence on US policies and that 62 per cent believed the United States failed to consider British interests. That same year the House of Commons Foreign Affairs Committee warned against using the term 'special relationship' as it raised unrealistic expectations of British influence vis-à-vis the United States. Impressions of British subservience to Washington became so toxic that when the Cameron government succeeded Brown's Labour government it developed a mantra of 'solid not slavish' relations with the United States and flirted with replacing the nomenclature special relationship with the 'essential relationship'.³⁸

While British media especially intensified its 'end of the affair' commentary in the post-Cold War years, American officials looked on in puzzlement at an over-reading of signs and signals about the special relationship that in February 2009 the US charge at the London Embassy, Richard LeBaron, reported 'would often be humorous, if it were not so corrosive'.³⁹ The 'coral reef' of Anglo-American relations remained sufficiently robust that close Anglo-American functional cooperation prospered during periods of warm high-level relations and sustained through periodic political squalls.[40] Just as during the Cold War, there were issues of sharp disagreement and friction. John Major rated policy disagreements over Bosnia as the most serious since the Suez crisis.[41] There were damaging recriminations during post-mortems on military interventions in Iraq and Afghanistan. Washington was taken aback in 2013 when the British Parliament rejected taking military action against Syrian president Bashar al-Assad's government to deter the use of chemical weapons. And in May 2017 the British government suspended intelligence sharing temporarily following American leakage of information about the Manchester terror attack. Conversely, there were plenty of examples of close cooperation. Intelligence sharing intensified after 9/11 and despite frictions the Anglo-American intelligence community became an 'increasingly fused entity', possessing exceptional 'networked' as well as 'quasi-epistemic qualities'.[42] Similarly, in December 2004 Lincoln P. Bloomfield, US assistant secretary of state for political-military affairs, declared, 'The U.S.-U.K. political-military partnership has produced today the closest and most capable bilateral military alliance in the world.'[43] British forces stood alongside American counterparts in the First and Second Gulf Wars, the Balkans, Afghanistan and Libya, and undertook tasks the United States preferred to avoid – such as early leadership of the International Security Assistance Force in Afghanistan. They also endured casualties in support of the United States that other NATO allies avoided by imposing restrictive caveats on where their troops were deployed and the tasks they could fulfil. Furthermore, this togetherness in adversity was reflected frequently in traditional Anglo-American shoulder to shoulder rhetoric and imagery. Consider, for instance, Prime Minister Blair's politically significant presence at President Bush's address to the joint session of Congress on 20 September 2011 and how their meeting at Camp David in March 2003 prior to the invasion of Iraq invoked memories of Roosevelt–Churchill meetings at the same location during the zenith of Anglo-American cooperation in the Second World War.

Looking ahead

Predicting how the special relationship may fare in the future has long proven hazardous. It has defied the logic of realist thought, survived the prescriptions of those favouring a European vocation for Britain and persisted despite both serious crises and becoming quantitatively much reduced. At some point functionalist calculations of mutual utility might finally tip such that the special relationship ends as Ambassador Bruce predicted in 1967. But this seems unlikely in the foreseeable future.

For a start Britain has in the process of Brexit reaffirmed a global foreign policy and cut off processes of Europeanization that were variously hoped and feared to pull it into a European future. The cost of this in terms of its European influence and utility to the United States is significant. The compensation for the United States, though nowhere near equivalent, is a clear affirmation of British Atlanticism that underscores NATO and weakens a possible EU defence alternative. Also, the

Global Britain project is highly leveraged to cooperation with the United States, giving the latter additional influence vis-à-vis London now that British European options have diminished. Early indications of the consequences of this were evident in how the Johnson government reluctantly placed Britain's opening to China second to American views when it announced in July 2020 that Huawei would be removed from UK 5G networks by 2027.[44] Similarly, of course, the Biden administration knows that the Johnson government wants a US–UK trade deal not only for economic gains but also to symbolize success in Britain's breaking away from the EU.

Britain's becoming more dependent on the United States re-sensitises the debate between partner and vassal status. Yet a variety of factors mean another period ahead of rising importance to the United States of capable and reliable allies. These include the reputational damage wrought by Trump's diplomacy and America First programme, the Biden administration's considered recommitment of America to internationalism, the global and diverse array of perceived threats to the United States, shifts in global power detrimental to the United States and American domestic political constraints upon US international engagement. In its recent think piece, 'A More Contested World', the US Intelligence Agency projected greater political instability over the coming two decades and competition for global influence to reach its highest level since the Cold War as the old order continues to weaken and institutions like the UN struggle.[45]

When the United States casts around for allies in protecting the rules-based international order and energising democracy in its defence, few rival Britain in terms of vested interest and established patterns of cooperation. Britain still has privileged positions in most of the key international fora, relies heavily on global free trade for its prosperity and views an American-led international order as key to its security. It also still has significant hard power as an official nuclear state with modern armed forces and substantial soft power, ranking third in the world for the latter in 2021.[46] Moreover, the 'common cast of mind' developed through many years of Anglo-American cooperation means that Britain remains more likely to perceive threats and potential recourses in ways similar to the United States than most allies. Indeed, levels of trust, confidence and policy congruity remain unusually high between Britain and the United States. In short, key reasons why the special relationship survived the end of the Cold War still hold good.

Looking ahead, it is difficult to see how record British borrowing during the covid pandemic will not require spending cuts from which defence and security budgets are immune. The economic impact of Brexit is also yet to be fully determined. Nevertheless, Britain is committed to investing in future capabilities of value to the United States that will facilitate continued cooperation. In July 2014 the United States and United Kingdom renewed the Mutual Defence Agreement for a further ten years and in 2016 the British Parliament overwhelmingly approved retaining Britain's nuclear deterrent. At a direct projected cost of £31 billion and a further £50.9 billion portfolio of support programmes (2018–28), the current Vanguard submarines will be replaced with four new Dreadnaught Class ballistic missile submarines such that the British deterrent runs to 2060 and beyond.[47]

Britain's carrier gap will be closed as the *Queen Elizabeth* and *Prince of Wales* enter service and become equipped with F-35B Lightning II stealth jump jets. And the Johnson government announced in November 2020 the largest real-terms increase in the defence budget since Margaret Thatcher's premiership – a four-year £16.5 billion spend over and above an existing commitment to increase the extant £41.5bn budget by 0.5 per cent above inflation.[48] The Biden administration disliked planned reductions in Britain's troop levels and criticized a contemporaneous British cut in overseas aid spending. Nevertheless, coming on the back of particularly fractious transatlantic burden-sharing exchanges during the Trump administration, it also recognized the strong signal sent to NATO states about their spending promises – Britain would be above target by committing 2.2 per cent GDP to defence. It was useful, too, in the context of Biden's efforts to stiffen NATO's resolve and solidarity in the face of Russian resurgence. The boost in Britain's military reach beyond Europe would also be advantageous, something the Johnson government was keen to emphasize. With China being an increasing preoccupation of US strategists, it announced in April 2021 that the *Queen Elizabeth* would shortly lead to the Indo-China region the largest fleet of Royal Navy warships to deploy internationally since the 1982 Falklands War.

There is also little to suggest that the web of economic and cultural connections that bind the United Kingdom and United States together, and which help sustain popular support for Anglo-American cooperation, will weaken in the foreseeable future. Reciprocal cultural consumption remains strong and poll data indicates that British and American people retain a strong sense of affiliation and belief in the importance of the relationship between their countries. For example, a YouGov/Economist poll in early 2021 found 84 per cent of Americans considered Britain to be a friend and the United Kingdom was considered the United States' greatest ally.[49] That same year Pew Centre research indicated 64 per cent of Britons had a favourable view of the United States,[50] and even when their popular dislike of Trump was high they still rated the United States as Britain's most important ally.[51] Furthermore, Brexit will likely further encourage the convergence of British and American economic philosophy and financial management evidenced in UK–US cooperation during the 2007–8 financial crisis and traceable back to the Reagan–Thatcher years. The mutual private sector confidence this encourages is reflected in the scale of the Anglo-American trade and investment relationship. The UK is America's seventh largest trading partner, fifth largest export destination and single largest investor, accounting for more than 15 per cent of all inbound FDI. The United States is by far the United Kingdom's largest export market and source of FDI; investment by American enterprises of nearly $758 billion represents nearly a quarter of their total investment in Europe and more than 12 per cent of all US FDI worldwide.[52] Fears that Brexit may drive some of the 7,500 American firms operating in Britain to relocate to EU countries were calmed by the UK–EU Trade and Cooperation Agreement deal signed on 30 December 2020.

Finally, it is worth considering the Johnson government's ambition that Britain's status as a Science and Technology Superpower be secured by 2030. This requires, according to the British 2021 Integrated Security, Defence, Development and

Foreign Policy review, establishing a leading edge in critical areas such as artificial intelligence and remaining at least third in the world in relevant performance measures for scientific research and innovation.[53] No doubt in 2030 there will be debate about whether this goal has been achieved, which measurement statistics have been selected and so forth. The important point now, however, is that more than ever technology will be vital to sustaining the special relationship. Technological prowess has potential to strengthen core facets of UK–US cooperation and reinforce Anglo-American trust relationships, including nuclear simulation and detection, intelligence gathering and analysis, communications, cyber security and the interoperability of forces. It also opens new possibilities for collaborative capability development and cooperation in the detection, regulation and denial of technology and associated weaponry. Furthermore, while Britain cannot match US innovation and investment in Research and Development, it can potentially make niche contributions and mitigate the danger of American technological superiority decoupling by default UK–US functional cooperation.

Conclusion

The Anglo-American relationship of today would be little recognizable to Churchill. For him, the special relationship was to be an exclusive relationship between the United Kingdom and United States as equal partners. Nowadays the relationship is highly asymmetric and no British prime minister lays claim to exclusivity with Washington. Indeed, Prime Minister Heath found the nomenclature special relationship inconvenient when negotiating British entry to the EC in 1973 and more recently there have been signs that some British leaders have become uncomfortable with the term – Cameron preferred the 'essential relationship' and Johnson reportedly regarded it as '"needy and weak"'.[54]

It is nevertheless unlikely that media and politicians will refrain from using the term 'special relationship' as shorthand for Anglo-American relations; President Biden used it repeatedly during his first visit to Britain in 2021. It is a term that has become culturally embedded in the UK especially to denote not just Anglo-American cooperation but also sentiments of affinity and entwining of peoples. Nor is it yet a term without substance. Over time the rationale for Anglo-American functional cooperation has changed rather than disappeared, as has the relative importance of British hard and soft power to the United States. Equally, advances in technology and communication have facilitated a depth and breadth of economic and cultural intermeshing of Britons and Americans beyond the realms of government that was inconceivable when Churchill delivered his Fulton speech in 1946.

Though diminished in scale, the special relationship is therefore likely to endure in the foreseeable future. It has evolved beyond a strategic partnership into patterned behaviour of cooperation and consultation throughout the coral reef of Anglo-American relations. Its cultural undercurrents, dismissed offhandedly by Ambassador Bruce in 1967, provide stable and important popular support for

Anglo-American cooperation. And it remains the case that there is both a mutual, if uneven, need at the heart of the relationship and a sense of shared destiny insofar as British and American prosperity and security remain bound in the rules-based international order they did so much to create in the aftermath of the Second World War.

Notes

1. Alex Danchev, *On Specialness: Essays in Anglo-American Relations* (London: Macmillan, 1998); Edward Ingram, 'The Wonderland of the Political Scientist', *International Security* 22 (Summer 1997): 53–63; Max Beloff, 'The Special Relationship: An Anglo-American Myth', in *A Century of Conflict: Essays for A.J.P. Taylor*, ed. Martin Gilbert (London: Hamish Hamilton, 1966), 151–71; Charles A. Kupchan, *How Enemies Become Friends: The Sources of Stable Peace* (Princeton: Princeton University Press, 2010); John Dumbrell and Axel Schafer, *America's 'Special Relationships': Foreign and Domestics Aspects of the Politics of Alliance* (London: Routledge, 2009); Ruike Xu, *Alliance Persistence within the Anglo-American Special Relationship: The Post-Cold War Era* (London: Palgrave Macmillan, 2017).
2. See, for instance, Christopher Thorne, *Allies of a Kind: The United States, Britain and the War against Japan* (London: Hamish Hamilton, 1979); C.J. Bartlett, *The Special Relationship: A Political History of Anglo-American Relations since 1945* (London: Longman, 1992); John Baylis, *Anglo-American Defence Relations 1939–1984: The Special Relationship* (London: Macmillan, 1984); J.T. Richelson and D. Ball, *The Ties That Bind: Intelligence Cooperation between the UKUSA Countries* (Hemel Hempstead: Allen and Unwin, 1985); John Dumbrell, *A Special Relationship: Anglo-American Relations in the Cold War and After* (London: Macmillan, 2001); Nigel Ashton, *Kennedy, Macmillan and the Cold War: The Irony of Interdependence* (Basingstoke: Palgrave, 2002); Ian Clark, *Nuclear Diplomacy and the Special Relationship: Britain's Deterrent and America, 1957–1962* (Oxford: Oxford University Press, 1994).
3. Robert M. Hendershot and Steve Marsh, eds., *Culture Matters: Anglo-American Relations and the Intangibles of Specialness* (Manchester: Manchester University Press, 2020); Alan P. Dobson and Steve Marsh eds., *Anglo-American Relations and the Transmission of Ideas: Towards a Political Tradition?* (New York: Berghahn, forthcoming); Robert M. Hendershot, *Family Spats: Perception, Illusion and Sentimentality in the Anglo-American Special Relationship* (Saarbrucken, Germany: VDM Verlag, 2008); Sam Edwards, *Allies in Memory: World War II and the Politics of Transatlantic Commemoration* (Cambridge: Cambridge University Press, 2015); David Haglund, *The US 'Culture Wars' and the Anglo-American Special Relationship* (New York: Palgrave Macmillan, 2019).
4. For an insightful set of analyses of this speech see Steve Marsh ed., 'Special Issue: Churchill's Fulton Missouri Iron Curtain Speech: Its Impact on Anglo-American Relations Seen from the 70th Anniversary Year', *Journal of Transatlantic Studies* 14, no. 4 (2016).
5. R.G.D. Allen, 'Mutual Aid between the US and the British Empire', *Journal of the Royal Statistical Society* 109, no. 3 (1946): 243–77 at 245.
6. Bradford Perkins, *The Great Rapprochement: England and the United States, 1895–1914* (New York: Atheneum, 1968); Harry C. Allen, *Great Britain and the United States: A History of Anglo-American Relations 1783–1952* (London: Odhams

Press, 1954); Marshall Bertram, *The Birth of Anglo-American Friendship: The Prime Facet of the Venezuelan Boundary Dispute* (Lanham, MD: University Press of America, 1992).

7   Alan P. Dobson and Steve Marsh, *United States Foreign Policy since 1945* 2nd ed. (London: Routledge, 2006), 55–6; Alec Cairncross, *Years of Economic Recovery: British Economic Policy 1945–51* (London: Methuen, 1985): 7.

8   United Kingdom National Archive (UKNA), FO 371 38523, 'The Essentials of an American Policy', 21 March 1944.

9   Richard N. Gardner, *Sterling-Dollar Diplomacy in Current Perspective: The Origins and Prospects of Our International Economic Order* (New York: Columbia University Press, 1980), 188–253; Susan Strange, *Sterling and British Policy: A Political Study of an International Currency in Decline* (London: Oxford University Press, 1971): chapter 8; Peter Burnham, 'Re-evaluating the Washington Loan Agreement: A Revisionist View of the Limits of Postwar American Power', *Review of International Studies* 18, no. 2 (1992): 241–59.

10 In 1945 the Americans had 11.8 million men under arms. By 1947 it had just 1.6 million. For Forrestal's disquiet see Walter Millis, ed., *The Forrestal Diaries: The Inner History of the Cold War* (London: Cassell and Co., 1952), 213.

11 Cited in Steve Marsh, *Anglo-American Relations and Cold War Oil* (London: Macmillan, 2003), 19.

12 See, for instance, Steve Marsh, 'Personal Diplomacy at the Summit', in *Churchill and Anglo-American Special Relationship*, ed. Alan P Dobson and Steve Marsh (London: Routledge, 2017), 116–41; Steve Marsh, 'Pageantry, Legitimation, and Special Anglo-American Relations', in *Culture Matters: Anglo-American Relations and the Intangibles of Specialness*, ed. Robert M. Hendershot and Steve Marsh (Manchester: Manchester University Press, 2020), 130–57.

13 Text is in George Kennan, *Memoirs 1925–50* (London: Hutchinson, 1968), Appendix C, 547–59.

14 US National Archive (USNA), RG 59, box 2768, H.R. Labouisse Jr. to Perkins, 27 February 1950.

15 John Darwin, *Britain and Decolonisation: The Retreat from Empire in the Post-War World* (Basingstoke: Macmillan, 1988), 43–4.

16 Malcolm Chalmers, *Paying for Defence: Military Spending and British Decline* (London: Pluto Press, 1985), 126.

17 Brief for the UK Delegation, 'The General Approach in Bipartite Conversations with the American Delegation, 21 April 1950', in *Documents on British Policy Overseas*, ed. Roger Bullen and Margaret Pelley (London: HMSO, 1985), Doc.24, 70.

18 USNA, RG 218, box 20, U.S. Jt. Chiefs of Staff Geographical File 1951–53, memo. Chief of Staff U.S. Army to Jt. Chiefs of Staff, 19 April 1950.

19 This section draws in part on Steve Marsh, 'Anglo-American Relations and Soft Power: Transitioning the Special Relationship', *The International History Review* 43, no. 3 (2021): 525–46.

20 Lyndon Baines Johnson Library, NSF Country File, box 210–12, folder: UK memos. Vol. xi, 4/67–6/67, Bruce to Rusk.

21 Richard Aldrich, *GCHQ* (London: Harper Press, 2010), 288–92. For UK–US differences over the Arab-Israeli War see Matthew Ferraro, *Tough Going: Anglo-American Relations and the Yom Kippur War of 1973* (London: iUniverse, 2007).

22 Gerald Ford Library (GFL), National Security Adviser, Presidential Country Files for Europe and Canada, Country File: United Kingdom (1), Box 15, United Kingdom (1), Kissinger to Ford 'Meeting with Edward Heath on 10 September 1974', undated.

23 UKNA, FCO 82/558, JT Masefield (Planning Staff) to McNally 'European/American relations', 8 August 1975.
24 Bodleian Library, Callaghan, 350, Report of the FCO, 'Programme Analysis and Review 1973. The Future of the Dependent Territories'.
25 GFL, Memcon between Ford, Kissinger, and Scowcroft, 18 October 1974, box 6, National Security Adviser's Memoranda of Conversation Collection, http://www.fordlibrarymuseum.gov/library/document/0314/1552829.pdf.
26 UKNA, PREM 16 / 419, Memo by HTA Overton with Steering Brief attachment, 14 March 1974.
27 Bodleian Library, MS Wilson, 1263, Transcript of Prime Minister's Q & A session at the National Press Club Luncheon, 31 January 1975.
28 GFL, National Security Adviser, Presidential Country Files for Europe and Canada, Box 15, Country File United Kingdom, Folder (3), U.S. Department of State, Briefing Memorandum, 'UK Defense Review', 8 November 1974.
29 John Dickie, 'Special' No More – Anglo-American Relations: Rhetoric and Reality (London: Weidenfeld & Nicolson, 1994); William Wallace, 'British Foreign Policy after the Cold War', International Affairs lxiii 3 (1992): 423–42; George Robertson, 'Britain in the New Europe', International Affairs lxvi, no. 4 (1990): 697–702.35. Geoffrey Warner, 'Foreign, Defence and European Affairs: Commentary', in New Labour in Power: Precedents and Prospects, ed. Brian Brivati and Tim Bale (New York: Routledge, 1997).
30 Henry A. Kissinger, 'Reflections on a Partnership: British and American Attitudes to Post-war Foreign Policy', International Affairs 58, no. 4 (1982): 571–87, at 576.
31 Justin Parkinson, 'Johnson: US Democracy Strong after Trump Impeachment 'Kerfuffle'', BBC News, 14 February 2021, www.bbc.com›news›uk-politics-56061624 (last accessed 8 April 2021).
32 Speech by Tony Blair to the Lord Mayor of London's Banquet, 22 November 1999.
33 Margaret Thatcher, The Downing Street Years (London: Harper Press, 1993), 783.
34 Raymond Seitz, Over Here (London: Phoenix, 1998), 322; Raymond Seitz cited in Robin Harris, 'The State of the Special Relationship', Policy Review 113, June/July (2002): 29–42, at 23.
35 Will Humphries, 'Special Relationship Just a Joke under Obama, Says Former US Aide', The Times, 11 October 2017, https://www.thetimes.co.uk/article/special-relationship-just-a-joke-under-obama-says-former-us-aide-vdl0sn3rk (last accessed 20 June 2021).
36 Peter Walker, '"The Highest Level of Special": Trump Praises US Relationship with UK', 13 July 2018, https://www.theguardian.com/us-news/2018/jul/13/the-highest-level-of-special-trump-praises-us-relationship-with-uk (last accessed 2 June 2021).
37 Alex Danchev, 'Anglo-Saxon Susceptibilities: The Special Relationship and the World', Intelligence and National Security xxv, no. 6 (2010): 843–55.
38 'An interview with David Cameron', The Economist, 31 March 2010, http://www.economist.com/node/15814344 (last accessed 10 April 2012); David Alexander, 'UK's Hague Lavish, Not "Slavish", On First U.S. Trip', Reuters, 14 May 2010, http://www.reuters.com/article/idUSTRE64D5XA20100514 (last accessed 24 June 2021); Steve Marsh, 'Beyond essential: Britons and the Anglo-American Special Relationship', Journal of Transatlantic Studies 18 (2020): 382–404.
39 'US Embassy Cables: Americans Discuss British 'Paranoia' over Special Relationship', The Guardian, https://www.theguardian.com/world/us-embassy-cables-documents/191116 (last accessed 24 June 2021); Testimony of BBC Reporter Justin

Webb, House of Commons Foreign Affairs Committee, *Global Security: UK–US Relations*, 18 March 2010, paragraph 32, https://publications.parliament.uk/pa/cm200910/cmselect/cmfaff/114/11402.htm (last accessed 22 June 2021).

40 Dumbrell structures the Anglo-American coral reef with personal leader relations at its apex, bureaucratic interweaving in the middle and public-level cultural interactions at its base. John Dumbrell, 'Personal Diplomacy: Relations between Prime Ministers and Presidents', in *Anglo-America Relations: Contemporary Perspectives*, ed. Alan P. Dobson and Steve Marsh (London: Routledge, 2013), 82.

41 John Major, *John Major: The Autobiography* (London: HarperCollins, 1999), 540.

42 Adam Svendsen, 'Strained Relations? Evaluating Contemporary Anglo-American Intelligence and Security Co-operation', in *Anglo-American Relations*, ed. Dobson and Marsh, 210.

43 Cited in Philip Berry, Alan P. Dobson, and Steve Marsh, 'Far from "The Highest Level of Special": Anglo-American Relations under Donald Trump', in *Foreign Perceptions of the United States under Donald Trump*, ed. Greg Mahler (Lexington Books: Lanham, MD: forthcoming).

44 Department for Digital, Culture, Media & Sport, National Cyber Security Centre, Press release, 'Huawei to Be Removed from UK 5G Networks by 2027', 14 July 2020, https://www.gov.uk/government/news/huawei-to-be-removed-from-uk-5g-networks-by-2027#:~:text=HUAWEI%20will%20be%20completely%20removed,sanctions%20against%20the%20telecommunications%20vendor (last accessed 20 June 2021).

45 US Intelligence Council, 'Global Trends 2040: A More Contested World', March 2021, https://www.dni.gov/files/ODNI/documents/assessments/GlobalTrends_2040.pdf (last accessed 15 June 2021).

46 https://brandfinance.com/press-releases/uk-ranked-3rd-in-world-for-soft-power-prowess (last accessed 1 June 2021).

47 United Kingdom Ministry of Defence, 'The United Kingdom's Future Nuclear Deterrent: The 2018 Update to Parliament', https://assets.publishing.service.gov.uk/government/uploads/system/uploads/attachment_data/file/767326/2018_Nuclear_Deterrent_Update_to_Parliament.pdf (last accessed 20 April 2021).

48 Dan Sabbagh and Patrick Butler, 'Boris Johnson Agrees £16bn Rise in Defence Spending', *The Guardian*, 18 November 2020, https://www.theguardian.com/politics/2020/nov/18/boris-johnson-agrees-16bn-rise-in-defence-spending (last accessed 25 May 2021).

49 Kathy Frankovic, 'United Kingdom Seen as United States Greatest Ally', 8 March 2021, https://today.yougov.com/topics/international/articles-reports/2021/03/08/united-kingdom-seen-united-states-greatest-ally (last accessed 20 June 2021).

50 America's Image Abroad Rebounds with Transition from Trump to Biden, 19 June 2021, https://www.pewresearch.org/global/2021/06/10/americas-image-abroad-rebounds-with-transition-from-trump-to-biden/ (last accessed 19 June 2021).

51 https://www.itv.com/news/2018-07-12/77-of-british-public-have-an-unfavourable-view-of-donald-trump-ahead-of-his-visit-to-the-uk/; https://www.ipsos.com/ipsos-mori/en-uk/two-three-britons-feel-unfavourable-towards-donald-trump; https://www.theguardian.com/commentisfree/2017/feb/05/donald-trump-dangerous-opinium-poll-uk-voters (last accessed 10 June 2021).

52 US Chamber of Commerce, U.S.–UK Trade and Investment Ties, https://www.uschamber.com/international/europe/us-uk-business-council/us-uk-trade-and-investment-ties (last accessed 18 October 2020).

53 Integrated Review of Security, Defence, Development and Foreign Policy, 16 April 2021, https://lordslibrary.parliament.uk/integrated-review-of-security-defence-development-and-foreign-policy/ (last accessed 1 June 2021).
54 Peter Walker, 'Boris Johnson Prefers Not to Use Term 'Special Relationship', Says No 10', *The Guardian*, 7 June 2021, https://www.theguardian.com/politics/2021/jun/07/boris-johnson-prefers-not-to-use-term-special-relationship-says-no-10 (last accessed 8 June 2021).

Chapter 14

UK–US RELATIONS: CAN SUBNATIONAL DIPLOMACY SAVE THE 'SPECIAL RELATIONSHIP'?

Alison R. Holmes

Introduction

The year 2021 marked at least three historical milestones in what we commonly call the 'special relationship'. The first was the eightieth anniversary of the *Atlantic Charter*, often considered a cornerstone set deep in the collective memory of the Second World War by Prime Minister Winston Churchill and President Franklin Roosevelt. On that foundation and forty years later, Prime Minister Margaret Thatcher and President Ronald Reagan built their ideological partnership and then spent nearly a decade creating the circumstances that arguably brought down the Berlin Wall and opened the Soviet Union – though neither was in power to see that outcome. Finally, twenty years ago, conflict in the form of terrorism once again realigned UK–US relations in the aftermath of 9/11. Of course, one doesn't need moments of urgent and symbolic importance to claim specialness. Even from the earliest days of diplomatic relations people such as John Hay, only the second full US ambassador to the United Kingdom, expounded the nature of the relationship as somehow different. He believed that Britain and the United States 'are bound by a tie we did not forge and which we cannot break; we are joint ministers of the same sacred mission of liberty'.[1] Thus, almost from the outset, transatlantic relations writ large have attracted promoters and detractors as well as scores of scholars. 'Transatlantica' remains a rich source of inspiration for what drives statespeople, businesspeople, civil leaders and individual citizens to call down this link to the other side. Regardless of speaker or audience, the constant ebb and flow of both the political and the personal relations between the United Kingdom and the United States pose questions as to the relative importance of the high politics of national interest and statecraft, the practical realities of economics, and the regularly referred to, but often-intangible discussions of culture in terms of language, history, art, music and increasingly, identity. These issues also present a constant challenge to larger questions of agency vs structure; the role of a specific leader vs their government and the peoples they govern; and official history vs collective memory at both the level of country and community.

The density in terms of diplomatic, political and individual communication that exists between these two countries is unusual, even if not entirely unique in the world and Alan Dobson spent a career addressing himself to this complexity while recognizing that this pairing has essentially always been a story of asymmetrical relations.[2] While Dobson focused primarily on economic ties, others have investigated the ways in which power has shifted from one player to the other in this ungainly pair, depending on which dimension of the relationship is under discussion. Thus, to understand UK–US relations requires not only an examination of shared national interest as expressed in state-to-state relations, but an appreciation of the depth and breadth of the different layers of the relationship – as well as the fact that each separate level has undergone its own balancing and rebalancing over time.

This discussion argues that this (a)symmetry is now of less importance as the age of great powers, superpowers or even hyperpowers has been undermined and overwhelmed by the forces of globalization. Or to be more precise, the suggestion here is that globalization has opened space on the international stage for subnational (and non-state) actors to engage in their own special relationships. Further, the intimacy of the 'special relationship' that has arguably always existed at the national level has become more visible, making it clear that such links extend well beyond traditional statecraft or diplomatic and political/policy interactions. That said, such fragmentation does not mean that UK–US specialness has diminished. On the contrary, as this subnational non-state environment opens, there is new room for an acknowledgement and deeper investigation into the long-standing operations at those other, multiple levels for a renewed kind of local/global special relationship(s) between these long-term partners. A prime example of this evolution is the relationship between what is called here the 'new middle powers' of California and the UK – or perhaps even more striking will be the potential for direct relations between US states and the nations of the UK.

In any given year there are many anniversaries to celebrate between the United Kingdom and the United States. In years hence, 2021 will, in its turn, be marked as the year a new *Atlantic Charter* was signed with great symbolic fanfare. Perhaps future authors will note that this latest document followed the time-honoured pattern in US–UK relations by building on the old while at the same time leading the way in terms of creating new forms of interaction between nation-states. Thus, even as the traditional nation-state comes under ever-increasing pressure, the United States and the United Kingdom navigate their bilateral as well as subnational politics by building the increasing number of special relationships necessary in a world of truly local/global politics.

Who is 'special' to who?

Academics have commented at length on the concept of 'specialness' and whether it is possible for any given country to have links beyond national interest, or if it's possible for a hegemon such as the United States to have a special friend, or indeed how middle and smaller powers add their names to another country's 'BFF' roster. Robert Jervis in particular has pondered the question of whether or not the fact the United Kingdom seems to have embraced the 'special' position with the United States, it becomes 'harder for others to emulate it'.[3] However, one feature of specialness that has escaped detailed comment by academic observers is the observation that the United States believes itself to be special – all by itself. John Dumbrell and Axel Schäfer do recognize that the notion of specialness in 'both in the world's comparative and normative sense (as "different" and "better") ... remains at the heart of US foreign policy'[4] while Dumbrell also concedes, 'There certainly is such thing as "Anglo-American culture", rooted to some degree in history and language, to some degree in the economic convergence of the US–UK model of contemporary capitalism'.[5] So, on the one hand, there is what Dumbrell and Schäfer call the 'universalizing dynamic of American exceptionalism'[6] that often results in the United States going it alone without any apparent need for special friends. On the other, there is what Dumbrell calls the 'illusion of "knowing" America' based on the world's familiarity with American popular culture. He believes that it is this disconnect of knowing almost too much about a country still that feels no need for any ally that 'bedevils real understanding' of the United States.[7]

This tension remained largely unchallenged until the arrival of a president whose most fundamental core belief was the idea that the United States is 'special' in the sense of both different and singular. President Trump had neither the desire nor the patience for any nicety that smacked of deferring to traditional allies and asserted the country's specialness – personified by his own – at every turn. As Gideon Rose pointed out, 'Perhaps no group has been more flummoxed by the Trump era than US allies, who awoke ... to find Washington no longer interested in playing the game, let alone managing the team.'[8]

At this point, what has been termed the recent 'cultural turn' in transatlantic studies could have much to offer our understanding of 'specialness' as it is in this realm that the question of how America views the world – and how the world views America – has more often come under scrutiny. A particularly good example of this type of analysis is found in the literary magazine *Granta*. Founded in 1889 in Cambridge, the publication seeks to 'discover and publish the best in new literary fiction, memoir, reportage and poetry from around the world'.[9] Often focusing on single topics, the immediate and painful aftermath of 9/11 offered the opportunity for the magazine's contributors to examine *What we think of America*. Later, as the United States seemed to squander the goodwill of those tragic events, the magazine posed the reverse question in *Over There: How Americans see the world*.

What the cultural/literary view reveals is not entirely surprising. Without reference to the international relations language of 'hegemonic power', editor Ian Jack simply argued that 'America shapes the way non-Americans live and think'. Blending the political with the cultural, he suggests that, before the end of the Cold War, American influence had been recognized as including 'half the world for several decades. Now, with the possible exception of North Korea and Burma, it is true of all of it. American cultural, economic and political influence is potent almost everywhere, in every life. What do we think of when we think of America? Fear, resentment, envy, anger, wonder, hope? And when did we start to think it?'[10] This, argues Ian Buruma in the same issue, is why 'America' as an ideal

> 'expressed in Hollywood movies, rock music, advertising and other pop culture is so attractive, so sexy, and to some, so deeply disturbing. All of us want a bit of 'America' but few of us can have it'. Buruma concludes by agreeing with a character in a German movie by Wim Winders and using yet another international relations term that has increasingly moved to the cultural mainstream 'America has colonized our mind'.[11]

Always a vast term, colonization – or more recently the idea of decolonizing – not only our minds but our disciplines – is particularly vague when used in this cultural context. However, its intention is further revealed in the later issue by turning the lens from what we think of America to how America sees the world. Again, Ian Jack explains:

> [I]n the wake of September 11 and the invasion of Afghanistan, this magazine asked writers across the world to describe how America had influenced their lives … culturally, politically, economically, for good or ill … when attitudes to America were on the cusp of changing from widespread sympathy to an anxiety … How much does imperious America know of the world it wants to shape? As a state with such lavish resources … Can America be so immune to the rest of the world, how it lives, what it thinks? … their [the writers] differences give the lie to the idea of America as a monolith. The frequency of their dissent suggests that the new empire will sooner or later be in trouble at home as well as abroad – or rather, in more trouble than it is already.[12]

Certainly, few would argue with the prediction that the American 'empire' – yet another specialist term being called upon in the cultural context – would get into trouble at home has come to pass.

Special: Sentiments and interests

In more traditional terms, the idea of national interest carries a great deal of weight in the analysis of statecraft, war and peace, foreign and economic policy. If the Second World War was a high point of UK–US parallel power and interests, the relative power of the two countries diverged in the period that followed. Kathleen Burk therefore agrees with Dobson that the relationship was 'bound to be asymmetrical' particularly as it became increasingly clear that the UK was moving from a 'global to regional power'. Yet what Burk calls an 'instinctive feeling' that the two powers are 'more alike than any other two powers on the globe' created the context for what she calls a 'true love-hate Anglo-American special relationship'.[13]

Walter Russell Mead takes an even broader perspective when he argues that the relationship is 'less a result of policy choices made by either the British or the Americans than it is the cause of the similar choices the two countries so frequently make' and even when the two 'disagree quite bitterly over how to do it'.[14] Lawrence Freedman draws up a list of events that reflect a rather jagged, yet parallel, trajectory of two maritime powers built on a foundation of free trade. Also starting from the Atlantic Charter, which he suggests formed the basis of the post-war liberal order, he traces the connection through the long history of presumed shared intelligence and nuclear weaponry, the collapse of the USSR, and even through the relationship built by Tony Blair with both George Bush and Bill Clinton and finally to the interesting dynamic of Boris Johnson and Donald Trump around Europe and specifically Brexit.[15]

Dobson and Marsh would recognize this as the heart of the 'school of sentiment and interests' which, they argue, does not mean polar opposite positions, but 'inextricably linked' factors that effectively become 'two sides of the same coin'. More importantly, they argue that the relationship cannot be understood solely on the basis of one or the other, but only with the 'realization that sentiments and interests cannot be usefully separated'.[16]

Given the shifts in national fortunes and the impact of global events on the bilateral relationship, it is also interesting to pose the question of what has caused breaks in the relationship? The 'low points' of the relationship are also, in many ways, as much about culture and perception as they are about the high politics of defence and foreign policy; the UK's humiliation at the Suez Canal, the crisis over missiles, the US humiliation in Viet Nam and most recently the push/pull of President Trump's approach to not only the UK, but to all of Europe and all of its 'traditional' allies – and enemies.

On the other hand, the slow but inexorable generational shift may have longer term consequences as the golden age literally dies away[17] which may also help explain the long-term framing of the relationship into the 'old' vs the 'new' by both political actors and scholars. From scholars such as Burk to Prime Minster Harold Wilson, President John F. Kennedy and Defense Secretary Donald Rumsfeld, the recurring theme or challenge is to – ideally – be located in both the old AND the new category. There are privileges to being the longest serving ally while at the same time remaining relevant to current problems and solutions.[18]

Perhaps it is this old vs new idea – or just the diminishing influence of two world powers that highlights the idea that both the United States and the United Kingdom are becoming more accurately identified as former 'great powers' that have both been reduced in stature in some significant way. The United States may, in many ways, remain a powerhouse, but no longer across the board. The United States is no longer the undoubted hegemon as its withdrawal from numerous multilateral agreements has, at least for the moment, reduced the world's view of its global role and thus its ability to operate and negotiate among and between the world's players on a range of issues. As Lawrence Freedman suggests, 'The US and the UK no longer have a grand strategic project … the challenge … is to manage the tension between independence and interdependence'.[19]

Middle Powers, the Anglo-sphere and its allies: Opening new levels of 'special'

In the face of the pressures of globalization, a general fragmentation of power and most recently the splintering consequences of a global pandemic, the US–UK relationship has arguably become less 'special' in a singular sense. However, even if the pairing is no longer strongly bilateral, it seems clear that their decline has created more space for action by Middle Powers or the wider group of countries termed the 'Anglo-sphere' by Freedman, Mead and others, as well as partners within a complex interconnected web of allies. It is this shift from a bilateral to a multilateral system of alliance and relationship-building that has not only altered the basic shape of the two-way core, but that arguably creates an entirely new culture of interaction and the space needed for more and different types of subnational actors to be more actively engaged on multiple issues simultaneously and at the level once reserved for national governments.

Countries that have made claim to a special kind of relationship with the United States (or had such an attribute ascribed to them) range from Canada as America's next-door neighbour to Israel – a more purely political alliance. However, it may be more helpful to see these relationships as concentric circles. In that sense, Canada, Ireland, Australia and New Zealand would make an obvious first tier as part of the English-speaking, democratic, capitalist world of the Anglo-sphere. The bonds that Mead outlines in terms of a shared worldview resulting in shared actions are the basis of much of the world's global governance and operated through vehicles such as the UN Security Council and NATO to the growing number of multilateral agreements on specific issues. Some would also include Israel given its particularly close links to the New States, but it is often outside (and increasingly on the wrong side) of many global structures.

Beyond that circle, there is a related case to be made for the specialness of other allies – particularly those with major economic links or close physical proximity to either the United States or the United Kingdom; for example, France and Germany for the United Kingdom or Mexico and even Japan for the United States. However, their case for being 'inside' the next circle is often not so much based on their cultural closeness to either country, but by how different they are to those further 'outside' that circle. Thus, Italy and India fall further away as both their interests and their sentiments diverge not only from those at the centre but also their neighbours and/or allies in the next tier. Even author such as Alex Danchev, who argues that the UK–US relationship is effectively an empty vessel, manages to come up with ten characteristics of what it means to be special: 'transparency, informality, generality, reciprocity, exclusivity, clandestinity, reliability, durability, potentiality and mythicizability'.[20] Clearly many terms are contrived, but somehow that only reinforces their cultural essence and a visceral quality. The point here is that this apparent 'rise' of Middle Powers – many already members of the Anglo-sphere or allies from other contexts – brings another layer of engagement and a new set of special relationships into the realm of UK–US specialness and often through a channel of subnational diplomacy.

Freedman suggests that, strangely enough, both Germany and France have become stronger separately and together in the face of Trump[21] and even as the constituent parts of the United Kingdom become more independent through the painful process of Brexit. In North America, both Canada and Mexico have developed new strategies that involve intense outreach and diplomatic interactions across the board. Jonathan Kay sees this as new space for Canada given that

> at the same time that the United States has descended into partisan rancor, Canada's political class has embraced a bipartisan consensus ... and has decisively rejected the type of nativist politics so popular in much of the United States and Europe these days ... Trump has made Canadians more conscious of the pluralistic values that inform their society ... In an unintended way, Trump has done much to give Canada the elevated international stature it has long craved ... this includes the opportunity to redefine its role in the world ... Canada can now find its own way, without regard to how its interests might intersect with those of the United States.[22]

Meanwhile, Mexico has also found a new layer of interaction with its neighbour to the north. As Shannon O'Neil points out, 'Faced with this [Trump's] unprecedented belligerence, Mexico has few options – and even fewer good ones. The best approach would be to avoid confronting Trump – not by capitulating to him but by going around him ... Mexico needs to venture outside the Beltway and deepen its already rich connections to US states, municipalities and communities.'[23]

As suggested before, these levels of diplomacy and communication between nation-states are not new. Indeed, one of the most prominent and commonly recognized features of the UK–US relationship (or any relationship that would be special) is exactly the breadth and depth of relations between different levels of governance. However, these layers have often not been investigated and certainly it has not been suggested that this space now has the potential to become the focus and foundation for the special relationships necessary for the forms of domestic and global governance required in a globalized/post pandemic world.

Regardless of longevity, the work to create subnational bonds is growing exponentially. In both Mexico and particularly Canada, the subnational structures are well designed to take on more international issues and agreements. Their state and provincial leaders are, in many ways, not as constrained as US states in terms of international agreements and issues, but it is arguably the result of a national breakdown of specialness that has opened the floodgates. As David Parks points out, both Canada and Mexico (like the United States) have strong national associations of subnational leaders and suggests that these systems could be even more organized in a way that ideas such as 'Strategic departmental secondments between governments would not only yield benefits in specific areas of technical cooperation (e.g. forestry management, pest control in agriculture, police training, etc.) but would foster greater understanding of culture and ways of conducting business in general' (Parks, n.d.).[24]

Specifically, Kay observes that Canada has 'launched the diplomatic equivalent of a carpet-bombing campaign: Canadian emissaries have relentlessly knocked on doors throughout the United States, spreading their message as widely as possible'.[25] In Mexico, O'Neil points out:

> [C]onnections between the two countries have proliferated at the state and local levels as well … it has focused on reaching out … These include governments and other elected officials in the 23 US states for whom Mexico is their largest or second-largest export market … With the help of 50 consular offices in the United States and the assistance of Mexican business elites, Pena Nieto's governments has begun to work the US system, courting all levels of government and seeking out potential grass-roots allies.[26]

Case in point: California and the United Kingdom as a new kind of special?

One of the more interesting examples of where the erosion of the nation-state has opened space for new special relationships is the evolution between California and the United Kingdom – as well as its constituent parts. This national/subnational special relationship is interesting for two main reasons. First, California recently bumped the UK, replacing it as the world's fifth largest economy, but more specifically, California is the top exporting US state to Europe while the UK is California's tenth largest export market. California did more than $5 billion in exports to the UK in 2017 and imports into California from the UK were approximately $5.5 billion, supporting approximately 90,000 jobs (CalChamber).[27] The UK consul general to Los Angeles, Michael Howells, identifies the fact that this increasing division between national governments and their subnational units is not simply a UK–US phenomenon but one that is gathering force in many places. As he points out:

> [T]here is definitely a shot of adrenaline that comes from having a political divergence between a subunit and the national unit … and that's happening in California [and in] the UK as well … You've had an erosion of government autonomy over international activity and in particular government ability to affect international issues of concern to people and companies and governments so – there's a general … diminution in the power of governments relative to other actors … that's changed the paradigm ….[28]

Second, in many ways, California is the birthplace of many of the cultural identities we associate with the United States. Returning to *Granta*'s literary perspective, Ian Buruma argues that 'America, especially California, holds out a more radical promise to its new citizens … the ideal that each person is free to choose his own destiny, unfettered by the social chain of whatever old world one has escaped ... America gives every man a second chance.'[29] Such prosaic sensibilities might come naturally in the literary world, but such sentiments are echoed directly first by Governor Newsom in his inaugural address claiming the standard of 'California for all' within the frame coined by Kevin Starr (California's public historian) of the 'Party of California' as the watch phrase of his administration. Thus, from the outset and following in the footsteps of Governors Schwarzenegger and Brown, he intentionally positioned himself and the state as a whole as a state above other states; an equal and worthy colleague at the international level. It may have been Governor Gray Davis who first made any claim to California as a 'nation-state', but issues of climate change and economic innovation through the following two administrations began to make such a claim credible leaving Newsom as the inheritor of the new paradigm identified by Howell from his diplomatic/international perspective. Nowhere was this more evident than during the recent pandemic as Newsom sought to coordinate efforts by other states and declared that he would use the bulk purchasing power of California 'as a nation-state' to acquire the hospital supplies that the federal government had failed to supply.[30]

This theme has been embraced by the governor's team and repeated by many others, including the state's first-ever female lieutenant governor (and former ambassador) Eleni Kounalakis. She makes overt the connection between the national and the state levels by arguing that the California dream has a claim to being synonymous with the American dream in a way that neither Ohio nor Florida possibly could. California is uniquely the land of rebirth and second chances because, she believes, 'California is where the future begins.'[31] Given her charge by Governor Newsom to be the State of California Representative for *International Affairs* and Trade Development (emphasis added), it is hardly surprising that she sees her responsibilities as including the elevation of California's voice to the world stage and putting more effort into building relationships with the consular corps at the state level rather than leave this to the State Department or to the cities, counties and businesses where several counties have already built a solid bridgehead. She clearly sees the same trend identified by Canada and Mexico, that policy is now shifting to the subnational level and not only from national to subnational but directly subnational to subnational and wants to ensure California is well represented. Consul General Howell makes this new connection between California and the UK explicit by suggesting:

> [T]he UK is the California of Europe ... they're basically the same size economy. The population of California is a little lower and a higher GDP per capita ... They have very similar global priorities. They have a lot of the same interests in that both wish to have a similar kind of economy ... and both wish to stand for a similar set of values ... [and] arguably see their position in the world as perhaps more similar than many other subunits do ... obviously we have different tools – different history ... different politics ... nevertheless you know we have this sort of perennial question: do we try and do a little bit of everything because as a global country you must – or do we prioritize things ... we care about ...

So what does that mean for California ... as a state of country scale ... Should California try to do as much as it can or should it prioritize focus on areas where it can make the most difference ... but where I think it is interesting is where California is seeking to develop a leadership role ... beyond just California ... it's a new phase.[32]

Taking the idea of the increasing importance of subnationals a step further, the pandemic has also brought the growth in the role of cities on the international scene into sharp relief. Nina Hachigian (another former ambassador) became the first deputy mayor for international affairs in Los Angeles under Mayor Garcetti (who was recently promoted to be the US ambassador to India under President Biden) is a prime example. An activist city diplomat, she makes the case for the ability and need for cities like LA to take on more in terms of global issues. To her, the pandemic has highlighted the way mayors and governors are able to take advantage of their global connections to share experience; illustrating her long-standing argument that we should look to cities for a renaissance of multilateral governance. She believes that 'City leadership is thus becoming fundamental to solving many of the world's toughest problems, going far beyond pandemic responses to other global challenges such climate change, migration and inequality'.[33]

Hachigian is far from alone in her recognition of this shift. Again, Consul General Howell has identified the same change in 'governance structures' from his national diplomatic viewpoint and believes that, in the United States in particular, 'the primary organizing unit is actually the city and they're almost "city states" in a kind of grainy sense and I think that is particularly true of the big mega cities like New York and Los Angeles'. Domestically, Jay Wang at the University of Southern California suggests that there is much to learn from the emergency response of cities as they leverage their international relationships. He argues that the pandemic could, in fact, become 'a teachable moment for connecting local priorities with global matters to enhance the security and prosperity of citizens'[34] even though he fears it may also 'expose the fault lines between national and cultural communities'.[35]

This may seem irrelevant to the Special Relationship, if it were not that the UK – like Canada and Mexico – has also recently added capacity to their Embassy in Washington. Right across the country, British staff are actively tracking and building relationships with states, cities, counties and more direct links to business and civil leaders relevant to their own agenda. At the same time, the constituent parts of the UK are also changing their forms of diplomatic connection and practical involvement as both Scotland and Wales have begun to build new structures not only within the more traditional embassy state-to-state framework, but also well beyond. Richard Jones and Elin Royles have outlined the significant ways in which the Welsh Assembly has enhanced its international presence particularly in the area of economic development,[36] and in ways that look very familiar in terms of what California has done. For example, in the same way Kounalakis and Hachigian were the first to be appointed to coordinate and 'elevate' the voices of their state and city to the international stage, Wales has also appointed the first-ever representative of Wales, head of North America Welsh Government in Washington, DC. A delicate position, it has been described as a kind of 'little brother' relationship to the British Embassy while at the same time charged with presenting the specific Welsh case. Scotland, as a secessionist power, is in a slightly different position to California, but has a similar need and desire to present the Scottish case both as part of the UK and with its distinct voice. Brexit clearly altered the position of the nations within the UK, but it seems only logical that the subnational units will continue to seek their own channels of communication and policy advocacy. Further, major subnationals such as California are a likely target of such outreach given the overlap of interest and sentiment in the face of a relative lack of resources. Indeed, it seems possible that all of these subnational units may find ways to create more elaborate international structures to support these complex special relationships.

Such issues may seem a long way from the traditional idea of the UK–US relationship and what constitutes specialness in a global world. However, the argument here is simply that it is time to recognize that the passing of the age of great powers and the more nuanced and networked behaviours of new middle powers has combined with the need and ability of subnational actors to reach into the global space. This has created a new form of interaction not only between states, but between states and subnationals and from subnational to subnational. The classic 'inside/outside' divide or the distinction of 'high/low' politics of international relations has collapsed, opening the way for relationships (both conflictual and cooperative) at all the different levels of interaction. Which relationships become 'special' in the future remains to be seen, but certainly California and a number of other US states as well as the nations within the UK have quite a head start.

Conclusion

Alan Dobson spent a career examining the relationship between the United States and the United Kingdom and 'Transatlantica' as a whole. While he focused primarily on economic relations, he did not limited himself to that realm, and remained open to other perspectives while at the same time being an active supporter of other scholars in his field. Like the relationship he studied, he continued to adapt and renew his approach to take into account both new approaches and world events. Even as this text in his honour was taking shape, President Biden and Prime Minister Johnson opened yet another chapter in this relationship as they effectively 'renewed their vows' in the form of the New Atlantic Charter.

In what can only be described as classic US–UK symbolism, and in the aftermath of what some might have seen as a populist affinity between Johnson and Trump, they chose the major global moment of President Biden arriving in the UK for the first G7 of his presidency for this set-piece. Arguably a mutually beneficial move, Biden played the wise older statesman extending a hand to a

Brexit-bedevilled prime minister. For his part, Johnson sought to reassert the classic role of the UK as America's gateway to Europe and problem-solving, multilateral diplomat. Andrew Marshall is correct in his observation that, in many ways, the new Charter is 'not comparable to the original … ' and that 'Neither (with the greatest respect) are Joe and Boris to the original FDR and Winston'.[37] However, the fact remains there was a felt need – apparently on both sides – to create a public statement. This desire and the existence of a document to 'revitalize' principles and to 'reaffirm their commitment to work together to realise our vision for a more peaceful and prosperous future'[38] perhaps only serves to prove the case that there is still a cultural pull and a perceived strength in the mythology of the special relationship going forward. However, they may find they increasingly need many different types and levels of relationship to face the modern threats of cyberspace, disinformation and nuclear deterrence set out in the new Atlantic Charter.[39]

The post-Trump, post-Brexit, post-pandemic world has thrown up countless crises to both the United States and the United Kingdom. Much remains unknowable as to the role their respective subnational actors will assume in this fragmented world, but four things seem clear. First, the UK–US relationship has survived reports of its death enough times for scholars to at least pause before writing off the closeness or specialness of this specific state-to-state bilateral alliance. Second, the symbolic diplomatic drama of asserting shared goals and the burdens of global governance will continue despite, or perhaps because of, the sense of erosion of certainty in the international realm. Third, Middle Powers and other types of subnational units within the United States and the United Kingdom – and indeed around the world – sense they now have the space to actively engage with that global arena. Moreover, they have a unique and specific role to play in the development of multiple special relationships that will enable and reinforce what is arguably the most enduring 'special relationship' in the world.

Notes

1 R. Raymond, 'The US–UK Special Relationship in Historical Context: Lessons of the Past', in J. McCausland and D. T. Stuart (eds.). *UK/US Relations at the start of the 21st Century*, http://www.StrategicStudiesInstitute.army.mil/. (2006), 4.
2 A. Dobson and S. Marsh, eds., *Anglo-American Relations: Contemporary Perspectives* (Abingdon: Routledge, 2013), 270.
3 J. Dumbrell, *A Special Relationship: Anglo-American Relations from the Cold War to Iraq* (Basingstoke: Palgrave Macmillan, 2006), 271.
4 J. Dumbrell and A. Schäfer, eds., *America's 'Special Relationships': Foreign and Domestic Aspects of the Politics of Alliance* (London: Routledge, 2009), 4.
5 J. Dumbrell, *A Special Relationship: Anglo-American Relations from the Cold War to Iraq* (Basingstoke: Palgrave Macmillan, 2006), 274.
6 J. Dumbrell and A. Schäfer, eds., *America's 'Special Relationships': Foreign and Domestic Aspects of the Politics of Alliance* (London: Routledge, 2009), 3.
7 J. Dumbrell, *A Special Relationship: Anglo-American Relations from the Cold War to Iraq* (Basingstoke: Palgrave Macmillan, 2006), 274.

8   G. Rose, Introduction. *Foreign Affairs*. 'Trump and the Allies: The View from Abroad', September–October (2017), n.p.
9   About, https://granta.com/about/.
10 I. Jack, ed., Introduction. *Granta: Magazine of New Writing*. 'What We Think of America', #77. Spring, (2002), 11.
11 I. Buruma, 'Episodes and Opinions from Twenty-Four Writers', in I. Jack (ed.) *Granta: Magazine of New Writing*. 'What We Think of America'. #77. Spring, (2002), 19–20.
12 I. Jack, ed., Introduction. *Granta, Magazine of New Writing*. 'Over There: How American Sees the World', #84 Winter, (2003), 6–8.
13 K. Burk, *Old World, New World: The Story of Britain and America* (London: Little Brown, 2007), 659.
14 W. Russell Mead, *God and Gold: Britain, America and the Making of the Modern World* (London: Atlantic Book, 2007), s. xii.
15 L. Freedman, 'Britain Adrift: The United Kingdom's Search for a Post-Brexit Role', *Foreign Affairs* (2020), May–June.
16 A. Dobson and S. Marsh, eds., *Anglo-American Relations: Contemporary Perspectives* (Abingdon: Routledge, 2013), 15.
17 B.W. Jentleson, 'The Atlantic Alliance in a Post-American World', *Journal of Transatlantic Studies* 7, no. 1 (March 2009), 61–72.
18 N. Cullather, in J. Dumbrell and A. Schäfer, eds., *America's 'Special Relationships': Foreign and Domestic Aspects of the Politics of Alliance* (London: Routledge, 2009), 4.
19 L. Freedman, 'Britain Adrift: The United Kingdom's Search for a Post-Brexit Role', *Foreign Affairs* (2020), May–June, 118–30, 128.
20 A. Dobson and S. Marsh, eds., *Anglo-American Relations: Contemporary Perspectives* (Abingdon: Routledge, 2013), 12.
21 L. Freedman, 'Britain Adrift: The United Kingdom's Search for a Post-Brexit Role', *Foreign Affairs* (2020), May–June, 118–30.
22 J. Kay, 'Trudeau's Trump Bump: How a Smaller American Gives Canada Room to Grow', *Foreign Affairs*, May–June, (2017), 35–42, 42.
23 S. O'Neil, 'The Mexican Stand-off: Trump and the Art of the Workaround', *Foreign Affairs*, September/October, (2017), 43–9, 44.
24 D. Parks, n.d. 'Canada and Mexico Strengthen Sub-national Diplomacy', https://www.focal.ca/publications/focalpoint/121-canada-and-mexico-strengthen-sub-national-diplomacy.
25 J. Kay, 'Trudeau's Trump Bump: How a Smaller American Gives Canada Room to Grow', *Foreign Affairs*, May–June (2017), 35–42, 42.
26 S. O'Neil, 'The Mexican Stand-off: Trump and the Art of the Workaround', *Foreign Affairs*, September/October (2017), 43–9, 47–9.
27 California Chamber of Commerce, https://www.calchamber.com/.
28 M. Howells, Interview with author. (2018).
29 I. Buruma, 'Episodes and Opinions from Twenty-Four Writers', in I. Jack (ed.) *Granta: Magazine of New Writing*. 'What We Think of America', #77. Spring. 1, (2002), 9.
30 F. Wilkinson, 'Gavin Newsom Declares California a "Nation-State"', *Bloomberg*, April (2020), 9, https://www.bloomberg.com/opinion/articles/2020-04-09/california-declares-independence-from-trump-s-coronavirus-plans.
31 E. Kounalakis, Lt Governor 'A Conversation with Lt Governor Kounalakis', Transcript. University of Southern California Event, 2 June 2020, https://calendar.usc.edu/event/a_conversation_with_lt_gov_eleni_kounalakis#.X0Lst8ipE2w.
32 Howells, Michael (2018). Interview with author.

33 N. Hachigian and A. Pipa 'Can Cities Fix a Post-Pandemic World Order?', *Foreign Policy*, 5 May 2020, https://foreignpolicy.com/2020/05/05/cities-post-pandemic-world-order-multilateralism/.
34 J. Wang, (Jay) '5 Takeaways on U.S. City Diplomacy during the COVID-19 Crisis', April (2020) 27, https://www.uscpublicdiplomacy.org/blog/5-takeaways-us-city-diplomacy-during-covid-19-crisis.
35 J. Wang, (Jay) 'Public Diplomacy in the Age of Pandemics', 18 March 2020, https://www.uscpublicdiplomacy.org/blog/public-diplomacy-age-pandemics.
36 R. W. Jones and E. Royles, 'Wales in the World: Intergovernmental Relations and Sub-state Diplomacy', *British Journal of Politics and International Relations* 14 (2012), 250–69, 257.
37 A. Marshall, 'That Was Then but This Is Now: Assessing the New Atlantic Charter', 2021, https://www.atlanticcouncil.org/blogs/new-atlanticist/that-was-then-but-this-is-now-assessing-the-new-atlantic-charter/.
38 White House BRIEFING ROOM. The New Atlantic Charter (2021), https://www.whitehouse.gov/briefing-room/statements-releases/2021/06/10/the-new-atlantic-charter/. June 10.
39 A. Marshall, 'That Was Then but This Is Now: Assessing the New Atlantic Charter', 2021, https://www.atlanticcouncil.org/blogs/new-atlanticist/that-was-then-but-this-is-now-assessing-the-new-atlantic-charter/.

INDEX

Locating the Transatlantic in Twentieth century Politics, Diplomacy and Culture.

9/11 162, 163, 218, 220, 229

Abraham Lincoln Brigade 51, 52, 53, 57, 58, 59, 60, 61, 62
Abyssinia, war with Italy 74, 119
Action Française 120
Addis, John 137
Afghanistan, Soviet occupation of 170, 171, 172, 173, 174, 175, 176, 177, 178, 179, 180, 220
air power
    American 11
    British 10, 11
Al-Assad, Bashar 220
Alvear, Marcelo 87
American Bicentennial 9
American-British-Dutch-Australian (ABDA) staff talks 107
American Civil War 69, 187, 188, 189, 190
American Revolution 6
Andropov, Yuri 176, 180
Anglo-American relations 2, 3, 4, 5, 6, 7, 8, 9, 10, 11, 12, 15, 16, 17, 18, 19, 20, 21, 22, 23, 31, 32, 33, 34, 35, 36, 37, 38, 39, 40, 41, 42, 43, 44, 49–50, 56, 67, 83, 84, 85, 86, 87, 88, 89, 90, 91, 92, 93, 94, 95, 101, 102, 103, 104, 106, 107, 108, 109, 110, 111, 112, 113, 117, 118, 119, 119, 120, 121, 122, 123, 124, 125, 126, 127, 129, 130, 131, 153, 154, 155, 156, 157, 158, 159, 160, 161, 162, 163, 211, 212, 213, 214, 215, 216, 217, 218, 219, 220, 221, 222, 229, 230, 231, 232, 233, 234, 235, 236, 237, 238
    Antisemitism 52–3
    commercial 4, 5, 6, 8–9, 11, 40, 83, 84, 85, 86, 87, 88, 89, 90, 91, 92, 93, 94, 95, 96, 220, 221
    cultural links 6, 7, 8, 9, 10, 11, 12, 15, 16, 53, 54, 55, 56, 101, 102, 103, 104, 106, 107, 108, 109, 110, 111, 112, 113, 153, 154, 155, 156, 157, 158, 159, 160, 161, 162, 163, 229, 230, 231, 232, 233, 234, 235, 236, 237, 238
    international law 6, 7, 67, 68, 70, 71, 72, 73, 74, 75, 76, 77, 78, 79, 80
    isolationism 11, 15, 18, 19, 41, 43, 101, 102
    relations with France 117, 118, 119, 120, 121, 122, 123, 124, 125, 126, 127, 128, 129, 130, 131
Anglo Meat Packing Company 84, 87, 90
Anti-Ballistic Missile Treaty 216, 222
Antisemitism 52–3
appeasement, Anglo-French policy of 31, 32, 33, 34, 36, 37, 38, 39, 40, 41, 42, 43, 44, 56, 86, 95, 96, 101, 102, 103
    Munich conferences 38, 39, 41, 42, 83, 95, 101, 105, 125
    Sudetenland, occupation 37, 38, 39, 83
Arbatov, Georgy 179
Argentina, Falklands claim 96
    Relations with the United States 84, 85, 86, 87, 88, 89, 90, 91, 92, 93, 94, 95, 96
    Roca-Runciman Mission 83, 84, 85, 86, 87, 88, 89, 90, 91, 92, 93, 94, 95, 96
Armstrong, Anne 160, 161
Aron, Robert 120, 123, 124, 125, 126, 127, 131
Aspen Institute 205
Astray, José Millán 61
Atlantic Charter 179, 229, 230, 231, 232, 233, 234, 235, 236, 237, 238, 240
Atlantic world 4, 187–8, 189, 190
Attlee, Clement 119, 214
Auriol, Vincent 119
Austro-Hungarian Empire 23

aviation 117, 118, 119, 121, 122, 123, 124, 125, 126, 127, 128, 129, 130, 131, 135, 136, 137, 138, 139, 140, 141, 142, 143, 144, 145, 146, 147, 201, 202, 203, 204, 205, 222
Azaña, Manuel 49

Baker, James 173
Baldwin, Stanley 95
Balfour, John 39
Ball, George 214
Battle of Britain 118
Bayard, Thomas 68
Beatles, the 192, 193
Beatty, Ned 188
Beauvoir, Simone de 118, 130
Benin Bronzes 155
Berlin Airlift 201
Berlin Wall 170, 206, 216, 229
Biden, Joseph (Joe) 219, 221, 222, 224, 238
Blair, Tony 218, 219, 220, 233
Bloomfield, Lincoln P. 220
Bodington, 'Richard' 128
Boland Amendment 174
Boorman, John 188
Borah, William 95
Bourgeois, Léon 123
Bowers, Claude 50
Boxer Rebellion 68
Bretton Woods Conference 214, 215, 216
Brexit 218, 220, 233, 235, 236, 237, 238, 239, 240
Brezhnev, Leonid 171, 174
Britain, airpower 10, 135, 136, 137, 138, 139, 140, 141, 142, 143, 144, 145, 146, 147
   appeasement 31, 32, 33, 34, 36, 37, 38, 39, 40, 41, 42, 43, 44, 56, 86, 95, 96, 101, 102, 103
   Argentina 83, 84, 85, 86, 87, 88, 89, 90, 91, 92, 93, 94, 95
   China 153
   European Economic Community membership 153, 215, 216, 224
   France 10, 11, 20, 21, 31, 38, 42, 56, 117, 118, 119, 120, 121, 122, 123, 124, 125, 126, 127, 128, 129, 130, 131, 157, 158, 159, 160, 161, 162, 163
   Germany 31, 32, 33, 42, 56, 95

non-intervention 49, 50, 51, 52
Royal state visit 1976 9, 10, 153, 154, 155, 156, 157, 158, 159, 160, 161, 162, 163
Royal state visits 1939 9, 33, 35, 36, 41, 42, 101, 102, 103, 104, 107, 108, 109, 110, 111, 112, 113, 114
sea power 20
Spanish Civil War 49, 50, 51, 52, 56, 57, 58, 59, 60, 61, 62, 63, 64
United States 3, 4, 5, 6, 7, 8, 9, 10, 11, 12, 15, 16, 17, 18, 19, 20, 21, 22, 23, 24, 32, 33, 34, 35, 36, 37, 38, 39, 40, 41, 42, 43, 44, 56, 67, 83, 84, 85, 86, 87, 88, 89, 90, 91, 92, 93, 84, 95, 96, 101, 102, 103, 104, 106, 107, 108, 109, 110, 111, 112, 113, 117, 118, 119, 120, 121, 122, 123, 124, 125, 126, 127, 128, 129, 130, 131, 135, 136, 137, 138, 139, 140, 141, 142, 143, 144, 145, 146, 147, 153, 154, 155, 156, 157, 158, 159, 160, 161, 162, 163, 198, 199, 200, 201, 202, 203, 204, 205, 206, 207, 208, 211, 212, 213, 214, 215, 216, 217, 218, 219, 223, 229, 230, 231, 232, 233, 234, 235, 236, 237, 238
United States Declaration of Independence 156
British Bicentennial Liaison Committee 154–5, 156, 157, 159
British Diplomatic Service 9
British Empire Industries Exhibition 87
British International History Group 12
British Library 155
British Museum 155
Brown, Gordon 219
Bruce, David 214, 220, 223–4
Brunei Revolt 141
BRUSA Agreement 214
Brzezinski, Zbigniew 171
Buchanan, John 171
Buñuel, Luis 126
Burgin, Leslie 88, 89
Burrows, Ian 144
Bush, George H.W. 8, 169, 173, 175, 179, 180, 204–5, 218, 219, 233
Bush, George W. 162, 233

Cadogan, Alexander 38
Callaghan, James 157, 160, 192, 199
Cameron, David 219, 224
Cameron, James Donald 33
Cameron, Martha 33
Camus, Albert 118, 121
'CARTE' (resistance network) 128
Carter, Jimmy 156, 161, 171, 190, 191, 192, 197, 198
Catholic Worker Movement 51
Céline, Louis Ferdinand 120, 121, 122, 123
Central Intelligence Agency (CIA) 138, 140, 146, 178, 179, 221
Chamberlain, Neville 37, 39, 83, 89, 94, 101, 103, 125, 127
Chernenko, Konstantin 175, 180
China
    diplomatic relations with the United States 16
    Civil War 119
Chmura, Tadek 122, 123
Churchill, Winston 5, 10, 31, 112, 11, 127, 154, 158, 159, 179, 180, 197, 198–9, 200, 207–8, 211–12, 213, 214, 215, 216, 217, 218, 219, 220, 221, 223, 229, 230, 231, 232, 233, 234, 235, 236, 237, 238, 240
Civil Rights Movement 192
Clinton, Bill 10, 219, 233
Colby, William 138, 147
Cold War 3, 7, 8, 10, 22, 113, 169, 170, 171, 172, 173, 174, 175, 176, 177, 178, 179, 180, 197, 198, 199, 200, 201, 202, 203, 204, 205, 206, 207, 208, 211, 212, 213, 214, 215, 216, 217, 218, 219, 221, 229, 230, 231, 232, 233, 234, 235, 236, 237, 238
collective security 22, 72, 73, 74, 75, 76, 77, 78, 79, 80
Collins, Godfrey 88
Combat 121
Concorde 157, 158
Ćopić, Vladimir 52, 57–8
Coughlin, Father Charles 51
Cox, Ronny 190
Craigie, Robert 91
Cromer, Lord 153
Crosland, Anthony 160

Crow, Jim 188
Cuban Missile Crisis 145, 216

D'Abernon, Lord 34
    trade mission to Argentina 87
Daily Telegraph 161
Daladier, Édouard 37
Dandieu, Arnaud 120
D'Annunzio, Gabriele 119
Darroch, Kim 219
Davies, Joseph 56
Davis, Gray 237
Davis, Norman 92
Day, Dorothy 51
Declaration of Independence 156
Defense Appropriation Act 174
democracy 10, 31, 32, 37, 38, 40, 49, 50, 51
    Christian principles 10
Deneuve, Catherine 126
Deng Xiaoping 179
Der Spiegel 192
D'Estaing, Giscard 158
Dickens, Charles 190
Dickinson, Flight Lieutenant 142
Diem, Ngo Dinh 135, 136, 137, 138, 139
Dobranski, Adam 122, 123
Dodd, Christopher 175
Dominican Arbitration Tribunal 68
Dreyfus, Alfred 120
    Dreyfusism 120
Dudley, David 190
Duff Cooper, Alfred 38
Dukakis, Michael 160
Duranty, Walter 55

Eccles, Lord 155
Eden, Anthony 41
Eden-Malbran Agreement 93
Eisenhower, Dwight 111, 158, 159
Electoral College, United States 197
Elgin Marbles 155
Elibank, Lord 94
Elizabeth, Queen, state visit to Washington, (consort of George VI) 9, 10, 35, 36, 41, 102, 104, 106, 107, 108, 109, 111, 112, 113
Elizabeth II, Queen 9, 153, 154, 155, 156, 157, 158, 159, 160, 161, 162, 163, 199, 200
Elliott, Walter 88

246   Index

El Salvador 169, 170, 171, 172, 173, 174,
    175, 176, 177, 178, 179, 180
Elsey, George 201
Esprit 121
European Economic Community (EEC)
    7, 153, 215, 216, 224
  British membership 153, 215, 224
European Union (EU) 7

Falange 49
Falkland Islands, Argentinian claim 96, 222
Ferber, Edna 60
First Transport Regiment 52
First World War 6, 8, 10, 11, 15, 16–17, 18,
    19, 20, 21, 22, 23, 24, 33, 43, 120,
    121, 122, 123, 124, 125, 126, 127,
    128, 129, 130, 131, 156
  American entry 11, 15, 16, 17, 18, 19,
    20, 21, 22, 23, 24
  France 119, 120, 121, 122, 123, 124,
    125, 126, 127, 128, 129, 130, 131
  neutral powers 23
Ford, Gerald 154, 157, 160, 161, 176, 178,
    179, 191–2, 215, 217
Foreign Office
  culture 33, 34, 36, 38, 40, 41
  Pre-First World War 34
Forrestal, Michael V. 138
Fourth International American
    Conference, Buenos Aires 68
France
  relations with Britain 20, 21, 22, 31, 33,
    36, 37, 38, 39, 40, 41, 42, 43, 44, 56,
    117, 118, 119, 120, 121, 122, 123,
    124, 125, 126, 127, 128, 129, 130,
    131, 207, 208
  appeasement 31, 36, 38, 40, 41, 42, 43,
    44, 56, 101
  First World War 119, 120, 121, 122, 123,
    124, 125, 126, 127, 128, 129, 130, 131
  Mers-el-Kébir, sinking of French navy
    at 127, 129, 131
  Oradour-sur-Glane, massacre 122
  'Post-War Planning' 118, 119
  resistance 128, 129
  Second World War 117–18, 119, 120,
    121, 122, 123, 124, 125, 126, 127,
    128, 129, 130, 131, 229, 230, 231,
    232, 233, 234, 235, 236, 237, 238

Spanish Civil War 49, 50, 51, 57
United States 117, 118, 119, 120, 121,
    122, 123, 124, 125, 126, 127, 207,
    208
Vichy regime 121, 122, 127, 128, 129,
    130, 131
Franco, Francisco 49, 50, 56, 120
Frederick, Crown Prince 9
Free French 121, 122, 123, 128, 129, 130,
    131
Frigorifico Anglo del Uruguay 84
Fuqua, Stephen 56, 57, 59

Gable, Clark 187
Gary, Romain 118, 119, 120, 121, 122, 123,
    124, 125, 126, 127, 131
Gates, Robert 173
Gaulle, Charles de 118, 121, 122, 123, 124,
    125, 126, 127
Geneva Accords 135, 136, 137, 138, 139,
    140, 142, 146, 147
Gentile, Emilio 119
George III, King 157, 161
George VI, King, state visit to Washington
    9, 33, 34, 35, 36, 41, 102, 103, 104,
    106, 107, 108, 109, 109, 110, 111,
    112, 113, 158, 159, 160, 161, 162,
    163
George Washington Brigade 52
Germany
  antisemitism 53
  appeasement 31, 32, 33, 36, 37, 38, 39,
    40, 41, 42, 43, 44, 56, 96, 101
  Britain 31, 32
  invasion of Poland 43
  Submarine warfare 23
  United States 20
Gershwin, Ira 60
Gilmour, John 89
Glass, Andrew J. 177
Gorbachev, Mikhail 7, 170, 171, 172, 173,
    174, 175, 176, 202, 203, 204, 205,
    206, 207, 208
Grafham, Flight Lieutenant 142
Granta 231
Graydon, Michael 147
Great Depression 52, 54, 85–6, 198,
    215
Gromyko, Andrei 175

Haakon VII, King 103, 106, 107, 109, 110, 111, 112, 113
Hachigian, Nina 238
Hague conferences 67, 69, 70, 71, 72, 73, 117, 118, 119
Haig, Alexander 169
Haley, Arthur 189, 190
Halifax, Lord 38, 39, 41
Hammett, Dashiell 60
Hardinge, Charles 34
Harkin, Tom 174
Harriman, William Averell 136, 137, 138, 139, 140, 147-8
Harris, James 57
Hawley-Smoot Tariff Act 87, 91
Hay, John 68
Healey, Denis 157
Heath, Edward 153, 199, 214–15, 223
Hellman, Lillian 60
Hemingway, Ernest 53, 58, 60, 62
Hilsman, Roger 137, 138, 147
Hitler, Adolf 17, 39, 101, 102, 103, 111, 112, 113, 125, 127
    Antisemitism 53
Ho Chi Minh Trail 135, 136, 137, 138, 139, 140, 141, 142, 143, 144, 145, 146, 147
Hollywood 187-8
Holocaust 18
Hoover, Herbert 34, 36-7, 74
Hope, Bob 159
Hopkins, Harry 106
Howard, Esme 32
Hoyte, Elizabeth Sherman 33
Hull, Cordell 35, 84, 85, 90, 91-2, 93, 94, 96
human rights 6, 7, 67, 68
Huntington, Flying Officer 142
Hussein of Jordan, King 206
Hyde Park, New York 9

Ikle, Fred 179
Import Duties Act 88
Indo-Pakistan War 215
Ingrid, Crown Princess 9
international brigades 10, 50, 51, 52, 53, 56, 57, 58, 59, 60, 61, 62
    Abraham Lincoln Brigade 51, 52, 53, 57, 58, 59, 60, 61, 62

George Washington Brigade 52
Mackenzie-Papineau Brigade 52
International Commission of Jurists, Rio de Janeiro 68
International Court of Justice 174
international history 2, 9, 10, 117, 118, 119, 120, 121, 122, 123, 124, 125, 126, 127, 128, 129, 130, 131, 197, 198, 199, 200, 201, 202, 203, 204, 205, 206, 207, 208, 211, 212, 213, 214, 215, 216, 217, 218, 219, 220
international law 67, 68, 69, 70, 71, 72, 73, 74, 75, 76, 77, 78, 79, 80, 117, 118, 119, 120, 121, 122, 123, 124, 125, 126, 127, 128, 129, 130, 131, 197, 198, 199, 200, 201, 202, 203, 204, 205, 206, 207, 208
International Monetary Fund (IMF) 162
international relations 15, 16, 18, 19, 20, 21, 22, 69, 117, 118, 119, 120, 121, 122, 123, 124, 125, 126, 127, 128, 129, 130, 131, 197, 198, 199, 200, 201, 202, 203, 204, 205, 206, 207, 208, 211, 212, 213, 214, 215, 216, 217, 218, 219, 220
Iran-Contra 171, 175
Iraq War, 2003 218, 219
Ireland, American ancestral roots 6
Iron Curtain 179, 201, 202, 203, 204, 205, 206, 207-8, 11-12, 213, 214, 215
isolationism 11, 15, 41
Italy 31, 56
    Spanish Civil War 49, 50
    War with Abyssinia 74, 119, 120

Jacobsen, Carl 171
Japan, invasion of Manchuria 74
Jim Crow legislation 53
John Brown Artillery Battery 52
Johnson, Boris 217, 221, 222, 233, 239-40
Johnson, Lyndon B. 155
Jones, Elwyn 156
Joyner, Charles 190
Juliana, Crown Princess, later Queen 104, 106, 107, 108, 109, 110, 111, 112, 113
Justo, Augustin 88

Kamenev, Lev 56
Kellogg, Frank 72, 73
Kellogg Pact (Pact of Paris) 67, 68, 73, 75
Kennan, George 213
Kennedy, Edward 157
Kennedy, John Fitzgerald 136, 137, 138, 145, 146, 147, 155, 233
Kennedy, Joseph 38, 51
Kerr, Philip, Lord Lothian 42
Kessel, Joseph 118, 120, 121, 122, 126–8, 129, 130–1
Khoman, Thanat 137
Killick, John 155
King, Martin Luther 193, 194, 216, 217
Kingsolver, Barbara 190
Kissinger, Henry 139, 153, 157, 160, 178, 179, 180, 214, 215, 216
Kohl, Helmut 206, 207, 208
Korean War 214
Kounalakis, Eleni 238
Krauthammer, Charles 172

Lamas, Carlos Saavedra 93
Lambert, Bernard 123
Lao, Pathet 136, 137, 138, 140
Laos 135, 136, 137, 138, 139, 140, 141, 142, 143, 144, 145, 146, 147
Laos Neutralisation Agreement 140, 141
Larmour, E.N. 162
Latin America 3, 4–13, 15–25, 83, 84, 85, 86, 87, 88, 89, 90, 91, 92, 93, 94, 95, 96
Laycock Abbey 155
Lazareff, Pierre 125, 126
League of Nations 6, 22, 24–5, 67, 70, 73, 74, 87, 93, 113, 120, 121, 122
   Assembly 87
   Council 70, 74
   Covenant 70
LeBaron, Richard 219–20
Lend Lease Act 95
   programme 106, 112, 212, 213
Leopold II, King 104
Liberty Bell 156, 159
Lincoln Cathedral 155
Lindbergh, Charles 123
Lindsay, Sir Ronald 8, 31, 32–3, 34, 35, 36, 37, 38, 39, 40, 41, 42, 43, 44, 90–1
   ambassador to Berlin 33
   ambassador to Constantinople 33
   ambassador to Washington 32, 33, 34, 35, 36, 37, 38, 39, 40, 41, 42, 43, 44, 90–1
   relations with the Foreign Office 33, 34, 35, 36
Lippmann, Walter 20, 21, 38, 43
Lloyd George, David 42
London Economic Conference 90, 91, 92, 95
Long Telegram 213
Lorca, Federico García 49
Lothian, Lord, Philip Kerr 42, 154
Ludlow Amendment 42, 43
Ludlow, Louis 42
Lukacs, Georg 131
Luther, Hans 34
Lutyens, Sir Edwin 33

Mackenzie King, William Lyon 103
Mackenzie-Papineau Brigade 52
Macmillan, Harold 139, 146, 147, 158, 159, 215
Madison, James 156
Magna Carta 155, 156, 157
Major, John 8, 219
Malayan Emergency 142
Malbran, Manuel 88
Malraux, André 51, 119
Malta, summit 173
Manchuria, Japanese invasion of 74
Manhattan Project 211
Margriet, Princess 105
Marine Battalion Landing Team 137
Marinetti, Filippo 119
Maritain, Jacques 124–5
Marshall Aid 213
Martha, Crown Princess 9, 101, 102, 103, 105, 106, 107, 109, 111, 112, 113
Martino, Nobile Giacomo de 83
Marty, André 59
Maud, Queen 103
Maudru, Désiré 128, 129
Maurras, Charles 120
May, Paul 35
McCone, John 146, 147
McFarlane, Robert 169–70
McMahon Act 212, 214
McMichael, David 175
Mearsheimer, John 19, 20, 22

Melhuish, Ramsay 162
Mercer, Lucy 105
Merrill's Marauders 137
Merriman, Marion 10, 49, 53, 55, 56, 57, 58, 59, 60, 61, 62
Merriman, Robert 10, 49, 50, 53, 54, 55, 56, 57, 58, 59, 60, 61, 62
Mers-el-Kébir 127, 129, 131
Military Advisory Assistance Group 137
Military Intelligence 6 (MI6) 128
Minh, Ho Chi 10, 135, 136, 137, 138, 139, 140, 141, 142, 143, 144, 145, 146, 147
Mitchell, Margaret 187
Mitterand, François 207, 208
Mola, Emilio 49
Monroe Doctrine 93
Montgolfier brothers 117
Moore, John Bassett 6, 7, 67, 68, 70, 71, 72, 73, 74, 75, 76, 77, 78, 79, 80
Moreton, J.G. 156
Moscow Institute of Economics 55
Munich conferences 38, 40, 42, 74, 83, 95, 101, 125
Murray, Arthur 94
Mussolini, Benito 103
Mutual Defence Agreement 214, 221

Neutralisation Agreement 137, 138
New Deal 50, 51, 198
New York Times 155, 179, 180
New York World's Fair 101, 102
Nicaragua 170, 171, 172
Nixon, Richard 153, 154, 155, 173, 178, 179
Nixon Doctrine 173
Nobel Peace Prize 193, 194
Non-Intervention Committee 49
North Atlantic Treaty Organisation (NATO) 5, 6, 10, 113, 175, 205, 206, 207, 212, 217–18, 219, 220, 221, 222, 223, 224, 225, 226, 238, 239, 240, 241, 242
North Georgia 187, 190, 191, 193, 195
North, Lord 161
La Nouvelle Revue Française 121
Novasan, Phoumi 136
Nuclear Non-Proliferation Treaty 216

Obama, Barack 219
O'Duffy, Eoin 51

Office of Strategic Services 137
Olav, Crown Prince 9, 101, 102, 104, 106, 108, 109, 111, 112, 113
Operation Market Garden 110
Ordre Nouveau 120–1
O'Selznick, David 187
Osgood, Robert Endicott 21, 22
Ottawa Agreements 84, 88, 89, 91, 92, 94

Pacific War Council 107
Palliser, Michael 157
Pan-American Society 73, 74
Paris Peace Conference 22, 37
Paris-soir 127
Parker, Dorothy 58
Part, Anthony 157
Pearl Harbor 31, 108, 109, 197
Pearl, Richard 179
Permanent Court of Arbitration 68, 69–9
Permanent Court of International Justice 68–9, 70, 71, 72, 73, 75
Peron, Juan 84, 96
Perron, Henri 118
Pershing, John J. 18
Pétain, Philippe 117–18, 126, 127
Pezzullo, Lawrence 175
Philip, Duke of Edinburgh, Prince 154, 155, 156, 157, 158, 159, 160, 161, 162, 163
Phouma, Prince Souvanna 136, 138
Pike, Thomas 146
Pinedo, Federico 84
Pittman, Key 38
Poett, Nigel 146
Poland, German invasion of 43
Portes, Hélène de 127
Powell, Colin 179–80
Primo de Rivera, José Antonio 49, 61
Prittwitz und Gaffron, Friedrich Wilhelm von 34

Ramsbotham, Peter 153, 159–60
Reagan Doctrine 7, 8, 169, 170, 171, 172, 173, 174, 175, 197
Reagan, Ronald 5, 8, 31, 60, 169, 170, 171, 172, 173, 174, 175, 176, 177, 178, 179, 180, 197, 198, 199, 200, 201, 202, 203, 204, 205, 206, 207, 208, 211, 212, 213, 214, 215, 216, 217, 218, 219, 220

Red Army 55
Red Cross, American 33, 111, 112
Reed, John Shelton 189, 190–1, 195
Rein, Heinz 118
Revel, Jean-François 123
Reynaud, Paul 125, 127
Reynolds, Burt 188
Rhodesia 161, 162
  Unilateral Declaration of
    Independence (UDI) 161, 162
Richardson, Elliot 157, 160–1
Rizzo, Frank 157
Roberts, Donald 135, 136, 137, 140–2,
    144, 145–6
Roca, Julio 84, 88, 89
Roca-Runciman trade agreement 8–9, 83,
    84, 85, 86, 87, 88, 89, 90, 91, 92, 93,
    94, 95, 96
Rochelle, Pierre Drieu la 120, 121, 124, 125
Roosevelt, Eleanor 9, 33, 36, 50, 103, 105,
    114
Roosevelt, Franklin Delano 8, 9, 21, 31,
    32, 36, 37, 41, 50, 51, 56, 84, 85, 86,
    90, 93, 94, 95, 96, 101, 102, 103,
    104, 105, 111, 112, 113, 114, 197,
    198, 199, 200, 201, 202, 203, 204,
    205, 206, 207, 208, 220, 221, 229,
    230, 231, 232, 233, 234, 235, 236,
    237, 238
  Latin America 84, 85, 86, 89, 90, 91, 93,
    94, 95, 96
  New Deal 50, 198
  origins of the Second World War 32,
    104, 106, 107, 108, 109, 110, 111,
    112, 113, 114
  Spanish Civil War 50, 51
Roosevelt, James 105
Rougemont, Denis de 123
Royal Air Force 10, 118, 121, 131
Royal Navy 20, 24, 127, 222
Rumsfeld, Donald 233, 234
Runciman, Garry 83
Runciman, Leslie 83
Runciman Mission 83
Runciman, Walter 83, 88, 89, 93–4, 95
Russia, attitude to Spanish Civil War 49,
    50
Russian Revolution 21, 76
Rutledge, Peter 143

Sablon, Germaine 128
Saint-Exupéry, Antoine de 118, 120, 121,
    123, 124, 125, 126, 130, 131
Salazar, Antonio 119
Sandinistas 169, 170, 171, 172, 173, 174,
    175, 176, 177, 178, 179, 180
SARS-CoV-2 16
Sartre, Jean-Paul 121, 131
Savalas, Telly 159
Schlesinger, Arthur M. 155
Schmidt, Helmut 190
Scowcroft, Brent 173, 204–5
Seberg, Jean 121
Second World War 2, 6, 7, 11, 17, 18, 21,
    105, 119, 120, 121, 122, 123, 124, 125,
    126, 127, 128, 129, 130, 131, 137, 138,
    139, 140, 141, 142, 143, 144, 145, 146,
    147, 153, 154, 155, 197, 198, 199, 200,
    201, 202, 203, 204, 205, 212, 213, 214,
    215, 216, 217, 218, 219
  French resistance 128, 129, 130, 131
  Oradour-sur-Glane, massacre 122
  Origins 31, 32, 33, 34, 37, 38, 40, 41,
    42, 43, 56
  Vichy regime 121, 122, 123, 124, 125,
    126, 127, 128, 129, 130, 131
Senedd (Welsh National Assembly) 7, 238–9
Seymour, Charles 23
Shapp, Milton 157
Shevardnadze, Eduard 173, 178, 179, 180
Shultz, George 177, 178, 179, 180, 204
Simon, John 89
Simon, Pierre-Henri 123
Simpson, Wallace, Duchess of Windsor 35
Sinclair, Archibald 90
Smith, Daniel Malloy 20
Smith, Wayne 171, 175
South America 3, 9, 83, 84, 85, 86, 87, 88,
    89, 90, 91, 92, 93, 94, 95, 96
Southeast Asian Treaty Organisation
    (SEATO) 137, 139, 140, 143
Soviet Union 7, 54, 55, 56, 169, 170, 171,
    172, 173, 174, 175, 176, 177, 178,
    179, 180, 200, 202–3, 204, 205, 206,
    207, 208, 229, 230, 231, 232, 233,
    234, 235, 236, 237, 238
  Afghanistan, occupation of 170–1, 172,
    173, 174, 175, 176, 177, 178, 179,
    180, 220

El Salvador 169, 170, 171, 172, 173, 174, 175, 176, 177, 178, 179, 180
Red Army 55
Vietnam War 136, 137, 169, 170, 171, 172, 173, 174, 175, 176, 177, 178, 179, 198
Spain, Second Republic 49, 50
Popular Front 49
Spanish-American War 68, 75
Spanish Civil War 10, 49, 50, 51, 52, 54, 55, 56, 57, 58, 59, 60, 61, 62, 119, 120, 121, 122
  British attitudes 49, 50, 52, 229, 230, 231, 232, 233, 234, 235, 236, 237, 238
  Falange 49
  First Transport Regiment 52
  French attitudes 49, 50, 52, 119, 120, 121, 122
  international brigades 10, 51, 51, 52, 54, 56, 57, 58, 59, 60, 61, 62
  Italian attitudes 49, 50
  John Brown Artillery Battery 52
  non-intervention 49, 50, 51, 52
  Russian response 49, 50, 51, 52, 54, 55, 56, 57
  Teruel, Battle of 119
  United States attitude 51, 52
special relationship 4, 9, 31, 153, 154, 155, 156, 157, 158, 159, 160, 161, 162, 163, 197, 198, 199, 200, 201, 202, 203, 204, 205, 206, 207, 208, 211, 212, 213, 214, 215, 216, 217, 218, 219, 223, 229, 230, 231, 232, 233, 234, 235, 236, 237, 238
Stalin, Josef 50, 55
Stalingrad, battle of 110
State Department 35, 92, 93, 94, 137, 155, 156, 157, 160, 161, 162, 163
  Bureau of Intelligence and Research 137
State visit, Crown Prince Olav and Crown Princess Martha 101, 102
  King George VI and Queen Elizabeth to Washington 9, 33, 35, 36, 37, 38, 41, 42, 102
  Queen Elizabeth II 9, 10, 153, 154, 155, 156, 157, 158, 159, 160, 161, 12, 163
Stimson Doctrine 74, 76

Stimson, Henry 35, 72, 74
Stoker, Bram 190
Strong, Anna Louise 55, 56, 58
'structural realism' 16
Suckley, Margaret 105
Sudetenland, cessation of 37, 39, 41, 83
Suez Crisis 158, 220, 233
Sullivan, John 146–7
Supplementary Tariff Agreement 90, 94

Tassigny, General de Lattre de 127
Thatcher, Margaret 5, 8, 31, 197, 198, 199, 200, 201, 202, 203, 204, 205, 206, 207, 208, 218–19, 222, 229, 230, 231, 232, 233
Thompson, Sir Robert 139
Thucydides 197
Time Magazine 172
The Times 147
Torres, Lissandro de la 84
Transatlantic Studies 4, 10, 187, 192, 197, 229
Transatlantic Studies Association (TSA) viii 1, 3, 8, 187
Tripartite Currency Agreement 95
Truman Doctrine 201, 213
Truman, Harry S. 155, 156, 157, 158, 200–1, 207
Trump, Donald 7, 8, 218, 219, 221, 222, 231, 232, 233, 235, 236, 239
Twardowski, Janek 122

Unamuno, Miguel de 61
Unger, Leonard 138
United Nations (UN) 6, 67, 109, 113, 179, 216, 219, 234, 235
  Security Council 216
United States, Air Force 118, 135, 136, 137, 138, 139, 140, 141, 142, 143, 144, 145, 146, 147
  American-British-Dutch-Australian (ABDA) staff talks 107
  appeasement 86, 95, 96, 102, 171
  Argentina 84, 85, 86, 87, 88, 89, 90, 91, 92, 93, 94, 95, 96
  Britain 4, 5, 6, 7, 8, 9, 10, 11, 12, 15, 16, 19, 20, 21, 22, 23, 24, 31, 32, 33, 34, 35, 36, 37, 38, 39, 40, 41, 42, 43, 85, 86, 87, 88, 95, 96, 101, 102, 117,

118, 119, 120, 121, 122, 123, 124, 125, 126, 127, 128, 129, 130, 131, 135, 136, 137, 138, 139, 140, 141, 142, 143, 144, 145, 146, 147, 153, 154, 155, 156, 157, 158, 159, 160, 161, 162, 163, 198, 199, 200, 211, 212, 213, 214, 215, 216, 220, 221, 223, 229, 230, 231, 232, 233, 234, 235, 236, 237, 238
Central Intelligence Agency (CIA) 138, 140, 141, 146, 221
China 16, 153, 154, 155
Civil Rights Movement 192
Civil War 69, 187, 188, 189, 190
commercial 4, 5, 6, 8–9, 11, 83, 84, 85, 86, 87, 88, 90, 91, 92, 93, 94, 95, 96, 220, 221
Constitution 42
cultural links 6, 7, 8, 9, 10, 11, 12, 15, 16
Declaration of Independence 156, 157
Electoral College 197
entry into the First World War 11, 15, 16, 17, 18, 19, 20, 21, 22, 23, 24
France 117, 118, 119, 120, 121, 122, 123, 124, 125, 126, 127, 128, 129, 130, 131
Germany 20, 23, 24, 31, 32, 33
international law 6, 7, 67, 68, 69, 70, 71, 72, 73, 74, 75, 76, 77, 78, 79, 80
isolationism 11, 15, 19, 20
Ludlow Amendment 42, 43
Nicaragua 169, 170, 171
Royal state visits 9, 10, 33, 34, 35, 36, 41, 42, 43, 153, 154, 155, 156, 157, 158, 159, 160, 161, 162, 163
sea power 24
SEATO 137, 138, 139, 140, 143, 144, 145
Spanish Civil War 49, 50, 52, 54, 56, 57
Supreme Court 50
Vietnam War 135, 136, 137, 138, 139, 140, 141, 142, 143, 144, 145, 146, 147, 169, 175, 198, 214, 215, 216, 233, 234, 235, 236, 237, 238
War of Independence 159
war with Spain 68, 75

Uriburu, José Felix 87
Ustinov, Dmitry 175

Vachon, Thélis 126
Vandenberg Resolution 213
Vansittart, Robert 38
Velvin, Mal 143
Verran, Tommy 193
Versailles, Treaty of 17, 40, 73, 119, 123
Vichy, regime 121, 122, 123, 126, 127, 128, 129, 130, 131
Victoria, Queen 103
Viet Cong 136, 137, 138, 139, 140, 141
Viet Minh 135, 136, 137, 138, 139, 140, 141, 142, 143, 144, 145, 146, 147
Vietnam War 10, 20, 135, 136, 137, 138, 139, 140, 141, 142, 143, 144, 145, 146, 147, 153, 169, 175, 198, 199, 200, 214, 215, 216, 233, 234, 235, 236, 237, 238
   Military Advisory Assistance Group 137
   Neutralisation Agreement 137, 138
Voight, Jon 188

Wales, devolved government 7
Walpole, Horace 190–1
War of Independence 159
Warhol, Andy 171
Washington
   British Embassy design 33
   Naval Yard 109
   Treaty of 69
Watergate scandal 154, 156, 198
Weddell, Alexander 93
Weil, Kurt 156
Weinberger, Caspar 178, 179
Welles, Sumner 95–6
Werth, Léon 127
White House 5, 8, 32, 42, 50, 104, 106, 108, 153, 159, 161, 177, 180, 197, 199, 200, 201, 202, 203, 204, 205, 206, 207, 208, 217, 218, 219
White, Robert 175
Wilhelmina, Queen 9, 104, 106, 108, 111, 112, 113

Wilson, Harold 153, 199, 215, 217, 235
Wilson, Woodrow 17, 18, 19, 20, 21, 22, 23, 24, 37, 68, 71, 76, 78, 105, 179
   Fourteen Points 179
   Wilsonianism 68, 78
Windsor, Duke of 36, 87
Wood, Douglas 142, 144
World Economic Conference 91

Yom Kippur War 153, 214, 216
Yrigoyen, Hipólito 85, 87

Zinoviev, Grigory 56